Fundamental Reference Sources

Fundamental Reference Sources

Second Edition

by Frances Neel Cheney
Emeritus Professor, Department of Library Science,
George Peabody College for Teachers, Vanderbilt University

and Wiley J. Williams
Professor, School of Library Science, Kent State University;
formerly, *Professor, Department of Library Science,*
George Peabody College for Teachers, Vanderbilt University

American Library Association
Chicago 1980

Library of Congress Cataloging in Publication Data

Cheney, Frances Neel, 1906–
    Fundamental reference sources.

    Includes index.
    1. Reference books—Bibliography.   I. Williams,
Wiley J., joint author.   II. Title.
Z1035.1.C5 1980   011'.02   80–21617
ISBN: 0-8389-0308-8

Printed in the United States of America

Contents

Preface   ix

1. The Nature of Reference/Information Service   1

    Definitions 2
    Search 6
    Guides to Reference Materials 9
    Current Reviewing Journals 12
    Evaluation of Reference Books 13

2. Sources of Bibliographic Information   15

    Definitions 18
    Library Catalogs 22
    National Library Catalogs 25
    National Book Bibliographies 31
    Bibliographies of Other Publications
        and of Audiovisual Materials 40
    Subject Bibliographies 52
    Selection Aids 57
    Current Selective Bibliographies 61
    Indexes and Abstracts 62
    Other Indexes and Concordances 81
    Bibliographies of Bibliographies 89
    Summary 91

3. **Sources of Biographical Information** 92

    Nature of Biographical Sources 92
    Indexes to Biography 95
    International Biographical Sources 99
    Current Sources 102
    National Biographical Sources 104
    Professions 112
    Summary 123

4. **Sources on Words** 124

    Why a Dictionary Is Made 125
    How Dictionaries Are Made 127
    Unabridged Dictionaries 138
    Abridged Dictionaries 145
    School Dictionaries 150
    Etymological Dictionaries 153
    Usage 155
    Synonyms and Antonyms 157
    Pronunciation 160
    Slang 161
    Dialect 162
    Abbreviations 164
    Special Fields 165
    Foreign-Language Dictionaries 169
    Summary 178

5. **Encyclopedias** 179

    The Making of Encyclopedias 182
    Multivolume Adult Encyclopedias 197
    Encyclopedia Supplements 203
    One- to Three-Volume Encyclopedias 204
    Children's and Young Adults' Encyclopedias 210
    Foreign-Language Encyclopedias 218
    General Reference Features of Encyclopedias 225

6. **Sources of Statistics** 226

    Statistical Reference Service
       and Evaluation of Statistical Sources 228
    Terminology 239
    Bibliographies 242
    Periodicals Indexes 255
    Other Types of Statistical Sources 256

7. Sources of Geographical Information 264

    General Reference Works 271
    Cartographic History and Map Librarianship 281
    English and American World Atlases 287
    School Atlases 293
    Foreign-Language Atlases 293
    National Maps and Atlases 295
    Thematic Maps and Atlases 297
    Gazetteers 303
    Encyclopedias, Directories, Handbooks 305
    Dictionaries of Geographical Terms 307
    Travel Guides 308

Appendix: Guidelines for Particular Types
   of Reference Works 315

    Atlases 315
    Bibliographic Reference Sources 318
    English-Language Dictionaries 320
    General English-Language Encyclopedias 322

Index 327

Preface

The second edition of FUNDAMENTAL REFERENCE SOURCES, like the first, is an introduction to selected sources of bibliographical, biographical, linguistic, statistical, and geographic information. The organization remains the same. The introductory chapter has been revised and updated to reflect the literature of reference/information service of the past decade, including the development of guidelines by the ALA's Reference and Adult Services Division, its role in reference/information service, the nature of the reference process, and the reference interview. Guides to reference materials which have appeared since 1970 have been added.

Chapter 2 discusses sources of bibliographic information, broadly defined as compilations of information regarding recorded sources of information and embracing library catalogs, national book bibliographies, bibliographies of government publications, audiovisual materials and other forms, subject bibliographies, indexes, and abstracts. The impact of computer-generated tools has been particularly evident in the past decade and a number of titles so produced, as well as a section on data bases, have been added. The latter cites a few examples and suggests sources of further information on these important forms of bibliographic control.

Chapter 3, on sources of biographical information, is updated to cover new indexes to biography, additional sources of national biography, and current biographical directories for various professions. It follows the chapter on bibliographic sources because, in many ways, bibliography and biography are closely allied.

Chapter 4 characterizes the principal sources of information on words, with some attention to how dictionaries are made. Unabridged English-language dictionaries are also included, as well as sources of etymology, usage, synonyms and antonyms, pronunciation, slang, dialect, abbreviations, and acronyms. A number of dictionaries in special fields, specifically the social sciences, have been added, most of them published since 1970. Also added are recently published bilingual dictionaries.

Chapter 5 covers the problems and responsibilities of editors and publishers of encyclopedias. A section on the coverage of broad subject fields by encyclopedias has been expanded. Newly added are outlines of the strengths and weaknesses of selected multivolume encyclopedias for both adults and children, and for one- to three-volume sets. Retained and updated is a discussion of some foreign-language encyclopedias.

Chapter 6 has been revised to round out the background of the field of statistics, with attention to important statistical terminology. Bibliographic control and statistical sources in various fields have been expanded and updated with recently published titles.

Chapter 7, covering sources of geographical information, has also been expanded and updated, with more attention to the role of United States government agencies in geography and cartography. Also expanded is coverage of travel and other guide books.

Titles were selected on the basis of their importance in general reference collections in American libraries, and while foreign-language sources were not deliberately avoided, they are not emphasized. The debt that any compilers of another guide to reference materials owe to the more exhaustive guides of Sheehy and Walford is fully acknowledged. Only a few titles published after June 1979 have been included.

Appended are guidelines for the evaluation of atlases, bibliographic reference works, dictionaries, and encyclopedias, prepared by the Reference and Subscription Books Review Committee of the American Library Association and reprinted here with its permission.

We are deeply grateful to Herbert Bloom and Helen Cline, ALA Publishing Services, for their editorial guidance and assistance.

1

The Nature of Reference/ Information Service

Libraries exist for their users. Many of these users have not yet appeared, but will at some time in the future, and so it is also for the potential user that librarians select and acquire what has been recorded in any available form. It is at this point that reference/information service begins, for without a body of knowledge and information, it is not possible to give service.

It is for the potential user that librarians attempt to organize these materials for easy access to the information they contain, through some system or systems that will provide clues to their location, such as cataloging and classification. Librarians also acquire or prepare indexes and abstracts of the contents of certain types of recorded information, such as periodicals, pamphlets, films, recordings, and maps. The nature and extent of this organization in individual libraries will vary according to the needs of the potential user.

It is for the potential user that libraries have provided persons who are qualified to assist the user in his or her search for information, and who have been designated as reference librarians, or information specialists, or some other term.

To fulfill these responsibilities to the user for selecting, acquiring, organizing, and retrieving this body of recorded knowledge, librarians have

veloped codes for cataloging, systems of classification, and standards of service. These are always in a state of change, subject to continuous inquiry into their effectiveness in meeting current demands.

Definitions

Efforts to set standards for reference and information services must begin with definitions, and reference librarians through the years have tried to define reference service, their terminology reflecting the times in which they lived. Thus William Warner Bishop, in the days before the computer, stated with some conviction that "reference work is organized effort on the part of libraries in aid of the most expeditious and fruitful use of their libraries." With this general statement it is hardly possible to disagree, but it is too broad to be of any value.

In 1930, James I. Wyer, in his still useful *Reference Work: A Textbook for Students of Library Work and Librarians* (Chicago, ALA; 315p.), described reference work as "sympathetic and informed personal aid in interpreting library collections for study and research." This is worth remembering as a reminder that respect for the user is essential to sympathetic and personal aid.

In 1943, the *A.L.A. Glossary of Library Terms* reflected both Bishop and Wyer in defining reference as "that phase of library work which is directly concerned with assistance to readers in securing information and in using the resources of the library in study and research."

In 1961, Samuel Rothstein and Henry Dubester developed a statement, for use by a committee on reference standards and statistics of the Reference Services Division of the American Library Association, that is notable for its outline of the kinds of services reference librarians should be prepared to offer. It was reproduced in Louis Shores, "The Measure of Reference" (*The Southeastern Librarian* 11:297–302 [Winter 1961]), and reprinted in Arthur Ray Rowland, *Reference Services* ([Hamden, Conn.: Shoe String, 1964; 259p.] p. 135–44). Briefly, it described two types of service to the library's patrons: direct and indirect.

Representative of the first type is instruction in the use of the library and information services, ranging from answering simple questions to "supplying information based on search in the collections of the library, combining competence in bibliothecal techniques with competence in the subject of inquiry." Indirect reference service "involves the preparation and development of catalogs, bibliographies, and all other reference aids which help in providing access to the library's collections. . . . This recognizes the significant role of the technical or processing services of the library as indispensable to the reference function."

A further expansion of Rothstein and Dubester's statement appears in "A Commitment to Information Services: Developmental Guidelines" (*RQ* 15:327–30 [Summer 1976]; *RQ* 18:275–78 [Spring 1979], with an added section on "Ethics of Service," adopted January 1979). Prepared by the Standards Committee of the Reference and Adult Services Division, and adopted by that Division in January 1976, it is directed to all who have responsibility for providing reference and information services. A description of reference or information services, both direct and indirect, prefaces an important set of developmental guidelines for services, resources, environment, personnel, and evaluation. These are followed by a draft outline of an information service policy statement.

The developmental guidelines for *services* (1.0–1.9) stress the responsibility for not only meeting but anticipating user needs, for "cooperation among other information handling units, centers, or agencies at local, regional, state, and national levels; and for regular evaluation of services." These are important points and require that librarians be acquainted with wide services and resources beyond their own libraries.

The guidelines for *resources* (2.0–2.4) also stress cooperation in developing selection policies within a given service area, diverse collections, duplication of frequently used materials, and a regular review of information materials.

The guidelines for *environment* (3.0–3.5) emphasize the importance of locating information services and collections in readily accessible points in the library, the provision of places for study, and additional service points for easy access to librarian/information specialists.

The guidelines for *personnel* (4.0–4.6) require that a professional librarian/information specialist be available to users during all hours the library is open, that staff be chosen not only for academic background and knowledge but also their ability to communicate easily with people, and that continuing education be provided.

The guidelines for *evaluation* (5.0–5.3) state that needed data should be collected, that responsibility for evaluation should be assigned to a staff member with skills in this field, and that statistics should be collected on a systematic basis.

"Ethics of service" (6.0–6.5) deals with accuracy of information supplied, confidentiality, impartiality, and avoidance of personal financial gain.

For further comment see Bernard Vavrek, "Reference Evaluation— What the 'Guidelines' Don't Indicate" (*RQ* 18:335–40 [Summer 1979]). According to Vavrek, the twofold purpose of the article is "first, to discuss what is happening in relation to the Guidelines, and second, to talk about an area of reference/information service that received only perfunctory treatment in the Guidelines, i.e. evaluation" (p.335).

Although many of these tenets have been observed by librarians in the past, the formulation of this document, which reflects the requirements of new and sophisticated information retrieval systems, represents a step forward in an important branch of service.

It is unlikely that it will produce uniform reference/information departments, for as Robert Balay points out in his article "Reference Services" (*The ALA Yearbook, 1978*, p. 260–63 [Chicago: ALA, 1978]), "Reference librarians have not always been sure where the boundaries of reference service lie, and they have seemed to engage in many kinds of activities that have had an uncertain bearing on their regularly assigned duties." Balay then summarizes the findings of Paula Watson and Martha Landis, who "reported that the range of responsibilities assigned to reference departments varies greatly. Some do one-to-one reference work and little else. Others take care of documents, periodicals, interlibrary lending and borrowing, microforms, newspapers, bibliographic instruction, maps, exhibits, book selection, computer-aided information retrieval, and so forth."

Balay concludes that "it would appear that reference work consists of whatever it is that reference departments do." But it must be recognized that whatever reference departments do, they must accept responsibility for not only meeting but anticipating user needs in order to qualify as reference/information centers.

One of the most important ways to determine users' needs is the *reference interview,* a subject which has received considerable attention in library periodicals. Geraldine B. King, in "The Reference Interview" (*RQ* 12:157–60 [Winter 1972]), offers five "filters" for structuring the interview: determination of subject, objective and motivation of the inquirer, personal characteristics of the inquirer, relationship of inquiry description to file organization, and anticipated or acceptable answers. She cites the advantages of open questions, including their encouraging the user to talk. Sara D. Knapp examines the reference interview in a computer-based setting and concludes that it differs from interviewing at the reference desk more in degree than in kind. "Mastery of the technology, systems, and vocabulary of searching are vital prerequisites, but I believe the real essence of the search analyst's role lies in the understanding of purposes, in communication, and especially in the application of analytical skills" ("The Reference Interview in the Computer-based Setting," *RQ* 17:320–24 [Summer 1978]).

Samuel Rothstein's "Across the Desk: 100 Years of Reference Encounters" (*Canadian Library Journal* 34:391–99 [Oct. 1977]) is valuable for its review of the pertinent literature on the subject from Samuel Green's paper in 1876 to the present. He believes that geniality, knowing how to find the truth, and a spirit of service are the essential ingredients of the reference encounter over the last hundred years. "I suggest that, with some modernization but also with some moderation, that same recipe might serve equally well for the foreseeable future." Which nobody can deny.

In 1966, Alan M. Rees, speaking before a conference at Columbia University, posed the question "What, in fact, is the fundamental nature of the reference process?" In answering his question, he began by saying, "I wish to make a clear differentiation between reference *process*, reference *work*, reference *sources*, and reference *services*. The reference process incorporates the sum total of variables involved in the performance of reference work by an intermediary designated as reference librarian. It includes both the psychology of the questioner and the environmental context within which the need for information is generated, together with the psychology of the reference librarian and the reference sources employed. Reference service is the formalized provision of information in diverse forms by a reference librarian, who is interposed between the questioner and available information sources. Reference work is the function performed by reference librarians in providing reference service. The perception on the part of the librarian of the need of the questioner is an important part of the reference process. The formalized representation of this need is the question, which may or may not be an adequate expression of the underlying information requirement."

He continued, "The reference process, therefore, comprises a complex interaction among the questioner, reference librarian, and information sources, involving not only the identification and manipulation of available bibliographic apparatus, but also the operation of psychological, sociological, and environmental variables which are imperfectly understood at the present time" ("Broadening the Spectrum," in Winifred B. Linderman, ed., *The Present Status and Future Prospects of Reference/Information Service* [Chicago: ALA, 1967], p. 57–58).

The librarian's concern for whether users do or do not retrieve their information has made him more conscious of the need to know more about these users. Most librarians would agree with Helen M. Focke "that we do not know enough about our patrons, how their minds operate and what kinds of things they need and ask for, to do a really good job of serving them. We have not gathered objective data continually or been as research-conscious as we should be." Focke's paper, delivered at the same conference where Alan Rees described the reference process, concluded with a proposal that a network of reporters, recorders, and data gatherers be established to build up a data bank of information on library patrons and the questions they ask (Linderman, p.33). Thus far, this network has not been established.

The present emphasis on the need for gathering data and conducting research on the information searching process will continue, stimulated in part by the increasing mechanization of libraries. In fact, Pierre Papazian attributes this questioning to the advent of mechanization. In "Librarian, Know Thyself" (*RQ* 4:7–8 [July 1965]), he proposes an analytical study of the human search process, advocating two levels of research on this question: the practice of information searching and the psychology of information searching.

James Rettig, in "A Theoretical Model and Definition of the Reference Process" (*RQ* 18:19–29 [Fall 1978]), analyzes various statements on reference service found chiefly in journal articles and theoretically defines reference service "as the interpersonal communication process, the purpose of which is to provide a person who needs information with that information, either directly by culling the needed information from an appropriate information source (or sources) or indirectly by (1) providing the person with the appropriate information source(s) or (2) teaching the person how to find the needed information in the appropriate information source(s)." It is well documented, as is Kenneth Whittaker's "Towards a Theory for Reference and Information Service" (*Journal of Librarianship* 9:49–63 [Jan. 1977]). After reviewing the development of this service from its origins to the present, he offers a base plan for systematic and comprehensive research, including terminology, nature and purpose of the service, its scope and relationships with other subjects.

Another type of continuing investigation is concerned with information needs in specific subject fields. While numerous examples of these investigations exist in science and technology and in psychology, one is singled out here because the author is a cataloger who, at the time of writing her article, was a doctoral candidate in anthropology. Diana Amsden, in "Information Problems of Anthropologists" (*College and Research Libraries* 29:117–31 [Mar. 1968]), brought to her investigation of the anthropologist's difficulties not only a subject competency, but also a knowledge of the organization of library collections in that subject. If her conclusions are not startling, they are at least based on a more complete understanding of the limitations of the existing bibliographical apparatus from the anthropologist's standpoint. She found that anthropologists needed, among other things, a prompt, cumulative, comprehensive index-abstract service and a guide to the literature of the field. This is not unique with anthropologists.

Search

Meanwhile, as the analysis goes on, individual librarians, attempting to provide direct and indirect reference service in a given library environment, must try to deal intelligently with the individual questioner who seeks his or her assistance. Seasoned reference librarians develop confidence in their ability to help patrons as they develop a knowledge of sources of information, although they may not express themselves as lyrically as S. R. Ranganathan did in "Reference Service and Humanism" (Rowland, p.31–34). In his inimitable style, he wrote, "When the reader comes amidst the library . . . he will meet a person, who with radiant geniality whispers into his ears, 'Take my hand; For I have passed this way, And know the truth.'"

Less certain of the truth, but with some degree of confidence, the reference librarian should be able to say to the questioner, "Take my hand, for I have passed this way, and know some of the sources of information." Once the questioner has taken this hand or, more literally, has stated his or her question, the reference librarian joins them in their quest, though not always with "radiant geniality." These first steps are usually referred to as the "reference interview," and more recently as the "librarian–questioner dialogue." By whatever name, it is the heart of the matter, and if it is not successfully conducted there will be no resulting restatement of the question, which is so often necessary.

It is at this point that some of the variables mentioned earlier become evident. One definition of *variable* is "having no fixed quantitative value," which may be one reason why reference librarians have never been successful in measuring reference service quantitatively. Another, more applicable definition is "anything that varies or is prone to variation." In this sense, what are some of the "things" that vary? Recognizing that continuing analysis will be expressed in more technical terms, but still daring to use less technical language, we may note that a few of the things that affect the nature of the search and that are subject to infinite variations are:

1. How much the questioner already knows about the subject field in which his or her question falls
2. How articulate he or she is in expressing need for information
3. How interested he or she is in the search
4. How defensive his or her attitude is toward the librarian
5. How much information he or she wants
6. How soon he or she needs the information
7. How much assistance he or she wants
   a. Would he or she rather do it alone?
   b. Would he or she rather have it all done by someone else?

These same variables may be expressed from the standpoint of librarians as

1. How much the librarian knows about the subject field in which the question falls
2. How skillful he or she is in determining what the questioner wants
3. How interested he or she is in the search
4. How defensive his or her attitude is toward the questioner

5. How much information he or she is prepared to provide
6. How quickly he or she can locate what is wanted
7. How much direct assistance he or she is willing to give
   a. Minimum
   b. Middling
   c. Maximum (Samuel Rothstein advocates this in his "Reference Service: The New Dimension in Librarianship," *College and Research Libraries* 22:11–18 [Jan. 1961])

These are only a few of the variables, expressed in very general terms and not in the language of a discipline such as psychology, sociology, or another behavioral science. But to follow them with a few questions, we might ask:

1. If questioners know more about the subject field of their question than the librarian, is the librarian's attitude apt to be more defensive?
2. If the librarian knows more about the subject field than the questioner, is the questioner's attitude apt to be more defensive?
3. What happens if the questioner is more interested in the search than the librarian?
4. What happens if the librarian is not skillful or sympathetic enough to interpret the question and relate it to the proper source of information?
5. What happens if the library's resources are not adequate to meet the questioner's need?
6. What happens if the questioner wants the answer more quickly than the librarian can supply it?

The continuing concerns of those engaged in reference/information services are reflected in the activities of the Reference and Adult Services Division of the American Library Association. Formed in 1972 by a merger of the former Adult Services Division and the Reference Services Division, it is engaged in "study of community information needs; exploration of avenues of community involvement; maximal exploitation of non-print resources and computerized information services; innovative efforts in instruction in the use of libraries; continuing education programs for reference and adult services librarians to enable them to give the best possible service to present and potential clientele."

Already noted are its developmental guidelines for information services, adopted in 1976. Also, the Library Services to an Aging Population Committee has prepared "Guidelines for Library Services to an Aging Population" and has compiled a directory of state and regional agencies that work with the aging.

Evidence of growing interest in computer-based reference service is the formation in 1977 of a new section, Machine-Assisted Reference Section

(MARS), within Reference and Adult Services Division of ALA. This group, together with other groups in the American Library Association, has been concerned with charging a fee for computer-assisted searching. An excellent summary of the arguments pro and con is found in Robert Balay's article "Reference Services" in *The ALA Yearbook, 1978* (p.261–62). The Local History Committee of the History Section conducted a survey of local-history collections and services, which will be used in developing guidelines.

An Interlibrary Loan Committee, a Catalog Use Committee, and a Committee on Wilson Indexes represent further interests of the Division. The latter assists subscribers to Wilson indexes in selection of appropriate periodical titles for inclusion.

RASD's official journal is the quarterly *RQ*, which has expanded from a small leaflet in November 1960 to a valuable source of articles on pertinent subjects, with regular sections of reviews of reference books, government publications, interlibrary loan issues, and news. The Division also prepares an annual list of outstanding reference books, published in April of each year in *Library Journal.* Librarians concerned with reference/information service find it a ready source of essential information.

A good overview of kinds of services rendered and current issues being faced is found in the signed articles, "Reference Services," which has appeared annually in *The ALA Yearbook* since 1976. Appended references include significant journal articles and working papers published during the year. *The ALA Yearbook* also includes an annual summary of the activities of the Reference and Adult Services Division of the ALA.

Two other convenient sources of well-selected articles in recent years are Arthur Ray Rowland's *The Librarian and Reference Service* (Hamden, Conn.: Shoe String, 1977; 281p.), which supplements his earlier collection of articles, and *Reference and Information Services: A Reader,* edited by Bill Katz and Andrea Tarr (Metuchen, N.J.: Scarecrow, 1978).

The most exhaustive bibliography of books, journals, and other sources in English is in Marjorie E. Murfin and Lubomyr R. Wynar, *Reference Service: An Annotated Bibliographic Guide* (Littleton, Colo.: Libraries Unlimited, 1977; 294p.), which describes a wide range of sources in English: 1,259 books and articles classified under fourteen aspects of reference service (its history, theory, and teaching in various types of libraries, the reference process, research, etc.).

Guides to Reference Materials

While inquiry into the reference process will continue, one thing is agreed on by all librarians: they must know sources of information. It is because of this that guides to reference materials and selection aids have been prepared. There are many notable examples, and only a few are singled out here.

The most frequently used guide is Eugene P. Sheehy's *Guide to Reference Books* (9th ed.; Chicago: ALA, 1976; 1015p.). Carrying on the reputation established by its earlier editors, including Isadore Mudge and Constance Winchell, its 10,000 entries emphasize scholarly English-language titles, with considerable representation of European works. It retains the same arrangement, grouping briefly but objectively annotated titles under five broad subjects: general reference works, the humanities, social sciences, history and area studies, and pure and applied sciences. These are further subdivided by fields (e.g. philosophy, religion, literature, etc., under the humanities) and by form of work (such as bibliography, dictionary, etc.). Helpful introductory notes preface some sections, such as those on biography, education, and history and area studies (most of them retained or only slightly altered from the eighth edition). A detailed and accurate index refers to item numbers—an aid in quick location of individual titles. The ninth edition was somewhat out of date before it was published, and a tenth edition is in progress. Supplements and an annotated biannual list of selected reference books, appearing in *College and Research Libraries*, help to bring it up to date.

A. J. Walford's *Guide to Reference Materials* (3rd ed.; 3v.; London: Library Assn., 1973–77; 4th ed. v. 1– , 1980–), distributed in the United States by ALA, has about 2,000 more titles than Sheehy but is similar in arrangement. European titles are more fully represented and, in some cases, annotations are fuller and more critical.

Although out of date, Louise-N. Malclès, *Les Sources du Travail Bibliographique* (3v. in 4; Geneva: Droz; Lille: Giard, 1950–58), must be mentioned as a classic, strong in French titles. Although *Sheehy, Walford*, and *Malclès* differ to some extent in arrangement and individual titles, they are international in scope, and all include the following types of reference books:

1. Bibliographies and indexes, which direct the user to other sources of information
2. Sources of biographical information
3. Dictionaries of all kinds
4. Encyclopedias
5. Yearbooks and handbooks
6. Directories of persons and organizations
7. Atlases and gazetteers

All are annotated; and as reference materials continue to proliferate, they serve as a record of those titles that were considered worthy of inclusion at the time the guides were published.

More current than *Sheehy* or *Walford* is *American Reference Books Annual* (Littleton, Colo.: Libraries Unlimited, 1970–date). Nearly 1,800 titles, published or distributed in the United States, are arranged alphabetically by subject, accompanied by brief, signed, critical reviews by subject specialists, with citations to other reviews in such library periodicals as *Choice* and *Library Journal.* Cumulative indexes to author, title, and subject are issued at five-year intervals. It is a good source of discriminating criticism as well as a guide to additional reviews of a title.

Additional citations to book reviews are found in "Reference Sources," a regular feature in *Reference Services Review,* published quarterly since 1972 (Ann Arbor, Mich.: Pierian Pr.). It indexes over 100 professional library, scholarly, and popular periodicals. Also included are brief scope notes for each title, and often brief excerpts from the reviews. Since 1977, they have been cumulated annually in *Reference Sources* (also published by Pierian Press). *Reference Sources 1977,* edited by Linda Mark, contains over 4,500 reviews for about 3,500 reference titles published in 1976 and some published in preceding years, if they were reviewed or received during 1976. Particularly useful are its three subject indexes, arranged first by broad subject fields and subdivided by form (e.g. bibliography); next by Dewey Decimal Classification; and finally alphabetically, by Library of Congress subject headings.

Reference Services Review is also a source of state-of-the-art surveys of reference sources in various fields. Compiled by librarians with experience in the field, they have covered such subjects as engineering, fine arts and crafts, film, radio and television, and Australia and New Zealand. The selected titles, well annotated, are usually prefaced with general commentary.

As reference books increase in number, need increases not only for more selective, less exhaustive guides, but for guides to the literature of a special subject field or country, or intended for a particular type of library.

Introductory textbooks, such as Jean Key Gates, *Guide to the Use of Books and Libraries* (4th ed.; New York: McGraw-Hill, 1979; 292p.), and the frequently revised *Introduction to Reference Work, Volume I, Basic Information Sources,* by William A. Katz (3rd ed.; New York: McGraw-Hill, 1978; 367p.), are examples of useful selective, less exhaustive guides.

An excellent example of a guide restricted to the publications of one country is Dorothy E. Ryder's *Canadian Reference Sources: A Selective Guide* (Ottawa: Canadian Library Assn., 1973; 185p. [supp. 1975, 121p.]). Arranged by broad subject fields, it provides well-selected, well-annotated titles, updated by her annual list in the August issue of *Canadian Library Journal.*

(For a list of guides to the literature in special subject fields see chapter 2, Sources of Bibliographic Information. A section on these guides is included.)

Examples of lists prepared for a particular type of library are Enoch Pratt Free Library's *Reference Books*, compiled by Marion V. Bell and Eleanor A. Swiden, which has proved its usefulness as a well-selected and -annotated list by appearing in eight editions between 1947 and 1978. Reflecting the experience and judgment of reference librarians who have helped to develop the services of Enoch Pratt, it is highly regarded in all types of libraries.

Reference Books for Small and Medium-sized Libraries is compiled at intervals by an ad hoc committee of the ALA Reference and Adult Services Division (3rd ed.; Chicago: ALA, 1979; 216p.). Briefly annotated, it is intended as a buying guide for these libraries.

For schools, there are Christine L. Wynar's *Guide to Reference Books for School Media Centers* (Littleton, Colo.: Libraries Unlimited, 1973; 473p.) and Carolyn Sue Peterson's *Reference Books for Elementary and Junior High School Libraries* (2nd ed.; Metuchen, N.J.: Scarecrow, 1975; 314p.). Both are well annotated.

Small libraries with limited budgets will find useful Bohdan S. Wynar's *Reference Books in Paperback: An Annotated Guide* (2nd ed.; Littleton, Colo.: Libraries Unlimited, 1976; 317p.). It is also valuable in advising possible purchasers of reference books for home use.

Current Reviewing Journals

Library periodicals that regularly review reference books, chiefly those in the English language, are:

1. *Booklist.* Regular section, "Reference and Subscription Books Reviews," includes lengthy evaluations of encyclopedias, dictionaries, atlases, and other types of reference books prepared by RSBRC, and shorter reviews as "Notes and Comments." (These are discussed at greater length below.) Biweekly.
2. *Choice.* Brief, critical, unsigned reviews by college and university professors and librarians; aimed at the college library. Monthly.
3. *Library Journal.* Brief, signed reviews by librarians and others. April 15th issue annually publishes "Reference Books of the Year," compiled by a committee of ALA Reference and Adult Services Division, which lists and annotates about 100 significant titles of general interest. Biweekly.
4. *The Reference Book Review.* Begun in July 1976, emphasizes currency of titles reviewed by librarians, averaging about 100 each issue. Quarterly.
5. *Reference Services Review*, as noted earlier, contains extended articles annotating reference books in various fields. Quarterly.

6. *RQ.* Signed reviews, some, lengthy, by librarians. Quarterly.
7. *Wilson Library Bulletin.* Contains between 20 and 30 reviews by Charles Bunge in a column called "Current Reference Books."

Selected lists and current reviewing media are helpful to librarians in developing collections on which effective service is based, but they are no substitute for discriminating judgment in the selection of titles best suited to the library's clientele. This requires a thorough knowledge of the library's existing reference collection, not only to use it effectively but also to avoid needless and expensive duplication of subject matter already available.

It is also imperative that librarians learn how to evaluate reference books. Not only is this necessary in collection building but also in evaluating the adequacy of review journals that are read regularly, for as various studies have shown, the reference-reviewing media have their shortcomings. These have been examined in Margaret Knox Goggin and Lillian M. Seaberg, "The Publishing and Reviewing of Reference Books" (*Library Trends* 12:437–55 [Jan. 1964]); Harry E. Whitmore, "Reference Book Reviewing" (*RQ* 9:221–26 [Spring 1970]); and Alma A. Covey, *Reviewing of Reference Books* (Metuchen, N.J.: Scarecrow, 1972; 142p.).

Evaluation of Reference Books

All of these sources, from general guides to reference materials to individual journals, supply guidance in the evaluation of reference and information sources, and one set of guidelines is reproduced in the appendix. The guidelines for reviewing English-language dictionaries and encyclopedias, bibliographies, and atlases represent the considered judgment of the Reference and Subscription Books Review Committee of the American Library Association, and are scrupulously followed by that Committee in preparing its reviews. They emphasize the thoroughness required for careful evaluation of these types of reference works and should aid the individual librarian and library school student in determining the value of a title, as well as give them a fuller understanding of how the Reference and Subscription Books Review Committee functions.

What is this Committee and how does it function? Increased in number from thirty-five to fifty in 1968, members are appointed by the Executive Board of the American Library Association. They represent the major types of libraries and library activity, and in their selection an effort is made to include on the Committee persons who have special competencies in one of the broad subject fields of the humanities, behavioral sciences, or science and technology.

As stated in the preface to the annual cumulation, *Reference and Subscription Books Reviews, 1976–1977* (Chicago: ALA, 1978), "Upon acceptance of a title for review, one member is assigned primary responsibility for preparation of a draft review. The completed draft is circulated to the entire Committee for comment on content, structure, and style. Referring to guidelines set forth in the Committee *Manual*, members note any errors, omissions, awkward or opaque language, or inattention to standard procedure. Clear characterization of the work under review—its organization and scope; publication history and editorial credentials; designation of the appropriate user; evaluation of accuracy, currency, and objectivity; comments on the adequacy of bibliographies, indexes, and cross-references; appraisal of the format—these are among the elements examined and remarked upon in every review. Above all, there is an attempt to combine clear description and analysis, comparison with similar titles, and astute judgment in an integrated and thoroughly substantiated statement that is fair to the author, publisher, and probable purchaser. Every review, before publication, is criticized and revised until divergent opinions on form and content have been resolved [p.ix–x]." This statement might well serve as a guide to beginning reviewers of reference books.

In the reviewing activities of the Committee, priority is given to general encyclopedias and other general fact-finding reference sources, such as unabridged and abridged dictionaries, biographical dictionaries, atlases and gazetteers, directories, yearbooks and annuals, and statistical compendia; general bibliographical reference sources and periodical indexes; and reference sources confined to a single subject field (except those so limited in scope or technical in treatment that they are of use only to the specialist). These priorities for review are based on such factors as general interest, importance of titles, and (to a certain extent) price.

Also issued by the Committee is a Terminology Report, prepared in cooperation with the Reference Book Section of the American Textbook Publishers Institute and first published in 1953. Intended to provide "a common vocabulary to be used in the description and evaluation of reference works," it is reprinted in *Booklist* (71:301–4 [Nov. 1, 1974]).

This brief overview of the nature of reference/information service is intended only as an introduction to the chapters on various types of sources of information which follow. If it appears liberally studded with references to other sources, it is deliberately so, not only to give credit where credit is due (a cardinal rule in reference/information work) but also to stimulate the reader to use these sources for fuller understanding of this process in a spirit of free inquiry.

2

Sources of
Bibliographic Information

Our efforts to record and to organize for future use our discoveries, meditations, and observations of the universe have never been adequate to the never ending flow of manuscripts, published works, films, recordings, and machine-based data that constitute our means of communication with one another. This variety of forms of communication is greatly exceeded by the varieties of bibliographic activity, and a serious study of their development might well take years of reading. They range from short title lists to data banks, from indexes that use broad Library of Congress subject headings to those with highly specific index entries in abstracting services in technical and scientific fields.

A good brief history relating bibliography to the social and intellectual movements that provided the climate for its development and stimulated men and women to compile such lists is found in Louise-Nöelle Malclès, *Bibliography* (New York: Scarecrow, 1961; 152p.; rev. 1973). She is concerned with systematic bibliography, that form of publication compiled to meet the need so aptly stated by the historian Charles Victor Langlois in 1904: "What can be done so that the public will have the means to find out, rapidly and accurately, the resources of all kinds, offered by that great library formed by the work of authors of all times and all countries?"

15

But, as Malclès points out, the desire to record sources of information pervades the history of scholarship, and we find early examples of it in the ancient Babylonian catalogs of cuneiform tablets; in the list compiled by the Greek physician Galen in the second century; in the list of Bede's own works appended to his *Ecclesiastical History*, written in the eighth century. But it was the invention of printing that gave the greatest impetus to bibliographical activity, and lists of published works began to appear as early as 1494. The founders of bibliography in the sixteenth century were men of science, whose research into printed books was an extension of their special studies. They did original work, searching out books in libraries, in homes, and in book stores. And they were interested in the authors of the works, producing biobibliographies that more nearly resemble biographical dictionaries, with less sttention to the full bibliographic description of the works themselves.

Interest in books for their own sake came later, with the increasing dependence on lists already in existence; but the sixteenth century gave bibliography its direction for the next two centuries (Malclès, p.52). The seventeenth century saw the rise of enumerators, concerned with a census of all books, and not merely those in which they happened to take personal interest. By then there was not only specialized bibliography but also the beginning of universal and national bibliography. Bibliography flourished in the eighteenth century, with a new generation of researchers to whom the book was as important as its author. This century saw the development of systems of classification and rules for cataloging. Between 1790 and 1810, booksellers began to publish periodicals which recorded the new books of their countries, a kind of beginning of current national bibliography.

Nineteenth-century bibliography was affected by the great scientific movement which completely changed the conditions of intellectual activities. Other important factors affecting its development were the exploration of new countries, the progress in public education through curriculum reform and the reorganization of universities, the increase in number of major schools and learned societies, the growth of the book trade and periodical press, and the establishment of archives and libraries open to the public. These factors led to an increase in investigation and research, which in turn helped change the emphasis of bibliography from recording the works of the past to dissemination of current advances in learning.

By the beginning of the twentieth century, the goals and methods of bibliography had been defined. It became much more than the science of the book. Unlike those of the sixteenth century, bibliographies concentrated on the author's works, not the author. If, in the language dictionaries, it kept the meaning "the science of the book," the facts contradicted this assertion. More than at any other period, bibliography was awareness of the distinct products of the mind. The growth of knowledge and the publication of other bibliographies encouraged this change. Authors had been subordinated to their particular works. Today, bibliography carefully identifies distinct works and editions to record intellectual activity.

From 1914 on, we see the rapid development of current bibliography in almost every subject field. Also, we find specialists working together to produce "collective syntheses," which list the source material considered essential to the subject. But the most dramatic development has been that of documentation centers, which have continued to increase in all subject fields, with those in science and technology taking the lead.

A powerful force in extending and improving bibliographic activity throughout the world is UNESCO, which works with other international organizations that have major bibliographic programs. These programs are reported in UNESCO's bimonthly *Bibliography, Documentation, Terminology*. In 1950, UNESCO and the Library of Congress prepared a working paper on the present state and possibilities of improvement of bibliographical services, with an appendix by Kathrine Murra, entitled "Notes on the Development of the Concept of Current Complete National Bibliography."

The resolutions of the UNESCO Conference on the Improvement of Bibliographical Services emphasized the need for national planning bodies for bibliography and named eleven categories that member states should consider for coverage in current national bibliographies and lists: (1) general national bibliography of books and pamphlets, theses, and government publications published and on sale; (2) books and pamphlets published but not on sale; (3) index to important articles in periodicals and newspapers; (4) maps and atlases; (5) musical works; (6) audiovisual materials; (7) unpublished theses and academic publications; (8) local-government publications; (9) current periodicals and newspapers; (10) publishers and booksellers; and (11) learned societies, institutions, and libraries. These categories were intended as a base for subject bibliography since they would provide exhaustive collection of material and prompt and frequent publication of material from which selection could be made.

Eloquent testimony to the many and varied bibliographic activities which UNESCO has engaged in or subsidized is found in *Bibliography of Publications Issued by UNESCO or under Its Auspices* (Paris: UNESCO, 1973). It lists about 5,000 items by subject, with appended author and title indexes, and ranges from manuals on fundamental education, mass communications, and the arts to an anthology of Tamil love songs in English translation.

Reports on American activities are also available in "United States of America National Bibliographical and Abstracting Services and Related Activities," which has appeared in the winter issue of *RQ* since 1970, with reports covering several years in earlier issues of *RQ*.

The number of agencies concerned with bibliographic control increases yearly, with such varied interests as those of the Library of Congress, the

American Council of Learned Societies, the Council on Library Resources, the National Endowment on the Arts and the Humanities, and state and local historical societies. Though many projects have been initiated in recent years, a general overview of activities over the world will be found in UNESCO, *Guide to National Bibliographical Information Centres* (3rd ed., rev. and enl. Paris: UNESCO, 1970; 195p.). It lists the chief centers in seventy-seven countries, with name and address, founding date, purpose, special fields of interest, resources, availabllity, and reproduction services.

With the coming of the computer we have seen the development of information systems and services which have dramatically affected our access to stored facts. They are most prominent in the fields of science and technology and, increasingly, in the social sciences and humanities. They are being developed by government agencies, university research centers, and agencies concerned with current problems, and include computerized data bases, SDI (Selective Dissemination of Information) services, clearing houses and information centers, library and information networks, and data collection and analysis centers. Their proliferation in recent years is most evident in Anthony T. Kruzas, ed., *Encyclopedia of Information Systems and Services* (3rd ed.; Detroit: Gale Research, 1978; 1030p.). This directory describes systems or services, including foreign, and gives their scope or subject coverage, their input or data sources, their holdings or storage media, their publications, their computer applications and services, the equipment used, and the restrictions placed on their use. Since 1979 it has been updated by its interedition supplement, *New Information Systems and Services*.

It is not the purpose of this chapter to trace the history of bibliographic activities, but to describe some of the kinds of systematic bibliography and their general characteristics and uses. For practical purposes, Luther Evans' definition of bibliography will be used (with full recognition that many other definitions exist): "A bibliography is a compilation of information regarding recorded sources of information."

Definitions

The two principal elements in bibliographic activities may be understood immediately by any library-school student who has learned to catalog and classify a book. They have been designated descriptive bibliography and systematic bibliography. With the book in hand, the student must first describe its physical state, its format. This description involves recording its author or authors, title, place of publication, publisher, date of publication, size, number of pages, illustrations, and, when applicable, the series to which it belongs. This record is a simple form of *descriptive* bibliography.

His (or her) next concern is the intellectual content of the book, its subject matter. He must designate its place in some system of classification—must assign its proper subject headings in terms of some established system. In so doing, he has engaged in a simple act of *systematic* bibliography.

Descriptive bibliography then, is concerned with accurate identification and description of a book (or nonbook) as a physical object. In his introduction to "Current Trends in Bibliography" (*Library Trends* 7, no.4:495 [Apr. 1959]), Roy Stokes provides a useful table that sets forth the two purposes of bibliography and clarifies the preceding, oversimplified statements:

I. Study of the Book itself as a *Physical Entity*, a material object:

PURPOSE accurate, precise identification and description	Analytical or Critical Bibliography	Textual Bibliography Study and comparison of texts and their transmission through editions and printings
		Historical Bibliography Placing and dating of individual books
		Descriptive Bibliography Identification of the "ideal copy" and all its variants

II. Study of the Book as an *Intellectual Entity*:

PURPOSE assembling of information about individual books into a logical and useful arrangement	Enumerative or Systematic Bibliography	Compilation of lists of books

For a fuller treatment of the subject, see also Roy Stokes, *The Function of Bibliography* (London: Deutsch, 1969; 174p.). Stokes believes that much confusion in use of the term bibliography stems from its application to a book as both a physical and an intellectual entity.

Paul S. Dunkin states simply, "A bibliographer tells us one or more of at least three things about a book he has examined as a physical object: (1) He classifies it as an edition, issue, state, or variant; (2) He transcribes its title; (3) He states its collation (p.13)." Each of these tasks Dunkin reviews in some detail in his *Bibliography: Tiger or Fat Cat?* (Hamden, Conn.: Archon Books, 1975; 128p.). His analyses of the writings of Fredson Bowers, Walter Greg, Ronald McKerrow, and other important writers on the book as a physical object remove some of the controversy and confusion which characterized earlier discussions of the role of descriptive bibliography.

Systematic bibliography is concerned with the subject matter of a book.

Current problems in bibliographical control include such matters as international cooperation, centralization, standardization, automation of cataloging procedures, and defining the role of bibliographic centers. An overview of these and other issues is found in the January 1977 issue of *Library Trends*: "Bibliographical Control: International Issues."

This chapter is concerned with bibliography, as broadly defined by Luther Evans, with full recognition that certain types, such as library catalogs and periodical indexes, are not admitted to this category by all who have written on the subject. These types are parts of systematic bibliography; and for those who seek information on recorded sources of information, it is practical to outline the whole range, without quibbling over differences in definition. Simply stated, the purpose is to make certain generalizations about existing bibliographic tools that allow a user to identify what has been recorded.

Systematic bibliographies take many forms, which have been developed in response to a recognized need for a systematic arrangement of recorded knowledge, whether it be recorded in a book or on a map, film, tape, or musical recording. Broadly defined, they include library catalogs, union catalogs, national bibliographies, subject bibliographies, selective bibliographies, indexes, abstracts, and concordances. These designations furnish some clue to their content and purpose, and within this framework may be briefly described.

Library Catalogs

Since libraries are the principal repositories of recorded knowledge, it follows that the library catalog, which systematically records the books in a library collection by author, title, and subject, is an important form of systematic bibliography.

Union Catalogs/Union Lists

From catalogs of individual libraries have developed general union catalogs, which record in one sequence the holdings or part of the holdings of two or more libraries, either on cards, in book form, or in microform, such as the *National Union Catalog* of the Library of Congress. Containing books and pamphlets unrestricted by subject, place, or date of publication, it constitutes the nearest approach to universal bibliography.

National Book Bibliographies

Place and date of publication are the principal factors that determine what is included in national bibliographies, of which the *Cumulative Book Index* is an important example for American librarians. A national bibliography may be further restricted by form of publication. Thus, principally, the *Cumulative Book Index* includes books in the English language published by trade publishers and is commonly referred to as a trade bibliography. Just as a library catalog serves as an inventory of a library's collections, a national bibliography serves as an inventory of titles published in a country.

Subject Bibliographies

As the name implies, subject bibliographies are restricted to one subject, but usually not to one form of publication or one language. They may be retrospective or current, comprehensive or selective. Interest in contemporary writers has been responsible for a large number of author bibliographies which record works by and about these authors.

Selective Bibliographies

Selective is most often applied to bibliographies that record the best titles for a particular type of user, library, or subject. But it should be noted that all of the types listed thus far are selective in another sense. A library catalog is selective in that it lists only the holdings of a particular library. National bibliography is selective in being restricted to the output of one country or type of publication. Subject bibliographies are selective in dealing with only one subject or aspect of a subject, and also may be selective in the other sense, by including only the best or most useful material on that subject.

These forms of bibliography are viewed as selective—not to create a confusion of terms but to serve as a reminder of the interdependence of the various forms and of the necessity of using more than one form in many kinds of searches for information. In general, selective bibliographies are compiled with stated criteria for selection of their contents.

Indexes

Indexes differ from book catalogs and trade bibliographies in recording alphabetically and analytically, under appropriate entries, the contents of a book, periodical, or other document. Increasingly, they are prepared by machines. They range from the general to the ever increasing number of indexes in special fields, especially in science and technology.

Abstracts

Abstracts resemble indexes in recording the contents of a book, periodical, or other document. They differ from indexes in their hierarchical arrangement and in that they contain digests, or abstracts, of the listed publications. It should also be noted that all systematic bibliography contains the element of descriptive bibliography, since a book, periodical article, map, phonograph record, or film must be described in order to be identified. The one most used by librarians is *Library and Information Science Abstracts*. All of them follow the pattern of the best known, *Chemical Abstracts* (described below).

Concordances

Alphabetical lists of the important words in a text as they occur in context are called concordances. Older examples include those to the Bible or to the works of important authors—Shakespeare, for example. These lists have increased in number since the application of computer technology to their compilation.

These elementary definitions and broad generalizations are insufficient to indicate the characteristics and uses of each form, which must be approached in greater detail, proceeding from the most familiar form, the library card catalog, to those forms that augment it by supplying more items on a particular subject or by giving a more specific approach to recorded knowledge. The following pages will set forth the characteristics of the individual forms, with annotations of selected titles for each.

Library Catalogs

When two or more books are acquired by a library, the problem of their relationship to one another arises; thus some method must be devised to show these relationships and, at the same time, preserve the identity of each. Go to a card catalog in your nearest library and observe that it contains cards for authors, subjects, and titles represented in the library's collection. Look at an author card and observe that the author's name is usually given in full, with dates of birth and death—to distinguish, for example, John Amos Brown from John Andrew Brown, or one John Brown from another. For a better understanding of the author concept in codes of cataloging rules in the English language, consult James A. Tait, *Author and Titles* (Hamden, Conn.: Archon Books, 1969; 154p.).

Next, look at the cards under a subject. Note that this subject was assigned according to a system of subject headings—whose arbitrariness

Hayes were not the first to recognize: "One of the drawbacks of a subject heading system is the arbitrary or artificial decisions which the indexer must make at the input stage when he makes his initial assignment of subject headings to documents. The user will not always agree with the indexer's choice—the semantics of the heading may change with time, and the concepts underlying the indexer's choice may themselves change. While the subject heading system has the virtue of expandability, it has the corresponding disadvantage of increasing rapidly in terms of size and complexity" (Joseph Becker and R. M. Hayes, *Information Storage and Retrieval* [New York: Wiley, 1963], p. 25).

The chief problem for the user of the catalog, then, is terminology. Most large American library catalogs contain subject headings whose authority was established by the Library of Congress and published in *Subject Headings Used in the Dictionary Catalogs of the Library of Congress*. According to its preface, this list is the product of evolutionary forces: the growth of the library's collections, semantic change, and varying theories of subject heading practice over the years; and while it is an accurate reflection of practice, it is not a complete embodiment of theory. Familiarity with this list is a prerequisite for any librarian who attempts to give instruction in the use of the card catalog. This familiarity involves an awareness of its *scope* notes, which explain the distinction between headings; of its *see* references, which direct the user from a term not used to the term under which it may be found; and of its *see also* references, which bring together related headings that are often more specific aspects of the subject.

Another system of subject headings, developed originally by the *British National Bibliography,* is PRECIS (Preserved Context Indexing System). This is a subject indexing system "in which the initial string of terms, organized according to a scheme of role-indicating operators, is computer-manipulated so that selected words function in turn as the approach term. Entries are restructured at each step in such a way that the user can determine from the layout of the entry which terms set the appropriate term into its context and which terms are context-dependent on the approach term" (L. M. Harrod, *The Librarian's Glossary* [4th rev. ed.; Boulder, Colo.: Westview Pr., 1977], p.655). It is held in high esteem by A. C. Foskett in his *Subject Approach to Information* (3rd ed.; Hamden, Conn.: Shoe String, 1977; p.224–44), who concludes: "It does not claim to be perfect, and it does have its critics, but it does appear to be one of the best, if not the best, system that we have at present. It is based on over twenty years of experience in the detailed indexing of large numbers of books for BNB, as well as on the theories developed by the CRG [Classification Research Group] in the quest for a new classification. Some experimental work has also shown that, because it is based on linguistic principles, it can give good results when used with other languages than English. It now forms part of the MARC records generated in Australia as well as those in BNB, and has been used successfully in indexing of non-book materials. It is certainly a major contribution to the theory and practice of alphabetical subject headings" (p.244).

Smaller libraries often use *Sears' List of Subject Headings*, which follows the Library of Congress form of headings, abridged and simplified to meet the needs of smaller libraries. But the point to be remembered is that a thorough knowledge of the system of subject headings used in a particular library catalog is essential to the intelligent use of that catalog. Those without this knowledge, but knowing the author of at least one book on a subject for which information is sought, must check under that author and resort to the subject headings transcribed near the bottom of the Library of Congress card. These will serve as guides to additional titles held by a library.

Other information on the card is the classification number, which not only indicates the location of a book in the library's collection but gives a clue to its subject matter. The classification number is often a clue to the nationality of an author; e.g., 810 is the Dewey number for American authors, while the Library of Congress uses PR and PS for American and British authors. The catalog card also indicates whether a book contains a bibliography, not only through a subject heading for a work devoted entirely to bibliography—"American literature—Bibliography," for example—but by noting in the collation if a bibliography is included in addition to the text.

Equally important is the catalog in microform, and there are those who believe that the hard-copy printed book catalog will eventually be replaced by those in Computer Output Microform (COM). Known as COMCAT (Computer Output Microform Catalog), these catalogs are reproduced in microform from card catalogs and kept current with frequent supplements which cumulate. Intended to provide faster access to more up-to-date information on library holdings, they have been adopted by a number of large American libraries or systems—among them, public libraries of Houston, St. Louis, Chicago, Dallas, Western Kentucky University, and the state libraries of Maryland and Kansas. Many articles on this relatively new form are listed in *Library Literature* under *Catalogs—Microform reproductions*. Often these are testimonials of their success or lack of success in libraries which have abandoned their card catalogs in favor of the microform.

Several book catalogs, however—those of the great national libraries—can be used as examples of universal bibliography, or our nearest approach to it, since they record collections that embrace all subjects, all countries, and all dates of publication.

There have been two theories in American cataloging: (1) that the catalog should serve as a finding list for location of a book if the author, title, or subject is known, and (2) that it is an encyclopedia which gives more than a brief description of an individual book, including birth and death dates for authors, series note, whether there are illustrations and maps, etc. Paul S. Dunkin, in "The Eternal Triangle" (*RQ* 3:3–6 [Mar. 1964]), reviews these theories and concludes that "the catalog is a good reference work. It can do for you one thing nothing else can do. It can find a book in the library for you if you know the author, title, or subject."

While the *card* catalog is the most familiar form of finding list in most American libraries, recent years have seen renewed interest in library catalogs in book form. Among the reasons are the growing complexity of card catalogs for large library collections, the newer methods of reproduction, and a recognition of the advantage of a more compact form, which allows book catalogs to be more easily placed in locations where they are needed. For a review of this form, see Theodore C. Hines, "Book Catalogs," in *Encyclopedia of Library and Information Science* (New York: Dekker, 1969; v.2, p.659–67).

National Library Catalogs

At first glance, it may seem to be a great jump from a card catalog of a small, general collection to the multivolume catalogs of such great libraries as the Library of Congress, the British Museum, and the Bibliothèque Nationale, but this jump should be made with the realization that they have certain features in common. They also supply dramatic contrasts between the collections in a small library and those in the great libraries of the world. No less dramatic is the fact that these great collections are accessible to qualified users over the world. What, then, are their general characteristics?

Published national library catalogs are usually restricted to printed books and pamphlets. When periodicals are included, they are usually listed by title, not analyzed by contents. Each gives fuller representation to books published in its own country than to those of other countries, and is usually the most comprehensive record of publications in that country, containing types of publications not listed in trade bibliographies, such as government publications. They are usually arranged alphabetically by author (with certain notable exceptions). Subjects are usually shown in separately published catalogs or indexes.

Catalogs of the great national libraries often differ from one another in form of entry and amount of bibliographic detail. Differences in form also occur within a catalog, reflecting changing rules for entry that have developed through the years. At the same time, it must be recognized that the catalogs have been prepared by professional catalogers who have observed a body of rules for cataloging and who have seen the books described. This preparation distinguishes library catalogs from trade bibliographies (the latter are often compiled from information supplied by publishers).

Some of the purposes that national library catalogs serve have been stated succinctly by A. D. Roberts in *Introduction to Reference Books* (2nd ed.; London: Library Assn., 1951; p. 75):

  a. They tell us what books an author has written (usually they supply the equivalent of a fairly full author bibliography), while the British Museum Catalogue lists books about an author, following works by that author.
  b. They verify the existence of a book since each entry has been catalogued with book in hand.
  c. They may, because of the detail of their entries, provide additional information about a book, or correct some incorrect information that we have.
  d. They locate one copy which is probably available for consultation.
  e. They help cataloguers in other libraries.

Recognizing the general characteristics and purposes of national library catalogs (their common elements), we can turn to their differences in scope, arrangement, and amount of bibliographic data. Here are only a few examples from the many listed and described in the guides to reference books by Sheehy and Walford.

→ National union catalog: a cumulative author list. Wash., Lib. of Congress, 1956– . Monthly, with quarterly, annual, and polyennial cumulations.

  SCOPE: Lists books, pamphlets, maps, atlases, periodicals, and other serials cataloged by LC or reported by 750 cooperating libraries.
  ARRANGEMENT: Alphabetical by author or other main entry, but with no added entries for joint authors.
  BIBLIOGRAPHIC DATA: Photographically reproduced from LC cards, giving full name and dates of author; full title; place, publisher and date; collation (paging, illustrations, maps); series; edition; contents notes; history; tracings for subject headings and added entries; LC and often Dewey classifications; and International Standard Book Numbers (ISBN). Library locations are shown by symbols, with key in front of cumulated volumes.

It was noted earlier that the subject approach to national library collections is found in separately published catalogs or indexes. Such is the case with the Library of Congress, which has published a subject catalog for its holdings only since 1950. Issued as *The Library of Congress Subject Catalog* and later as *Library of Congress Catalog. Books: Subjects*, since 1975 it has appeared under the following title:

→ U.S. Library of Congress. Subject catalog. 1950– . Wash., Lib. of Congress, 1950– . Quarterly, with annual and quinquennial cumulations.

SCOPE: Quinquennial cumulations cover publications dated 1945 or later, cataloged during the periods covered by LC and cooperating libraries. Quarterly issues exclude entries for belles lettres and imprints earlier than the current and two preceding years. Annual cumulations include currently cataloged titles published from 1945 to date. The introductions must be read with care to note variations in scope and type of material included. For example, motion pictures and music scores have been excluded after 1952, being indexed by subject in separate catalogs from 1953.

ARRANGEMENT: Alphabetical by LC subject headings.

BIBLIOGRAPHIC DATA: Substantially the same as that in LC author catalog, with minor variations.

If the *Subject Catalog* is used for location of titles in libraries other than the Library of Congress, the *National Union Catalog* for authors should be checked further, since it includes added library locations that are not in the *Subject Catalog*.

→ National union catalog. Pre-1956 imprints. A cumulative author list, representing LC printed cards and titles reported by other American libraries. Comp. and ed. with the cooperation of LC and National Union Catalog Subcommittee of the Resources and Technical Services Division, American Library Assn. [London]: Mansell, 1968– . v.1– . (In progress)

SCOPE: Planned to include some 12 million entries for books, pamphlets, maps, atlases, music, serials (if represented by LC card or reported by another library) and to be published in about 750 volumes.

ARRANGEMENT: By main entry, with *see* references and some added entries.

BIBLIOGRAPHIC DATA: Substantially the same as *National Union Catalog*.

When complete, it will supersede the following Library of Congress catalogs: *A Catalog of Books Represented by Library of Congress Printed Cards (Cards Issued from August 1898 through July 1942); Supplement (Cards Issued from August 1942 through December 1947*); The Library of Congress Author Catalog, 1948–1952*; The National Union Catalog, 1952–1955 Imprints; The National Union Catalog, a Cumulative Author List, 1953–1957*.* (Starred titles are included in a cumulation in one alphabet published by Gale Research of Detroit, which covers the years 1942–62.)

As noted, the pre-1956 catalog is based on a number of predecessors, but is restricted to books, pamphlets, maps, atlases, music, and periodicals. It has undergone editing which attempted to standardize all entries, but some inconsistencies are still found. Users must remember that

1. Different works by the same author are sometimes found under different forms of the author's name.
2. Copies of the same work reported by cooperating libraries may be found under different forms of the author's name.

Also certain types of materials found in some of its predecessors have been omitted, among them:

1. Books for the blind (in Braille, etc.)
2. Phonorecords, motion pictures, and filmstrips. Separate volumes covering these in superseded catalogs must be retained.
3. All works in non-Latin characters (Arabic, Chinese, etc.), unless represented by LC cards

Also, certain types of material are more fully recorded elsewhere, including:

1. Periodicals. Holdings in libraries are more fully listed in *Union List of Serials* and *New Serial Titles*.
2. Manuscript collections are listed in *National Union Catalog of Manuscripts*, and *only* individual manuscripts reported to LC are in *NUC*.

An added bibliographic approach by title to the classified collections of the Library of Congress is:

→ The cumulative title index to the classified collections of the Library of Congress, 1978. Arlington, Va., Carrollton Pr., 1979–82?

> SCOPE: Includes 1 million MARC entries and 5.5 million non-MARC entries for LC classified collections. The non-MARC entries, which make up 85 percent of the collection, include pre-1968 and transliterated non-Roman-alphabet items. Estimated completion date, July 31, 1982.
> ARRANGEMENT: Alphabetical by title.
> BIBLIOGRAPHIC DATA: For each entry: title, author, complete LC classification number, and LC card order number, giving year and MARC designation (M).

The British and French national library catalogs will be discussed briefly to emphasize how they differ from the Library of Congress catalog in scope, arrangement, and kinds of bibliographic data. It should be remembered that both of them began publication before the Library of Congress catalog, that both include only works found in their own libraries, and that both represent collections assembled over a longer period of time.

→ British Museum. Department of Printed Books. General catalogue of printed books. Photolithographic ed. to 1955. London, Trustees of the British Museum, 1959–66. 263v. Polyennial supps.

SCOPE: Contains entries for books, pamphlets, and periodicals in Western languages, and reproductions of these from the 15th century to the end of 1955. Representing the holdings of one of the largest libraries in the world, it includes many titles not found in the LC catalog. A random sample of 250 authors by Walford revealed that 77 percent of the works listed do not appear in the LC *Catalog of Books*, and for the period before 1800, 95 percent of those listed are not in the LC catalog. Strong in British authors, British history, and British imprints. Note sections on the Bible, England, London, and periodical publications.

ARRANGEMENT: Alphabetical by author, titles or catchword titles for anonymous works, and cross-references for editors, translators, etc. Note carefully the following subject features: (1) biographies and biocriticism of authors are listed with their works, making the catalog an excellent source on individual authors; (2) family histories are listed under family name; (3) periodicals are listed in v.184–87 under the headings *Periodicals* and place of publication, e.g. Aberdeen; (4) texts and commentary on sacred books are listed under their names, e.g. Bible; (5) official publications, some works about a country, and many titles in which the name of the country occurs are listed under the name of the country.

BIBLIOGRAPHIC DATA: In general, briefer than those in the LC catalog, usually omitting birth and death dates of authors, pagination, size, name of publisher, and subject headings. Often noted is occupation of an author, e.g. Pike (Joseph) *Artist*. The differences in the two catalogs are most easily understood by comparing the entries for several titles found in both. Supplements contain corrections of some entries in the photolithographic edition.

In addition to the biographical and geographical subject approaches provided in *General Catalogue of Printed Books*, there is *Subject Index of the Modern Works Added to the Library* (London: British Museum, 1881–), arranged by large subject groupings, omitting personal names but entering biographees under the subjects with which they are connected.

→ Paris. Bibliothèque Nationale. Catalogue général des livres imprimés: Auteurs. Paris, Impr. Nationale, 1900– . v.1– .

SCOPE: Since the Bibliothèque Nationale traces its origin to the private library of John II, 14th-century king of France, its catalog is rich in early works, particularly strong for French history and literature and

French and Continental imprints. Works of certain important authors (Cervantes, Molière, Shakespeare, and others) are included, in some cases constituting union catalogs of Parisian library holdings. Each volume includes titles acquired up to the date of its publication; e.g. v.1 represents the collection as of 1897. Beginning with v.189, however, only additions through 1959 are included, with more recent acquisitions listed in a new series. (See below.) Omitted are anonymous classics, periodicals, society transactions, government publications, and works by corporate authors.

ARRANGEMENT: Alphabetical by name of personal author. Under authors of voluminous works are detailed title indexes, including alternative and changed titles, citing volumes or editions in which each may be found.

BIBLIOGRAPHIC DATA: Given more fully than in the British Museum catalog, including author's full name, title, place, publishers, date, edition, paging, size, and illustrations, with occasional contents notes and citation to original publication in case of titles reprinted from periodicals.

→ _____. _____. Departement des Imprimés. Catalogue général des livres imprimés. 1960/69– . Paris, 1972– .

SCOPE: Titles added to the Bibliothèque Nationale from 1960 on, and all French titles in *Bibliographie de la France*. Excludes periodicals.

ARRANGEMENT: Alphabetical by personal author, corporate entry, title entry for anonymous works and publications of some corporate bodies, with added entries for joint authors, translators, etc. Works in the Cyrillic alphabet and in Hebraic characters are in separate alphabets.

These three national library catalogs, one of which has been expanded into a union catalog, are examples of a form of bibliography distinguished for

Breadth of scope, being unrestricted by subject, date, or place of publication

Inclusion of rare, obscure, and privately printed titles not found in trade bibliographies

Scrupulous attention to bibliographic detail, representing a body of practice developed by professional catalogers

Recording location in at least one library for each title.

Their importance for research workers cannot be overestimated and their general characteristics should be kept in mind as other forms of bibliography are considered.

These great national library catalogs have long served scholars, but many lesser-known catalogs of art museums, societies, former private collections, government agencies, research institutes, and some of the major public and university libraries in the English-speaking world are also important. These are listed in

→ Collison, Robert. Published library catalogues. London, Mansell, 1973. 184p.

Describes catalogs in various subject areas, including auction sales, book industries, philosophy and religion, science and technology, art and architecture, and geography, with appended bibliography and detailed subject index.

National Book Bibliographies

Current

If we adopt LeRoy H. Linder's definition of national bibliography, we must include in this category not only the Library of Congress catalogs already discussed, but also bibliographies of government publications, pamphlets, periodicals, and newspapers, which will be treated separately later on to set forth more clearly their distinguishing characteristics. For Linder, in his study of current national bibliographies, states: "For this study, then, current complete national bibliography is a complete or nearly complete listing, in one or more parts, of the records of a nation, about a nation, copyrighted in a nation, or in a single language, issued serially at appropriate intervals as the records appear" (*The Rise of Current Complete National Bibliographies* [New York: Scarecrow, 1959], p. 18).

Helen Conover viewed current national bibliography as "a complete listing of all books, documents, pamphlets, serials, and other printed matter published within the bounds of a single country and within the time limits of the previous year or less" (*Current National Bibliographies* [Washington: Library of Congress, 1955; repr.: Greenwood, 1968], p.1). Her carefully annotated list of sources of bibliographic information in sixty-seven countries includes sources for books, pamphlets, theses, maps, music, periodicals, newspapers, and government publications, as well as notable selective lists. This is augmented in part by UNESCO, *Bibliographical Services throughout the World*—by various compilers, published at intervals, and updated by *Bibliography, Documentation* and *Terminology* (cited earlier).

For a good overview of the subject, consult Frank M. McGowan's "National Bibliography," in *Encyclopedia of Library and Information Science*, v.19, p.50–60 [New York: Dekker, 1976]).

Current national bibliography (described in the following section) is restricted to inventories of books published in a single country or language, with only American, British, and French examples cited. These book inventories are usually referred to as trade bibliographies since they emphasize books published by trade publishers and serve the book trade as well as other persons seeking information on recently published book titles.

To relate them to national library catalogs, it is pertinent to note what information they supply that is not found in national library catalogs. It includes:

Price of a book at the time of publication, in all cases
Descriptive annotations, in some cases
Lists of publishers and their addresses
Title entries that are not given in national library catalogs
Titles in trade series (those from a single publisher, e.g. *Rivers of America*)
Evidence that a book was in print when the trade bibliography was issued
Some books not recorded in national library catalogs, either because of their recent or forthcoming publication or because they had not been acquired or cataloged by these libraries.

It is wise to remember that some books announced for publication never appear, as was the case of Katherine Anne Porter's *No Safe Harbor*, published years later as *Ship of Fools*.

How do they differ from national library catalogs in their arrangement? Here it is more difficult to generalize, since trade bibliographies do not follow one pattern. The following examples illustrate the wide differences in arrangement in only a few of the most frequently used British and American trade bibliographies:

Dictionary arrangement, with authors, titles, and subjects in one alphabet, e.g. *Cumulative Book Index*
Alphabetical by name of publisher, e.g. *Publishers' Trade List Annual*
Alphabetical in two indexes: (1) by author and editor; (2) by title and series, e.g. *Books in Print*, to accompany *Publishers' Trade List Annual*
Alphabetical by subject, e.g. *Subject Guide to Books in Print*, to accompany *Books in Print*
Alphabetical by author, e.g. *Weekly Record*
Classified by Dewey Decimal Classification, e.g. *British National Bibliography* and *American Book Publishing Record*.

Since every classified bibliography must have an index, it should be noted that the *British National Bibliography*'s classified arrangement is followed by an alphabetical author, title, and subject index, which includes editors, translators, and series.

As noted earlier, place and date of publication are the principal factors that determine the scope of trade bibliographies. To these may be added the form of publication, such as books, and the kind of issuing agency, such as trade publishers. The following titles are those most frequently used.

AMERICAN
→ Cumulative book index: a world list of books in the English language. N.Y., Wilson, 1898– . Monthly, with quarterly, annual, and 5-year cumulations.

> SCOPE. Books, scholarly pamphlets, and proceedings in the English language, published by trade publishers, university presses, religious denominations, societies, scientific institutions, conferences, and councils in all countries. Government documents, periodicals, and ephemeral materials are omitted.
> ARRANGEMENT: Authors, subjects, and titles in one alphabet.
> BIBLIOGRAPHIC DATA : Author, title, edition, series, paging, illustrations, price, date of publication, publisher or publishers, and LC card number given for main (author) entries. Subject entries omit paging, illustrations, series, and LC card numbers.

→ Publishers' trade list annual, 1873– . N.Y., Bowker, 1873– . 6v. Annual.

> SCOPE: Active lists and forthcoming publications of American and a few Canadian trade publishers, including some university presses, religious denominations, and scientific and learned societies in the United States, but not all of those represented in *Cumulative Book Index* or *Books in Print*. Occasionally lists titles announced for publication but never published.
> ARRANGEMENT: Alphabetical by names of larger publishers; v.1 includes catalogs of smaller publishers and index.
> BIBLIOGRAPHIC DATA: Based on information supplied by the publisher and thus varies from publisher to publisher.

→ Books in print, 1948– . N.Y., Bowker, 1948– . 4v. Annual, with supp. in 1v. 1973– .

> SCOPE: Books available from American publishers, based on active lists and forthcoming publications in *Publishers' Trade List Annual,* augmented by additional sources of new titles since 1973. Government publications, elementary/high school texts, some paperback lines, and periodicals are omitted. Supplements include new titles published since the basic volume, some forthcoming titles, and those which have gone out of print since the basic volume. Recent issues contain nearly 500,000 titles from over 5,000 publishers.

ARRANGEMENT: In two alphabets: (1) author and editor, and (2) title and series. Supplements include subjects.

BIBLIOGRAPHIC DATA: Author, title, publisher, price, date of publication, number of volumes, LC card number, and International Standard Book Numbers (ISBN), used by publishers to distinguish one title from another.

→ Subject guide to books in print, 1957– . N.Y., Bowker, 1957– . 2v. Annual.

SCOPE: Includes roughly 70 percent of titles in *Books in Print,* omitting individual titles of plays, fiction, poetry, Bibles, but not collections and criticisms of literary forms.

ARRANGEMENT: Alphabetical by LC subject headings, with some minor variations. Subject key to publishers' and distributors' abbreviations.

BIBLIOGRAPHIC DATA: Same as *Books in Print.*

→ El-hi textbooks in print. N.Y., Bowker, 1970– . Annual.

SCOPE: Based on and replacing *Textbooks in Print*, it is somewhat more complete than *BIP* in its listing of elementary and high school textbooks. Includes encyclopedias, dictionaries, atlases, maps and booklists, programmed learning materials in book form, professional books for teachers, teaching aids, and audiovisual materials such as films, filmstrips, and records, from more than 300 publishers.

ARRANGEMENT: Under 21 broad subject headings, with many subcategories; author, title, and series indexes; directory of publishers.

BIBLIOGRAPHIC DATA: Author, title, publisher, grade level, publication date, and latest price. Also indicates for each listing whether related AV material or teachers' edition is available.

→ Children's books in print, 1969– . N.Y., Bowker, 1969– . Annual.

SCOPE: Over 40,000 titles, drawn from *Books in Print.*

ARRANGEMENT: Separate sections for authors, titles, and illustrators.

BIBLIOGRAPHIC DATA: Same as *BIP*, including grade level.

→ Subject guide to children's books in print, 1970– . N.Y., Bowker, 1970– . Annual.

SCOPE: Drawn from *BIP.*

ARRANGEMENT: Alphabetical under about 7,000 categories.

BIBLIOGRAPHIC DATA: Same as *BIP.*

→ Weekly record, 1974– . N.Y., Bowker, 1974– . Weekly.

> SCOPE: Lists books of American publishers, omitting government pub-
> lications, subscription books, dissertations, periodicals, pamphlets
> and specialized publications, e.g. telephone books. Previously
> pulished in *Publishers Weekly*.
> ARRANGEMENT: Alphabetical by author or other main entry.
> BIBLIOGRAPHIC DATA: Based on LC cataloging, giving full title, pub-
> lisher, paging, price, Dewey Decimal number, LC card number and
> subject headings, and brief, descriptive annotations.

→ American book publishing record, v.1, no.1, Feb. 1, 1960– . N.Y.,
Bowker, 1960– . Monthly, with annual and quinquennial cumulations.

> SCOPE: Includes titles "as catalogued by Library of Congress and anno-
> tated by *Weekly Record*."
> ARRANGEMENT: By Dewey Decimal Classification, with monthly author
> and title index; annual author and title index, 1962–65; annual
> cumulations since 1965, with subject index since 1976. Separate
> sections on juvenile and adult fiction alphabetical by author.
> BIBLIOGRAPHIC DATA: Same as *Weekly Record*, with some revisions.

→ American book publishing record cumulative, 1950–1977: an American
national bibliography. N.Y., Bowker, 1979. 15v.

> Includes titles from National Union Catalog for years 1950–68 and from
> LC MARC tapes for years 1968–77, which did not appear in previous
> *ABPR* cumulations.

→ Forthcoming books. v.1, no.1– , Jan. 1966– . N.Y., Bowker, 1966– .
Bimonthly.

> SCOPE: Books to be published in succeeding 5 months by trade pub-
> lishers. Each issue overlaps and updates preceding one. Beginning in
> November 1967, was expanded to include titles published since the
> most recent *Books in Print*.
> ARRANGEMENT: Alphabetical in separate author and title indexes.
> BIBLIOGRAPHIC DATA: Author, title, publisher, price, and publication
> date.

→ Subject guide to Forthcoming books. v.1, no.1– , Jan. 1967– . N.Y.,
Bowker, 1967– . Bimonthly.

> "Presents by [broad] subject the same titles that are listed by author and
> title in *Forthcoming Books*" (Foreword to v.1, no.1).

BRITISH

→ British national bibliography, 1950– . London, British Library, Bibliographic Services Division, 1950– . Weekly, with interim, annual, and five-year cumulations.

> SCOPE: British imprints of trade publishers, university presses, societies, scientific institutions, and some non-British publishers. Omitted are periodicals (except first issue of a new periodical or a periodical under a new title), music, maps, certain government publications (parliamentary papers and routine administrative publications), and paperback reprints of previously recorded novels.
> ARRANGEMENT: Classified by Dewey Classification, with weekly author and title index; monthly author, title, and subject index; and quarterly, annual, and five-year cumulations in three parts: classified subject, author/title, and subject index.
> BIBLIOGRAPHIC DATA: Classified section includes author, title, place, publisher, date (usually month and day), paging, illustrations, size, series, and price. Prepared by qualified bibliographers with resources of British Library at their disposal.

→ British books in print; the reference catalogue of current literature . . . , 1965– . London, Whitaker, 1965– . Annual. Previously published at four-year intervals. (Formerly Reference catalogue of current literature.) Distributed in the U.S. by Bowker.

> SCOPE: Records about 283,000 books in print and on sale in United Kingdom.
> ARRANGEMENT: Authors and catchwords in one alphabet.
> BIBLIOGRAPHIC DATA: Author surname, with initials or Christian name; title; date of original publication or latest edition; editor, translator or reviser, when applicable; size; paging; illustrations; series; binding; publisher; price; standard book number.

FRENCH

→ Le catalogue de l'édition française, 1970–76. (Paris), VPC Livres; [Port Washington], Paris Publications [1971–76]. 23v.

> SCOPE: Includes hard- and softbound books in French from more than 2,000 publishers in more than 40 countries, and United Nations publications in French.
> ARRANGEMENT: (v.1) Authors, (v.2) titles, and (v.3–4) subjects, arranged by Universal Decimal Classification. Appended in each volume are lists of publishers with addresses and publishers' series.

BIBLIOGRAPHIC DATA: Author, title, subtitle, publishers, special imprint, collection number, translation, index, glossary, bibliography, illustrations, pagination, size, reference number, and price.

→ Repertoire des livres de langue française disponibles, 1972–75. (Paris), France-Expansion, 1972–75. 8v.

Full bibliographic information for in-print French-language titles, regardless of place of publication. Indexed by author, subject, and title and verified from publishers' stock, including data on some titles not in publishers' own catalogs and price lists.

→ Les livres disponibles. 1977– . Paris, Cercle de la Librairie, 1977– . Issued in two parts: auteurs, titres.

Established by merger of *Le Catalogue de l'Édition Française* and *Repertoire des Livres de Langue Française Disponibles,* it covers the same types of publications.

→ Bibliographie de la France—Biblio. 1971– . Paris, Cercle de la Librairie, 1972– . Weekly, with monthly and quarterly cumulations.

SCOPE: Titles received by legal deposit section of Bibliothèque Nationale, including weekly list of books and, at intervals, materials grouped under (a) publications en série, (b) gravures, estampes et photographies, (c) oeuvres musicales, (d) thèses, (e) atlas, cartes et plans, (f) publications officielles, (g) catalogues de ventes publiques.

ARRANGEMENT: As noted above, with the weekly book section broadly classified by Dewey Classification and indexed in two parts, by author and by "anonymes." This part is cumulated as a monthly supplement, titled *Les Livres du Mois,* with the same arrangement; and by *Les Livres du Trimestre—Biblio,* listed in one alphabet by author, title, and subject. Supersedes *Bibliographie de la France,* 1811–70, and *Biblio,* 1933–70.

→ Les livres de l'année—Biblio. 1971– . Paris, Cercle de la Librarie, [1972]– . Annual

Formed by merger of *Biblio* and *Librarie Française les Livres de l' Année,* it cumulates the quarterly issues of the supplement to *Bibliographie de la France—Biblio, Les Livres du Trimestre—Biblio.* Contains foreign titles, added by the editors to the titles in the weekly and monthly issues.

SUMMARY

The scope, arrangement, and frequency of these current national book bibliographies indicate the ways in which they may be used in searching. These may be summarized as follows.

> As a record of what is currently in print, listed annually in *Publishers' Trade List Annual, Books in Print, Subject Guide to Books in Print, British Books in Print,* and German, Italian, and Australian equivalents.
>
> As a record of books to be published, listed bimonthly in *Forthcoming Books* and *Subject Guide to Forthcoming Books.*
>
> As a record of recently published books issued at intervals, as follows:
>
> Weekly. Listed only by author in *Weekly Record*; by Dewey Classification, with author and title index, as in *British National Bibliography*; and indexed by author in *Bibliographie de la France— Biblio.*
>
> Monthly. Listed by author, subject, and title in *Cumulative Book Index* and by author, title, and Dewey Decimal Classification in *American Book Publishing Record* and *British National Bibliography.*
>
> Quarterly. Listed in *Cumulative Book Index* and *British National Bibliography.*
>
> Annually. Listed in *Cumulative Book Index, American Book Publishing Record,* and *British National Bibliography.*

There is a great deal of duplication in American imprints listed in the trade bibliographies and the *National Union Catalog,* although some titles will be found in only one source.

That United States trade bibliographies are in a state of change is evident from the number of tools that have begun publication since 1960. This changing pattern will continue for some time, stimulated not only by the need for prompt and complete recording of an increasing number of imprints but by the developing use of computer methodology in their compilation.

For a fully annotated list of trade and national bibliographies, consult A. J. Walford's *Guide to Reference Materials* (3rd ed., v.3.; London: Library Assn., 1977).

Retrospective

It should be remembered that the examples of current national bibliography mentioned thus far have been considered current because they provide a continuing record of what was published or in print at a given time, this record appearing soon after the titles were published or, in a few cases, were announced for publication. Although none of the American examples began publication before 1872, it is apparent that their early volumes may also be used as retrospective bibliographies when viewed from the standpoint of the late twentieth century. But what of the earlier periods not covered?

Here are cited a few examples of the American predecessors, less frequently used than current bibliographies but, nevertheless, historically important not only as sources of earlier published books but also as evidence of how greatly national and trade bibliographies have increased in number and extent of coverage during the twentieth century. They are listed below by period covered.

1500–1800. Sabin, Joseph. Dictionary of books relating to America, from its discovery to the present time. N.Y., Sabin, 1868–92. Bibliographical Society of America, 1928–36. 29v.

> The indefatigable work of this one-man bibliographer in listing about 250,000 editions of books, pamphlets, and periodicals, published in or dealing with America, has been augmented by later inventories. But the author listing, with anonymous works under title and, in some cases, under geographical location (e.g. New York), will remain a great source of early imprints. It requires careful searching in some cases. For additional bibliographic data on individual items, see *The New Sabin* . . . indexed by title, subject, joint authors, and institutions and agencies, ed. by Lawrence S. Thompson. v.1– . (Troy, N.Y., Whitston, 1974– .)

> Also useful is J. E. Molnar's *Author-Title Index to Joseph Sabin's "Dictionary of Books relating to America"* (Metuchen, N.J., Scarecrow, 1975; 3v.). This includes, in a single alphabetical sequence, 270,000 entries: authors, editors, illustrators, titles, etc., and many cross-references.

1801–1819. Shaw, Ralph Robert, and Shoemaker, Richard H. American bibliography: a preliminary checklist for 1801–1819. N.Y., Scarecrow, 1958–66. 22v.

1820–1829. Shoemaker, Richard H. Checklist of American imprints for 1820–1829. N.Y., Scarecrow, 1964–71. 10v.

———. ———. Title index, comp. by M. Frances Cooper. Metuchen, N.J., Scarecrow, 1972. 556p.

———. ———. Author index, comp. by M. Frances Cooper. Metuchen, N.J., Scarecrow, 1973.

Gives locations for all entries and corrections.

1830–1861. Cooper, Gayle. A checklist of American imprints for 1830– .

Metuchen, N.J., Scarecrow, 1972– . (In progress; planned to cover 1830–61.)

1639–1800. Evans, Charles. American bibliography; a chronological dictionary of all books, pamphlets, and periodical publications printed in the United States of America from the genesis of printing in 1639 down to and including the year 1800; with bibliographical and biographical notes. Chicago, pr. for the author, 1903–59. 14v.

    Chronologically arranged, it has author, subject, printer, and publisher indexes in each volume.

    Shipton, Clifford K., and Mooney, James E., eds. National index of American imprints through 1800: the short-title Evans. Worcester, Mass., Barre Pub. and American Antiquarian Soc., 1969, 2v.

    Contains about 10,000 items not in *Evans.*

1820–1861. Roorbach, Orville Augustus. Bibliotheca americana, 1820–1861. N.Y., Roorbach, 1852–61. 4v.

    Gives publisher, date, size, and price. Incomplete.

1861–1870. Kelly, James. American catalogue of books (original and reprints), published in the United States from Jan. 1861 to Jan. 1871, with date of publication, size, price, and publisher's name. N.Y., Wiley, 1866–71. 2v.

    Same information as Roorbach, but has list of sermons and list of society publications. Incomplete.

1876–1910. American catalogue of books, 1876–1910. N.Y., Publishers' Weekly, 1876–1910. 9v. in 13.

    Includes about 70,000 titles from over 900 publishers, reprints, publications of learned societies, important U.S. government publications, and court reports.

1899–1927. United States catalog: books in print. Jan. 1, 1928. 4th ed. N.Y., H. W. Wilson, 1928. 3169p.

Bibliographies of Other Publications and of Audiovisual Materials

However convenient it might be to consult one current national bibliography for all forms of publication, it is hardly feasible. At present, trade bibliographies—which are limited principally to books published by trade publishers, university presses, religious denominations, societies, and scientific institutions—must be supplemented by other bibliographies that record other forms of publication or nonbook materials. These lists are sometimes restricted to the output of a single country, such as *Monthly Catalog of United States Government Publications*; sometimes by form, regardless of place of publication: *Union List of Serials* and *Ulrich's International Periodicals Directory*, for example. Singled out for description are examples of useful sources for government publications, pamphlets, periodicals, newspapers, paperbound books, reprints, films, manuscripts, music, and translations, all of them representing efforts to record sources of information which have grown in number and complexity in recent years.

Government Publications

These important sources of scientific, technical, and socioeconomic information, from national, state, and local-government agencies, are too voluminous to be included in trade bibliographies. Nor are they always adequately listed in library catalogs. They are recorded, with varying degrees of completeness and accuracy, by government agencies, which may include publications of many agencies, as in the *Monthly Catalog*, or the publications of one agency, as the *Bureau of the Census Catalog*. For an overview, see "Government Publications (Documents)," by the well-known authority James B. Childs, in *Encyclopedia of Library and Information Science* (v.10, p.36–140). This includes many citations to pertinent bibliographies and indexes.

→ U.S. Superintendent of Documents. Monthly catalog of United States government publications. 1895– . Wash., Govt. Prt. Off., 1895– . Monthly, with varying cumulations.

> SCOPE: Congressional, department, and bureau publications, including books, pamphlets, maps, and serials.
> ARRANGEMENT: Alphabetical by Superintendent of Documents classification numbers, with monthly indexes for author, title, subject (using LC headings), and one for series and reports.
> BIBLIOGRAPHIC DATA: Author, title, date, pagination, LC card number and subject headings, Superintendent of Documents classification number, price, and whether available for purchase.

→ _____. Cumulative subject index to Monthly Catalog of United States Government Publications, 1895–1899. Wash., Carrollton Pr., 1977. 2v.

→ _____. Cumulative subject index to Monthly Catalog of United States Government Publications, 1900–1971. Wash., Carrollton Pr., 1973–76. 15v.

These omit name entries and personal authors but include entries for government agencies as authors and for titles.

For a brief history of the *Monthly Catalog* and a detailed description of its present form, its availability on tape, its use as a selection and bibliographic tool, its serials supplement, an outline of types of material excluded, and several added references, see Yuri Nakata, *From Press to People* (Chicago: ALA, 1979; p.54–61).

The following give a more selective subject approach to government publications than the *Cumulative Subject Index:*

→ Leidy, William Philip. A popular guide to government publications. 3rd ed. N.Y., Columbia Univ. Pr., 1976. 440p.

→ Newsome, Walter L. New guide to popular government publications for libraries and home reference. Littleton, Colo., Libraries Unlimited, 1978. 370p.

Both are useful in public libraries, being arranged by subject, with some titles annotated.

→ U.S. Superintendent of Documents. Selected U.S. government publications. 1928– . Wash., Govt. Prt. Off., 1928– . Monthly.

Useful for small libraries because each issue lists, with some annotations, more than 200 government publications, general in nature and with popular appeal.

For an annual annotated guide to important government publications, see John L. Andriot, *Guide to U.S. Government Publications* (McLean, Va.: Documents Index, 1972–).

Comprehensive listings of all United States and foreign government publications in computer-produced format by the Research Libraries of the New York Public Library and the Library of Congress are issued annually by G. K. Hall: *Bibliographic Guide to Government Publications, U.S.*, 1975 to date, and *Bibliographic Guide to Government Publications, Foreign*, 1975 to date. They give main and added entries, titles, series, and subject headings in one alphabetical listing.

→ U.S. Library of Congress. Exchange and Gift Division. Monthly checklist of state publications, v.1, 1910– . Wash., Govt. Prt. Off., 1910– . Monthly.

scope: Official publications of U.S. states, territories, and insular possessions, received by Library of Congress.

ARRANGEMENT: Alphabetical by state and under state by issuing agency, with annual subject and agency index. Periodicals listed semiannually in June and December since 1963.

BIBLIOGRAPHIC DATA: Issuing agency, title, date, paging, illustrations, frequency, and LC card number when available.

State publications may also be located in lists issued by individual states, though these lists vary greatly in currency and completeness.

United Nations documents and publications are found in:

→ United Nations. Dag Hammarskjöld Library. United Nations documents index. Jan. 1950–Dec. 1973. N.Y., 1950–75. v.1–24. Superseded for 1950–62 by Cumulated index, v.1–13, 1950–62. Millwood, N.Y., Kraus, 1974. 4v.

Combines 13 authors and subject indexes, with added cross references for new terminology. Entries identified by reference numbers.

→ _____. UNDEX. United Nations documents index. Series A.: Subject index, v.1– , Jan. 1970– ; Series B: Country index, v.1– , Jan. 1970– ; Series C: List of documents issued, v.1– , Jan. 1974– . N.Y., 1970, 1974– . All monthly, except July and Aug.

Pamphlets

Though some scholarly pamphlets are listed in *Cumulative Book Index*, much more extensive listing is given in:

→ Vertical file index: subject and title index to selected pamphlet material. N.Y., Wilson, 1935– . Monthly (except Aug.), with annual cumulations.

SCOPE: Lists English-language "pamphlets, booklets, brochures, leaflets, circulars, folders, maps, posters, charts, mimeographed bulletins, and other inexpensive material . . ." (Pref.). Titles range from those suitable for school libraries to specialized technical reports, but with emphasis on the general.

ARRANGEMENT: By subject, with liberal use of cross-references, and appended title index.

BIBLIOGRAPHIC DATA: Author, title, series, edition, paging, illustrations, date, publisher, price, and descriptive annotation.

Periodicals

Though periodicals are included in national library catalogs and those published by government agencies are listed in catalogs of government publications, they are more fully covered, and with library locations indicated, in the following retrospective and current lists:

→ Union list of serials in libraries of the United States and Canada. 3rd ed., ed. by Edna Brown Titus. N.Y., Wilson, 1965. 5v.

> SCOPE: Worldwide, listing more than 156,000 titles in existence as of Dec. 1949 with holdings in 956 American and Canadian cooperating libraries, including periodicals, proceedings, and annual reports of associations. Excludes titles having highly limited or ephemeral value, newspapers, and some government serials.
> ARRANGEMENT: Alphabetical by latest title, with references to earlier forms.
> BIBLIOGRAPHIC DATA: History of title changes, place of publication, publisher, date of first volume, and date of last volume if serial has ceased publication, the latter indicated by parallel bars. Followed by holdings of cooperating libraries. See list of libraries with symbols inside front cover.

This union list, indispensable for interlibrary loan, is kept up to date by:

→ New serial titles, 1950–1970. Wash., Lib. of Congress; N.Y., Bowker, 1973. 4v.

> SCOPE: Cumulates monthly *New Serial Titles*, with many revisions and additional library locations, for about 220,000 titles from 800 libraries in United States and Canada.
> ARRANGEMENT: Alphabetical by latest title, with references to earlier forms and a separate list of titles which have ceased publication.
> BIBLIOGRAPHIC DATA: Same as *Union List of Serials*, plus International Standard Serial Numbers (ISSN).

→ _____. Subject guide. N.Y., Bowker, 1975. 2v.

> SCOPE: Same as *New Serial Titles, 1950–1970*.
> ARRANGEMENT: By modified Dewey Decimal Classification under about 250 broad categories.
> BIBLIOGRAPHIC DATA: Resemble that of *New Serial Titles, 1950–1970*, without library locations.

→ New serial titles; a union list of serials commencing publication after Dec. 31, 1949. Wash., Lib. of Congress, Jan. 1953– . Since 1969, 8 monthly and 4 quarterly issues; annual cumulation, self-cumulative through periods of four or more years.

SCOPE: Periodicals, with some omissions, such as newspapers and law reports, published since 1950, acquired in about 700 U.S. and Canadian libraries.

ARRANGEMENT: Alphabetical, with appended section listing changes for all serials, regardless of first date of publication.

BIBLIOGRAPHIC DATA: Same as *New Serial Titles, 1950–1970.*

→ New serial titles—classed subject arrangement. Jan./May 1955– . Wash., Lib. of Congress, Card Div., 1955– . Monthly. No cumulations.

SCOPE: Same as *New Serial Titles.*

ARRANGEMENT: Dewey Decimal Classification.

BIBLIOGRAPHIC DATA: Same as *New Serial Titles.*

Union lists of serials have multiplied greatly in recent years. For a bibliography of more than 1,200, arranged geographically by country and region, consult:

→ U.S. Library of Congress. General Reference and Bibliography Division. Union lists of serials; bibliography. Comp. by Ruth S. Freitag. Wash., 1964. 150p. Repr.: Boston, Gregg Pr., 1972.

Broad geographic coverage and subject approach distinguish the following selected list:

→ Sources of serials; an international publisher and corporate author directory. Ed. 1– . New York, Bowker, 1977– .

Approximately 90,000 titles listed in Ulrich's volumes (below) arranged by country, publisher, and/or corporate author.

→ Ulrich's International periodicals directory; a classified guide to a selected list of current periodicals, foreign and domestic. Ed. 1– . N.Y., Bowker, 1932– . Biennial.

SCOPE: Recent editions contain nearly 60,000 periodicals from worldwide publishers.

ARRANGEMENT: Alphabetical by subject, under which titles are listed alphabetically, with appended title and subject index.

BIBLIOGRAPHIC DATA: Title, subtitle, date of v.1, frequency, circulation, subscription rate, editor's name, publisher's name and address, language of text, where indexed or abstracted and whether it contains advertising, reviews, abstracts, bibliographies, special numbers, or annual index.

It is augmented by Bowker's *Irregular Serials and Annuals*, in alternate years.

→ Ulrich's Quarterly (a supplement to Ulrich's International periodicals directory and Irregular serials and annuals). v.1, Sept. 1977– . N.Y., Bowker, 1977– . Quarterly.

This serves to keep the biennial volumes current.

Also useful for their full description of contents of periodicals are these selective, annotated lists:

→ Katz, William Armstrong, and Richards, Berry Gargal. Magazines for libraries. 3rd ed. N.Y., Bowker, 1978. 937p. Frequently revised.

About 6,500 fully annotated titles under 104 broad subjects, with abstracting and indexing services, basic periodicals, and a general introduction prefacing each subject. Indicates reference value, audience level, and judgment values for each periodical.

→ Farber, Evan I. Classified list of periodicals for the college library. 5th ed. rev. and enl. Westwood, Mass., Faxon, 1972. 449p. Updated periodically in *Choice*.

About 1,000 titles published before 1969, discriminatingly annotated from the standpoint of the liberal arts college.

→ Richardson, Selma K. Periodicals for school media programs. Chicago, ALA, 1977. 397p.

Covers over 500 journals and newspapers for kindergarten through high school.

A valuable guide to about 11,000 periodicals, indexed in 33 indexing services, is Joseph Marconi's *Indexed Periodicals* (Ann Arbor, Mich.: Pierian Pr., 1976. 416p.).

Newspapers

Locations of back files and a directory of currently published newspapers will be found in the following titles:

→ American newspapers, 1821–1936; a union list of files available in the United States and Canada, ed. by Winifred Gregory under the auspices of the Bibliographical Society of America. N.Y., Wilson, 1937. 791p. Repr.: Kraus Rep. Co., 1970.

> SCOPE: Holdings in nearly 5,700 libraries, county courthouses, newspaper offices, and private collections.
>
> ARRANGEMENT: Alphabetical by state or province, then cities and towns; under city, alphabetical by first important word in title of newspaper.
>
> BIBLIOGRAPHIC DATA: Title, frequency, birth and death dates, earlier titles, and holdings. See preliminary pages for symbols used.

→ Brigham, Clarence S. History and bibliography of American newspapers, 1690–1820. Worcester, Mass. Amer. Antiquarian Soc., 1947. 2v. Repr.: Hamden, Conn., Archon, 1962, with corrections and additions.

> Lists 2,120 newspapers alphabetically by state and town, giving historical notes for each (title, date begun, title changes and dates, names of editors and publishers, frequency, etc.). Originally appeared in *Proceedings* of American Antiquarian Society.

→ Ayer, *firm, Philadelphia.* Ayer directory of publications. Philadelphia, Ayer, 1880– . v.1– . Annual.

> SCOPE: Subtitle (1979 ed.) reads: "The professional's directory of print media published in the United States; Puerto Rico; Virgin Islands; Canada; Bahamas; Bermuda; the Republics of Panama and the Philippines. Economic descriptions of the states, provinces, cities and towns in which all listees are published; 15 separate, classified lists; 69 custom-made maps on which all publication cities and towns are indicated."
>
> ARRANGEMENT: Geographical by state or province, then by city or town, with added sections of maps and certain subject fields, e.g. religious and black publications.
>
> BIBLIOGRAPHIC AND OTHER DATA: Name, frequency, character or politics, beginning date, size of column or page, subscription price, circulation figures, names of editors and publishers.

Users should remember that extensive microfilming activities in libraries have increased the availability of local newspapers. These are reported in:

→ U.S. Library of Congress. Catalog Publication Division. Newspapers in microform, 1948–1972. Wash., Lib. of Congress, 1974. Annual, 1973– .

> The annual issue reports new titles and additional locations for titles in the earlier volumes.

Paperbound Books

Although many paperbound books are listed in *Cumulative Book Index* and *Books in Print*, these sources are augmented by:

→ Paperbound books in print. N.Y., Bowker, 1955– . Semiannual.

SCOPE: In-print and forthcoming titles, chiefly from U.S. publishers.
ARRANGEMENT: In three parts under title, author, and subject.
BIBLIOGRAPHIC DATA: Title, author, illustrations, paging, price, publisher, and ISBN number.

This resembles *Paperbacks in Print* (London, Whitaker: 1960–) for titles on sale in Great Britain. For earlier years, see:

→ Reginald, R., and Burgess, M. R. Cumulative paperback index, 1939–1959; a comprehensive bibliographic guide to 14,000 mass-market paperback books of 33 publishers issued under 69 imprints. Detroit, Gale, 1973. 362p.

SCOPE: Lists output of American mass-market publishers, excluding textbooks and scholarly books.
ARRANGEMENT: Alphabetical by publishers, with author and title index.
BIBLIOGRAPHIC DATA: Gives publisher, stock number, publication date, and price in author index only.

Reprints

The increasing number of reprints issued each year is responsible for the publication of an annual guide that lists material not apt to be listed in *Paperbound Books in Print*, though usually in *BIP*.

→ Guide to reprints, 1967– . Kent, Conn., Guide to Reprints, Inc., 1967– . Annual, cumulative.

SCOPE: Books, journals, and other materials that are available in reprint form from both American and foreign publishers, principally those titles reproduced by a photo-offset process in editions of not fewer than 200 copies.
ARRANGEMENT: Alphabetical by authors of books and by titles of periodicals.
BIBLIOGRAPHIC DATA: Author, title, original date of publication, and price as given in publishers' catalogs for books; title, volume numbers, years, and prices for journals and sets.

Also useful is:

→ International bibliography of reprints. N.Y., Bowker, 1976– . 3v.

> V.1 lists reprints by author and title; v.2 includes annuals and periodicals.
> V.3, title and serial indexes, not yet published.

Films and Microforms

The enormous increase in the production of microform in recent decades has stimulated the compilation of bibliographic guides to this form. Among them are:

→ U.S. Library of Congress. Audiovisual materials. Wash., 1979– . Three quarterly issues per year, with annual and quinquennial cumulations. Supersedes *Films and other materials for projection, 1972–1979*.

> SCOPE: Includes not only films "of educational or instructive value" but, from 1951 through Apr. 1957 (pub. with title *Motion Pictures and Filmstrips*), nearly all films copyrighted during that period. Since May 1957, restricted to those added to LC collections or for which data have been supplied by producers or distributors. Sets of transparencies and slide sets included from Jan./Mar. 1973 quarterly issue, when title was changed to its present form.
> ARRANGEMENT: Alphabetically by title, with added entries for form, names of advisers, producers, distributors, and authors of published work on which film is based. Appended subject index, with special subject headings for juvenile literature since Jan./Mar. 1973.
> BIBLIOGRAPHIC DATA: Producer, running time, size, credits, cast, and added entries given under film or slide title. Briefly listed under added entries.

→ Guide to microforms in print, 1961– . Westport, Conn., Microform Review, Inc., 1961– . Absorbed *International Microforms in Print* in 1977 ed. Annual. Updated by monthly *Microlist* since 1975.

A subject approach to this author-title guide is found in:

→ Subject guide to microforms in print, 1962/63– . Westport, Conn., Microform Review, Inc., 1962– . Annual.

→ Microform market place, 1974/75– . Westport, Conn., Microform Review, Inc., 1974– . Biennial.

> Contains subject and geographic indexes to micropublishers' directory, giving addresses, programs, and subjects. Appended are mergers, jobbers, organizations, bibliography, and a names and numbers directory. International in scope.

For citations to reviews of films and filmstrips, records, tapes, and videotapes, see:

→ Media review digest, 1970– . Ann Arbor, Mich., Pierian Pr., 1970– . Annual, with supp. Pub. 1970–72 as *Multi Media Reviews Index.*

Includes reviews from about 150 journals, some of them with excerpts and symbols indicating whether review is favorable or unfavorable.

Less comprehensive, but useful in schools, is *Educators Guide to Free Films* (Randolph, Wis., Educators Progress Service), revised annually, annotated, and with subject and title indexes. The same publisher issues annual volumes for filmstrips; tapes, scripts, and transcriptions; and *Elementary Teachers Guide to Free Curriculum Materials.*

Manuscripts

Libraries have been feverishly collecting manuscripts in recent years, and the following is a monumental effort to describe the contents of some of these manuscript collections:

→ National union catalog of manuscript collections. 1959/61– . Wash., etc., Lib. of Congress, etc., 1962– . Annual.

SCOPE: Describes collections, chiefly personal papers, in more than 850 American repositories.
ARRANGEMENT: Earlier volumes by assigned numbers, with index of names, places, subjects, and named historical periods. Since 1963, alphabetically by respository and under repository by collection, with index for 1963–66 in fifth series.
BIBLIOGRAPHIC AND OTHER DATA. Main entry, title, number of items, physical description, scope and content, location, identifying number, restrictions on access, availability of microfilm copies, etc.

Music

→ U.S. Library of Congress. Library of Congress catalog—Music and phonorecords, 1953–72. Wash., 1953–72. Semiannual, with annual and quinquennial cumulations, the latter appearing as part of *National Union Catalog.*

"Contains entries for music scores in the broadest sense, i.e., music for performance, regardless of its classification. It includes also phonorecords, e.g., sound recordings, musical or non-musical, reproduced on all kinds of material, including cylinders, discs, tape, and wire" (Intro.). Also books about music and musicians, which also appear in

National Union Catalog. Arranged alphabetically by composer, or by title if entry contains works by different composers, with appended subject index. Superseded by:

→ _____. Library of Congress catalog—Music, books on music, and sound recordings. Jan./June 1973– . Wash., 1973– . Semiannual, cumulating in the 2nd issues.

The Foreword states that "music in the broadest sense, including music scores, sheet music, libretti, and books about music and musicians, is covered in the catalog. It also contains entries for sound recordings of all kinds, whether these are musical, educational, literary, or political."

All music published in the United States and foreign countries and deposited for copyright registration is listed in:

→ U.S. Copyright Office. Catalog of copyright entries. 3rd ser. Pt. 5: Music. v.1– . Jan./June 1947– . Wash., Govt. Prt. Off., 1947– . Semiannual.

Translations

Though many translations into English are listed in *Cumulative Book Index* and *Books in Print*, translations from English into other languages are much more fully covered in:

→ Index translationum. Répertoire international des traductions. International bibliography of translations. Paris, Internat. Inst. of Intellectual Cooperation, 1932–40. no.1–31; n.s. v.1, 1948– . Paris, UNESCO, 1949– . Annual.

SCOPE: Translated books published in 60 or more countries.
ARRANGEMENT: Alphabetical by country, under it by the 10 broad divisions of the Universal Decimal Classification, with indexes of authors, publishers, and translators.
BIBLIOGRAPHIC DATA: Name of author, editor, or compiler; title of the translation; name of translator, place of publication, publisher, date; pages; price, when known, in currency of country where translation was published; references to original work, giving language in which it was written or from which it was translated, and original title.

Summary

These lists and catalogs, which augment national library catalogs and trade bibliographies, represent only a small segment of the sources that may be consulted. Others—more limited in scope, such as guides to manuscripts in individual repositories or translations from one language, such as Mor-

gan's *A Critical Bibliography of German Literature in English Translation*—
are described in *Sheehy*.

Of the many uses for these supplemental bibliographies, three should be
emphasized:

> For library location of individual titles, e.g. *Union List of Serials, New
> Serial Titles, American Newspapers, 1821–1936,* and *National Union
> Catalog of Manuscript Collections*
>
> For forms of publication not included in book trade bibliographies, e.g.
> *Vertical File Index*
>
> For price of individual titles, e.g. *Monthly Catalog of United States Gov-
> ernment Publications, Vertical File Index, Ulrich's International
> Periodicals Directory, Ayer Directory, Paperbound Books in Print,
> Guide to Reprints,* and *Index Translationum.*

Subject Bibliographies

Bibliographies devoted to a single subject or aspect of a subject constitute
the largest body of bibliographic publication and are often the first point of
departure in a search for information. They may be either retrospective or
current, comprehensive or selective, annotated or unannotated. They may
exist as separate books or parts of books, in periodicals, or on cards, film,
tape, wire, or punched cards. But regardless of form, their purpose is "to
give information on intellectual activity, international or national, in each
branch of knowledge" (Malclès, *Bibliography*, p.2). The development of
subject bibliography since the Middle Ages and its role in the flow of
information are analyzed in Barbara M. Hale's *The Subject Bibliography of
the Social Sciences and the Humanities* (New York: Pergamon, 1970; 149p.).

Though library catalogs and trade bibliographies provide a series of
subject bibliographies through their subject headings, they are less comprehensive than bibliographies of a single subject. As noted earlier, they are
only inventories of books in a particular library collection or a record of
books published or in print in one country during a specified period of time.

Useful in evaluating subject bibliographies is "Criteria for Evaluating a
Bibliography," prepared by the ALA Reference and Adult Services Division, Bibliography Committee, 1971 (*RQ* 11:359–60 [Summer 1972]).

Carl White has pointed out some of the problems in social science bibliography, problems common to subject bibliographies in most fields: (1) the
proliferation of the literature, (2) the need for and enlarged use of social
science skills and trustworthy information, (3) the lack of scholars who can
handle bibliographical instruction in all branches of their subject, and (4)
the lag in development of social science bibliography as a branch of study

which has not kept up with the growth in the field (*Sources of Information in the Social Sciences* [Chicago: ALA, 1973], p.5–6). Learned societies and government agencies, such as the Social Science Research Council and the President's Science Advisory Committee, have recognized the need for improved expertise in handling information, and in recent years, improved bibliographic aids have appeared, especially in the area of current periodicals.

Retrospective—Comprehensive

Subject bibliographies represent the work of subject authorities and reflect their informed judgment and knowledge of sources, including books, periodicals, manuscripts, and other forms of publication pertinent to the subject. When they are logically arranged and critically and descriptively annotated, they provide the most useful overview of the literature of a subject for those who are less familiar with it.

Since their arrangement is so important and can add so much to ease of use, those who wish to familiarize themselves quickly with the various methods of compilation should consult *Systematic Bibliography* by A. M. L. Robinson (Hamden, Conn.: Archon Books, 1966; p.36–65). This practical guide, intended for those inexperienced in bibliographical techniques, discusses the methods used and their suitability to certain subjects or types of publications.

One form of comprehensive subject bibliography that has assumed increasing importance in recent years is the reproduction of catalogs of special collections in large libraries. Often representing a body of material on a subject, acquired over a long period of years, they are significant not only for the rich collections they record, but for including analytics for periodical articles, pamphlets, and parts of books. One outstanding example is *Dictionary Catalog of the Schomburg Collection of Negro Literature and History in the New York Public Library,* reproduced by G. K. Hall. Another project of interest to scholars is the Widener Library shelflist, a series of classified and indexed catalogs produced by computer for portions of Harvard University's central research collection. Though they are usually too expensive to be acquired by most libraries, students of bibliography should be aware of their existence and their great reference value. Many of them are listed in *Sheehy*.

One example, however, should be familiar to librarians, since it records an outstanding collection in the field of library science and has real historical significance:

→ Columbia University. Libraries. Library of the School of Library Service. Dictionary catalog. Boston, Hall, 1962. 7v. 1st supp. 1976. 4v.

SCOPE: Records titles collected since 1876, both American and European, in library resources, readers' services, organization and administration of libraries, histories of libraries and their function in society, history of books and bookmaking, public communication and the library, book evaluation, and research methods. Includes Children's Historical Collection, made up of books of all periods, and a collection of juvenile books.

ARRANGEMENT: Author, subject, and title in one alphabet.

BIBLIOGRAPHIC DATA: Reproduced from the library's catalog, they follow Library of Congress form, with some variations.

Other examples include carefully prepared bibliographies of individual authors, which provide accurate and complete bibliographic descriptions of first editions of an author's works, with contributions to periodicals, anthologies and other collections, and sources of biography and criticism. Author bibliographies are being published at a great rate, for living writers as well as those no longer living, as even a casual examination of *Bibliographic Index* will reveal.

Increased publication and the specialization that characterizes so much of scholarly and scientific research have led to bibliographies restricted to narrower and narrower subjects, such as *The Bibliography of the Fig*. These are best located through bibliographies of bibliographies (which will be described later). Because of their specialized nature, no examples are cited here, but they must be kept in mind as important adjuncts to national library catalogs and trade bibliographies.

Not to be overlooked are guides to the resources of libraries which differ from library catalogs by describing the collections of one or more libraries. These guides note their subject strengths and occasionally list outstanding titles, rather than list the entire contents by individual titles. These are discussed by William V. Jackson in "Library Resources and Bibliography," *Research Librarianship: Essays in Honor of Robert B. Downs,* edited by Jerrold Orne (New York: Bowker, 1971; p.75–90). Viewing surveys of resources as a real contribution to the world of learning, he cites Downs' *American Library Resources* and its supplement as an outstanding example. Among guides to individual library collections, that of the New York Public Library is notable.

For special collections in many fields in United States and Canadian libraries, consult the frequently revised *Subject Collections*, compiled by Lee Ash and Stephen J. Calvert (5th ed., rev. and enl.; New York: Bowker, 1978; 1184p.). Prepared from materials supplied by libraries or other repositories, it varies in fullness of description but is an excellent source for determining what library has important holdings on a particular author or subject.

Retrospective—Selective

A selective bibliography records the best titles for a particular subject or subjects or for a particular type of library or user, as noted earlier. Any selective bibliography reflects the bias of the compiler or compilers, their depth of knowledge of the subject, the amount of writing on the subject, and the era and country in which it was compiled. All these factors should be borne in mind in their evaluation and use.

One type of selective subject bibliography that deserves special consideration is the guide to the literature in a broad subject field. These guides have developed as a result of the increased number and complexity of reference materials in various fields and are intended to guide the beginning research worker in the selection of the most pertinent sources. They augment the general guides to reference materials, such as *Sheehy* and *Walford*, and many of them conform at least in part to the following pattern:

Overview of the subject field
Description of the nature of research in the field
Often a more exhaustive list of reference titles, sometimes (but not always) more fully annotated, in terms of the subject, than in general guides such as *Sheehy*
Lists of important texts and syntheses in the field
Separate chapters on types of material that are of particular importance in individual fields, e.g. patents in guides to chemical literature, maps and atlases in geographical literature, government publications in education and geology, and statistics in business
Lists of important journals in the field, including indexing, abstracting, and review journals
Lists of libraries, museums, and other repositories of outstanding collections in the fields
Lists of important societies and associations in the field, often with brief descriptions and lists of their serial publications
Lists of authorities in the field, with their special interests
Typical reference questions in the field.

Many examples of these guides will be found in *Sheehy*, and a few are listed below:

ART
→ Muehsam, Gerd. Guide to basic information sources in the visual arts. Santa Barbara, Calif., Jeffrey Norton/ABC-Clio, [1978]. 266p.

BIOLOGY
→ Bottle, Robert T. The use of biological literature. 2nd ed. Hamden, Conn., Archon Books, 1971. 379p.

Kirk, Thomas G. Library research guide to biology: illustrated search strategy and sources. Ann Arbor, Mich., Pierian Pr., 1978. 83p. (Library research guides, no.2)

BUSINESS
→ Daniells, Lorna M. Business information sources. Berkeley, Univ. of California Pr., 1976. 439p.

CHEMISTRY
→ Antony, Arthur. Guide to basic information sources in chemistry. N.Y., Halstead, 1979. 219p.

EDUCATION
→ Woodbury, Marda L. A guide to sources of educational information. Wash., Information Resources Pr., 1976. 371p.

GEOGRAPHY
→ Brewer, J. Gordon. The literature of geography: a guide to its organization and use. 2nd ed. Hamden, Conn., Linnet Books, 1978. 264p.

GEOLOGY
→ Wood, D. N., ed. Use of earth science literature. Hamden, Conn., Archon Books, 1973. 459p.

HISTORY
→ American Historical Association. Guide to historical literature. George Frederick Howe, chairman, Board of Editors, N.Y., Macmillan, 1961. 962p.

→ Poulton, Helen J. The historian's handbook: a descriptive guide to reference works. Norman, Univ. of Oklahoma Pr., [1972]. 304p.

HUMANITIES
→ Rogers, A. Robert. The humanities, a selective guide to information sources. 2nd ed. Littleton, Colo., Libraries Unlimited, 1979. 355p.

MATHEMATICS
→ Dick, Elie M. Current information sources in mathematics; an annotated guide to books and periodicals, 1960–72. Littleton, Colo., Libraries Unlimited, 1973. 281p.

MUSIC
→ Duckles, Vincent Harris. Music reference and research materials; an annotated bibliography. 3rd ed. N.Y., Free Press, [c1974]. 526p.

PHILOSOPHY
→ DeGeorge, Richard T. A guide to philosophical bibliography and research. N.Y., Appleton-Century-Crofts, [1971]. 141p.

The bibliographic section of DeGeorge is updated and greatly expanded in:

→ Guerry, Herbert. Bibliography of philosophical bibliographies. Westport, Conn., Greenwood Pr., 1977. 332p.

PHYSICS
→ Whitford, Robert H. Physics literature; a reference manual. 2nd ed. Metuchen, N.J., Scarecrow, 1968. 272p.

SOCIAL SCIENCES
→ White, Carl M., and associates. Sources of information in the social sciences. 2nd ed. Chicago, ALA, 1973. 702p.

For additional examples, see also *Sheehy* and *Walford*.

These guides to the literature in broad subject fields are useful not only to beginning research workers but to reference librarians as well. Not only may they be used as selection aids, but also as sources for possible answers to specific questions, such as biographical, statistical, and miscellaneous facts.

Selection Aids

Quite different in scope, arrangement, and method of compilation are selective bibliographies that include all subjects and are aimed primarily at one type of library. They often augment library catalogs and trade bibliographies by including descriptive annotations. Though more often referred to as selection aids than as subject bibliographies, they may be viewed as starting points by those seeking titles considered suitable for purchase in a school, public, or college library. These titles may have been selected in one of two ways:

By vote of experienced librarians and subject specialists, e.g. the *Standard Catalog* series

By one or more compilers, with the assistance of subject specialists, e.g. *Books for College Libraries.*

Listed below are a few examples, widely used in libraries in the United States as selection aids and in readers' advisory service:

→ The reader's adviser: a layman's guide. Ed.1– . N.Y., Bowker, 1921– . Title varies. 3v.

> SCOPE: Covers American and foreign fiction, poetry, essays, drama, biography, bibliography, general reference books, Bibles, world religions, philosophy, psychology, science, social sciences, history, government and politics, the lively arts and communications, folklore and humor, travel and adventure.
> ARRANGEMENT: Broad subject with appended author and title indexes.
> BIBLIOGRAPHIC DATA: Include publisher and price, annotations, and some citations to book reviews. See *Booklist* 74:1129 (Mar. 1, 1978) for review of 12th ed. (1974–77).

→ Public library catalog, a classified and annotated list of . . . non-fiction books recommended for public and college libraries. N.Y., Wilson, 1934– . Quinquennial with annual supps.

> SCOPE: See subtitle. Selected by votes of consultants drawn from staffs of college and public libraries.
> ARRANGEMENT: In three parts: (1) classified catalog by Dewey classification; (2) author, title, subject, and analytical index in one alphabet; and (3) directory of publishers and distributors.
> BIBLIOGRAPHIC DATA: Pt. 1, author, title, publisher, date, paging, illustrations, price, Dewey classification, subject headings based on *Sears' List of Subject Headings*, LC card numbers, and extracts from book reviewing media.

→ Books for public libraries; nonfiction for small collections. N.Y., Bowker, 1975. 220p.

> SCOPE: 5,000 nonfiction titles considered suitable as a starter list by a committee of ALA.
> ARRANGEMENT: By Dewey classification with author and title index.
> BIBLIOGRAPHIC DATA: Author, title, publisher, date, and price.

→ Senior high school library catalog, 1926– . N.Y., Wilson, 1926– . Every five years with four annual supps. Earlier editions entitled *Standard Catalog for High School Libraries.*

SCOPE: More than 4,000 titles useful for grades 10 through 12, selected by votes of representative group of experienced librarians and specialists in literature for young people. Includes many adult books considered suitable for young adults.

ARRANGEMENT: In three parts: (1) classified catalog, arranged according to Abridged Edition of Dewey Decimal Classification; (2) author, title, subject, and analytical index in one alphabet; and (3) directory of publishers and distributors.

BIBLIOGRAPHIC DATA: Pt. 1, author, title, publisher, date, paging, illustrations, price, Dewey classification, subject headings based on *Sears' List of Subject Headings*, annotations and extracts from book-reviewing media.

→ Books for secondary school libraries. Ed.1 – . N.Y., Bowker, 1968– .

SCOPE: Designed for college-bound students; includes books, periodicals, records, slides, reproductions, and a few foreign titles. Compiled by Library Committee of National Assn. of Independent Schools.

ARRANGEMENTS: Dewey Decimal Classification, with author, title, and subject indexes, the latter using Sears' subject headings.

BIBLIOGRAPHIC DATA: Author, title, publisher, date, price, Dewey number, and LC subject headings.

→ Junior high school library catalog, 1965– . N.Y., Wilson, 1965– . Quinquennial with annual supps.

SCOPE: Titles used for grades 7 through 9, selected by votes of consultants.

ARRANGEMENT: Same as *Senior High School Catalog*.

BIBLIOGRAPHIC DATA: Same as *Senior High School Catalog*.

→ Children's catalog, 1909– . N.Y., Wilson, 1909– . Quinquennial with annual supps.

SCOPE: Basic volume contains more than 4,000 titles for public and elementary school libraries, with about 1,700 titles in each supplement, selected by children's librarians.

ARRANGEMENT: In three parts: (1) classified catalog arranged by abridged Dewey classification; (2) author, title, subject, and analytical index in one alphabet; and (3) directory of publishers and distributors.

BIBLIOGRAPHIC DATA: Full description of titles, with annotations and grade levels.

→ Elementary school library collection, 1965– . General ed., Mary V. Gaver. Newark, N.J., Bro-Dart Foundation, 1965– . Frequently revised.

> SCOPE: More than 8,000 books and nearly 700 entries for AV materials intended to represent a balanced elementary school library collection, selected on basis of literary quality, appeal to children, format, authenticity of content, and suitability for range of reading interests normally represented in elementary school.
>
> ARRANGEMENT: Classified catalog in six sections: (1) reference, classified by Dewey; (2) nonfiction, classified by Dewey; (3) fiction, alphabetical by author; (4) easy; alphabetical by author; (5) periodicals, alphabetical by title; and (6) professional tools, classified by Dewey. Computer-produced author, title, and subject indexes are appended.
>
> BIBLIOGRAPHIC DATA: Reproduce actual catalog cards, with added information on price, grade level, and phase number. Annotated.

For a long review, see *Booklist* 71:190–92 (Oct. 1, 1974).

→ Books for children, 1960/65–1970/71. Chicago, ALA, 1966–71.

> SCOPE: Reprints reviews from *Booklist* Children's Books section.
>
> ARRANGEMENT: By modified Dewey Decimal Classification, with appended author, title, and subject index.
>
> BIBLIOGRAPHIC DATA: Author, title, date, paging, publisher, binding, price, Dewey Decimal Classification number, subject headings, and critical evaluations, with suggested grade levels.

→ Books for college libraries. 2nd ed. Chicago, ALA, 1975. 6v.

> SCOPE: Covers undergraduate courses in all subject fields.
>
> ARRANGEMENT: By LC numbers, with appended author and subject index.
>
> BIBLIOGRAPHIC DATA: Author, title, publisher, date, etc.

→ Pirie, James W., comp. Books for junior college libraries. Chicago, ALA, 1969. 468p.

> SCOPE: Approximately 20,000 titles.
>
> ARRANGEMENT: By broad subject, with appended author and subject index.
>
> BIBLIOGRAPHIC DATA: Author, title, publisher, date, price, pages, and LC card number.

→ Reinhart, Bruce. Vocational-technical learning materials; books and manuals for schools and community colleges. 2nd ed. Williamsport, PA., Bro-Dart, 1974. 307p.

Current Selective Bibliographies

The need for the most recent publications on a subject has led to an increasing number of current subject bibliographies, issued separately or as part of a journal in a subject field. Since many of them take the form of indexes to periodicals, examples are given in the next section of the chapter. A useful approach by subject is provided in *Bibliographic Index* and in Richard A. Gray, *Serial Bibliographies in the Humanities and Social Sciences* (described later, in the section on bibliographies of bibliographies).

Here, only current selective bibliographies are discussed that include all subjects and are aimed primarily at one type of library. As in the case of retrospective selective bibliographies (discussed above), they are quite different from periodical indexes in scope, arrangement, and method of compilation. They are usually prepared in one of the following ways:

By staff of professional reviewers, e.g. *Booklist*
By individual reviewers selected by the editor, e.g. *Choice* and *Library Journal*.

Listed below are a few examples, widely used in libraries in the United States:

→ Booklist. 1905– . Chicago, ALA, 1905– . v.1– . Semimonthly (monthly in Aug.).

> SCOPE: Recommended titles for small and medium-size libraries, in English, with separate lists of foreign-language titles.
> ARRANGEMENT: Broad Dewey Decimal Classification, with separate sections for fiction, books for young adults, children's books, adult education, U.S. government publications, films and filmstrips, recordings, followed by reviews of Reference and Subscription Books Review Committee, with semimonthly, semiannual, and annual indexes to authors, titles, and subjects.
> BIBLIOGRAPHIC DATA: Author, title, date of publication, paging, publisher, price, ISBN number, Dewey Decimal Classification, LC subject headings, LC card number, and descriptive (sometimes critical) annotations written by *Booklist* staff (librarian consultants advise in the selection of items for review). Data for films and other audiovisual items include release date, length, production credits, distributors' addresses, purchase and rental price, annotation, Dewey Decimal Classification, LC card number, and LC subject headings.

Since 1956, reviews prepared by the RSBR Committee have been reprinted in *Subscription Books Bulletin Reviews* (1956–60, 1960–62, 1962–64, 1964–66, 1966–68) and *Reference and Subscription Books Reviews* (1968–).

→ Choice: books for college libraries. A publication of the Association of College and Research Libraries, a division of the American Library Association. Middletown, Conn., Olin Lib., Wesleyan Univ., 1964– . v.1– . Monthly (except bimonthly, July–Aug.).

    SCOPE: More than 6,000 appraisals of scholarly books by subject specialists, chiefly college professors. Covers subjects in the liberal arts curriculum. Designed particularly for libraries with modest book budgets.

    ARRANGEMENT: Alphabetical by broad subjects, under which entries are alphabetical by author.

    BIBLIOGRAPHIC DATA: Author, title, publisher, date, paging, illustrations, LC card number, ISBN, price, and brief reviews.

→ Library journal. N.Y., Bowker, 1876– . v.1– . Semimonthly.

    SCOPE: Book Review section contains short, signed reviews, evaluating current titles in all subject fields, chiefly in English language.

    ARRANGEMENT: Alphabetical by broad subject fields, e.g. art, biography, education, fiction, home economics, humor, theater, etc. Separate sections on reference books, professional reading, recordings, films, and other media.

    BIBLIOGRAPHIC DATA: Author, title, paging, publisher, price, LC card number, ISBN, and signed review.

Briefly, subject bibliographies may supplement library catalogs and trade bibliographies in supplying:

A more exhaustive list of titles *or* a more selective list of titles
A broader range of materials, e.g. periodical articles and other material pertinent to the subject
A more specific or logical approach through their internal arrangement
Critical or descriptive annotations.

Indexes and Abstracts

As pointed out earlier, indexes differ from book catalogs and trade bibliographies in recording alphabetically and analytically, under appropriate entries, the *contents* of a book, periodical, or other document. Already noted are examples of indexes in subject bibliographies—author, title, and subject indexes to the classified parts of the Standard Catalog series, for example. Included in this section are indexes to periodicals and newspapers, with brief discussion of other forms, such as indexes to individual books and concordances of the work of a single author. Indexes to individual books are compiled on different principles from indexes to a body of literature.

John L. Thornton has said that the characteristics of a "born indexer" are an orderly mind, infinite patience, and an ability to approach a book from the reader's angle ("Indexing," in Robert L. Collison, ed., *Progress in Library Science* [Washington: Butterworths, 1965], p.34). These same characteristics are needed by users of indexes.

John Rothman has noted four problems of index making that cause problems in index using: (1) selectivity, or scope of coverage in the index; (2) depth, or the extent to which items selected for indexing are analyzed through index entries; (3) structure of the index, or the pattern in which entries are arranged; and (4) terminology, such as how to handle synonyms, technical versus popular terms, current terms versus their obsolete predecessors ("Communicating with Indexes," *Special Libraries* 57:569–70 [Oct. 1966]). Also informative is his "Index, Indexer, Indexing," in *Encyclopedia of Library and Information Science* (v.11, p.286–99).

Some knowledge of the basic principles and methods of indexing is essential to users of indexes, not only because it leads to more intelligent use but also because it provides a base for judging the adequacy of an index. Users must determine whether terms employed in the index are specific and consistent, whether location is accurately indicated, and whether decisions to omit certain types of material in a collection being indexed have been wisely made (e.g. ads in periodicals).

The Society of Indexers and its American counterpart, the American Society of Indexers, are dedicated to the improvement of this important form of information retrieval. This is reflected in the Society's official journal, *The Indexer,* and in its course for indexers. Lectures by experts on name and subject headings; indexing in scientific, technical, medical and legal fields; and editing an index were published in *Training in Indexing: A Course for the Society of Indexers*, edited by G. Norman Knight (Cambridge, Mass.: M.I.T. Pr., 1969; 219p.). Also useful is Knight's *Indexing, the Art of* (Winchester, Mass.: Allen & Unwin, 1979; 208p.).

Different methods are used for indexing different forms. These are described in Robert Collison's *Indexes and Indexing* (New York: De Graff, 1972; 232p.) and include books, periodicals, music, recordings, films, and other material.

Abstracts differ from indexes in their arrangement, which is hierarchical in terms of the appropriate aspects or subdivisions of a subject. Because of this arrangement, they also contain alpabetically arranged subject and author indexes. They also differ from indexes in supplying an accompanying brief digest or summary of books, articles, or other documents. Abstracts may vary in form, from a brief descriptive note to one which critically evaluates the title.

Leonard M. Harrod's *The Librarian's Glossary of Terms Used in Librarianship, Documentation, and the Book Crafts and Reference Books* (4th rev. ed.; Boulder, Colo.: Westview Pr., 1977; 903p.) defines an abstract as either indicative, informative, evaluative, general, selective, author, traditional, locative, or illative—reflecting the ways they've been described.

Often referred to as abstracting services or abstract journals, they are usually compiled and published by an independent publisher or a learned association. Some originate in United States government agencies. Abstracts are sometimes supplied by the authors of the original work, by volunteer abstractors who are specialists in the subject, or by a central staff of professional abstractors. One problem that has concerned both users and compilers of abstracts is the lag in time between publication of the original work and publication of the abstract. Strenuous efforts have been made to reduce this time lag. Further information will be found in Charles L. Bernier, "Abstracts and Abstracting," in *Encyclopedia of Library and Information Science* (v.1, p.16–38).

Also useful is Robert Lewis Collison, *Abstracts and Abstracting Services* (Santa Barbara, Calif.: ABC-Clio, 1971; 122p.). Collison gives attention to trends in mechanization and to the role played by abstracting services in the information industry. Included is a critical examination of over 1,000 abstracting services, with 500 services listed in an appendix.

Periodical Indexing and Abstracting Services

Probably the most-used form of subject bibliography is the periodical index, not only because of the number and variety of periodicals currently published but also because of the need for the most recent information on topics not yet covered in books. These indexes augment library catalogs, trade bibliographies, and retrospective subject bibliographies in many important ways:

> They provide a subject, and sometimes author and title, approach to individual articles in periodicals.
> They are more up to date, reflecting contemporary opinion on subjects included or what is known about a subject at a specific time.
> They usually employ more specific subject headings, reflecting current terminology.
> They reveal trends in certain subject fields. (For discussion of this point, see Katharine S. Diehl, "Indexes Examined: Reference without Periodicals," *RQ* 4:11–14 [Nov. 1964].)

Like any other serial publication, individual periodical indexes are subject to change, not only in the periodical titles indexed but also in forms of entries. For example, indexes published by the H. W. Wilson Company are regularly reviewed for possible additions and deletions of titles, with the assistance of the Committee on Wilson Indexes of the ALA Reference and Adult Services Division (as mentioned in chapter 1).

The user should also note that some indexes, primarily designated periodical indexes, include books, pamphlets, and other forms of material—*Public Affairs Information Service*, for example.

Since, at the present time, there are two or three of these periodical indexes for many subjects, published in different countries and including many of the same titles, the problem of expensive duplication of effort has engaged international agencies and learned societies for many years. These agencies have been further concerned with (1) the great amount of current publication not presently listed in current bibliographies, (2) the time lag in publication, and (3) the need for further specificity in indexing. The need for a more specific approach to a subject field has encouraged experimentation in new forms of storing information for retrieval, including film, tape, wire, and punched cards. The cooperative attack upon these and other bibliographic problems will affect the kinds of indexes produced in the future.

Computerized indexes have increased greatly in recent years, especially in science and technology, where the KWIC (Key Work in Context) index is used extensively. The KWIC (or permuted title) index is produced by listing titles successively by each significant word. Another example of a computer-produced index is the *Science Citation Index*, which records works cited in footnotes of journal articles.

Points to be considered in evaluating periodical indexes are:

1. Scope of index
2. Length of period covered
3. Frequency and promptness of publication
4. Completeness of the indexing of the material
5. Quality of indexing.

Because of the dilemmas just cited and growing recognition that traditional methods of storing and retrieving information from abstracting and indexing sources (meaning, usually, printed sources) were not keeping pace with the demands for information, it seems—in retrospect—inevitable that newer technologies should be applied to the processing of information. Roger Christian has supplied this bit of perspective on the coming of electronic bibliographic data bases:

Both SDI (Selective Dissemination of Information) and retrospective searches have for some time fallen within the purview of special and major academic libraries, and bibliographic materials in machine-readable form are simply extensions of abstracting and indexing reference works in print—a familiar and traditional library medium. (Indeed, a library itself is a data base of sorts, in the sense of being an organized and indexed repository of information.) . . .

Parallel and sometimes related developments were being experienced in publishing circles. Publishing, like library service, is labor-intensive, and like libraries, publishers are caught between steadily escalating costs and relatively flat productivity. . . . Without new tools for the production of abstracting and indexing services, the organizations publishing these bibliographic aids would have been overwhelmed by the volume of the literature with which they had to cope. Fortunately, technological developments, especially those resulting in the rapid drop in the cost of computer storage, and in practical photocomposition, which usually costs far less than conventional typesetting, helped such services survive and grow. . . . (Photocomposition involves capturing or converting material in machine-readable form. In the process, one unavoidably creates a machine-readable data base.)

Once a data base exists in machine-readable form, it can be accessed or manipulated for any number of purposes. What came into being as a by-product has become a valuable asset in its own right—one that can be marketed in conjunction with, or independently of, the associated printed publication. Recognizing the commercial potential of these machine-searchable files, publishers have modified the preparation of their data bases to make them more suitable for these purposes. Many organizations now produce machine-readable data bases directly, as distinct products that may or may not have printed counterparts [Roger Christian, *The Electronic Library: Bibliographic Data Bases, 1978–79* (rev. 2nd ed.; White Plains, N.Y.: Knowledge Industry Publications, 1978), p.10–18, passim].

Christian also points out that "the availability of such data bases is one aspect of a broader trend toward resource sharing, which enables libraries better to serve the needs of their patrons" (p.8).

In terms of a time span, computerized data bases are, of course, a recent phenomenon, and with but few exceptions they do not cover the years before the mid-1960s. For example, MEDLINE (Medical Literature Analysis and Retrieval System/MEDLARS on Line), a National Library of Medicine data base, provides coverage from 1966 to date. (But another NLM data base, EPILEPSYLINE, goes back to 1945.) *Science Citation Index* (an Institute for Scientific Information product) has been searchable in both printed and machine-readable format since 1961. Of the many Chemical Abstracts Service data bases, none covers a period that begins earlier than 1962. The Psychological Abstracts data base (1967–) corresponds with the printed *Psychological Abstracts*, in which format coverage extends back to 1927. Coverage of *Comprehensive Dissertation Index* (Xerox University Microfilms) is 1861 to date. For the record, the time span of three of the largest data bases—BIOSIS PREVIEWS (BioSciences Information Service, corresponding with two printed sources, *Biological Abstracts* [1926–] and *BioResearch Index* [1976–]); COMPENDEX (Engineering Index, Inc., publisher of *Engineering Index*, covering 1884–); and the *New York Times Information Bank*—is from January 1969 on.

The preceding paragraphs, it should be made clear, deal largely with bibliographic machine-readable data bases. Nonbibliographic and noncomputerized data bases—statistical and/or economic data, patents, marketing projections, credit records, medical histories, full text, etc.—are beyond the scope of this chapter. For a fuller, current guide to data bases of all types, consult *Encyclopedia of Information Systems and Services*, by Anthony T. Kruzas and others (3rd ed.; Detroit: Gale, 1978; 1030p.), and its interedition supplement, *New Information Systems and Services* (1979–). *Information Market Place, an International Directory of Information Products and Services* (New York: Bowker, 1979; 270p.) gives names, contact information, and descriptions of services for some 400 data base publishers, 1,000 data bases, 100 online readers, centers, etc.

Readers may also find the following sources useful: Pauline Atherton and Roger W. Christian, *Librarians and Online Services* (White Plains, N.Y.: Knowledge Industry Publications, 1977); *Computer-readable Bibliographic Data: A Directory and Sourcebook* . . . (Washington, D.C.: American Society for Information Science, 1976– [1 v., looseleaf]); Marvin C. Gechman, "Machine-readable Bibliographic Data Bases," *Annual Review of Information Science and Technology* 7:323–78 (1972); Martha E. Williams, "Use of Machine-readable Data Bases," *Annual Review of Information Science and Technology* 9:221–84 (1974); and periodicals such as the *Bulletin* (June/July 1974–) and *Journal* (Jan. 1950–) of the American Society for Information Science; *Database: The Magazine of Database Reference and Review* (Sept. 1978–); *Journal of Library Automation* (Mar. 1968–); and *Online: The Magazine of Online Information Systems* (Jan. 1972–).

GENERAL

General periodical indexes are a good source for articles on subjects of general current interest, treated in nontechnical terms. Most used in the United States is:

→ Readers' guide to periodical literature (cumulated), 1900– . N.Y., Wilson, 1905– . v.1– . Semimonthly, with annual cumulations.

> SCOPE: About 180 U.S. periodicals of broad general and popular character, including nontechnical magazines, representing all important scientific, technical, and subject fields. Titles are selected by subscribers' voting lists, supervised by the ALA Committee on Wilson Indexes, and are revised at intervals to add significant new titles and drop others.
>
> ARRANGEMENT: Alphabetical by author, subject, and title when necessary (notably for texts of short stories and plays, but not poems, these being listed only under author). Separate list of book reviews since

Mar. 1976. Note that subject headings are based on the LC *List of Subject Headings*, with certain deviations.

BIBLIOGRAPHIC DATA: Under author and subject, but not title entries, are author, title, volume, paging, and date of periodical, with indication of illustrations, portraits, maps, and bibliographies, when these are in the articles.

The following is a cumulative author-subject index to *Readers' Guide:*

→ Cumulative index to periodical literature, Mar. 1959–Feb. 1970. Princeton, National Library Service Corp., c1976. 7v.

For earlier years, see *Poole's Index to Periodical Literature, 1802–1906* and its cumulative author index, the latter from Pierian Press (1971). Also, *Nineteenth Century Readers' Guide to Periodical Literature, 1890–1899* (New York: Wilson, 1944; 2v.), an author-subject index to 51 significant periodicals.

→ Abridged readers' guide to periodical literature, v.1– , July 1935– . Author and subject index to a selected list of periodicals. N.Y., Wilson, 1936– . Monthly, with annual cumulations.

SCOPE: More than 50 periodicals selected from those indexed in *Readers' Guide* to meet the needs of school and small public libraries. About one-fourth of the titles are available for blind readers on "talking books," in braille, or on magnetic tape, and are so indicated in the list of periodicals indexed.

ARRANGEMENT and BIBLIOGRAPHIC DATA: Same as *Readers' Guide.*

Readers' Guide to Periodical Literature is generally held in American libraries, but recent general indexes to general periodicals, not included in *Readers' Guide,* have appeared in recent years. *Access* (Syracuse, N.Y.: Gaylord), issued three times a year since 1975, emphasizes popular music, travel, arts and crafts, and city magazines. The semiannual *Popular Periodical Index* (Camden, N.J.: The Index) began publication in 1973 and includes some titles also in *Access* and about 30 not in *Readers' Guide.* Another is *The New Periodicals Index* (Boulder, Colo.: Mediaworks), semiannual since 1977. This includes titles from the "alternative press."

As the following examples indicate, indexing and abstracting services have developed in many subject fields, many of them since 1900. They are usually the result of proliferating journal publication, which, in turn, reflects the ever increasing amount of investigation and research. No attempt is made to be exhaustive, for there are a number of sources for more complete lists (cited below).

ART
→ Art index, v.1– , Jan. 1929– , a cumulated author and subject index to a selected list of fine-arts periodicals. N.Y., Wilson, 1933– . Quarterly, with annual cumulations.

SCOPE: Includes yearbooks, museum bulletins, and American and foreign periodicals in archaeology, architecture, art history, arts and crafts, fine arts, graphic arts, industrial design, interior decoration, photography and films, planning and landscape design, and related subjects. Selected by subscribers.

ARRANGEMENT: Alphabetical by author and subject, with separate section of book reviews. Exhibitions and illustrations without text are listed under name of artist.

BIBLIOGRAPHIC DATA: Same as *Readers' Guide.*

BIOLOGICAL SCIENCES
→ Biological abstracts from the world's biological research literature. Philadelphia, Biological Abstracts, 1926– . Semimonthly.

SCOPE: Abstracts about 8,000 serials, books, symposia proceedings, and government reports in theoretical and applied biology, agriculture, behavioral sciences, basic medicine, and veterinary sciences.

ARRANGEMENT: Under general headings, with many subdivisions. Each issue contains author index, list of subject headings, Biosystematic Index (coordinating abstracts under lists of taxonomic categories), and alphabetical list of subject headings with pertinent abstract numbers. Also in each issue is a computer-produced key-word index, BASIC (Biological Abstracts Subjects in Context). There is also a separate book review section.

BIBLIOGRAPHIC DATA: Exact citation, with titles in English translation supplied for foreign articles.

→ Biological & agricultural index, a cumulative subject index to periodicals in the fields of biology, agriculture, and related sciences, 1964– . N.Y., Wilson, 1964–. v.50– . Monthly (except Sept.), with cumulations. Continues Agricultural index.

SCOPE: About 200 English-language periodicals in fields noted above.

ARRANGEMENT: Alphabetical by subject only, with separate book review section.

BIBLIOGRAPHIC DATA: Same as *Readers' Guide.*

BUSINESS
→ Business periodicals index; a cumulative subject index to periodicals in the fields of accounting, advertising, banking and finance, general business, insurance, labor and management, marketing and purchasing, office

management, public administration, taxation, specific businesses, industries, and trades. N.Y., Wilson, 1958– . v.1– . Monthly (except July), with annual cumulations.

SCOPE: See subtitle. Includes some U.S. government periodicals.

ARRANGEMENT: Alphabetical by subject only. Name entries refer to articles *about*, not *by*, the person or agency named. Separate book review section.

BIBLIOGRAPHIC DATA: Same as *Readers' Guide*.

CHEMISTRY

→ Chemical abstracts, a publication of the Chemical Abstracts Service, pub. by American Chemical Society, 1907– . Columbus, Ohio, 1907– . v.1– . Weekly.

SCOPE: Most comprehensive of abstract journals, including about 14,000 journals from many countries, patents, formulas, theses, proceedings, reports, and new books in the field. Peripheral literature in science and technology is included if related to chemistry or chemical engineering.

ARRANGEMENT: Classified under sections, with new ones added as necessary. Excellent computer-based key-word index to current volumes and separate indexes to formulas, patents, and ring systems, some of them cumulated at intervals.

BIBLIOGRAPHIC DATA: Complete citation.

EDUCATION

→ Current index to journals in education. v.1, 1969– . N.Y., Macmillan Information Corp., 1969– . Monthly with annual cumulation. Published since 1979 by Oryx Pr., Phoenix, Ariz.

Indexed by source journal, subject, author, and journal contents are over 500 journals, some not indexed in *Education Index*. Titles of articles in foreign journals given in original language and English translation. Valuable source for recent terminology in list of new thesaurus terms in monthly issues. Prepared by ERIC Clearinghouses.

→ Education index, v.1– , Jan. 1929– ; a cumulative author and subject index to a selected list of educational periodicals, proceedings, and yearbooks. N.Y., Wilson, 1932– . Monthly, with annual cumulations.

SCOPE: Currently indexes about 240 American and a few English titles, chiefly official journals of American educational associations and agencies, with a few U.S., but no state, government publications.

ARRANGEMENT: By author and subject. Separate book review section.
BIBLIOGRAPHIC DATA: Same as *Readers' Guide*.

HISTORY
→ America: history and life. A guide to periodical literature. v.1, no.1–.
July 1964– . Santa Barbara, Calif., ABC/Clio Pr., 1964– . Quarterly.

> SCOPE: Abstracts more than 3,000 articles a year from U.S. and some
> foreign journals "on the history of the United States and Canada
> published throughout the world, and . . . articles dealing with current
> American life and times."
> ARRANGEMENT: Since 1974, in four parts: A, article abstracts and cita-
> tions (Spring, Summer, Fall); B, book reviews (Spring, Fall); C,
> American history bibliography; D, annual index. Also five-year in-
> dexes, which now (since the one for 1969–73) employs the American
> Bibliographical Center's Subject Profile Index (ABC Spindex), a
> computer-assisted but humanly attuned indexing system that con-
> tains both generic and specific terms. Each index entry consists of an
> average of 3.5 subject, geographic, and biographic descriptors, fol-
> lowed by chronology of the article. Appended list of journals indi-
> cated countries of publication and cessations whenever appropriate.
> An introduction gives instructions for use.
> BIBLIOGRAPHIC DATA: Exact citation to source.

→ Historical abstracts, 1775–1945: bibliography of the world's periodical
literature . . . Eric H. Boehm, ed. v.1, no.1, Mar. 1955– . Santa Barbara,
Calif., Clio Pr. with International Social Science Inst., 1955– . Quarterly.

> SCOPE: Abstracts, more than 2,000 journals, transactions, and proceed-
> ings of historical associations which relate to the period 1775–1945 in
> world history. United States and Canada omitted since 1964. See
> above.
> ARRANGEMENT: Classified by subject and geographic areas, with annual
> and five-year author, biographical, geographical, and subject in-
> dexes. Since 1971, published in two parts.
> BIBLIOGRAPHIC DATA: Exact citation to source.

HUMANITIES
→ Arts & humanities citation index, 1977– . Philadelphia, Inst. for Scientific
Information, 1978– . 8 times a year.

> Indexes citations in articles appearing in over 1,000 journals and, since
> 1979, in symposia, monographic series, proceedings, and multiauthor

books, indexed to the level of individual chapters and authors. Patterned on *Science Citation Index*.

→ Humanities index, 1974– . N.Y., Wilson, 1974– . Quarterly with annual cumulations. Successor to *Social Sciences and Humanities Index*, 1907–74.

> SCOPE: More than 250 scholarly journals in archaeology, folklore, history, literature, philosophy, and related subjects.
> ARRANGEMENT: Author and subject entries, with appended list of book reviews in each issue.
> BIBLIOGRAPHIC DATA: Complete citation to source.

LIBRARY AND INFORMATION SCIENCE
→ Library and information science abstracts, 1969– . London, Library Assn., 1969– . Bimonthly. Supersedes *Library Science Abstracts,* 1950–68.

> SCOPE: Abstracts books, pamphlets, reports, and *selected* articles from 300 library and bibliographical periodicals, British and foreign.
> ARRANGEMENT: By broad subject, e.g. types of libraries, services, and bibliography, with annual author and subject indexes.
> BIBLIOGRAPHIC DATA: Title, author, name of periodical with volume, pages, and dates, and abstract and initials of abstractor.

It differs from *Library Literature* (described below) in scope, arrangement, and amount of information supplied for each work. Its full abstracts give enough content of a work to allow users to decide whether they want to read the original or may dispense with reading original. Foreword to each volume should be read for a fuller statement of purpose. Abstracts are prepared by 100 abstractors and translators, chiefly British librarians, who are identified in annual list. See B. A. Lipetz, "Information Science Abstracts," *Encyclopedia of Library and Information Science* (v.11, p.487–94), which describes the classification scheme of *Information Science Abstracts*, 1966– (Philadelphia: Documentation Abstracts, Inc., 1966–).

→ Library literature, 1921/32– . N.Y., Wilson, 1934– . Bimonthly, with annual and biennial cumulations.

> SCOPE: Indexes, by author and subject, current books, pamphlets, unpublished theses, films, filmstrips, microcards and microfilms dealing with libraries and librarianship, and articles in English- and foreign-language journals in the field and pertinent articles from other periodicals. Includes a number of journals of particular impor-

tance in bibliography: *American Documentation; Bibliographical Society of America, Papers; Bulletin of Bibliography; Indexer; Journal of Documentation;* and *Library Trends.*

ARRANGEMENT: Alphabetical by author and subject. Separate book review section.

BIBLIOGRAPHIC DATA: Exact citation to articles; author, title, place of publication, publisher, date, and paging for books; author, title, date, paging, degree, and name of institution for theses.

For earlier years, consult Harry George Turner Cannon's *Bibliography of Library Economy; a Classified Index to the Professional Periodical Literature in the English Language Relating to Library Economy, Printing, Methods of Publishing, Copyright, Bibliography, etc., from 1876 to 1920* (Chicago: ALA, 1927; 680p.; repr.: B. Franklin, 1970). This includes alphabetical index to classified lists. For author index, see A. H. and M. Jordan, eds., *Cannons' Bibliography of Library Economy, 1876–1920: An Author Index with Citations* (Metuchen, N.J.: Scarecrow, 1976; 473p.).

LITERATURE
→ The Access index to little magazines. Syracuse, (Gaylord Professional Publications), 1976– . Annual.

SCOPE: About 75 literary periodicals, most of them not indexed elsewhere.

ARRANGEMENT: Separate author, title, subject indexes.

BIBLIOGRAPHIC DATA: Exact citation to source.

For earlier years, consult *Index to Little Magazines*, which has had various compilers and publishers, but is planned to cover journals of high quality but small circulation published since 1900. Volumes are available for 1900 through 1967. Also useful for earlier years is *Comprehensive Index to English-Language Little Magazines, 1890–1970* (series 1; Millwood, N.Y.: Kraus-Thomson, 1976; 8v.), which indexes 100 magazines. Additional titles to be included in later volumes.

MATHEMATICS
→ Mathematical reviews, v.1, 1940– . Providence, R.I., American Mathematical Soc., 1940– . Monthly.

Contains abstracts and signed critical reviews by authorities of mathematical literature appearing in about 1,500 foreign and U.S. journals and from books and proceedings. Monthly and cumulated author indexes; since 1973, semiannual classified indexes. *Index of*

Mathematical Papers, which has fully indexed *Mathematical Reviews* since 1973, has been more current since 1978, with the index for 1978 available in Feb. 1979.

MEDICINE
→ Index medicus. Wash., Nat. Lib. of Medicine. v.1–21 (1879–99); 2nd ser. v.1–18 (1903–20); 3rd ser. v.1–6 (1921–27); 1916–56 as Quarterly cumulative index to current medical literature; n. s. v.1, 1960– . Monthly.

Subject and name indexes, the first giving English titles and English translations of foreign articles from over 2,000 U.S. and foreign medical journals. Very comprehensive. All citations stored in MEDLARS (Medical Literature Retrieval and Analysis System) for use in machine retrieval.

MUSIC
→ Music index; the key to current music periodical literature. Detroit, Information Service, 1949– . Monthly, with annual cumulations.

SCOPE: More than 200 U.S. and European music periodicals, articles on music from general periodicals, and a few books.

ARRANGEMENT: Author and subject indexes, with music reviews listed under composer, title, and medium; book reviews grouped under that heading.

BIBLIOGRAPHIC DATA: Exact citation to source.

PHILOSOPHY
→ The philosopher's index; an international index to philosophical periodicals. v.1, no.1– , Spring 1967– . Bowling Green, Ohio, Bowling Green State Univ., 1967– . Quarterly, with annual cumulations.

SCOPE: Major American and British philosophical periodicals, selected journals in other languages, and related interdisciplinary publications.

ARRANGEMENT: Since 1969, separate author and subject entries coded to "Bibliographic data and abstracts" section, which gives exact citation to source.

An index to "approximately 15,000 articles from U.S. journals published during the 27 year period, 1940–1966, and approximately 6,000 books published during the 37 year period, 1940–1976" was issued by the same publisher in 1978 in three volumes as *The Philosopher's Index: A Retrospective Index to U.S. Publications from 1940*.

PSYCHOLOGY

→ Psychological abstracts, 1927– . Lancaster, Pa., and Wash., American Psychological Assn., 1927– . v.1– . Bimonthly.

> SCOPE: Abstracts U.S. and foreign books, journals, dissertations, monographs, and reports.
> ARRANGEMENT: Classified by broad subject, with separate author and subject indexes in each issue that cumulate annually.
> BIBLIOGRAPHIC DATA: Exact citation.

The annual author and subject indexes to *Psychological Abstracts* have been cumulated in the following:

→ Columbia University. Libraries. Psychology Library. Author index to Psychological index 1894 to 1935 and Psychological abstracts 1927 to 1958. Boston, G. K. Hall, 1960. 5v.

→ Psychological abstracts. Cumulative author index. 1959/63– . Wash., American Psychological Assn., 1965– .

→ _____. Cumulated subject index to Psychological abstracts, 1927/60. Boston, G. K. Hall, 1966. 1st supp., 1961/65, pub. 1968; 2nd supp., 1966/68, pub. 1971 in 2v.

→ _____. Cumulative subject index to Psychological abstracts, 1969/71. Wash., American Psychological Assn., 1969/71– . Usually covers 3- or 4-year periods.

> Data published since 1967 are also available for online computer searching.

RELIGION

→ Catholic periodical and literature index, v.1– . 1930– . Haverford, Pa., Catholic Lib. Assn., 1939– . Bimonthly, with biennial cumulations.

> SCOPE: "A cumulative author-subject index to a selective list of Catholic periodicals and an author-subject bibliography of adult books by Catholics, with a selection of Catholic-interest books by other authors" (subtitle). About 135 periodicals and 2,500 books indexed annually, chiefly in English language and covering many general topics. Published as *Catholic Periodical Index*, 1930–66, and combined with *The Guide to Catholic Literature* in July 1968.

ARRANGEMENT: Annotated author, title, and subject bibliography of books; author and subject index to journals.

BIBLIOGRAPHIC DATA: Exact citation to source.

→ Religion index one: periodicals. v.13– . July/Dec. 1977– . Chicago, American Theological Lib. Assn., 1978– . Semiannual. Pub. as *Index to Religious Periodical Literature*, v.1–12. 1949/52– Jan./June 1977. The Association, 1953–78.

SCOPE: More than 150 American and foreign journals in religion and archaeology. Collective works are indexed in companion volume, *Religion Index Two: Multi-Author Works*.

ARRANGEMENT: In three parts: subject, author (with abstracts), and book review indexes.

BIBLIOGRAPHIC DATA: Exact citation to sources.

SCIENCE AND TECHNOLOGY

→ Applied science and technology index; a cumulative subject index to English language periodicals in the fields of aeronautics, automation, chemistry, construction, earth sciences, electricity and electronics, engineering, industrial and mechanical arts, machinery, materials, metallurgy, physics, telecommunications and related subjects (formerly *Industrial Arts Index*). N.Y., Wilson, 1913– . Monthly except July, with annual cumulations.

SCOPE: About 225 American and British periodicals from fields listed in its subtitle.

ARRANGEMENT: Alphabetical by subject, with separate book review section arranged by author, 1976– .

BIBLIOGRAPHIC DATA: Same as *Readers' Guide*.

→ General science index, v.1– , N.Y., Wilson, July 1978– . Monthly except June and Dec., with bound annual cumulation.

SCOPE: Nearly 100 general science periodicals, about 40 of which are also indexed in *Readers' Guide* or *Applied Science and Technology Index*. Among those not indexed in these Wilson indexes are *American Biology Teacher, American Journal of Public Health, Isis, Journal of General Psychology, New Ecologist, Physics Teacher*, and *Psychology Today*, which also illustrate the wide range of subjects covered. All are in English.

ARRANGEMENT: Subject index with appended section of citations to book reviews.

BIBLIOGRAPHIC DATA: Same as *Readers' Guide*.

As the above is designed for the general reader, the following is intended for the scientist:

→ Science citation index, 1961– . Philadelphia, Inst. for Scientific Information, 1961– . Bimonthly, with annual cumulation.

> SCOPE: Computer-produced index to citations in articles in nearly 3,000 English-language and foreign journals and, since 1977, to citations in books, symposia, and proceedings. Covers biology, chemistry, engineering, mathematics, physics, and behavioral sciences, but latter are more fully covered in *Social Sciences Citation Index* (from same publisher).
>
> ARRANGEMENTS: The Source Index supplies full bibliographic data for the citations, preceded by author index to the citations and followed by a Permuterm Subject Index to key words in the title of each citing article, and corporate and patent citation indexes. As explained by Marion V. Bell and Eleanor A. Swidan in *Reference Books: A Brief Guide* (8th ed.; Baltimore: Enoch Pratt Free Library, 1978; p.109): "By checking the author of a cited item in the Citation Index portion of *SCI*, additional titles which cite any publications by this author in the period covered by the index may be identified. These citing items may report the latest development in a particular field, corroborate or refute earlier studies, identify scientists investigating similar phenomena, or the citing author may in turn be traced in the Citation Index for another gathering of related references."
>
> BIBLIOGRAPHIC DATA: Source Index supplies full bibliographic data.

SOCIAL SCIENCES
→ Public Affairs Information Service. Bulletin of the Public Affairs Information Service. v.1, Oct. 15, 1914– . N.Y., Service, 1914– . Semimonthly since v.64, Oct. 1977. Annual cumulation.

→ _____. Cumulative author index, 1965–1969. Comp. and ed. by C. Edward Wall. Ann Arbor, Mich., Pierian Pr., 1973. 490p.

→ _____. Cumulative subject index to Public Affairs Information Service bulletins, 1915–1974. Arlington, Va., Carrollton Pr., 1977–78. 15v.

→ _____. Foreign language index. v.1– , 1968/71– . N.Y., Service, 1972– . Quarterly with annual cumulations.

> SCOPE: *Selected* articles from a wide range of periodicals published throughout the world, dealing with social and economic conditions, government and international affairs, and public administration.

Differs from Wilson indexes not only in its selective indexing (rather than indexing whole contents of a periodical) but also in including pertinent books, documents, pamphlets, reports of public and private agencies, and certain statistical sources. *Foreign Language Index* includes "languages other than English."

ARRANGEMENT: Alphabetical by subjects, many of them further subdivided for greater specificity. Author index in annual volume.

BIBLIOGRAPHIC DATA: For books, full bibliographic date, including price; for articles, exact citation to source. Online data base since 1976.

→ Social sciences index, 1974– . N.Y., Wilson, 1974– . Quarterly, with annual cumulations. Successor to *Social Sciences and Humanities Index*, 1907–74.

SCOPE: More than 250 scholarly journals in anthropology, economics, geography, political science, sociology, public administration, and related subjects.

ARRANGEMENT: Author and subject entries, with appended list of book reviews in each issue.

BIBLIOGRAPHIC DATA: Complete citation to source.

→ Social sciences citation index. v.1– , 1973– . Philadelphia, Inst. for Scientific Information. Three times a year. Third issue is an annual, bound cumulation.

Indexes citations in about 2,000 journals from many countries in anthropology, archaeology, area studies, community health, demography, economics, educational research, ethnic studies, geography, history, law, linguistics, management, political science, psychology, psychiatry, sociology, statistics, and urban planning and development. Beginning in 1979, books, symposia, and proceedings are also indexed. Patterned on *Science Citation Index*.

Additional indexes may be found in sources listed not only in general guides to reference books, such as *Sheehy*, but also in guides to the literature of individual fields and in *International Periodicals Directory* (as noted earlier). *Subject Guide to Periodical Indexes and Review Indexes*, by Jean Spealman Kujoth (Metuchen, N.J.: Scarecrow, 1969; 129p.), draws on these sources for its descriptive list of more than 200 currently published indexes. Also, Bill Katz and Berry Richards, *Magazines for Libraries* (cited earlier), gives bibliographic data and descriptive and evaluative annotations for quite a number of periodical indexing and abstracting services in an introductory section.

International Periodicals Directory also indicates if there are annual or cumulative indexes for individual periodicals, which must be consulted for titles not indexed elsewhere, though they vary greatly in completeness, consistency, and conformity to established lists of subject headings.

Abstracting services have increased greatly in number in many fields, and the following describes many of them.

→ Chicorel index to abstracting and indexing services: publications in humanities and the social sciences. Ed. by Marietta Chicorel. 2nd ed. N.Y., Chicorel, 1978. 2v. (Chicorel Index Series, v.11, 11A, 2nd ed.)

Newspaper Indexes

Tremendous strides have been made in recent years in newspaper indexes, with over 500 in North America alone. They vary greatly in scope and form, and the best known are produced by commercial firms. In the past, librarians have used the *New York Times Index* as a partial index to their local papers, since most metropolitan newspapers publish reports of important events at approximately the same time. Of course, it is no help in locating purely local or special articles.

→ New York Times index, v.1– . 1913– . N.Y., Times, 1913– . Semimonthly, with annual cumulations.

> SCOPE: Indexes, with brief abstracts, the late city edition.
> ARRANGEMENT: Alphabetically by subjects, under which articles are chronologically arranged. Book and theater reviews are listed separately under these headings. Book reviews are cumulated in *The New York Times Book Review Index, 1896–1970* (5v.; N.Y., New York Times and Arno Pr., 1973). For full explanation of indexing policy and list of subjects, see New York Times, *Thesaurus of Descriptors* (N.Y., New York Times Co., 1968).
> BIBLIOGRAPHIC DATA: Author, title, date, column, page, and cross-references. Users must remember to add *year* to date in copying citations for further reference, since, for obvious reasons, it is not given for each entry. Novices are inclined to forget it when consulting more than one annual volume.

→ _____. Prior series. N.Y., Bowker, 1966–76. 15v.

Also valuable for its broad coverage is:

→ Times. London. Official index. 1906– . London, The Times. Frequency varies. Monthly since 1977.

A six-volume subject index to the London *Times* is in progress, with many of the entries briefly annotated. It will cover 1785–90, previously unindexed (*The Times Index*, v.1, Jan.–Dec. 1785 [Woodbridge, Conn.; distributed in the U.S. by Research Pubns., 1979; 156p.], pref. by Derek Jewell).

Particularly useful for economics and business is:

→ Wall Street Journal index. v.1– , 1958– . N.Y., Dow Jones, 1958– . Monthly, with annual cumulations.

The largest commercial index producer is Bell and Howell's Micro Photo Division, which publishes:

→ Newspaper index, Jan. 1972– . Wooster, Ohio, Newspaper Indexing Center, Bell & Howell, 1972– . Monthly, quarterly, and annual cumulations.

> Indexes nine of the country's largest and most strategically located newspapers: *Chicago Sun-Times, Chicago Tribune, Denver Post, Detroit News, Houston Post, New Orleans Times-Picayune, San Francisco Chronicle, Los Angeles Times,* and *Washington Post*. Micro Photo also sells microfilm copies of all except the last two papers. Nine separate key-word subject and personal name indexes cover international, national, state, local and regional news, photographs and cartoons, editorials and syndicated columns, and some ads. Citations to date, section, page, and column are given for each entry, together with a short, descriptive sentence. Indexes for each newspaper may be purchased separately.

For an overview of Micro Photo and other newspaper indexes, see Susan Spaeth Cherry, "Yesterday's News for Tomorrow: A Special Update on News Indexes, Indexing, and Indexers" (*American Libraries* 10:588–92 [Nov. 1979]). Cherry also describes the *National Newspaper Index* on computer-output microfilm. Each issue is cumulative, and now available for *Christian Science Monitor, New York Times,* and *Wall Street Journal*.

Current Events

Allied to newspaper indexes in their subject matter, but usually supplying more content, are news digests. Frequently found in American libraries are:

→ Facts on file, a weekly world news digest, with cumulative index. N.Y., Facts on File, Oct. 30, 1940– . Weekly, with annual bound volumes.

→ Keesing's Contemporary archives. London, Keesing's, July 1, 1931– . (Represented in U.S. by Charles Scribner's Sons, N.Y.) Weekly.

Both of these services draw their information from well-known newspapers (*New York Times,* [*London*] *Times,* etc.). *Keesing's* states that its coverage of world events is based on "newspapers, periodicals, and official publications of the United Kingdom, the British Commonwealth, and foreign countries, as well as from information supplied by international organizations and recognized foreign news agencies."

While both are international in scope, *Facts on File,* in its brief digests, emphasizes important events in the United States, and *Keesing's* places its major emphasis on British Commonwealth affairs. *Keesing's* also supplies informative background reports which add considerably to its reference value, although this results in the service's being less current than *Facts on File. Keesing's* also gives texts of major political speeches, communiqués, treaties, and laws. Illustrations, maps, tables, statistics, and a few photographs accompany the text.

Facts on File is arranged under broad subjects, *Kessing's* under name of country, territory, continent, or group of governments. Both issue detailed indexes every two weeks, with quarterly and annual cumulations. *Facts on File* also has a monthly index.

Keesing's has some special features (as noted) which are not found in *Facts on File.* However, *Facts on File* is received more promptly in American libraries, and this, plus its American emphasis, explains its popularity. Both are reliable sources for accounts of major developments, national and international.

Other Indexes and Concordances

For retrieving bits of information too specific for inclusion in national library catalogs and trade bibliographies, other indexes and concordances are useful. They also supplement periodical indexes by providing additional approaches, or added information for individual items, and by drawing on a wider range of indexed sources. They fall roughly into four categories: (1) indexes to single books, (2) indexes to the works of a single author, including concordances, (3) indexes to literary forms, and (4) indexes to nonliterary forms. Their general characteristics may best be described under these categories.

Indexes to Single Books

If carefully prepared, indexes to single books supply an alphabetical list of names, facts, places, and other subject content, sometimes in one alphabet, sometimes in two or more alphabets (basic principles of book indexing are discussed by Robert Collison in the titles cited earlier). But their present state is far from satisfactory. Librarians need to be aware of these inadequacies and should work with publishers toward bringing about better book indexes.

Editors of multivolume encyclopedias are particularly aware of the importance of a complete and well-organized index to the persons, places, things, and abstract ideas treated in articles, which more often than not are arranged alphabetically by subject. But no one should expect to find all the information pertinent to a subject in one article—one on the United States, for example. Nor even in an encyclopedia that favors short articles on specific subjects should one expect to find separate articles on every subject. Thus the need for an index is evident. Collison sees its compilation as a highly skilled task, noting that the index must "analyze every name, every topic, every idea, every illustration, map, and diagram, etc." (*Encyclopedias: Their History throughout the Ages* [2nd ed.; New York: Hafner, 1966; 334p.], p.15).

Indexes to Works of a Single Author

Indexes to an author's works may resemble indexes to single books or, in the case of important authors, take the form of concordances, which index all significant *words* in the text, such as a Shakespeare concordance. Concordances of the works of one author will continue to increase greatly in number, due to the use of electronic data processing machines in their compilation. These machines, if properly programmed, produce accurate and usable results in a very short time.

Indexes to Literary Forms

Indexes to literary forms augment national library catalogs, trade bibliographies, subject bibliographies, and periodical indexes by (1) supplying authors, titles, and subjects of individual essays, plays, poems, short stories, speeches, dissertations, and other writings in collections whose contents are not analyzed in other types of bibliography; (2) supplying citation to exact location of *words* in a quotation; (3) supplying citation to or quotations from reviews of individual titles; or (4) supplying additional descriptive information, as for plays.

In turn, periodical indexes that index periodical publications of essays, plays, poems, short stories, and speeches must be consulted for more recently published titles.

A few examples of titles most frequently consulted are listed below, alphabetically by literary form:

BOOK REVIEWS
→ Book review digest, v.1–, 1905– . N.Y., Wilson, 1905– . Monthly, with

semiannual and annual cumulations. Author/Title Index, 1905–1974. (Wilson, 1976. 4v.)

SCOPE: As indicated in its statement of policy, it includes works of nonfiction for which two or more reviews have appeared in about 75 periodicals, selected by subscribers, and works of fiction for which four or more reviews have appeared. Exception is made for books reviewed in Reference and Subscription Books Review section of *Booklist*, where one review is sufficient for listing. Emphasis is on books and reviews for the general user, rather than the specialist.

ARRANGEMENT: Alphabetical by author, with subject and title index, which is cumulated every five years. Fiction is classified by subject, e.g. historical and geographical setting, vocation, etc., in the index.

BIBLIOGRAPHICAL AND OTHER DATA: Author, title, pages, illustrations, maps, price, publisher, Dewey Decimal Classification, subject headings based on *Sears' List of Subject Headings*, exact citation to reviews, number of words in each review, and not more than three excerpts for fiction and four excerpts for nonfiction, except for books of unusual importance or controversial nature.

Since 1976, H. W. Wilson has issued the monthly *Current Book Review Citations*, which is distinguished for the large number of reviews cited for about 40,000 titles a year, appearing in about 1,300 major periodicals, both general and specialized. It must be remembered that not all reviews in these periodicals are indexed.

Narrower in coverage but more current in its indexing is:

→ Book review index, v.1, no.1, Jan. 1965– . Detroit, Gale Research, 1965– . Bimonthly, with annual cumulations.

SCOPE: Indexes *all* reviews in about 300 English-language periodicals, principally general and those in the humanities and social sciences.

ARRANGEMENT: Alphabetical by author or editor of work; by title if these are not known. Title index since 1976.

BIBLIOGRAPHIC DATA: Author, title, name of reviewer if known, and exact citation to reviews.

Book Review Digest and *Book Review Index* complement each other. The first is distinguished for its added features (noted above), the second for its inclusiveness.

Two useful cumulations which save time, if publication date of book is not known, are:

→ Cumulative book review index, 1905–1974. Princeton, National Library Service, 1975. 6v.

Indexes reviews from *Book Review Digest, Choice, Library Journal,* and *Saturday Review* in one alphabetical arrangement by author and title.

→ The New York Times book review index, 1896–1970. N.Y., New York Times and Arno Pr., 1973. 5v.

Five separate indexes, including author, title, byline, subject, and category.

Somewhat different, in that it brings together critical excerpts which have appeared over a period of time, is:

→ Children's literature review. v.1– , 1975– . Detroit, Gale Research, 1975– . Semiannual.

SCOPE: "Excerpts from reviews, criticism, and commentary on books for children and young people" (subtitle). Each volume includes about 40 authors of older and contemporary fiction and nonfiction, with excerpts from books and periodicals.
ARRANGEMENT: Alphabetical under author, followed by book titles, with cumulative indexes to authors, book titles, and critics.
BIBLIOGRAPHIC AND OTHER DATA. Brief identification of author, excerpts, and exact citation to sources.

This is augmented by *Children's Book Review Index*, 1975 to date, also published by Gale Research. It is a current index but contains no excerpts.

Particularly useful for further sources of book reviews, including serials and separately published titles, is:

→ Gray, Richard A.   A guide to book review citations: a bibliography of sources. Columbus, Ohio State Univ. Pr., 1968. 221p.

Fully annotated, with author, title, and subject indexes to its classified arrangement. Invaluable for scholarly and foreign periodical sources not indexed in *Book Review Digest* and *Book Review Index*.

DISSERTATIONS

→ Comprehensive dissertation index, 1861–1972. Ann Arbor, Mich., Xerox Univ. Microfilms, 1973. 37v. Supps.

Though admittedly incomplete, it is the best source for readily locating more than 400,000 dissertations, listed under 22 disciplines and further divided by subject, with a computer-generated key-word subject index. Chiefly American, but a few foreign graduate schools are represented.

→ Dissertation abstracts international, v.30, July 1969– . Ann Arbor, Mich., University Microfilms International, 1969– . Monthly.

> Formerly *Dissertation Abstracts* and *Microfilm Abstracts*. Includes about 30,000 abstracts of doctoral dissertations annually. Three parts cover humanities, sciences, and European abstracts. Key-word and author index in each issue, with cumulative annual author index.

DRAMA

→ Chicorel, Marietta, and Hall, Veronica, eds. Chicorel theater index to plays in anthologies, periodicals, discs and tapes. N.Y., Chicorel Lib. Pub. Co., 1970– .

> SCOPE: Plays in book and periodical sources, and those available on tapes or records.
> ARRANGEMENT: Alphabetical by author, title, and subject, followed by titles of individual plays and anthologies; with appended lists of authors, editors, titles of plays, publishers, and subject indicators, the latter including type of genre, national origin, and historical periods.
> BIBLIOGRAPHIC DATA: Complete, including price and indicating titles available in paperback.

→ Play index. N.Y. Wilson, 1953– . Irregular.

> SCOPE: Plays of all types, including some for children and young adults, published separately or in collections from 1949 to date.
> ARRANGEMENT: Alphabetical by author, title, and subject, followed by list of collections indexed, cast analysis, and directory of publishers.
> BIBLIOGRAPHIC DATA: Under author, gives title, brief plot, number of scenes and settings, number and sex of characters, and citation to collection or separate publication. Under title, gives author only. Under subject, gives author and title only. Plays for children are designated by symbol.

ESSAYS

→ Essay and general literature index. N.Y., Wilson, 1934– . Semiannual, with five-year cumulations.

> SCOPE: Essays and articles in English language appearing in collections published from 1900 to date, with emphasis on the humanities and, especially, literary criticism.
> ARRANGEMENT: Authors, subjects, and some titles in one alphabet, with appended list of books indexed.
> BIBLIOGRAPHIC DATA: Author and title of essay with author or editor and

title of collection, and inclusive paging for all entries. Many cross-references.

→ _____. 70-year index, 1900–1969. N.Y., Wilson, 1972. 437p.

Cites under author nearly 200,000 essays from 9,917 collections.

FICTION

→ Fiction catalog. 1st ed., 1908– . New editions every five years, with annual supps.

SCOPE: Outstanding novels selected by consulting librarians and specialists; intended primarily for small and medium-size libraries.

ARRANGEMENT: Pt. 1, author alphabet; pt. 2, title and subject index; pt. 3, directory of publishers and distributors.

BIBLIOGRAPHIC DATA: Pt. 1 gives title, publisher, date of publication, paging, price, descriptive notes (excerpts from reviewing media), and symbol for titles especially suitable for young adults.

POETRY

→ Granger's Index to poetry. 1st ed.– . N.Y., Columbia Univ. Pr., 1904– .

SCOPE: Indexes standard and popular collections usually found in college and public libraries, deleting out-of-print titles in earlier editions and adding new ones. *Granger's Index to Poetry, 1970–1977,* ed. by William James Smith and published in 1979, replaces the customary five-year supplement, indexing about 25,000 poems in 120 anthologies. For the first time, recommends certain collections for first purchase.

ARRANGEMENT: In three alphabets: by title and first line, author, and subject.

BIBLIOGRAPHIC DATA: Under title and first line, gives author and citation to collection; under author, gives title only; under subject, gives author and title only. Supplemented by John R. Brewton, *Index to Poetry for Children and Young People; a Title, Subject, Author, and First Line Index to Poetry in Collections for Children and Young People* (N.Y., Wilson, 1942, and supps.).

PROCEEDINGS

→ Directory of published proceedings. Series SEMT—science, engineering, medicine, technology. v.1– , Sept. 1965– . Harrison, N.Y., InterDok Corp., 1965– . Monthly, except July–Aug., with annual cumulation and 5-year cumulated index. Directory of published proceedings, series SSH—social sciences/humanities, v.1, no.1, Jan. 1968– . Harrison, N.Y., InterDok Corp., 1968– . Quarterly.

Preprints and published proceedings, with directory of meeting places, chronologically arranged; bibliographical data for ordering: subject/ sponsor, editor, and location indexes (annual). Worldwide coverage.

QUOTATIONS

Collections of quotations from prose and poetry exist in great numbers and vary greatly in exactness of bibliographic citation and completeness of indexing. They may be arranged alphabetically by author or subject, or chronologically by birth date of authors. For a representative list, see *Sheehy*, which also contains commentary on their reference use. Only a few examples are given here:

→ Bartlett, John. Familiar quotations; a collection of passages, phrases, and proverbs traced to their sources in ancient and modern literature. 14th ed., rev. and enl. Emily Morison Beck, ed. Boston, Little, [1968]. 1750p.

> SCOPE: Comprehensive selection, revised at intervals to include more recent authors and delete those no longer familiar.
> ARRANGEMENT: 2,250 authors and major collective or anonymous works, e.g. the Bible, arranged chronologically, with author and detailed key-word indexes.
> BIBLIOGRAPHIC DATA: Birth and death dates for authors; citation to source adequate for location of original, varying according to type.

→ Evans, Bergen. Dictionary of quotations. N.Y., Bonanza Books, 1968. 2029p.

> SCOPE: Based on other quotation books, but with some additions not found in other sources, especially contemporary.
> ARRANGEMENT: Alphabetical by specific subject, with author and detailed concordance index.
> BIBLIOGRAPHIC DATA: Exact citation to source, with explanatory notes for some entries.

→ Stevenson, Burton Egbert. The home book of quotations, classical and modern. 10th ed. rev. N.Y., Dodd, 1967. 2816p.

> SCOPE: More than 50,000 quotations, well selected.
> ARRANGEMENT: Alphabetical by subject. Author index, giving dates, brief identification, and references to all quotations cited. Key-word index omits subjects under which quotations are listed.
> BIBLIOGRAPHICAL DATA: Usually give exact citation to source.

→ Dictionary of contemporary quotations. v.1– . Syracuse, J. G. Burke; distributed by Gaylord Professional Pubns., 1976– .

Auguments above titles by recording more timely quotes on subjects of contemporary interest.

→ What they said, 1969– . Ed. by Alan F. and Jason R. Pater. Beverly Hills, Calif., Monitor Book Co., 1969– . Annual.

Quotations arranged under topics of current interest, with identification of speaker and indexes to speakers and subjects.

SHORT STORIES

→ Short story index. N.Y., Wilson, 1953– . 1553p. Supps., 1950–54, 1955–58, 1959–63, 1964–68, 1969–73, 1975– . Annual, with five-year cumulations.

SCOPE: Earlier volumes indexed only book collections published from 1900 to 1973, but since 1975, periodicals are also included.

ARRANGEMENT: In one alphabet under author, title, and many subjects, with separate list of collections indexed.

BIBLIOGRAPHIC DATA: Under author, gives title and citation to source; under title, gives author only; under subject, gives author and title only. Full bibliographic information in list of collections indexed.

Since the magazines indexed in *Readers' Guide to Periodicals* and *Humanities Index* publish many stories, these too may be used, for earlier years. Since 1974, stories indexed in these sources are included in *Short Story Index*.

SPEECHES

→ Sutton, Roberta Briggs. Speech index; an index to 259 collections of world famous orations and speeches for various occasions. 4th ed., rev. and enl. N.Y., Scarecrow, 1966; 947p. Supps. 1966–70, 1971–75.

SCOPE: Indicated in subtitle.

ARRANGEMENT: Author, subject, and type of speech, e.g., acceptance, in one alphabet. *Sears' List of Subject Headings* is the authority for subject entries. Many cross-references.

BIBLIOGRAPHIC DATA: Author, title, and citation to source for all entries. For review of 1971–75 supp., see *Booklist* 74:641 (Dec. 1, 1977).

Indexes to Nonliterary Forms

In each case, nonliterary forms (music, works of art, law reports, illustrations, patents, formulas) are indexed by their distinguishing characteristics. Great advances are being made in some of these fields, particularly in the indexing of law reports and formulas, where machine-produced indexes have been developed. For examples and descriptions, guides to the literature of pertinent fields should be consulted.

Periodical and newspaper indexes, indexes to literary and nonliterary forms, and concordances, in spite of their great variations in form, may be generally described in terms of the accepted definition of an index: a systematically arranged list that gives enough information about each item to enable it to be identified and traced.

Bibliographies of Bibliographies

Nearly all the forms of bibliography that have been noted thus far may serve as bibliographies of bibliography, for in many of these indexes an element of the citation notes the existence of a bibliography. Briefly, library catalogs, by use of the subdivision *Bibliography* in their subject headings and by indicating in the collation of a work whether it contains a bibliography, serve as a record of bibliographies that will be found in one library collection. To a certain extent, this is also true of some trade bibliographies, *Cumulative Book Index*, for example. Guides to the literature of subject fields always include lists of bibliographies. Periodical indexes and abstracting services also indicate bibliographical articles, as well as those that contain bibliographies in addition to their text. But the proliferation of bibliographies, especially subject bibliographies, has created a need for separate works devoted entirely to this form, which will allow the user quickly to discover what has been published. This need has been admirably met by two examples, one retrospective, the other current, which often serve as starting points for a serious bibliographic search.

→ Besterman, Theodore. A world bibliography of bibliographies and of bibliographical catalogues, calendars, abstracts, digests, indexes, and the like. 4th ed., rev. and greatly enl. Lausanne, Societas Bibliographica, (1965–66). 5v.

Besterman has examined nearly all the titles in this monumental one-man effort, which includes some 117,000 separately published works, carefully cataloged and indicating in brackets the number of items in each. It is alphabetically arranged under about 16,000 subject headings and subheadings, with adequate cross-references. There is an index to authors, titles of serial and anonymous works, libraries and archives, and subjects covered by abstracts to British patent specifications. Its chief limitation, as stated by its compiler, is that it omits bibliographies which appear as parts of books or articles. In this respect it differs from *Bibliographic Index*. *Besterman* is updated by:

→ Toomey, Alice F. World bibliography of bibliographies, 1964–1974; a list of works represented by Library of Congress printed catalog cards; a decennial supplement to Theodore Besterman, A world bibliography of bibliographies. Totowa, N.J., Rowman & Littlefield, 1977. 2v.

Listed under about 6,000 subject headings are 18,000 titles, also found in *Library of Congress: Books—Subjects*. Entries are reproduced from LC catalog cards, with some cross-references. Although convenient to consult, it serves as a reminder of the importance of the LC subject catalog as a bibliography of bibliographies. Many of the titles do not appear in:

→ Bibliographic index; a cumulative bibliography of bibliographies. 1937– . N.Y., Wilson, 1938– . Pub. Apr. and Aug., with bound cumulation each Dec.

This subject index gives complete citation for articles devoted wholly or in part to bibliography from more than 1,500 periodicals, including a number in foreign languages; to books and parts of books and pamphlets, indicating whether titles are annotated or not. It is also useful as a guide to current indexes (e.g. *Art Index* is cited under Art and *Library Literature* under Library Science), as well as to appended lists of references in books and articles on very specific subjects. Only bibliographies with 50 or more citations are indexed. These references are often the best source of important writing on that subject. The preface to the first cumulation, 1937–42, should be read for an understanding of the scope and method of compilation. During this period, about 50,000 bibliographies were listed under nearly 10,000 subjects. Lack of author and title entries does not restrict its use, since bibliographies are usually sought by subject, not by author. Personal name entries are for works *about* a person, not *by* him or her.

Archer Taylor has called the *Bibliographic Index* "the most comprehensive of all periodical surveys of bibliography." His *History of Bibliographies of Bibliographies* (New Brunswick, N.J.: Scarecrow, 1955; 147p.) has a critical introduction to bibliographies that preceded this important current index.

Extremely useful in the broad fields of the humanities and social sciences is:

→ Gray, Richard A., comp. Serial bibliographies in the humanities and social sciences. Ann Arbor, Mich., Pierian Pr., 1969. 345p.

Fully describes the contents of a wide range of serial bibliographies, published either separately or as parts of journals, both current and those no longer published. Deliberately omitted are national bibliographies, accession lists, book review sections of periodicals, monographic bibliographies in series, bibliographic bulletins, bibliographies of periodical titles, government publications, and those primarily concerned with audiovisual materials. Augments *Besterman* by including parts of journals and *Bibliographic Index* with additional foreign sources. Ten descriptive codes indicate characteristics of individual titles, such as language, selectivity, nationality of authors, frequency, publication form, and arrangement. Title; author, publisher, sponsor; subject, keywords in context; and selected characteristics indexes are appended.

Articles on bibliography and bibliographical societies and centers are found in *Encyclopedia of Library and Information Science*, volume 2.

Guidelines for reviewing bibliographic reference sources may be found in the appendix of this book.

Finally, Martha L. Hackman, *The Practical Bibliographer* (Englewood Cliffs, N.J.: Prentice-Hall, 1970; 118p.), is an excellent overview of national and trade bibliography, the bibliography of government publications, union lists and catalogs, and general subject bibliography.

Summary

This chapter has reviewed the development of bibliographic work and some of the agencies in the field, describing the characteristics of the following types of bibliographies:

1. Library catalogs
2. National library catalogs
3. National book bibliographies
4. Bibliographies of other publications and audiovisual materials
5. Subject bibliographies
6. Periodical indexing and abstracting services
7. Bibliographies of bibliographies.

These bibliographic forms are among the most used and most important reference sources in libraries, especially in those that serve scholars and research workers. They are helpful in the selection, cataloging, and identification of varied materials that are not available within a single library. Their use in interlibrary loan is well recognized. Their biographical features make them indispensable in biographical searching, as will be noted further in the next chapter.

3

Sources of Biographical Information

It is not rare to encounter persons who confuse the word *biography* with *bibliography*. Instead of being supercilious about this mistake, librarians should be reminded that biographical searching is very dependent on bibliographical sources and that the early bibliographies resembled biographical dictionaries, their compilers being more concerned with the writers of the works than with scrupulous recordings of their writings. They often included details on birth, death, and career, and should not be overlooked in biographical searching. Also, national library catalogs, such as those of the Library of Congress and British Museum, supply some biographical information.

Familiarity with sources of biographical information requires, first of all, some knowledge of their nature and some understanding of the generalizations that apply to their use.

Nature of Biographical Sources

Look in any good encyclopedia and you will find a brief history of biographical writing, its changing viewpoints and approaches throughout the centuries, and the names of the great biographers who produced this body of knowledge about men's lives. Dryden, who first used the word *biography* as "the history of particular men's lives," little dreamed of the proliferation of published biographical reference sources since his time, which must be seen in terms of their usefulness if biographical data are to be retrieved accurately, quickly, and with discriminating judgment.

The value of biographies to reference work lies in the biographical data they make available. But these data may be presented unclearly, incorrectly, or not at all. In her excellent chapter on biographical reference questions, Margaret Hutchins discusses identification problems—those involving obscure persons, disputed facts, and hidden facts about famous people. Attempting to verify disputed facts, she warns that "the correct information is not determined by a mere accumulation of testimonies but by an evaluation of them and by careful checking of a variety of sources against one another" (*Introduction to Reference Work* [Chicago: ALA, 1944], p.61). Thus checking a subject in a number of secondary sources, such as biographical dictionaries or encyclopedias, will not necessarily verify a disputed fact, since erroneous "facts" may have been drawn from a single source. Rather, one must attempt to find information whose origin is as close as possible to the subject, in place and in time.

In the discussion that follows, only sources—not types of questions—are considered. No effort has been made to be exhaustive, only to point out the patterns of publication of these sources: the bibliographies and indexes, encyclopedias and biographical dictionaries, together with some of the generalizations that apply to them.

Generalizations

What generalizations must be borne in mind?

1. Biographical sources are apt to reflect the prevailing critical opinion of the age in which they are published. *Webster's Biographical Dictionary*, for example, represents the judgment of editors in the mid-twentieth century, both in the selection of biographees and in the amount of space devoted to them.

2. International biographical dictionaries usually give more emphasis to nationals of the country in which they are published. Again, for example, *Webster's Biographical Dictionary* has British and American emphasis in its number of biographees and length of sketches.

3. Encyclopedias are a good source of information about persons no longer living, but less useful than current biographical directories for contemporaries, such as *International Who's Who*.

4. Responsibly edited encyclopedias and national biographical dictionaries are apt to include evaluation as well as narration of a biographee's

accomplishments, for responsible editing involves a discriminating selection of contributors, verification of facts, and an effort to reflect established judgment of a biographee's contribution to society. Photographs often accompany the sketches.

5. National biographical dictionaries record more nationals and usually give more information about them than international dictionaries. Thus *Dictionary of American Biography* gives more information on John Quincy Adams than *Webster's Biographical Dictionary*.

6. State and county histories, with long biographical sections, are a good source of information about less prominent persons, and often give fuller treatment to more prominent persons than national biographical dictionaries.

7. Newspaper and periodical indexes give good references for obituaries, outstanding accomplishments, contemporary opinion, and eyewitness accounts, such as *New York Times* references to a controversial figure. The indexes also serve to bring earlier sources up to date. Also useful is the *New York Times Obituaries Index*.

8. Special biographical dictionaries of writers and artists usually give more biocritical information and more bibliographic citations than general sources.

9. Special biographical dictionaries of scientists, like *American Men and Women of Science* and *Dictionary of Scientific Biography*, usually give more specific information on a scientist's special field than a general source.

10. Contributors' columns in general periodicals and literary quarterlies are seldom indexed, but often serve to identify a young writer in the issue that publishes his work.

11. It is usually less difficult to find biographical information on a writer than a nonwriter of equal prominence, since a writer's works will appear in bibliographies, catalogs, and indexes.

12. Literary histories and handbooks, such as *Cambridge History of English Literature* and Benét's *Reader's Encyclopedia*, are a good source of biographies of poets, dramatists, and novelists, often containing more discriminating biocriticism than more general sources.

From the above generalizations, it may be observed that:

When the nationality of a person is not known, an encyclopedia or international biographical dictionary should be consulted first.

When the nationality of a person is known, a national biographical dictionary should be consulted first.

If it is known that a person is no longer living, a retrospective source should be consulted first.

If it is known that a person is living, a current source should be consulted first.

If a person's profession is known, biographical sources for that profession should be consulted first.

Evaluation

What points must be kept in mind in evaluating the relative worth of a biographical dictionary? The following questions should be answered satisfactorily.

1. How were the biographees selected? Is the selection based on sound criteria, clearly stated in the preface and consistently applied? Are persons of interest included? Are notables within the particular field for which the dictionary claims coverage fully represented? Does it duplicate information readily available in more general reference sources?
2. What sources of information are used? Have they been compiled by an authority who used cited published and unpublished sources? Have they been supplied by the biographee? Were questionnaires used?
3. Are the sketches factual or evaluative? If evaluative, are they interestingly written?
4. Are references to further information appended?
5. Are photographs included?
6. If it is a current biographical dictionary, issued at intervals, is it kept scrupulously up to date?
7. Is there an appended index to a biographee's vocation and geographic location?

Some or all of these points will apply to the individual titles discussed below, though they are less applicable to the indexes to biography, which often serve as a starting point in searching for biographical information.

Indexes to Biography

Many general sources may be used as indexes to biographies, among them:

The dictionary catalog, with its subject entries for individual biographies
Trade bibliographies, with their subject entries for individual biographies
Periodical indexes, with their entries for persons who are the subjects of articles
Newspaper indexes, which include references to obituaries and to names in the news.

These should not be overlooked in libraries that lack more specialized titles, for they often give birth and death dates, and clues to a person's nationality and occupation.

The demand for biographical information, as well as its proliferation, has led to the publication of bibliographies and indexes that make biographical reference work much easier. One of the most important is:

→ Slocum, Robert B. Biographical dictionaries and related works. Detroit, Gale Research, 1967. 1056p. Supp. 1972, 922p.; supp. 1978, 852p.

   Its subtitle describes the types of sources found in its more than 12,000 entries: "An international bibliography of collective biographies, bio-bibliographies, collections of epitaphs, selected genealogical works, dictionaries of anonyms and pseudonyms, historical and specialized dictionaries, biographical materials in government manuals, bibliographies of biography, biographical indexes, and selected portrait catalogs." Invaluable, not only as a guide to specific sources but as a reminder of the wide range in types of materials which are useful in biographical searching.

Special indexes to biography fall into two broad categories:

Those that currently index a wide range of biographical information appearing in books and periodicals, *Biography Index*, for example, and

Those that index collective biography found in books published during a specified period in a specified country or countries, or otherwise restricted by occupation or profession, such as Riches, *Analytical Bibliography of Universal Collected Biography*.

Both types often supply birth and death dates and nationality and occupation of biographees, which will be useful even if the indexed references are not available in the libraries where they are consulted. Careful attention to their scope will save a searcher's time; for instance, if a name is not found in Hyamson's *Dictionary of Universal Biography*, it is not necessary to consult volumes of the *Dictionary of National Biography* published before 1934, which are completely indexed in Hyamson.

Current Indexes

The following current biographical indexes cite sources of information both for living persons and those no longer living. Most useful of the current sources is:

→ Biography index; a quarterly index to biographical material in books and magazines. N.Y., Wilson, 1947– . v.1– . Quarterly, with annual and 3-year cumulations.

Ranges in subject matter from saints to demimondaines, from kings to baseball players, from philosophers to glassmakers, being worldwide in coverage and unlimited in time. Thus "Amenotep IV, Kings of Egypt, 1388–1358 B.C." may be followed by labor leader "Anastasio, Anthony, 1905?–1963." Based on examination of about 2000 periodicals and equally varied in subject matter, e.g. *American Anthropologist* and *American Potato Journal, Church History* and *Gazette des Beaux-Arts.* Since the Wilson indexes are, of necessity, oriented toward English-language publications, most of the periodicals indexed in *Biography Index* are in English. Many of these publications, however, are international in scope, and foreign personages are well represented. Books dealing with individual and collective biography are completely analyzed, as well as biographical material in titles not devoted primarily to biography. A prefatory checklist of these titles contains symbols to denote juvenile literature. An appended index to professions and occupations reveals generous representation of authors and singers, scientists of various kinds and nationalities, and a sprinkling of kidnapers, auctioneers, beekeepers, and bullfighters. Since illustrations and portraits are indicated, it is useful as an index to portraits.

More restricted in scope is *Chicorel Index to Biographies* (New York: Chicorel, 1974; 2v.), which includes only books devoted to one biographee, analyzed by nationality, occupation, and other broad subjects.

Other indexes to biography which are restricted to one field (e.g. art or literature) are described under these subjects in the following pages.

The proliferation of biographical sources has stimulated compilation of computer-assisted indexes to some of the most used scources, such as Who's Whos, with some unfortunate duplication of effort, as noted in the two following titles:

→ Biographical dictionaries master index, 1975/76. Detroit, Gale Research, 1975– . Supps.

Living Americans are emphasized in the more than 725,000 entries found in 50 current biographical dictionaries and Who's Whos. It is duplicated to a great extent by:

→ Marquis who's who publications: index to all books. Chicago, Marquis, 1974– . Annual.

Indexes all current Marquis biographical directories, including the regional ones, as well as those in subject fields (e.g. government, science, and medicine) and Who Was Who volumes.

A time saver in searching for authors is the Index to the *Wilson Author Series* (New York: Wilson, 1976; 72p.). These titles are discussed later in the text.

Biographies of about 13,000 women from all periods of history, found in 950 collective biographies, are indexed in Norma W. Ireland's *Index to Women of the World from Ancient to Modern Times: Biographies and Portraits* (Westwood, Mass.: Faxon, 1970; 573p.). Dates, nationality, and occupations are given for each entry (when known).

A very ambitious work, now in progress, is:

→ Lobies, Jean-Pierre. Index bio-bibliographicus notorum hominum. Osnabrück, Biblio Verlag, 1972– . (In progress)

Planned to include between 3,000,000 and 5,000,000 persons, from all periods and countries, found in 2,000 collective works.

The value of newspaper indexes in biographical searches has already been noted, but two deserve special mention:

→ New York Times obituaries index, 1858–1968. N.Y., Times, 1970, 1,136p.

More than 350,000 names, many of them not found easily elsewhere, are listed with citation to date, page, and column of the original news story. Useful even in libraries without files of the newspaper as a source for death dates. Updated by *The New York Times Biographical Service*.

→ Obituaries from the Times, 1961–1970. London, Newspaper Archives Development; Westport, Conn., Meckler Books, 1975. 952p. First supp. 1971–75– .

International in scope, it reprints selected obituaries for the periods indicated, together with an index to all obituaries and tributes in the *Times* for the decade 1961–70, and following five-year periods. About 60 percent of the entries are British.

Retrospective Indexes

The second type of index, retrospective, is represented by a larger number of titles, many of them described in *Guide to Reference Books*. The following are cited as examples of ready-reference titles found in many libraries.

→ Hyamson, A. M. A dictionary of universal biography of all ages and of all peoples. 2nd ed. London, Routledge; N.Y., Dutton, 1951. 680p.

Excellent when nationality of biographee is not known. Includes persons no longer living whose sketches appear in 23 biographical dictionaries and encyclopedias; the *Dictionary of National Biography* and *Dictionary of American Biography* are completely indexed, others only selectively to include those whose work or memory has "survived until today." Name entries are accompanied by nationality, country of adoption, profession, dates (when known), and citation to sources of fuller biography.

→ Riches, Phyllis M. Analytical bibliography of universal collected biography, comprising books published in the English tongue in Great Britain and Ireland, America and the British dominions . . . with an introduction by Sir Frederic Kenyon. London, Lib. Assn., 1934. 709p.

Its 56,000 entries from 3,000 volumes include many lesser-known names. Entries often, but not always, accompanied by birth and death dates, nationality and profession, e.g., "Agassiz (Louis John Randolph) 1807–1873, Naturalist." Appended are chronological and occupation indexes of biographees and an author and subject bibliography of biographical dictionaries.

Useful in school library and media centers is:

→ Silverman, Judith. Index to young readers' collective biographies. 2nd ed. N.Y., Bowker, 1976. 322p.

Lists nearly 6,000 persons from more than 700 collective biographies, giving birth, death, nationality, and field of activity for each, followed by subject index and list of the collective biographies and their contents.

International Biographical Sources

Consult international biographical dictionaries first if nationality is not known. Some of the so-called universal dictionaries are products of the nineteenth century and reflect a certain bias of the period, in both the selection and the treatment of biographees. In using them, one should also check more recent sources, which may correct errors or include findings based on more recent research. Other, more recent one-volume international biographical dictionaries often give very brief sketches, with little or no bibliographical citation. In verifying biographical facts, varied types of sources should be consulted, for errors may be repeated from one biographical dictionary to another. Thus the number of times the same fact is found is not necessarily an assurance of its accuracy.

Only a few of the better-known biographical dictionaries, international in scope, are given below:

→ Biographie universelle, ancienne et moderne. Nouv. éd., publiée sous la direction de M. [Joseph François] Michaud . . . Paris, Mme. C. Desplaces, 1843–65. 45v.

Long, signed articles, with appended bibliographies, and some shorter sketches, by 300 writers whose high standard of scholarship was recognized in R. C. Christie's comment that "there is no book where errors are so few in proportion to the great extent of the work." The first edition reflected a strong royalist and Catholic bias, which was revised in the second edition. Usually cited as *Michaud*.

→ Nouvelle biographie générale depuis les temps plus reculés jusqu'à nos jours, avec les renseignements bibliographiques et l'indication des sources à consulter; publiée par MM. Firmin Didot Frères, sous la direction de M. le Dr. Hoefer. Paris, Firmin Didot, 1853–66. 46v. Photographic reprint, 1963–69.

Contains more than 50,000 fairly long, signed articles, with appended bibliographies. usually cited as *Hoefer*, it is often compared with *Michaud* (above), having been planned to include names of people still living in 1852 as well as many minor names not found in *Michaud*. Inclusion of 405 pirated articles from *Michaud* in the first two volumes of its first edition led to a famous lawsuit, described by R. C. Christie in *Quarterly Review* (157:204–26), reprinted in his *Selected Essays and Papers* (London, Longmans, 1902).

→ Chambers's Biographical dictionary. Ed. by J. O. Thorne and T. C. Collocott. Rev. ed. N.Y., Two Continents, 1978. 1432p.

Critical evaluation of "the great of all nations and all times, and a large number of persons not of that standing but none the less apt to occur in general reading." Approximately 15,000 entries, based upon articles in *Chambers's Encyclopaedia*, emphasize British and European names, give pronunciation, and include some contemporary figures. More bibliographic references than found in earlier editions, though many of the old articles are retained.

→ The Library of world biography. Ed. by J. H. Plumb. Boston, Little, Brown, 1974– .

Unique features of this work, according to the editor, are the emphasis on the interplay of social forces and human life, and the attitudes of subsequent generations to the biographee, e.g. to Cromwell. Each volume covers one person, averaging 60,000 to 80,000 words. Biographers were often selected from younger writers, since Plumb believes that "young people are less constricted by opinion than older ones and their books last longer." About 55 percent of the contributors are American and Canadian, and 45 percent from Britain.

→ The McGraw-Hill encyclopedia of world biography. N.Y., McGraw-Hill, [1973]. 12v.

Evaluative sketches of about 5,000 famous persons from all countries, periods, and fields, illustrated with portraits, reproductions of works of art, and maps. Final volume contains study guide and classified index to persons, places, etc. For a long, analytical review, see *Booklist* (70:1161–62 [July 1, 1974]).

→ New Century cyclopedia of names, edited by C. L. Barnhart with the assistance of W. D. Halsey. N.Y., Appleton, 1954. 3v.

Revised from, and twice as large as, *Century Cyclopedia of Names* (1911), it emphasizes important information in the English-speaking world (and English and native spellings and pronunciations) in its more than 100,000 entries for persons, places, historical events, literary works, and mythological and biblical characters. Distinguished for its broad scope. Appended are a chronological table of world history and lists of rulers, chiefs of state, etc., arranged by country. Its instructions for use should be read carefully.

→ Thomas, Joseph. Universal pronouncing dictionary of biography and mythology. 5th ed. Philadelphia and London, Lippincott, [c1930]. 2550p. Repr.: N.Y., AMS Pr., 1972.

Brief sketches, with occasional longer articles, often based on other standard biographical sources, with some bibliography. Appended vocabulary of Christian names, with their equivalents in the principal foreign languages, and disputed or doubtful pronunciation. One of the most generally useful of its kind because of its comprehensive coverage of all nations and all periods, including names from Greek, Roman, Teutonic, Sanskrit, and other mythologies, and its scrupulous attention to pronunciation.

→ Webster's Biographical dictionary; a dictionary of names and noteworthy persons, with pronunciations and concise biographies. Springfield, Mass., Merriam, 1974. 1697p.

More than 40,000 brief sketches, with British and American emphasis in number of biographies and length of sketches; minimum representation of persons prominent in sports, motion pictures, theater, and radio. About 80 percent are deceased. Gives syllabic division of surnames and titles of rank. It has not been thoroughly revised since 1942, which limits its usefulness. Death dates have been added, but persons who have recently achieved prominence are not fully treated, nor have recent accomplishments been added to biographies of living persons in 1942 printing.

→ Who did what. Gerald Howat, general ed. N.Y., Crown, 1974. 383p.

Brief biographies assessing contributions to civilization of 5,000 distinguished persons, living and deceased. Useful chiefly for its time chart of human achievement, divided into six chronological periods from 1,000 B.C. to 1974.

Current Sources

Current sources of biographical information require careful reading of their prefaces to determine the source and date of sketches. They should be further examined to determine whether sketches are simply an abbreviated recording of facts or whether they attempt to interpret the biographee in a readable style. They are usually compiled from questionnaires containing biographical data supplied by the biographees. However, when questionnaires are subjected to judicious editing and further checked against published sources of information, the result is apt to be more accurate and better balanced. Also, some persons are inclined to report fully their appointments to local committees, resulting in lengthy biographical sketches that do not necessarily indicate their relative importance.

Given below are some of the more generally used current sources:

→ Biography news. v.1, Jan. 1974–75. Detroit, Gale Research, 1974–75. Monthly, with cumulative index in each issue.

A compilation of news stories and feature articles from 50 American newspapers and some magazines covering personalities of national interest in all fields, with accompanying photographs. Chiefly Americans in sports, entertainment, and political affairs, with a few foreign notables. No longer published.

→ Current biography. v.1, 1940– . N.Y., Wilson, 1940– . Monthly except Dec.; cumulated annually. Cumulative index, 1940–70.

Distinguished by careful editing, readable style, clear photographs, and appended references. Sketches are written by a research staff which supplements data supplied by the biographee with further information from other biographical sources, periodicals, and newspapers. Though American artists, film stars, scientists, and writers are more fully represented than those of other countries, foreign diplomats and important government officals are often found. Note the cumulative indexes and classified lists of professions.

→ International who's who, 1935– . London, Europa, 1935– . Annual.

Intended to supplement and coordinate national biographical sources, it includes data supplied by persons of international importance in all fields, selected by editors who use the press of many countries to secure recent information on persons approaching prominence. Brief, factual sketches, a few lines in length, include title, dates, nationality, education, profession, career, political affiliation, publications, and address. Appended list of obituaries includes deaths noted since previous edition. A good source for persons from countries without a national *Who's Who*, but not to be preferred to a national *Who's Who*. British emphasis. *Who's Who in the World* has twice as many entries.

→ International year book and statesmen's who's who, 1953– . Surrey, Kelly's Directories, Ltd. 1953– . Annual.

More than half of its contents gives facts of birth, education, profession, organizations, publications, and address for more than 10,000 persons prominent not only in government but also in education, business, and finance. Includes many names not found in *International Who's Who*.

→ The New York Times biographical service: a compilation of current biographical information of general interest. N.Y., Arno, 1970– . Monthly, looseleaf. Cumulative indexes, 6 months and annually.

Reprints biographical items: obituaries, feature stories, etc., appearing in *New York Times*, including photographs. Convenient source of information on people in the news.

→ Who's who in the world, 1971/72– . Chicago, Marquis, 1970– .

Identifies most eminent world figures in current affairs and various important fields; compiled from questionnaires. Emphasis on government leaders, legal and diplomatic figures, scholars, journalists, and heads of philanthropic and educational societies. Indexed by countries.

National Biographical Sources

Consult national biographical dictionaries first if nationality of the biographee is known. If carefully edited, they contain well-written accounts of a person's life, outstanding accomplishments, references to further sources of information, and (sometimes) portraits or photographs. When the exact date of death is given, it serves as an aid in locating obituaries in newspapers. Current sources of the who's who type are usually compiled from data supplied by the biographees and resemble the international who's whos described above. The following are well known and often used for information on persons, living and dead.

United States

→ Dictionary of American biography. N.Y., Scribner, 1974. 11v. Supps. 5–6, 1977–78.

More than 16,000 long, signed evaluations of those "who have made some significant contribution to American life," who lived in the territory now known as the United States, excluding British loyalists and officers in the British army during the American Revolution. Appended bibliographies often contain reference to the location of manuscript collections relating to the biographee and to the definitive edition of his works. Distinguished for its judicious selection of biographees, the authority of its contributors, and its scholarly approach, it should be consulted first for Americans who died before 1970 (though less inclusive than Appleton's *Cyclopedia of American Biography*, which has some Canadian and Latin American names). Names of lesser national importance may be found in *National Cyclopedia of American Biography*. The index is a good source for a state's outstanding men and important college graduates, as well as lists of persons prominent in various occupations (e.g. librarians or ornithologists, where John James Audubon leads the list). Supplements include those who have died since preparation of the original set, plus a few individuals omitted from the original volumes. *Concise Dictionary of American Biography* (2nd ed.; N.Y., Scribner, 1977) contains condensations of all sketches in the set and supplements, in one alphabet.

→ Encyclopedia of American biography. John A. Garraty, ed. N.Y., Harper & Row, 1974. 1241p.

"More than 1,000 notable Americans who have contributed to our history and culture from Columbus to the present day." Its two-part articles are unique in giving a factual summary, followed by an interpretive essay signed by a qualified contributor. Brief appended bibliographies.

→ National cyclopedia of American biography. N.Y., White, 1892– . v.1– . (In progress)

Differs from *Dictionary of American Biography* in (1) more names of local importance, especially in business and industry; (2) sketches which are more descriptive than evaluative, prepared by a central staff from information supplied by the family of the biographee; (3) photographs of some of the biographees; and (4) no appended bibliography. However, data on which articles are based are in the publisher's files and may be consulted with permission. It is not alphabetically arranged and must be used with its indexes: *White's Conspectus of American Biography*, in its expanded and updated 3rd edition, titled *Notable Names in American History* (1973).

→ Notable American women, 1607–1950; a biographical dictionary. Cambridge, Mass., Belknap Pr. of Harvard Univ. Pr., 1971. 3v.

Resembles *Dictionary of American Biography* with its long, signed articles by qualified contributors. The 1,359 biographies were carefully selected, with emphasis on women who had "significant impact on American life." Appended bibliographies.

→ Webster's American biographies. Ed. by Charles Van Doren and Robert McHenry. Springfield, Mass., Merriam, 1974. 1233p.

Brief sketches of about 3,000 persons, some of them living. Geographical and occupational indexes appended.

→ Who was who in America, 1942– . Chicago, Marquis, 1942– . Historical volume, 1607–1896 (1967); v.1, 1897–1942 (1942); v.2, 1943–50 (1950); v.3, 1951–60 (1960); v.4, 1961–68 (1968); v.5, 1969–73 (1973); v.6, 1974– 76 (1976).

A good source for exact date of death (and often place of burial) of persons whose names formerly appeared in *Who's Who in America*, with sketches reproduced as they appeared there, plus requested revisions appearing in editor's files. V. 6 contains cumulated index to v.1–6.

CONTEMPORARY

→ Who's who in America. Chicago, Marquis, 1899– . v.1– . Biennial.

Data, supplied by biographee, are concisely and factually presented for "the best-known men and women in all lines of useful and reputable achievement," selected because of outstanding effort or official position. Principally American, but a few persons of other nationalities are included if likely to be of interest to Americans. Differs from *Current Biography* in (1) being more inclusive, (2) giving no evaluation, (3) employing abbreviations to save space, and (4) excluding bibliography, except lists of authors' works. Resembles *International Who's Who* in the form and content of its sketches. Augmented by regional volumes for the East, Midwest, West, South and Southwest, and some subject fields, e.g. law and religion.

Although not comprehensive, the biennial *Who's Who among Black Americans* (Northbrook, Ill.: Who's Who among Black Americans, 1976–) is useful for factual data about more than 13,500 persons, many of them not found in *Who's Who in America*. It contains geographical and occupational indexes. The second edition (1978) has about 3,500 names not found in the first edition.

→ Who's who of American women: a biographical dictionary of notable· living American women. v.1– . 1958/59– . Chicago, Marquis, 1958– . Biennial.

Concise sketches, based on information supplied by the biographee, include birth, education, marriage, career, membership in organizations, political and religious affiliations, publications, and address, with many names not found in *Who's Who in America*. A good source for professional and club women. For 1935–40, consult *American Women* (3v.), no longer published.

Africa

→ Dictionary of South African biography. Pretoria, published for the Human Science Research Council, 1968– . When coverage to 1950 is completed, volumes will appear decennially.

Projected to include about 3,000 deceased biographees in the basic volumes selected by the intellectual community. Detailed sketches, signed by specialists, with long appended bibliographies. Alphabetically arranged, with cumulative indexes and glossary.

→ Who's who in Africa. Ed. by John Dickie and Alan Rake. London, African Buyer and Trader, Ltd., 1973. 602p.

Biographies of leading figures in politics, business, and the military in 47 African countries.

Australia

→ Australian dictionary of biography. Melbourne, Melbourne Univ. Pr. 1966– . v.1– . (In progress)

Resembling *Dictionary of National Biography*, but arranged by broad periods, it has signed sketches and appended bibliographies that evaluate, in a most readable form, the contributions of all sorts of persons to the development of Australia, including some very colorful ones. Few entries for women, though some are briefly noted in biographies of their husbands. Will contain about 6,000 entries.

→ Who's who in Australia, 1906– . Melbourne, Herald and Weekly Times, 1906– . Triennial.

Canada

→ Dictionary of Canadian biography. Toronto, Univ. of Toronto Pr., 1966, v.1– . (In progress)

Resembling the *Dictionary of National Biography* in its signed evaluative sketches, with appended bibliographies, it differs only in its arrangement, by broad periods, e.g. v.1, 1000–1700. An index to persons mentioned in the text of individual articles makes it particularly useful for elusive minor figures. V.2, 1701 to 1740, published in 1969, like v.1, contains useful introductory essays, including a glossary of Indian tribal names and an excellent appended general bibliography of most frequently cited sources, describing the principal archival sources, primary printed sources, reference works, secondary works, and principal journals used in each volume.

→ Standard dictionary of Canadian biography; the Canadian who was who, 1875–1937. Eds., Charles G. D. Roberts and Arthur L. Tunnell. Toronto, Trans-Canada Pr., 1934–38. 2v.

Signed articles, varying from 1,000 to 2,000 words, whose length "does not always indicate the importance of the subject but has been determined by the amount of useful, authentic source-material." Includes eminent Canadians who died during the period 1875–1937, and some who were born abroad but significantly affected Canadian life. Bibliographies appended.

→ The Macmillan dictionary of Canadian biography, by W. S. Wallace. 3rd ed. rev. and enl. London, Toronto, Macmillan; N.Y., St. Martin's, 1963. 822p.

Brief entries for important persons have appended references to additional information.

CONTEMPORARY

→ Canadian who's who . . . v.1– . 1910, 1938– . Toronto, Who's Who Canadian Pubs., c1910– . v.1– . Triennial, with semiannual supps.

Over 8,000 concise, factual sketches, compiled from questionnaires, supplemented by *Who's Who in Canada*, since neither is comprehensive.

→ Who's who in Canada. Toronto, Internat. Pr., 1922– . Biennial.

About 2,000 entries, nearly half accompanied by photographs. Random arrangement requires use of the index.

China

→ Biographical dictionary of Republican China. Howard L. Boorman, ed. N.Y., Columbia Univ. Pr., 1967–71. 4v. Personal name index, v.5. 1979.

Includes about 600 scholarly, evaluative biographies of persons, living and dead at time of publication, emphasizing those prominent in all fields during the years 1911–49; some sketches based on private memoranda and personal reminiscences. The final volume has an appended bibliography which lists the known works of all the biographees and sources used in writing the articles. Chinese titles are given in characters and romanization.

→ Lewytzkyj, Borys, and Stroynowski, Juliusz. Who's who in the Socialist countries; a biographical encyclopedia of 10,000 leading personalities in 16 Communist countries. N.Y., Saur, 1978. 736p.

China is well represented.

France

→ Dictionnaire de biographie française. Paris, Letouzey, 1933– . v.1– . To be completed in 20v.

Treats outstanding persons, no longer living, of metropolitan France and territories from the earliest times and foreigners importantly involved in the life of France, in signed, evaluative articles by authorities, usually shorter than those in the *Dictionary of National Biography*, which it resembles. Extensive bibliographies.

CONTEMPORARY
→ Dictionnaire biographique français contemporain. 2nd ed., 1954–55. Paris, Pharos, Agence Internat. de Documentation Contemporaine. 1954. 708p. Supp. 1– , 1955– .

Photographs accompany some of the sketches, which vary in length. Includes Frenchmen and other prominent persons living in France. Differs from who's who type in including comment; e.g. the article on Sartre discusses his principal works and gives an appended list of books by and about him. A necrology includes names of those who died between July 1950 and publication of the second edition.

→ Who's who in France: dictionnaire biographique. 1953/54– . Paris, Lafitte, 1953– . Biennial.

Most up to date of the French sources; its more than 20,000 brief, factual sketches include French persons overseas and others abroad.

Germany
→ Allgemeine deutsche Biographie; hrsg. durch die Historische Commission bei der K. Akademie der Wissenschaften. Leipzig, Duncker, 1875–1912. 56v. (2., unveränderte Aufl.) Neudruck der 1 Aufl. von 1875. Berlin, Duncker & Humblot, 1967– . v.1–45, A–Z; v.46–55, Nachträge bis 1899, Andr–Z (A–Ad included in v.45); v.56, general register.

More than 20,000 lengthy, evaluative, signed biographies (with bibliographies) make this the standard source for persons no longer living at the end of the 19th century. Its arrangement requires that the general index be used first.

→ Neue deutsche Biographie, hrsg. von der Historischen Kommission bei der Bayerischen Akademie der Wissenschaften. v.1– . Berlin, Duncker, 1953– . (In progress). To be completed in 12v. and index.

Long, signed articles with appended bibliographies include many names also in *Allgemeine deutsche Biographie*, many from later periods and some from earlier periods, with indexes to each volume citing entries from *Allgemeine deutsche Biographie*.

CONTEMPORARY

→ Wer ist wer? Das deutsche who's who, v.1– . 1905– . Title, publisher, and frequency vary. 1905– . v.1– . Title varies.

19th edition, 1975, gives more than 35,000 factual sketches of persons from the Federal Republic and West Berlin, prominent in politics, industry, religion, arts, and sports, including some not found in *Who's Who in Germany*.

→ Who's who in Germany: a biographical dictionary . . . 1956– . Munich, Oldenbourg, 1955– . Irregular.

Short factual sketches in English of persons in government, religion, education, industry, and social and cultural associations in the Federal Republic, including German citizens, some of them living outside Germany, and others selected because of official position or special prominence. Gives some persons not found in *Wer ist Wer?* Appended directory of organizations, associations, and institutions gives brief descriptive information and addresses.

Great Britain

→ Dictionary of national biography, ed. by Leslie Stephen and Sidney Lee. London, Smith, Elder, 1908–9 (reissue); London, Oxford Univ. Pr., 1938 (reprint). 21v. and supp. 1; supps. 1– . Oxford, Oxford Univ. Pr., 1912– .

Largest of the national biographical dictionaries, its full, evaluative sketches, prepared and signed by authorities, treat more than 32,000 no longer living "men and women of British or Irish race who have achieved any reasonable distinction in any walk of life," from comedy queens to cabinet ministers, architects to archbishops, "early settlers in America . . . natives of these islands who have gained distinction in foreign countries and persons of foreign birth who have gained eminence in this country," from the earliest time to the present. Its sixth supplement includes an index for 1901–50. For careful biographical checking, consult *Bulletin of the Institute of Historical Research,* where corrections of or alterations to the sketches will be found. Corrections and additions covering the years 1923–63 have been cumulated in one volume. *The Concise Dictionary* (London, Oxford Univ. Pr., 1953–61; 2v.) contains corrections and additions to the main set.

→ Who was who, 1897– . London, Black; N.Y., St. Martin's, 1929– . Decennial.

Contains brief, factual sketches of persons who have died since 1897; drawn from *Who's Who*, with exact date of death and other necessary corrections. Published at intervals, currently decennial. V.6 includes those who died in the years 1961–70.

CONTEMPORARY

→ Who's who. London, Black; N.Y., St. Martin's, 1849– . v.1– . Annual.

Aims to furnish, in as compact a form as possible, a series of biographical sketches of eminent living persons of both sexes in all parts of the civilized world. Selected because of "personal achievement or prominence, and of a man's or woman's interest to the public at large or to any important section of that public." Based on returns from questionnaires submitted annually to biographees for updating. Sketches are removed to *Who Was Who* after death of biographees or are dropped because they are no longer of public interest or have not returned their sketch. Thus, in a few instances, names will be found in one or more earlier volumes but not in later ones. Prefatory pages contain obituary for previous year and additions and corrections received too late for inclusion in the body of the text.

Italy

→ Dizionario biografico degli italiani. v.1– . Rome, Istit. della Enciclopedia Italiana, 1960– . (In progress)

Patterned on *Dictionary of National Biography,* with long, signed evaluative sketches and appended bibliographies of Italians who lived between the 5th and 20th century. When completed, will contain about 40,000 persons no longer living.

→ Chi è? Dizionario degli italiani d'oggi. Ed.1– (1928)– . Rome, Scarano, 1928– .

Another work, with the same title, was issued in 1908 by Guido Biagi. Compiled by the editor from sources other than the biographees, it includes contemporary Italians of note.

Latin America

→ Who's who in Latin America. 3rd ed. rev. and enl. Stanford, Calif., Stanford Univ. Pr.; Chicago, Marquis, (c1946–51). 7v. Repr.: Detroit, Blaine Ethridge, 1971.

Brief, factual sketches of 8,000 leading persons of Mexico, Colombia, Ecuador, Venezuela, Bolivia, Chile, Peru, Argentina, Paraguay, Uruguay, Brazil, Cuba, Dominican Republic, Haiti, Panama, and the countries of Central America, each country being treated separately.

Augmented by *Encyclopedia of Latin America*, ed. by Helen Delpar (N.Y., McGraw-Hill, 1975; 651p.). Two-thirds of the encyclopedia's 1,600 articles are biographical, emphasizing politicians and statesmen but with some figures from industry, literature, and the arts.

USSR

→ Russkii biograficheskii slovar' . . . St. Petersburg, "Kadima," 1896–1918. 25v.

Incomplete; letters V, Gog–Gia, E, M, Nik–Nia, Tk–Tia, U never published. Resembles *Dictionary of National Biography*, with long, signed evaluative articles and appended bibliographies for no-longer-living persons prominent in prerevolutionary Russia.

→ Who was who in the USSR: a biographic directory containing 5,015 biographies of prominent Soviet historical personalities. Heinrich E. Schulz, Paul K. Urban, Andrew I. Lebed, eds. Metuchen, N.J., Scarecrow, 1972. 677p.

Indexed by career and profession are concise factual sketches of outstanding citizens, chosen from detailed biographical information on more than 135,000 Soviet citizens who have made major contributions to political, intellectual, scientific, social, and economic life of the country. Works by authors are included.

→ Lewytzkyj, Borys, and Stroynowski, Juliusz. Who's who in the Socialist countries; a biographical encyclopedia of 10,000 leading personalities in 16 Communist countries. N.Y., Saur, 1978. 736p.

Includes over 4,000 Soviet listings.

Professions

Many sources of biographies of persons who have been active in professions or vocations are available in a good library collection. Among them are literary histories for men and women of letters, military and diplomatic histories for soldiers and statesmen, histories of art and music for artists and musicians, and histories of science and technology for scientists. Directories of associations and professions also provide brief, identifying data—*Association of American Geographers Handbook*, *American Medical Directory*, and *Biographical Directory of the American Psychiatric Association*, for example—all of which sometimes list foreign affiliates. Also, special periodical indexes in these fields, such as *Art Index* or *Applied Science and*

Technology Index, are useful for supplementary information. But when a living person's profession or vocation is known, it is well to consult first a biographical dictionary in that field, for it often contains more names than the more general who's whos. The titles listed below are restricted primarily to current biographical dictionaries and represent only a sampling of this rapidly growing type of publication.

Current biographical dictionaries in special fields have increased in number and variety in recent years, due to the increase in the number of professional men and women, the growth of professional associations, and the prestige attached to being among those men and women considered outstanding in their vocations. Like the national who's whos, professional directories are usually compiled from information supplied by the biographee, as is the case with *American Men and Women of Science*.

These special biographical dictionaries may be supplemented by association membership directories, which vary greatly in amount of biographical data, from a simple name-and-address list to a compilation of biographical sketches, such as *American Architects Directory*, which gives for members of the American Institute of Architects (and a few nonmembers) their birth date, education, career, and address.

Another source of biographical information in special fields is the official journal of an association, which often contains news notes on persons active in that field, such as *American Libraries* for librarians.

Listed below are only a few special biographical dictionaries, some retrospective and evaluative, but many of the who's who type.

Artists

For older artists:

→ Bryan, Michael. Bryan's Dictionary of painters and engravers. 4th rev. ed. London, Bell, 1903–5. Repr.: Kennikat Pr., 1964. 5v.

> About 20,000 artists, with longer articles signed by specialists, usually listing principal works and their location. Represents turn-of-the-century critical views of artists of the past.

More recent biocriticism of many older artists if found in the excellent and well-illustrated *Encyclopedia of World Art* (New York: McGraw-Hill, 1959–68; 15v.). Contemporary artists are found in:

→ Who's who in art: biographies of leading men and women in the world of art today. 1st ed.– . London, Art Trade Pr., 1927– . Biennial.

> Short, factual biographies, with British artists, craftsmen, critics,

teachers, curators, and collectors in the majority. Appended are monograms and signatures.

→ Who's who in American art. v.1– . 1936/37– . N.Y., Bowker, 1935– . Triennial.

Birth, education, career, exhibitions, bibliography, and present positions and addresses for U.S. and Canadian painters, sculptors, cartoonists, art teachers and librarians, museum directors, collectors, and others. Appended are geographical and specialty indexes, obituaries, and a list of "open" exhibitions, national and regional.

→ Naylor, Colin, and Orridge, Genesis P. Contemporary artists. N.Y., St. Martin's, 1977. 1076p.

Brief biographies, mailing addresses for biographee and his dealer, one-man shows, books by or about the artist, some b&w reproductions of works, and critiques for about 1,300 international artists.

Although not biographical dictionaries, the following are valuable indexes to other sources:

→ Havlice, Patricia P. Index to artistic biography. Metuchen, N.J., Scarecrow, 1973. 2v.

Some 70,000 artists in 64 reference sources published between 1902 and 1970, with accompanying dates, nationality, media, pseudonyms, variant name spellings. International in scope.

→ Mallett, Daniel T. Mallett's Index of artists, including painters, sculptors, illustrators, engravers of the past and present. N.Y., Bowker, 1935. Supp. 1940. Repr.: N.Y., Peter Smith. 2v.

Brief biographical data for names in 22 general and over 1,000 specialized sources. Good for minor figures.

There are a number of biocritical works, among them John Canaday's *Lives of the Painters* (New York: Norton, 1969; 4v.), for those who lived before 1900, as well as Paul Cummings, *A Dictionary of Contemporary American Artists* (3rd ed.; New York: St. Martin's, 1977; 545p.). The latter includes 872 artists, chosen on the basis of representation in museums.

Authors

Distinguished for the quality of its contributors is:

→ American writers. Leonard Unger, ed. in chief. N.Y., Scribner, 1974– . 4v. and supps.

Long biocritical essays of writers from Jonathan Edwards to the present, written by recognized literary scholars. *British Writers*, also published by Scribner, follows the same pattern for the period 1332 to the 20th century.

→ Contemporary authors, a bio-bibliographical guide to current authors and their works. Detroit, Gale Research, 1962– . v.1– . Quarterly, with cumulations.

Covers authors (broadly defined) and many little-known authors from many fields and countries, with emphasis on American authors. About 50,000 represented, and more to come. Factual sketches, based on information supplied by the biographee, emphasize career and work in progress. Fairly complete lists of works by and about an author are included.

→ International authors and writers who's who. 7th ed.– . Cambridge, Melrose Pr., 1976– .

Combines *Country Authors Today* and *Author's and Writer's Who's Who*, continuing the numbered editions of the latter. Authors, editors, feature writers, and other journalists briefly treated.

→ Rush, Theresa, and Myers, Carol F. Black American writers past and present: a biographical and bibliographical dictionary. Metuchen, N.J., Scarecrow, 1975. 2v.

More than 2,000 creative writers and literary critics, with a few nonfiction writers from the 18th century on, living or publishing in the United States, are covered in brief biographical sketches, often with personal statements from the authors. Appended bibliographies. Includes many names not easily found in other sources.

→ Something about the author: facts and pictures about contemporary authors and illustrators of books for young people. Anne Commire, ed. Detroit, Gale Research, 1972– . Annual.

Interpretive sketches of contemporary writers and illustrators, written in lively style for young readers, with accompanying portraits and illustrations from their works, and appended lists of works. Cumulative index in each volume.

→ Vinson, James, ed. Contemporary novelists of the English language. N.Y., St. Martin's, 1972. 1444p.

> Like *Contemporary Dramatists* (1973) and *Contemporary Poets* (1971) by the same editor, includes not only biographical sketches but commentaries by the authors and signed critical essays on their works. All have appended bibliographies for each biographee and are indexed.

→ World authors, 1950–1970. Ed. by John Wakeman, N.Y., Wilson, 1975. 1594p.

> Well-written sketches, with accompanying portraits and bibliographies, of nearly 1,000 authors over the world who achieved a reputation between 1950 and 1970. Continues the well-known *Twentieth Century Authors*, compiled by Stanley J. Kunitz and Howard Haycraft (N.Y., Wilson, 1942; supp. 1955). Both are based on material supplied by the biographee or on research.

Other frequently used volumes in the H. W. Wilson Company Authors series include *American Authors, 1600–1900*; *British Authors before 1800*; *British Authors of the Nineteenth Century*; and *Junior Book of Authors*, all compiled by S. J. Kunitz and Howard Haycraft. *More Junior Authors*, by Muriel Fuller; *Third Book of Junior Authors*, by Doris De Montreville; *Fourth Book of Junior Authors and Illustrators*, by De Montreville and Elizabeth D. Crawford; and *European Authors, 1000–1900*, by Kunitz and Vineta Colby, are others in the series.

Literary handbooks, such as Max J. Herzberg's *Reader's Encyclopedia of American Literature* (New York: Crowell, 1962; 1280p.) and the *Oxford Companions* to English, French, and German literatures, should not be overlooked as a source of brief biocriticism of authors. Also useful are the standard histories of the literatures of various countries, such as the *Cambridge History of English Literature*.

Two useful indexes to biographical dictionaries are:

→ Author biographies master index. 1st ed. Detroit, Gale Research, 1978. 2v. Supp. 1979. (Gale Biographical Index Series, no. 3)

> Subtitle: "A consolidated guide to biographical information concerning authors living and dead as it appears in a selection of the principal biographical dictionaries devoted to authors, poets, journalists, and other literary figures." First edition contains over 416,000 references to biographies of 238,000 different authors, found in nearly 150 English-language biographical dictionaries.

→ Havlice, Patricia. Index to literary biography. Metuchen, N.J., Scarecrow, 1975. 2v.

Resembles the compiler's *Index to Artistic Biography*, listing writers in 50 literary reference sources published between 1931 and 1972, in four languages, with accompanying dates, nationality, pseudonyms, and literary genre.

Business Men and Women

→ Who's who in finance and industry. Ed. 1– . Chicago, Marquis, 1936– . Irregular.

Supersedes *Who's Who in Commerce and Industry, World Who's Who in Commerce and Industry,* and *World Who's Who in Finance and Industry.* International in scope, but with strong American emphasis, it contains brief, factual sketches of about 25,000 business executives, as well as lawyers and engineers in business and industry.

Educators

→ Biographical dictionary of American educators. Ed. by John F. Ohles. Westport, Conn., Greenwood Pr., 1978. 3v.

Includes 1,665 signed sketches from the 17th century to the present, restricting living educators to those retired or over 60 in 1975. Appendixes list biographees by birthplace and dates, states in which they worked, and field of specialization. Also has chronology of important dates in American education and an index.

→ Directory of American scholars. Ed. by Jaques Cattell Pr. 1st ed.– . N.Y., Bowker, 1942– . Irregular. Pub. about every 5 years.

Factual, concise biographies, based on questionnaires, from scholars in fields of history, speech and drama, foreign languages and linguistics, philosophy, religion, and law.

→ Leaders in education. 5th ed. Comp. by Jaques Cattell Pr. N.Y., Bowker, 1974.

Factual sketches of more than 14,000 administrators, teachers, and authors in the United States and Canada.

Labor Leaders

→ Who's who in labor. N.Y., Arno Pr., 1976. 807p.

Brief information for 73,800 persons currently engaged in the labor movement itself, in neutral capacities, such as arbitration, or as government officials. Appended lists of labor federations, periodicals, study centers, a glossary of terms and an index of biographees by organization. Contains many more names but less biographical information than Gary M. Fink's *Biographical Directory of American Labor Leaders.* (Westport, Conn., Greenwood, 1974. 559p.)

Librarians

→ Dictionary of American library biography. Littleton, Colo., Libraries Unlimited, 1978. 596p.

Evaluative, signed sketches of about 300 deceased librarians and a few others who were active in library service (e.g. Carnegie and Benjamin Franklin), many written by contributors with personal knowledge of biographee. Carefully documented, with appended bibliographies. Name index includes names mentioned in the sketches.

→ A biographical directory of librarians in the United States and Canada. 1st ed.– . Chicago, ALA, 1933– . Irregular.

Includes "active members of the library profession, archivists, or information scientists associated with all types of libraries in the United States and Canada." Gives place and date of birth, name of spouse, education, languages read or spoken, positions, activities and organizations, honors, publications, areas of professional interest, and mailing address. Formerly titled *Who's Who in Library Service* (with another publisher).

Military Leaders

→ Hayes, Grace P., and Martell, Paul, eds. World military leaders. N.Y., Bowker, 1974. 268p.

Gives training, experience, and other pertinent data for most of the biographees, with only address and official position in a few cases. Well edited.

Musicians

→ Baker, Theodore. Baker's biographical dictionary of musicians. 6th ed. Revised by Nicholas Slonimsky. N.Y., Schirmer, 1978.

Brief biographies of composers, performers, publishers, etc., from all countries and periods, with appended lists of works by and about them. A standard work.

→ Ewen, David. Musicians since 1900. N.Y., Wilson, 1978. 970p.

Includes careers of 432 concert artists, with generous quotations from many current sources, bibliographies, and portraits. Intended for the general reader. Earlier works by this prolific music reference-book editor are *Great Composers, 1300–1900; Composers of Tomorrow's Music; Composers since 1900; Great Men of Popular Song*; and others. All are written in a lively style.

Philosophers

→ Directory of American philosophers. Ed. 1– , 1962/63– . Bowling Green, Ohio, Philosophy Documentation Center, 1962– . Biennial.

Nearly 10,000 entries, U.S. and Canadian, giving addresses, fellowships and assistantships, and lists of colleges with philosophy departments, as well as journals, book publishers, and societies.

→ International directory of philosophy and philosophers. Ed. 1– , 1966– . Bowling Green, Ohio, Philosophy Documentation Center, 1966– . Revised at intervals.

Gives same information as *Directory of American Philosophers* for 91 countries.

Philosophers are also found in the *Directory of American Scholars.*

Political Leaders

→ U.S. Congress. Biographical directory of the American Congress, 1774–1971. 11th ed. Wash., Govt. Prt. Off., 1971. 1972p.

Brief, factual accounts, giving birth dates, education, career, and terms of office of congressmen, based on the official *Congressional Directory*, which serves to keep the *Biographical Directory* up to date between new editions. For other political figures, see *Who's Who in American Politics*, 1967– .

→ Who's who in American politics: a biographical directory of United States political leaders. Ed. 1– , 1967/68– . N.Y., Bowker, 1967– . Biennial.

Nearly 20,000 notables from federal, state, and local governments, based on returns from questionnaires. Appended lists of members of cabinets and state delegations; governors; and a geographical index.

→ Who's who in government, Ed. 1– , 1972/73– . Chicago, Marquis, 1972– .

Differs from above in going beyond subcabinet positions. Indexed by government department and field or subject specialty.

Religious Leaders

→ Bowden, Henry Warner. Dictionary of American religious biography. Westport, Conn., Greenwood, 1977. 572p.

Sketches about 1 page in length, with appended bibliography for 425 leaders (chiefly clergy) no longer living. General index, with added indexes by denomination and birthplace. Well-balanced coverage.

→ Who's who in religion. 1st ed.– , 1975/1976– . Chicago, Marquis, 1975– .

Follows the conventional who's who style in its sketches. Also, *Directory of American Scholars* includes religious leaders.

Scientists

→ Dictionary of scientific biography. Ed. by Charles C. Gillispie, under the auspices of the American Council of Learned Societies. N.Y., Scribner, 1970–80. 16v.

Patterned on *Dictionary of National Biography*, the first 14 volumes include more than 5,000 evaluative biographies of deceased mathematicians and natural scientists, written by more than 1,000 scholars from more than 60 countries, and emphasizing their scientific contributions. Volume 15 (Supplement) contains additional 133 biographies and essays on early, nonattributable scientific developments in India, Central America, Egypt, Mesopotamia, and Japan. It is particularly useful for Japanese, Chinese, and Indian scientists not found in other biographical dictionaries. Excellent bibliographies of original works and secondary literature are appended. The final (index) volume allows problems, concepts, and subjects to be traced throughout the set.

→ American men and women of science. Ed. by Jaques Cattell Pr. 13th ed. N.Y., Bowker, 1976. 7v.

Begun in 1906, this essential source of brief, factual sketches has undergone many changes. In its first seven editions, names of outstanding scientists were starred. Its first 11 editions were published under the title *American Men of Science*. The increasing number of volumes in each edition is evidence of the great increase in the number of scientists and teachers of science whose stature in scientific work, research activity, or attainment of a position of substantial responsibility make them eligible for consideration by the Advisory Committee. The 13th edition

(1976, 7v.) includes nearly 111,000 Canadian and American biographies in the physical and biological sciences, plus a selection of those in the social and behavioral sciences. A separate Social and Behavioral Sciences volume, published in 1978, "covers the twelve areas . . . not covered in the major compendium (i.e. the 7v. set published in 1976); namely administration and management, area studies, business, communications and information science, community and urban studies, economics, environmental studies, futuristics, international studies, political science, psychology, and sociology" (Pref.). It contains about 24,000 sketches. Geographic and discipline indexes are included in both the seven-volume edition and the separate volume. Also published separately are volumes in specific fields, e.g. Biology; Chemistry; Consultants; Medical and Health Sciences; Physics, Astronomy, Mathematics, Statistics and Computer Science. These differ from the Social and Behavioral Sciences volume in being excerpted from the original seven-volume set. For an analysis of their contents, see *Booklist* 74:1132 (Mar. 1, 1978).

→ McGraw-Hill modern scientists and engineers. N.Y., McGraw-Hill, [1980]. 3v.

Emphasizes the achievements of leading contemporary scientists, with some biographical information supplied by the biographees. Cites appropriate background articles in *McGraw-Hill Encyclopedia of Science and Technology*. Index in v.1. A classified index groups scientists by subject fields.

→ World who's who in science: a biographical dictionary of notable scientists from antiquity to the present. Chicago, Marquis, 1968.

Retrospective and current, with brief sketches of 30,000 biographees selected by the staff and consultants, based in part on questionnaires from living scientists, with staff-written biographies of eminent scientists who did not return questionnaire. Selected bibliographies.

Social Scientists

See *American Men and Women of Science*, under SCIENTISTS.

Theater

→ Notable names in the American theatre. Clifton, N.J., James T. White, 1976. 1250p.

Detailed sketches of living actors, playwrights, directors, designers, and producers, with abbreviated histories of United States theater groups, theaters, awards, and recipients. Revised edition of *The Bio-graphical Encyclopedia & Who's Who of the American Theater*, ed. by Walter Rigdon (N.Y., Heineman, 1966. 1101p.).

→ Who's who in the theatre: a biographical record of the contemporary stage. Ed. 1– . London, Pitman, 1912– , distributed in U.S. by Gale Research. Irregular.

Includes performers, composers, dramatists, critics, managers, etc. Emphasis on Britain, but more Americans in recent years. Bibliographies and appended indexes include New York, London, and other playbills; theatre associations and movements; obituaries; long runs and notable productions; and working dimensions of British stages.

For deceased persons in the theater, see:

→ Who was who in the theatre, 1912–1976. A biographical dictionary of actors, actresses, directors, playwrights, and producers of the English-speaking theatre; compiled from *Who's Who in the Theatre*, v.1–15 (1912–72). Detroit, Gale Research, 1978. 4v. (Gale composite biographical dictionary of persons, no.3)

Many more national biographies and biographical directories in special fields will be found in Sheehy's *Guide to Reference Books* and its supplements, which devote section AJ to biography and section AK to genealogy.

A. J. Walford's *Guide to Reference Material* (v.2) devotes 91 to biography, 919 to genealogy and hearldry. It resembles *Sheehy* in its broad coverage and discriminating annotations, some of which give additional (others less) information than those in *Sheehy*. Like *Sheehy*, it groups biographical sources for artists, writers, and the like under appropriate subject.

A readable account of the most frequently used biographical sources will be found in William Katz's *Introduction to Reference Work* (v.1), whose recognition of the wide number of sources that may be used for searching resembles that found in Slocum's *Biographical Dictionaries*. Slocum's book serves to remind us that while certain generalizations continue to hold true, the tools we use continue to increase and sometimes dramatically change our search strategies.

An example of an annotated list of titles suitable for small libraries, *Reference Books for Small and Medium-sized Libraries* includes about fifty biographical titles judged to be most useful in this type of library by a committee of the Reference and Adult Services Division of the American Library Association.

Finally, an extended article on biographical dictionaries, prepared by the ALA Reference and Subscription Books Review Committee, was published in *Reference and Subscription Books Reviews, 1972–1974* (p.362–92), reprinted from *Booklist* (May 1, 1974). Excellent guidelines for evaluating individual titles are followed by summaries of the characteristics of eighty established current and retrospective biographical dictionaries, with citations to the most recent reviews by the Committee.

Summary

Sources of biographical information are among the most used and most numerous. They are widely varied—encyclopedias, bibliographies, indexes, manuscript collections—and their variety is exceeded only in their degree of reliability. This chapter has described the nature of biographical information, the most important indexes, international and national sources, and those restricted to one or more professions. Points to be observed in their evaluation have been noted.

4

Sources on Words

Language is a solemn thing:
it grows out of life—out of its agonies and
ecstasies, its wants and its weariness.
Every language is a temple in which the soul
of those who speak it is enshrined.

—O. H. HOLMES

In a world where the need to communicate is keenly felt, no source is more important than one on words and their meanings. Individuals must communicate with individuals, and nations with nations. This need increases with the complexity of society, with the advances in science and technology, and with our concern with our image. We are a far cry from the days when we could be satisfied with glossaries of difficult words. Today, we are less concerned with rare and obsolete words than with the rapidly increasing living language.

For this reason, this chapter will be concerned with sources of the living language, chiefly the English language, fundamental to our understanding of the symbols we use to communicate. Most important and most widely used are general langauge dictionaries, and some knowledge of why and how they are made is essential if they are to be used intelligently—not as a kind of mystical authority, but as a product of our efforts to record the meanings of words and their pronunciations. Guidelines for reviewing English-language dictionaries may be found in the appendix.

Why a Dictionary Is Made

General language dictionaries have been compiled in modern times by individuals or learned societies with one of two basic purposes, purposes that are inevitably related: (1) to set authoritative standards for spelling, meaning, and usage, or (2) to record the words of a language, with all their uses and meanings. Dictionaries compiled for the first purpose are known as perscriptive, an often cited example being Samuel Johnson's *Dictionary of the English Language* (1755). Dictionaries compiled for the second purpose are known as descriptive, the best-known example in English being the *Oxford English Dictionary* (1884). *O.E.D.*, as it is usually cited, owes its origin in large part to Dean Richard C. Trench's attack on Samuel Johnson's view, which had influenced English lexicography for more than a hundred years. Dean Trench believed that a dictionary should be an inventory of the langauge and that the lexicographer should be an historian, not a critic, of the language.

That the latter view is more generally accepted in twentieth-century lexicography is evident in *Webster's Third New International Dictionary*, which aims to represent the language as it is now used. (That there are objections to this purpose is evident in the storm of controversy that arose soon after publication of *Webster's Third*; for a sample, see James H. Sledd and Wilma R. Ebbitts, eds., *Dictionaries and That Dictionary* [Chicago: Scott, Foresman, 1962], 273p.). Noah Webster was a man of many interests—teacher, author, journalist, lawyer, judge, scientist, gardener, traveler—but was best known as a lexicographer. (Israel Shenker, in *Harmless Drudges*, has given some interesting sidelights on this father of American lexicography [Bronxville, N.Y.: Barnhart Books, 1979; p.125–31].) An ardent believer that the American nation needed a language and literature of its own, he wrote a three-volume *Grammatical Institute of the English Language* (pt. I), known as the *Blue-backed Speller* (1783), which became a best seller (some 60 million copies were sold in the course of a century). It helped to bring about reform in American orthography. The year he died (1843), G. & C. Merriam acquired the right to produce further editions of his great work, *An American Dictionary of the English Language*, and this firm continues to revise and publish this standard, unabridged dictionary (as well as many abridgments). In 1970, Johnson Reprint Corporation published a facsimile of the original 1828 edition of the dictionary in two volumes, with an introduction by Mario Pei.

Even Dr. Johnson, though unable to abandon the prescriptive approach, finally admitted, in the preface to his dictionary, that his desire to "fix" the language was one "which neither reason nor experience can justify."

An example of how modern lexicographers defend their objectivity in recording a language is given by Jess Stein, editor in chief of *Random House Dictionary of the English Language* who states in its introduction:

> And finally, that lexicographer's Scylla and Charybdis: Should the dictionary be an authoritarian guide to "correct" English or should it be so antiseptically free of comment that it may defeat the user by providing him with no guidance at all? There is, we believe, a linguistically sound middle course. Language, most people agree, is never static—except when dead. It has a capacity for constant change and growth that enables it to serve effectively the requirements of the society in which it exists. It is, therefore, the function of a dictionary to provide the user with an exact record of the language he sees and hears. That record must be fully descriptive. Since language is a social institution, the lexicographer must give the user an adequate indication of the attitudes of society toward particular words or expressions, whether he regards those attitudes as linguistically sound or not. The lexicographer who does not recognize the existence of long-established strictures in usage has not discharged his full responsibility. He has not been objective and factual; he has reported selectively, omitting references to a social attitude relevant to many words and expressions. He does not need to express approval or disapproval of a disputed usage, but he does need to report the milieu of words as well as their meanings [p.vi].

Nevertheless, present-day compilers of dictionaries must inevitably be concerned with what is considered the "standard" language and must give emphasis to standard words and meanings in their vocabularies. As an example, the editors of *Funk & Wagnalls Standard College Dictionary* give emphasis to standard English, defined in the dictionary itself as "those usages in English that have gained literary, cultural, and social acceptance and prestige for educated speakers of the language."

Clarence L. Barnhart believes that "the popular dictionary tends to be a dictionary of the standard language and is concerned with slang and various specialized vocabularies only so far as they may appear in current newspapers, magazines, and books" ("Problems in Editing Monolingual Dictionaries," in Fred W. Householder and Sol Saporta, eds., *Problems in Lexicography* [Publication 21; Bloomington: Indiana Univ. Research Center in Anthropology, Folklore, and Linguistics, 1962], p.162). However, slang is increasingly included in general dictionaries. For example, the supplement to the *Oxford English Dictionary* incorporates Eric Partridge's *Dictionary of Slang*, which was once described by Partridge as containing words not fit to print in the *O.E.D.* And certainly slang appears increasingly in newspapers, magazines, and books.

Sumner Ives provides a further statement on the purpose of dictionaries: "A modern dictionary should be a record of the modern language—what it is and how it reflects the present-day ideas and activities" ("An Outline Commentary on *Webster's Third New International Dictionary*" [mimeographed; n.p., n.d., p.10]).

That dictionaries inevitably serve as language standardizers is pointed out by Kenneth Whittaker:

> It was commonly accepted in the eighteenth century that dictionaries should try to standardize the spelling, pronunciation, meaning and general usage of words. In fact, it was sometimes held that dictionaries should fix the words of good English for all time, Nowadays, on the contrary, it is generally felt that dictionaries should limit themselves to recording exactly a language's development. However, although the twentieth century point of view is different from that of the eighteenth century, the fact remains that dictionaries do inevitably act as language standardizers. In Elizabethan times, when English dictionaries were still rudimentary, the spelling of words was far more varied than it is today. . . . One of the main reasons for the disappearance of varied spellings since Shakespeare's day is undoubtedly the growth of dictionaries.

Even when dictionaries record different usages and spellings, they can only record a very limited number, and so fix usage. Whittaker further points out that in newly developing countries of the world, variations in usage (such as different spellings) are eliminated from the start, since dictionaries are produced alongside the first newspapers, books, and other writings in a language hitherto unwritten (*Dictionaries* [New York: Philosophical Library, 1966], p. 25–26).

Why, then, do we discriminate between dictionaries which are prescriptive and those which are descriptive? The answer lies in the methods of compilation, the former being based on the opinions and judgments of compilers on what they consider to be approved, standard usage; the latter on the basis of evidence gathered from a careful inventory of recorded sources of the language. These sources are described below, in our review of how dictionaries are made.

It is a difficult and time-consuming task to produce a good general English-language dictionary. This task must be viewed as "a serious and conscientious attempt to produce a work which conforms to the requirements of responsible scholarship but provides the information desired by those who are not scholars" (Ives, p.2).

This same idea is expressed by C. L. Barnhart: "The function of a general reference book is to make available to the general public in understandable language the knowledge upon which scholars and specialists are agreed" (p.173).

How Dictionaries Are Made

The making of a dictionary is both a science and an art. The painstaking accumulation of reliable data, consisting of thousands upon thousands of individual facts of the language; the proper classification of this data; and finally the formulation of sound conclusions from this mass of material—all illustrate the inductive process that is basic to every science. At the same time, the presentation of information about the language, the phrasing of definitions, and the ordering of word treatments demand of the lexicographer the ability to manipulate the language with economy and precision. The science without the art is likely to be ineffective; the art without the science is certain to be inaccurate [from Marckwardt's preface to *Funk & Wagnalls Standard College Dictionary*].

Who makes up the staff of a general English-language dictionary? What are their responsibilities? What sources do they use? How do they select the vocabulary? How do they phrase the definitions? In what order are word senses given? How are illustrations of the use of a word shown? How is the etymology of a word developed? How are levels of usage shown? How is prononication shown?

Much of this information is given in the introduction to dictionaries, seldom read by the general user but essential for the serious student. It is here presented in abbreviated, outline form, and should be supplemented by further reading.

I. Staff and its responsibilities
   A. The editor, who is concerned with the needs of the user, the selection of material, the coordination of the work of special editors and staff, and the liaison between the publisher and those engaged in the actual compilation.
   B. The advisory board or committee, which is usually carefully selected to supplement the experience, training, and information of the editor, and must represent varying points of view. It considers policies on such matters as how pronunciation is to be shown, the order and levels of definitions, the selection of entries, and how various levels of usage are to be labeled.
   C. Consulting specialists in etymology, pronunciation, usage, synonyms and antonyms, dialect, etc., who are also carefully selected to provide the editor and the advisory board or committee with information on these matters which is needed as a basis for policy decisions.
   D. Consulting specialists in specific subject fields, who are responsible for the selection of terms and the accuracy of definitions in specific subject fields, sometimes writing or making editorial revisions of definitions in their fields. Their assistance is particularly needed in scientific fields and has been recognized for a long time, long before Noah Webster sought the help of a professor of medicine in improving his definitions of scientific terms.
   E. The supporting staff in the editorial offices is responsible for continuous reading of pertinent contemporary publications and recording new words and new meanings of older terms for possible

inclusion. "Usually an office staff prepares copy for the dictionary in order that everything included may be adjusted to the space that we have and a proper balance between the various types of information presented may be maintained. This involves people who are highly skilled in the art of abstracting, careful and judicious in their judgments, and capable of writing good clear English" (Barnhart, p.180). The excellence of the final product depends in large part on the experience, intelligence, and accuracy of the supporting staff.

II. Sources used

It is generally recognized that the authority of a dictionary is ultimately dependent on the thoroughness with which its editors have examined the total language in use, as observed by Ives (p.7). Some of the sources examined by reputable staffs are:

A. Existing dictionaries. Indispensable is the *Oxford English Dictionary*, because of its inclusiveness of words in use since 1150, its nearly 2 million illustrative quotations, and the principles on which it is compiled. Also useful is the *Dictionary of American English* and *Dictionary of Americanisms*, prepared on the same principles as the *Oxford English Dictionary*. Though Dr. Johnson had no *O.E.D.* to consult, he made use of earlier dictionaries in compiling the word list for his dictionary, drawing heavily on technical dictionaries for legal, medical and ecclesiastical terms.

B. Files. A file of citations gathered over a long period of time and continuously updated in an effort to represent the total language in use, from which the entries may be selected. This file is maintained by highly trained persons who systematically cover pertinent sources. Examples of sources used in assembling the file of nearly 5 million citations to current English used in the preparation of *Webster's Third New International Dictionary* include: *Dictionary of American Biography*; college catalogs (especially course descriptions) from all sections of the country; American Guide Series, whose authors come from all sections of the country; newspapers from all parts of the English-speaking world; journals and abstracts in technical fields; general magazines; company publications of major corporations; a large number of specialized titles in various activities (Ives, p.7–8).

Funk and Wagnalls maintains a current citation file "based upon the regular survey of many periodicals published here and abroad. We have a number of paid readers who scan periodicals for use and mark them for citations. The periodicals are then returned to us, where index cards are prepared for each citation, and the citation is clipped and pasted on the card. The periodicals read include virtually all of the national magazines, major newspapers, significant literary journals, specialized publications, and some regional periodicals and newspapers. Our file includes the complete index of *American Speech*, so all the citations of that publication are at our disposal as well" (Sidney I. Landau, editor in chief, to Frances Cheney, Dec. 3, 1968).

Dr. Johnson also collected a file of citations in the preparation of his dictionary, using books easily at hand, beginning with those written by Sir Philip Sidney (about 1580), but including Chaucer. He was less objective than modern compilers (including a few of his friends among contemporary writers), but, like modern compilers, he employed copyists to transcribe words which he had underlined in the books he read.

In an abridged dictionary, intended for college students, the file of citations must represent an adequate sampling from contemporary sources, including newspapers; popular, literary, and technical magazines; yearbooks; and important novels and nonfiction, both British and American. "A balanced quotation file of perhaps half a million quotations that supplements the file of the *Oxford,* the *Century*, and the *Dictionary of Americanisms* would be adequate to give authority to the selection of new material" (Barnhart, p.167).

C. Firsthand observation. "The common but unsystematic observations of educated men" (Ives, p.3).

III. Scope
A. Selection of the vocabulary

The staff must decide what is to be included in the vocabulary, based on the sources at hand and the needs of potential users. This decision involves emphasis, inclusion of nonlexical terms, and coverage of scientific and technical terms. The following examples are listed to show the decisions made by staffs of several dictionaries.

1. *Webster's Third New International Dictionary*, in the selection of its more than 450,000 entries:
   a. Gives emphasis to the living language, deleting about 250,000 words and adding 50,000 new words and 50,000 new meanings to those in *Webster's Second*
   b. Deletes words that were obsolete before 1755, unless found in well-known major works of a few major writers
   c. Omits nonlexical terms, such as geographical and biographical entries, titles of books and works of art, names of fictional characters, and mottoes and other familiar sayings

    d. Includes scientific and technical terms that are not the exclusive property of the true specialist. The cutoff point was approximately the level of graduate school specialization

    e. Excludes many slang and substandard entries found in *Webster's Second* (Ives, p.9–11).

2. *Funk & Wagnalls Standard College Dictionary*, in the selection of its 150,000 entries:

    a. Gives emphasis to standard words and meanings, including nonstandard words of wide currency

    b. Holds rare, archaic, and obsolete terms to a minimum

    c. Includes nonlexical terms, such as geographical and biographical entries

    d. Includes many scientific and technical terms.

Barnhart observes that nearly all college dictionaries are about 90 percent in agreement on the choice of words to be entered, but differ in number of abbreviations and geographical and biographical names (p.164).

B. Wording of definitions

Since dictionaries are most often used to find the meaning of a word, the form of the definition is of great importance. It is generally agreed that the wording of a definition should go from known to unknown, from the general to the specific. In *Funk & Wagnalls Standard College Dictionary*, each definition defines only the entry word or phrase and can usually be substituted for it. "The editorial policy of the *Third New International* has been to select general terms from among the words in *Webster's Elementary Dictionary*" (Ives, p.21).

Ives describes the method used in *Webster's Third* as follows: "When a definer has collected an adequate group of citations for writing a definition, he divides and subdivides this group until no further subdivisions are required to distinguish between senses. . . . He has one or more piles of citations, each illustrating one meaning of the word in question. He then frames a phrasal statement or selects another word, or both, signifying this meaning. Each of these words or phrases is a semantic equivalent of the entry word . . . a 'substitute' for the entry word in that it may replace the entry word in an actual context and convey, in that context, the same sense as that conveyed by the entry word, insofar as any word or phrase in English may replace any other word or phrase. These items, taken together, give the range of meaning the word has in the language" (p.16).

Another consideration, in addition to the wording of a definition, is the matter of encyclopedic explanations, often used in unabridged dictionaries to augment the bare definition. Small dictionaries are less apt to include these because of space limitations.

C. Order of word senses

Word senses may be arranged in three ways: (1) in historical order; (2) in order of frequency of use, the most common usage being given first; and (3) in no fixed order. Each may be justified by the editors.

Ives defends the historical order of definitions in *Webster's Third* in noting: "The historical order of listing is based fundamentally on two considerations. First, it is generally possible to date the document in which a citation is found and therefore be reasonably sure of the basis for the order of listing. On the other hand, it is hardly possible to get more than a very general idea of the relative frequency with which a word is used in any of its varying senses, for semantic counts can hardly be made for any but the most common words, and these semantic counts must rely on an existing breakdown of a word's total meaning into discrete senses" (p.28).

Funk & Wagnalls follows the second order: "In entries for words having several senses, the order in which definitions appear is, wherever possible, that of frequency of use, rather than semantic evolution" (*Standard College Dictionary*, text ed., p.xxiii).

The *Random House Dictionary of the English Language* (college ed.) states: "The most common part of speech is listed first, and the most frequently encountered meaning appears as the first definition for each part of speech. Specialized senses follow, and rare, archaic, and obsolete senses are usually listed at the end of their part-of-speech group. This order is changed in those cases where it is desirable to group related meanings together" (p.xxviii, 1968 ed.).

But as Ives points out, "To a person consulting a dictionary for the particular meaning of a word in something he is currently reading, the order of listing is of little importance, for he must search through the various meanings for one that fits anyway. . . . If his dictionary lists senses according to some estimate as to frequency, a reader has a slight advantage in starting at the beginning; if his dictionary lists according to historical order, he has a slight advantage in starting at the end" (p.28–29).

In some instances, no one order of senses is given, for example, in *Webster's New Twentieth Century Dictionary of the English Language*. Its introduction states: "No fixed, arbitrary arrangement of the senses within a given entry has been attempted. Any effort to arrange each entry so that the prevailing current meaning is given first is doomed to failure, since for most words there are a number of senses, on different levels and in different fields, that have equal currency. The editors have therefore allowed practicality to determine their practice. Where historical order of senses seemed advisable, this order has been followed; where one meaning flows logically into another or others, this too has been indicated" (p.vi).

While a user must be generally aware of the order of word senses in a particular dictionary, it is more important that he heed Marckwardt's warning in his preface to *Funk & Wagnalls Standard College Dictionary*: "Yet it is of primary importance to find the meaning which applies to the use of the word about which one is in doubt. The dictionary is not a tool to be used hastily or casually" (p.vii).

D. Illustrations

Definitions of words must often be augmented by illustrative phrases, which may be supplied by the editorial staff or quoted from published sources. Pictorial illustrations are usually held to a minimum in general unabridged or college dictionaries, being chiefly used to accompany entries for flora and fauna, geographical areas, architectural details, etc., which are more easily explained by pictures, diagrams, or maps, than by words. They are more freely used in dictionaries for children. A notable exception is *The American Heritage Dictionary of the English Language*, whose spot maps and marginal illustrations, many in color, number nearly 4,000. They have been favorably received and may set a precedent for use of more pictorial matter in dictionaries.

Most distinguished for its illustrative quotations is the *Oxford English Dictionary*, which has nearly 2 million quotations from more than 5,000 authors of all periods. These were assembled over a long period of time, from manuscript as well as printed sources, and have been judiciously edited.

Funk & Wagnalls Standard College Dictionary and *Random House Dictionary of the English Language* include brief phrases or sentences which illustrate the use of the entry words or supplement and clarify the definitions. These are supplied by the editorial staff, and no quotations, literary or otherwise, are included.

In *Webster's Third*, "the selection of quotations has been made with the ordinary rather than the literary reader in mind. In other words, the quotations have been selected to illustrate words in their common, general, typical, and characteristic senses and contexts, rather than in atypical uses often found in imaginative literature, however interesting" (Ives, p.24).

Whether quotations should be selected from the "best writers" has been raised by James R. Hulbert in *Dictionaries, British and American* (2nd rev. ed.; London: Deutsch, 1969; 112p.). He feels that the best quotations are those that define a word or meaning, or have value as information, and sees no reason to criticize historical dictionaries for including quotations from "second or third rate writers," since the editors must select the best quotations correctly spaced in time, regardless of source. It is not the purpose of a historical dictionary to provide models of good writing, but to record objectively (p.81–83).

In general, dictionary makers supply illustrations of use, agreeing with Voltaire, who wrote to Charles Duclos in 1760 that "a dictionary without quotations is a skeleton."

E. Etymologies

Editors of dictionaries must decide in what form etymologies should be given and where they should be placed in the word treatment. For in spite of the fact that the average user most often consults dictionaries for the meanings of words, etymologies are of interest to linguists and others interested in the history of words.

In the matter of form, editors have a choice of recording root words in the alphabets of the original, e.g. in Greek, as in the *Oxford English Dictionary*, or transliterated according to the Roman alphabet, as in *Webster's Third* and *Funk & Wagnalls Standard Dictionary*.

In the matter of placement, editors must decide whether root words should precede the definition, as in *Webster's Third*, or be placed last, as in *Funk & Wagnalls Standard College Dictionary*.

But in all general dictionaries, etymologies must be based on authoritative sources and should be given in a form which can be understood by the general user. Ives has pointed out that "a general difficulty with etymologies in dictionaries has been that they have been so abbreviated as to be cryptic rather than informative, and consequently have communicated better to the language scholar than to the general reader" (p.27). At the same time, it must be noted that editors are faced with the problem of holding a dictionary's contents to a reasonable size, and the space allotted to etymologies must be determined in relationship to that allotted to definitions and illustrations of use. Space limitations are responsible for the extensive use of abbreviations in this part of an entry, and prefatory explanations must be consulted to interpret these abbreviations accurately, e.g. the use of *ISV* for International Scientific Vocabulary in *Webster's Third*.

F. Levels of usage

Allen Walker Read, in reviewing *Webster's Third*, observed that the labeling of levels of usage is one of the most misunderstood functions of a dictionary. He reminds readers that "a label is an objective observation about the usual nature of the contexts in which a word appears and is not a directive to the user. It gives information to the user, and the user can then decide whether the word fits his needs" ("That Dictionary or The Dictionary?" in *Consumer Reports* 28:492 [Oct. 1963]).

Various level and style labels are applied by editors. Examples of those employed in several dictionaries to indicate nonstandard words are *Dial.* (dialect), *Slang*, and *Illit.* (illiterate), used in *Funk & Wagnalls Standard College Dictionary*, which does not use *Colloq.* (colloquial) because the editors believe it to be so often misunderstood. In addition, it uses labels for certain standard words: (1) to indicate that a word is characteristic of a national division of English, e.g. *U.S., Brit., Scot., Austral.;* (2) to indicate that a word is characteristic of a broad region or of a national division. e.g. *Southern U.S., SW U.S.;* and (3) to indicate that a word is characteristic of informal use, by labeling it *informal.*

Webster's Third employs the label *Substand* (substandard) to indicate a pattern of linguistic usage "that exists throughout the American language community but differs in choice of word or form from that of the prestige group in that community." It uses *nonstand* (nonstandard) "for a very small number of words that can hardly stand without some status label but are too widely current in reputable context to be labeled *substand*" (p.19a).

Other designations for both standard and nonstandard words include: (1) currency labels, used to indicate both standard and nonstandard words in less than general currency, e.g. *Rare, Archaic,* or *Obs.* (obsolete); and (2) field labels, used to identify the field of learning or activity in which a word or sense belongs, e.g. *Bot.* (botany), *Chem.* (chemistry); and (3) foreign-language labels, used to identify the source of words or phrases not fully naturalized into English.

Ives reminds us that "any statement on usage is a judgment rather than a report, based on the comprehensiveness of the evidence, the skill and experienced discernment with which it has been classified, and, finally, on the linguistic perspicacity of the one making the statement" (p.33).

The lexicographers of *The American Heritage Dictionary of the*

English Language commissioned a usage panel of about one hundred novelists, essayists, poets, journalists, writers on science and sports, public officials, and professors, who had "in common only a recognized ability to speak and write good English." Their opinions on good usage are reflected in the 800 usage notes appended to certain troublesome terms, e.g. *ain't*. Morris Bishop has discussed the problem of authority in a prefatory article, "Good Usage, Bad Usage, and Usage," in the same dictionary (p.xxi–xxiv). Israel Shenker gives some amusing examples of varying options of the panel in his *Harmless Drudges* (p.141–52).

G. Pronunciation

James B. McMillan, in the introduction to *Funk & Wagnalls Standard College Dictionary*, states the commonly held view of dictionary makers: "A pronunciation is correct when it is normally and unaffectedly used by cultivated people. Strictly, any pronunciation is correct when it serves the purpose of communication and does not call unfavorable attention to the speaker" (p.xxii).

Ives has noted that the material on American pronunciation is quite uneven in quality and that there are only a few scholarly studies. Increasingly, transcriptions and recordings are used, usually taken from "running" speech. Pronunciation as shown in *Webster's Third* is based on a recording, or a reliable study, or an expert guess by analogy with a recorded pronunciation of a similar word (p.39–40).

But editors are further plagued with problems of how pronunciation is most clearly shown. *Webster's Third* uses a combination of letters and diacritical markings, which has been criticized by some as too technical. Like *Funk & Wagnalls Standard College Dictionary* and other well-edited dictionaries, it uses the schwa, the upside-down symbol ə, to stand for the neutral vowel spelled *a* in *alone*, *e* in *system*, *i* in *easily*, *o* in *gallop*, and *u* in *circus*. This is the most often used sound in American English, and the symbol is also used in the International Phonetic Alphabet. But this phonetic alphabet (developed by the International Phonetic Association) uses a number of symbols that are not familiar to American users. Thus American and English general dictionaries often indicate pronunciation by simple respelling, using the letters of the Roman alphabet and differentiating the vowel sounds by diacritical markings and certain consonantal sounds by combinations of letters. Accented syllables are usually indicated by stress marks. Fortunately for users, a key to pronunciation, usually in abbreviated form, is repeated throughout a dictionary.

Other problems, in addition to selection of a pronunciation key, confront editors, among them the extent to which variant pronunciations are to be represented. Differences in English and American pronunciation and in regions of the United States are often indicated in American unabridged dictionaries, usually with the assistance of consulting editors who are specialists in pronunciation.

H. Synonyms and antonyms

Dictionary makers are concerned with adequate treatment of synonyms and antonyms, often employing specialists for advice in such matters, for example, *Funk & Wagnalls New Standard College Dictionary*, whose synonym discriminations were written by the late George Mott-Smith and edited by S. I. Hayakawa. These discussions of the shades of meaning within a group of related words, together with illustrations, follow many of the definitions. *Webster's Third* appends a paragraph of synonym discriminations to many of its definitions.

IV. Other considerations

The editorial staff must make decisions on such matters as alphabetical order of the vocabulary and syllabication.

Vocabularies may be arranged in word-by-word or letter-by-letter order, the latter method being used by *American Heritage Dictionary, Webster's Third,* and *Funk & Wagnalls Standard College Dictionary*.

Nonlexical terms, such as geographical and biographical entries, may be included in the main alphabet, as in *American Heritage Dictionary* and *Funk & Wagnalls Standard College Dictionary*. Or they may be listed separately, as in *Webster's New Collegiate Dictionary*, with its appended list of biographies and a pronouncing gazetteer.

Syllabication may be shown by centered periods, by hyphens, or by spaces between parts of words. Both *Webster's Third* and *Funk & Wagnalls Standard College Dictionary* use centered periods.

The selection of other material also depends on editorial judgment. Instruction in use is important and is found in all good dictionaries. Sections on grammar and on history of the language, lists of colleges, tables of weights and measures, and other features must be decided in terms of the possible user.

Samuel Johnson is credited with observing that "dictionaries are like watches; the worst is better than none, and the best cannot be expected to go quite true." Nevertheless, we have a number of excellent general English-language dictionaries, whose characteristics may be generally summarized:

1. They are published by reputable publishers.
2. They have a strong central editorial staff of lexicographers, directed by an experienced editor.
3. They have a qualified staff of consultants and contributors.
4. They strive for clarity of definitions and attempt to keep abreast of recent research in etymology.
5. They contain illustrative quotations, selected from an extensive file assembled from a wide range of sources.
6. They reflect the changing language by their inclusion of new words and new meaning for older words.
7. They reflect the needs of the time in giving special attention to scientific and technical terms, while not neglecting the literary language.
8. They reflect the needs of the types of users for whom they are intended.

Mitford M. Mathews, in his introduction to *Webster's New World Dictionary*, has summarized the uses of a good English dictionary:

The dictionary has ceased to be merely one book; it is a small library of books brought together into one. These would be suitable titles for the different books that are combined in a good English dictionary:

1. How to Spell English Words
2. How to Capitalize English Words
3. How to Divide English Words into Syllables
4. How to Pronounce English Words
5. A Brief English Grammar
6. A Dictionary of English Etymologies
7. Levels of English Usage
8. The Meanings of English Words
9. A Dictionary of Synonyms
10. A Dictionary of English Phrases

Unabridged Dictionaries

Briefly discussed here are only well-known unabridged English-language dictionaries—their scope and word treatment. Fuller discussion will be found in Kenneth Kister's *Dictionary Buying Guide* (New York: Bowker, 1977; 358p.), an excellent source of thorough, discriminating evaluations of about 350 English-language dictionaries and wordbooks. There are sections on unabridged and abridged schools', children's, adults', and special-purpose dictionaries (etymological, usage, slang, synonyms, crossword puzzles, rhymes, pronunciation, abbreviations and acronyms, and foreign words and phrases). Informed commentary on purpose and scope, authority, vocabulary treatment, format, and special features is augmented by citations to further sources of information. There is also an annotated bibliography of sources, giving critical commentary on their quality. Among them are *American Reference Books Annual, Booklist, Choice, Library Journal, RQ*, and *Wilson Library Bulletin*, all of which review dictionaries. For brief descriptive notes on a wide range of titles, see Eugene P. Sheehy's *Guide to Reference Books* (9th ed.; Chicago: ALA, 1976; sec. AD).

A very useful review, "Purchasing a Desk Dictionary" (*Booklist* 75: 1591–94 [July 1, 1979]), not only evaluates eight adult-level abridged English-language dictionaries but gives points to consider in buying one. It was prepared by the ALA Reference and Subscription Books Review Committee, which also prepared the guidelines for the evaluation of dictionaries (found in the appendix).

Though the number of entries for each dictionary (listed below) is given as stated by the publishers, these statistics should be used with some knowledge of what is being counted. Sidney Landau, editor in chief of Funk and Wagnalls dictionaries, has discussed this point in an article which concludes: "To regard a dictionary's total entry count as significant in itself, is not very sensible, especially if one has only vague notions of what a dictionary entry is. Properly understood, however, and provided one also is familiar with other aspects of the dictionary in question, entry count can be a useful guide in estimating a dictionary's comparative size and comprehensiveness" ("The Numbers' Game: Dictionary Entry Count," *RQ* 4:6, 13–15 [Sept. 1964]).

Landau explains the various types of entries, defining a main entry as "a word, phrase, abbreviation, or word element (including prefixes, suffixes, and combining forms) that appears in its regular alphabetical place and is there defined." Other types of entries that may be included in the total vocabulary count have been designated by a federal specification, which provides for counting inflected forms, variant spellings, and defined parts of speech other than the main entry. Also included in entry counts may be idioms, "run on" derivatives, and words or phrases in self-explanatory lists—one beginning with the prefix *un*, for example. It should be remembered that what may appear in main entry form in one dictionary may appear in another form in another dictionary. Thus we see the validity of including in the total count not only the main entry but also inflected forms, variant spellings, defined parts of speech, idioms, run-on derivatives, and words or phrases in self-explanatory lists.

Felicia Lampert quotes one lexicographer as saying, "Most publishers either lie or equivocate in their entry claims; no one is likely to sit down and count." She cites no source for this statement, and continues somewhat frivolously, "Exaggerations of up to 20 percent are considered sporting in the trade" ("Dictionaries: Our Language Right or Wrong," in Jack C. Gray, comp., *Words, Words, and Words about Dictionaries* [San Francisco: Chandler, 1963; 207p.], p.70). But it is reasonable to believe that good editors know how many entries are included in the dictionaries for which they are responsible.

One other point should be remembered in comparing the vocabulary counts of one dictionary with another. Some dictionaries include nonlexical terms, such as biographical and geographical names, while others do not. This difference should be taken into consideration if sizes of vocabulary are compared.

Historical

→ Murray, *Sir* James Augustus Henry. New English dictionary on historical principles. Oxford, Clarendon Pr., 1888–1933. 12v. and supp.

> SCOPE: 414,825 entries for all words known to have been in use since 1150, including "(1) all common words of speech and literature, and all words that approach these in character, the limits being extended further into science and philosophy than into slang and cant; (2) in scientific and technical terminology, all words English in form except those of which an explanation would be intelligible only to a specialist, and such words not English in form as are in general use or belong to the more familiar language of science; and (3) dialectal words before 1500, omitting dialectal words after that date except when they continue the history of the word once in general use, illustrate the history of a literary word, or have a literary currency" (Sheehy, p.112). Supplement contains new words and senses and some corrections.
>
> WORD TREATMENT: Gives current or most usual spelling, pronunciation, part of speech, field or currency label when pertinent, earlier spelling, earliest appearance of a word (shown by symbols or precise date), etymology, meanings (numbered or lettered, with specification of their status and date of first appearance, or, if obsolete, indications of authorship, numbered according to the senses they exemplify), groups of idiomatic phrases or attributive uses, and combinations. Excellent source of histories of words and illustrative quotations, which number 1,827,306. But it should be remembered that while many sources were searched in an effort to determine the earliest recorded use of a word, some were inevitably missed. Also, it is likely that many words were in the *spoken* language for some years before their first recorded use.

For a moving account of Murray's editorship of the *O.E.D.* for 35 years, until his death at 78, see *Caught in the Web of Words* by his granddaughter, K. M. Elizabeth Murray (New Haven and London: Yale University Press, 1977; 386p.).

→ _____. Oxford English dictionary, being a corrected reissue, with an introduction, supplement and bibliography, of A New English dictionary on historical principles; founded mainly on the materials collected by the Philological Society and ed. by James A. H. Murray, Henry Bradley, W. A. Craigie, C. T. Onions. Oxford, Clarendon Pr., 1933. 12v. and supp.

Reprinted from original edition, with correction of some typographical errors.

→ _____. A supplement to the Oxford English dictionary. Ed. by R. W. Burchfield. Oxford, Clarendon Pr.; N.Y., Oxford Univ. Pr., 1972– . To be completed in 4v. v.1, A–G, 1972; v.2, H–N, 1976.

Gives greater coverage to scientific and taboo words, new meanings, and embraces "all 'common words' (and senses) in British written English" which came into use during the publication years of the *O.E.D.* (1884–1928), plus new words up to the present.

For analytical reviews of v.1–2 of the Supplement, see *Booklist*, May 1, 1973, p.818, and May 15, 1977, p.1455. Shenker gives some facets of its compilation in *Harmless Drudges* (p.84–95).

Several other dictionaries compiled on historical principles may be used to supplement the *Oxford English Dictionary*. While they cannot be classified as unabridged dictionaries, their method of compilation and emphasis on illustrative quotations justifies their being considered here, rather than with dialect dictionaries. Three of them deal with American English, one with Canadian English. Most exhaustive is *Dictionary of American English on Historical Principles*, edited under the direction of William Craigie, one of the editors of the *Oxford English Dictionary*. *Dictionary of Americanisms*, though more limited in scope than *Dictionary of American English*, should be used in conjunction with it for more recent terms and revision of some of the entries in *D.A.E.* Both of these drew on Thornton's *An American Glossary*, an earlier work based on Thornton's reading of the *Congressional Record* and other sources.

A more recent work is *A Dictionary of Canadianisms*, which follows the *Oxford English Dictionary* and *Dictionary of American English* in supporting every term with dated evidence from printed sources. The *Dictionary of Australian English* is in progress.

→ Craigie, *Sir* William Alexander, and Hulbert, James R. Dictionary of American English on historical principles. Chicago, Univ. of Chicago Pr.; Oxford, Oxford Univ. Pr., 1936–44. 4v.

SCOPE: For the period before 1900 includes "not only words or phrases which are clearly or apparently of American origin, or have greater currency here than elsewhere, but also every word denoting something which has a real connection with the development of the country and the history of its people" (Pref.). Excluded are technical terms or meanings not in general use, and slang words or uses originating after 1875.

WORD TREATMENT: Gives definitions and explanations, with chronologically arranged illustrative quotations giving exact citation to sources, and symbols to indicate those words or senses found in English before 1600, those originating within the United States, and those known only from the passage cited. Unlike the *Oxford English Dictionary*, gives little attention to pronunciation and etymology.

→ Mathews, Mitford McLeod. A dictionary of Americanisms on historical principles. Chicago, Univ. of Chicago Pr., 1951, 2v.

SCOPE: Contains 50,000 entries. Differs from *Dictionary of American English* in including only words and phrases originating in the United States and in period covered, to about 1950. Gives earlier uses of some words in *Dictionary of American English* and corrects some errors.

WORD TREATMENT: Gives definitions; chronologically arranged illustrative quotations (including many in *Dictionary of American English*) with exact citation to sources; pronunciation (more often than in *Dictionary of American English*); some drawings based on old periodicals, Sears, Roebuck catalogs, etc., when needed to clarify a definition.

→ Thorton, Richard H. An American glossary, being an attempt to illustrate certain Americanisms upon historical principles. London, Francis; Philadelphia, Lippincott, 1912; New Haven, Conn., Amer. Dialect Soc., 1931–39. 3v. (v.3 in *Dialect Notes*, 1931–39) Repr. with an introduction by Margaret M. Bryant: N.Y., Ungar, 1962. 3v.

SCOPE: Drawn from books, periodicals, newspapers, with special attention to *Congressional Globe* and *Congressional Record*, it includes not only words of American origin but English words that have acquired an American meaning or were still in use in the United States, though obsolete or provincial in England. Also includes persons and places.

WORD TREATMENT: Definitions and explanations, with chronologically arranged illustrative quotations giving exact citation to sources.

→ Dictionary of Canadianisms on historical principles. Produced . . . by the Lexicographical Centre for Canadian English, Univ. of Victoria . . . Walter S. Avis, ed. in chief. Toronto, W. J. Gage, 1967. 926p.

> SCOPE: Provides "historical record of words and expressions character-istic of the various spheres of Canadian life during the almost four centuries that English has been used in Canada" (Intro.). Includes many compound terms incorporating proper nouns, but omits geo-graphical and biographical entries.
>
> WORD TREATMENT: Gives definitions and many illustrative quotations, with careful citation to sources, and pronunciation and etymology only when relevant. Drawings are used when necessary to clarify a definition.

→ Funk & Wagnalls new standard dictionary of the English language, prep. by more than 380 specialists and other scholars under the supervision of I. K. Funk, Calvin Thomas, F. H. Vizetelly. N.Y., Funk & Wagnalls, 1964; distributed by Crowell. 2816p.

> SCOPE: 458,000 entries, including mythological, biblical, geographical, and biographical entries. More emphasis given to words currently in use throughout English-speaking world than to obsolete terms. Thoroughly revised in 1913, has been updated by insertions of new words in the text, by deletion or shortening of some older material, and more recently by supplementary lists of new words.
>
> WORD TREATMENT: Gives spelling (with preference to simpler form), syllabication (centered period), pronunciation (using revised scien-tific alphabet of National Education Association and ordinary re-spelling used in text books, referred to as "Textbook Key"), part of speech, definitions (in order of frequency of use, with most modern meaning first), illustrative phrases and quotations, synonyms and antonyms, concise etymologies, and many pictorial illustrations, in-cluding color plates.

→ Webster's New International dictionary of the English language. 2nd ed., unabridged . . . A Merriam-Webster. William Allan Neilson, ed. in chief; Thomas A. Knott, gen. ed.; Paul W. Carhart, managing ed. Springfield, Mass., Merriam, 1934. 3195p.

> SCOPE: 600,000 entries for words in use since 1500, with main words in upper part of divided page; lower part of page includes very rare and obsolete words, biblical proper names, foreign-language quotations, etc. Separate appended list of abbreviations, arbitrary signs and symbols, forms of address, pronouncing gazetteer, and pronouncing

biographical dictionary. Thoroughly revised in 1934, but updated by insertion of new words in the text, supplementary lists of new words and added meanings, and some corrections.

WORD TREATMENT: Gives spelling, syllabication (centered period), pronunciation (shown by respelling and diacritical marks), part of speech, detailed etymologies (using Latin alphabet), definitions (in historical order), labels (including field, usage, and geographic), illustrative quotations (incompletely cited), synonyms and antonyms, and many pictorial illustrations, including color plates.

→ Webster's Third new international dictionary of the English language, unabridged. A Merriam-Webster. Ed. in chief, Philip Babcock Gove and the Merriam-Webster editorial staff. Springfield, Mass., Merriam, 1961. 2622p.

SCOPE: 450,000 entries for words in use since 1755. Its preface states that it is "a completely new work, redesigned, restyled and reset." Differs from 2nd ed. in: (1) addition of 50,000 new words and 50,000 new meanings, (2) expanded etymologies, (3) deletion of many obsolete and rare words, (4) deletion of pronouncing gazetteer and biographical dictionary, (5) deletion of foreign words and phrases, except those which have become part of the English language, (6) deletion of literary and art allusions, (7) inclusion of abbreviations in main alphabet, (8) divided page not used, (9) less use of labels, and (10) new but fewer pictorial illustrations.

WORD TREATMENT: Gives spelling, syllabication (centered period), pronunciation, part of speech, etymology (in Latin alphabet), definitions ("analytical one-phrase" in historical order), illustrative quotations (chiefly from contemporary sources, incompletely cited), labels (including field, usage and geographic), synonyms (carefully discriminated and with illustrative quotations), and some pictorial illustrations.

Addenda are found in:

→ 6,000 words; a supplement to Webster's Third new international dictionary. Springfield, Mass., Merriam, 1976. 220p.

See *Booklist and Subscription Books Bulletin* (59:871–74 [July 1, 1963]) for fuller comparison with 1959 printing of second edition.

The following falls between the unabridged and abridged dictionary:

→ Random House dictionary of the English language. Jess Stein, ed. in chief. N.Y., Random, 1966. 2059p.

scope: More than 260,000 entries, emphasizing words in current use, including "foreign words and phrases, biographical terms, geographical terms, abbreviations, titles of major literary works and many other types of information" (Pref.). Appended are four concise bilingual foreign dictionaries; an atlas; a gazetteer; lists of national parks, colleges, and universities; presidents and vice presidents of the United States; reference books; signs and symbols; a basic style manual; and miscellaneous tables.

word treatment: Gives pronunciation (respelling and diacritical marks), syllabication (centered period), part of speech, definitions ("most frequently encountered" given first), illustrative phrases (written by the editorial staff), synonyms and antonyms, labels (regional, status, and field), etymologies, and 2,000 pictorial illustrations and spot maps.

This was the first general dictionary to use electronic data processing equipment in its production. For a description, see *Booklist and Subscription Books Bulletin* (63:803–7 [Apr. 1, 1967]).

For further reading, see Jack C. Gray's *Words, Words, and Words about Dictionaries*. Its contents include: (1) general discussions of words by Warren Weaver, Porter Perrin, and I. A. Richards, followed by (2) essays by Mitford M. Mathews, Mortimer Adler, and Felicia Lampert on the history and use of dictionaries, (3) reviews and comments on *Webster's Third New International*, representing widely varying points of view, and (4) prefaces and sample entries from Johnson's dictionary, *Webster's Second*, and *Webster's Third*. Intended for college freshmen, it is a provocative collection of reprints from various sources with questions and topics for writing.

Abridged Dictionaries

While all libraries need a well-edited, up-to-date, unabridged dictionary, many people find it too cumbersome and too expensive. Convenience, therefore, explains the popularity of abridged dictionaries, which usually are published because of the demand for a handy, inexpensive dictionary for quick reference. They may be abridgments of larger dictionaries, as in the case of *Funk & Wagnalls Standard College Dictionary* and *Webster's New Collegiate Dictionary*, or independent compilations, as the *Scribner-Bantam English Dictionary* and *The American Heritage Dictionary*.

Described below are a few of the better-known college or desk dictionaries, whose general characteristics are:

1. A vocabulary ranging from about 100,000 to 200,000 entries, usually giving preference to words in current use, with generous representa-

tion of scientific and technical terms and varying emphasis on slang and dialect
2. Less emphasis on etymology than is found in unabridged dictionaries
3. Fewer illustrations of use than are found in some unabridged dictionaries
4. Adequate attention to synonyms and antonyms
5. Supplementary lists of signs and symbols, forms of address, meaning of given names, colleges and universities, and biographical and geographical names, which are sometimes found in the main alphabet.

American

→ The American heritage dictionary of the English language. William Morris, ed. Boston, American Heritage and Houghton Mifflin, 1973. 1600p. First published, 1969.

> SCOPE: Over 155,000 entries, including biographical and geographical names, representing basic current vocabulary, with some attention to "words widely used in campus 'confrontations' and by persons living in U.S. ghetto areas." Prefatory essays on history, etymology, grammar, usage, dialects, spelling and pronunciation, and "Computers in Language Analysis and in Lexicography." First dictionary to use the computerized *Corpus of Present-Day Edited American English*, a wide-ranging sampling of 1 million words, prepared at Brown University.
>
> WORD TREATMENT: Syllabication (centered periods), pronunciation (respelling and diacritical marks), part of speech, field and usage labels, concise definitions ("The first definition is the central meaning about which the other senses may be most logically organized" [p.xlvii]), 20,000 sample sentences and phrases, 6,000 quotations, clear etymologies with supplementary list of Indo-European root words, synonyms, 800 usage notes for words requiring explanation of their grammatical use, and about 4,000 marginal illustrations and spot maps. Produced by the use of computers and cathode ray tube, from data stored on magnetic tapes.
>
> For a favorable review of the 1969 issue, see *Booklist* (Feb. 1, 1972), p.437. For a review of the new college edition, which is identical to the standard edition of *American Heritage*, see *Booklist* (July 1, 1979), p. 1592.

→ Funk & Wagnalls standard college dictionary. (New updated ed.) N.Y., Funk & Wagnalls, 1977. 1606p. First pub. in 1963. Rev. in 1973.

> SCOPE: 150,000 entries, including derived and compound forms, biographical and geographical entries, and abbreviations, with emphasis

on standard words and meanings but good representation of nonstandard words of wide currency, slang, and dialect. Rare, archaic, and obsolete terms are held to a minimum. Based on *Funk & Wagnalls New Standard Dictionary of the English Language*, with addition of new words and deletion of some obsolete words. Supplementary material includes colleges and universities in the United States and Canada, signs and symbols, and a list of given names.

WORD TREATMENT: Spelling (as established by use), syllabication (centered periods and stresses), pronunciation (using letters of the alphabet, combined with diacritical marks, plus the schwa), part of speech, definitions (in order of frequency, with most common meaning first), labels (field, usage, and geographic), illustrative phrases or sentences (no quotations), synonyms and antonyms, etymologies, and 3,000 pictorial illustrations.

For evaluation, see *Booklist* (July 1, 1979), p.1592–93.

→ Random House college dictionary. Rev. ed. Jess Stein, ed. in chief. N.Y., Random, 1975. 1568p. Pub. in 1968 as Random House dictionary of the English language, college ed.

SCOPE: More than 170,000 entries, based on *Random House Dictionary*. Appended are directories of United States and Canadian colleges and universities, signs and symbols, English given names, and a basic manual of style.

WORD TREATMENT: Same as unabridged edition.

See evaluation of 1975 edition in *Booklist* 75:1593 (July 1, 1979). An inexpensive paperback abridgment, the *Random House Dictionary* (N.Y., Ballantine Books, 1978; 1070p.) contains about 70,000 entries and fewer meanings, etymologies, examples of use, synonyms and antonyms, and geographical and biographical entries than *Random House College Dictionary*.

→ The Scribner-Bantam English dictionary. Edwin B. Williams, gen. ed. N.Y., Scribner, 1977. 1093p.

SCOPE: About 80,000 entries for words in current use, with emphasis on standard vocabulary, omiting common obscenities and racial slurs. Biographical and geographical names are in the main alphabet, with appended lists of colleges and universities, signs and symbols, etc.

WORD TREATMENT: Pronunciation, etymology, readable definitions, and discriminated synonyms.

→ Webster's New collegiate dictionary. [8th ed.] Springfield, Mass., Merriam, 1976. 1568p.

SCOPE: 152,000 entries based on *Webster's Third* and on more than 1 million citations collected since last edition, with emphasis on the standard language and with a small selection of slang, dialect, and obsolete terms and meanings. Appended to main vocabulary are an essay on the English language, a tabular history of the language, foreign words and phrases which have not become part of the language, biographical and geographical names, a list of U.S. and Canadian colleges and universities, a style handbook, and illustration of a business letter.

WORD TREATMENT: Same as *Webster's Third*, "with such modifications as are required by the smaller scope of the *Collegiate*" (Pref.). For evaluation, see *Booklist* 75:1593 (July 1, 1979).

→ Webster's New world dictionary of the American language. David B. Guralnik, ed. in chief. 2nd college ed. N.Y., Collins and World, 1976. 1692p.

SCOPE: More than 150,000 entries, including geographical and biographical names, selected on the basis of "frequency of occurrence in contemporary usage and in readings generally required of college and university students" (Pref.). Idiomatic and slang terms are well represented. Supplementary material includes articles on Americanisms, etymology and the English language, lists of colleges and universities in the United States and Canada, forms of address, weights and measures, and signs and symbols. First edition published in 1953; completely revised in 1970.

WORD TREATMENT: Pronunciation (using modified system of diacritical marks and respellings to represent practice of literate speakers in central United States), syllabication (centered period), part of speech, etymologies, definitions (in historical order), illustrative phrases (no quotations), labels (e.g. colloquial, slang, poetic), synonyms and antonyms, and 1,500 pictorial illustrations and spot maps.

For evaluation, see *Booklist* 75:1593 (July 1, 1979).

→ World book dictionary. Ed. by Clarence L. Barnhart and Robert K. Barnhart. A Thorndike-Barnhart dictionary. Chicago, World Book–Childcraft. Frequently revised. 2v.

SCOPE: The 1979 edition contains 225,000 entries, representing what the editors believe to be the most important, frequently used words in English. Complements *World Book Encyclopedia* and omits geographical, biographical, and other encyclopedic information. Prefatory sections on the use of languages (including foreign), on how to write effectively, and on how to use this dictionary are well developed. First published in 1963 and completely revised in 1976.

WORD TREATMENT: Syllabication (light vertical line), pronunciation (using adaptation of International Phonetic Alphabet and recording English as currently spoken), part of speech, definitions (by frequency of use, with most common meaning first), illustrative quotations (many from classic and contemporary writing, but some staff written), etymologies, synonyms and antonyms, labels (field, usage, geographic), and 3,000 pictorial illustrations. Words are treated according to age at which person first encounters them.

See *Booklist* 75:1593–94 (July 1, 1979) for evaluation of 1976 ed.

Barnhart is also editor of *The Barnhart Dictionary of New English since 1963* (Bronxville, N.Y.: Barnhart/Harper & Row, 1973; 512p.), which is recommended for its information on about 5,000 new words, accompanied by many quotations, whose sources are cited. A new compilation, including words which have come into the language since 1973, was published in 1980 by Barnhart Books, with expanded usage notes. See Shenker (p.121–24) for some of Barnhart's other activities.

British

→ Chambers's twentieth century dictionary: with supplement. Rev. ed. Ed. by A. M. Macdonald. Edinburgh, Chambers, 1977. 1652p.

SCOPE: "All words in general use in literary and conventional English, all words used in Shakespeare and the Authorized Version of the Bible, in the poems (and many of those in the prose writings) of Spenser and Milton, and in the novels of Walter Scott" (Pref.). Appended lists of signs, symbols, forms of address; Greek, Latin, and modern foreign quotations; common English Christian names; etc.

WORD TREATMENT: Pronunciation (respelling and diacritical marks), parts of speech, labels, definitions (sometimes current or most important given first, sometimes original or early meaning), citations to authors (using the word, but not quotations), and etymology.

→ Murray, *Sir* James Augustus Henry. Shorter Oxford English dictionary on historical principles. Prepared by William Little, H. W. Fowler, and Jessie Coulson. Rev. and ed. by C. T. Onions. 3rd ed. Completely reset with etymologies revised by G. W. S. Friedrichsen, with revised addenda. Oxford, Clarendon Pr., 1973. 2672p. Also 2v. ed.

SCOPE: 202,000 words, combinations, and idiomatic phrases. Approximately 40 percent of *O.E.D.*, with a few new words added. Chosen for inclusion were "not only the literary and colloquial English of the present day together with such technical and scientific terms as are most frequently met with or are likely to be the subject of inquiry, but also a considerable portion of obsolete, archaic and dialectical words and uses." The etymologies have been revised and rewritten, based on the *Oxford Dictionary of English Etymology* (1966), with an addendum containing words not recorded in the body of the dictionary and further senses and constructions of words already treated.

WORD TREATMENT: Same as *O.E.D.*, but with fewer quotations and revised etymologies.

The Concise Oxford Dictionary, frequently revised (New York: Oxford Univ. Pr.), includes nearly 75,000 words in current use, scientific and technical terms, and many colloquial and slang expressions. Unlike the *Shorter Oxford*, it is not compiled on historical principles but is a standard desk dictionary, more popular in Britain than the United States. Shenker interviews its editor in *Harmless Drudges* (p.73–78).

School Dictionaries

School dictionaries are a type of abridged dictionary that are often independently compiled (not based on a larger work). Careful attention is given to the selection of the vocabulary and to features that add to ease of use. Their general characteristics include:

1. A vocabulary ranging from about 2,500 to 80,000 entries, selected on the basis of their frequency in school textbooks and supplementary readings, with emphasis given to words in current use, though obsolete words from English classics (e.g. Shakespeare) may be included
2. Etymology usually omitted or briefly treated
3. Pronunciation shown in easily understood form
4. Definitions simply expressed in terms of a vocabulary suitable for the intended age level, emphasizing standard usage
5. Verbal illustrations of use, selected in terms of the interests of the intended age level and fewer than those in collegiate dictionaries
6. Pictorial illustrations more freely used at lower levels, selected in terms of the interests of the intended age level, and text in large type
7. Supplementary material, giving instructions on how to use the dictionary, tied in with school curriculum
8. Separately published workbooks to accompany the dictionary, which may take a programmed form.

Selection aids for school dictionaries that supply information on grade level and size of vocabulary are:

→ Kister, Kenneth F., ed. Dictionary buying guide. N.Y., Bowker, 1977.
358p.

Includes a large section, "School and Children's Dictionaries," subdivided by secondary, middle school, elementary, and preschool levels,
plus one on dictionaries for English as a foreign language.

→ Standard Catalog series, including *Children's Catalog, Junior High
School Library Catalog,* and *Senior High School Library Catalog.*

Titles selected by representative group of experienced librarians and
specialists in literature for children and young people, with excerpts
from reviewing media.

Filmstrips for teaching dictionary skills are readily available for school
use. These include one by the Society for Visual Education in 1976, "The
Dictionary," intended for elementary grades. "Using the Dictionary,"
issued by Interpretive Education in 1973, is designed for secondary special-
education students.
Scope and word treatment of some well-known school dictionaries are
given below:

→ American heritage school dictionary. N.Y., American Heritage and
Houghton Mifflin, 1972. 992p. (1977 reprint has some changes in introductory sections.)

SCOPE: About 35,000 entries, selected from over 6,000 readers, texts,
and other printed materials in grades 3 through 9, submitted by
American educators. Selection based on statistical analysis of frequency.
WORD TREATMENT: Pronunciation, part of speech, and definitions in
language of school children; illustrated with photographs or drawings; simple word histories.

The Concise Heritage Dictionary (Boston: Houghton Mifflin, 1976;
820p.), based on the *American Heritage Dictionary*, has been recommended
as an intermediate dictionary for advanced middle and secondary school
students as a bridge between *American Heritage School Dictionary* and a
desk dictionary in the 100,000-plus entry range. Its 55,000 entries are clearly
and briefly defined.

→ Macmillan dictionary. William D. Halsey, ed. dir. N.Y., Macmillan,
[c1977]. 1158p.

SCOPE: 90,000 main entries, including biographical, geographical, mythological, and biblical names. Intended for grades 9–12.

WORD TREATMENT: Clear etymologies, full definitions, with many illustrative examples, usage notes, and 1,800 drawings, some in two colors.

Others in this excellent series are *Macmillan School Dictionary*, intended for use in middle school, and *Macmillan Dictionary for Children*, for elementary schools.

→ Rainbow dictionary. Compiled by Wendell W. Wright. Cleveland, Collins/World, 1976. 464p.

SCOPE: 2,300 words found in eight word lists. Updated by editorial staff of *Webster's New World Dictionary*. No encyclopedic material. Intended for grades 1–4.

WORD TREATMENT: Simple definitions, with well-chosen illustrations of use in sentences and 1,100 illustrations in color. Quotations from Mother Goose, Robert Louis Stevenson, Lewis Carroll, etc.

→ Scott, Foresman beginning dictionary. Clarence L. Barnhart, ed. Garden City, N.Y., Doubleday (trade ed.); Glenview, Ill., Scott, Foresman (text ed.), 1976– . 718p.

SCOPE: 25,200 main entries, selected on basis of recent word-frequency counts. Supersedes *Thorndike-Barnhart Beginning Dictionary*. Intended for grades 3–8.

WORD TREATMENT: More than 32,000 definitions, about 23,000 illustrations of use, a few etymologies, pronunciation shown by Thorndike-Barnhart system. Well illustrated, with both color and black-and-white photographs. Kister (p.175) considers it "currently the most authoritative, up-to-date, and best school dictionary available."

→ Thorndike-Barnhart intermediate dictionary. Clarence L. Barnhart, ed. Garden City, N.Y., Doubleday (trade ed.); Glenview, Ill., Scott, Foresman (text ed.), 1971– . 2nd ed. 1974. 985p.

SCOPE: 57,000 entries, including biographical and geographical names. Intended for grades 5–8.

WORD TREATMENT: Clear definitions, well-selected illustrative phrases, and 1,300 illustrations.

→ Thorndike-Barnhart advanced dictionary. Clarence L. Barnhart, ed. Garden City, N.Y., Doubleday (trade ed.); Glenview, Ill., Scott, Foresman (text ed.), 1974. 1186p.

SCOPE: 95,000 entries, including biographical and geographical names, and some new words. Intended for grades 9–12.

WORD TREATMENT: Etymologies, good definitions, illustrative examples, 1,300 b&w illustrations, clearly shown pronunciation. Kister (p.155) considers it "a first choice dictionary for classroom use in American high schools."

→ Webster's New students dictionary. Ed. by Merriam-Webster staff. Springfield, Mass., Merriam (trade ed.); N.Y., American Book Co. (text ed.), 1964– . 1050p. (Five-year revisions.)

SCOPE: 81,000 entries, most frequently encountered by high school students, based on *Webster's Third*; includes foreign words and phrases, slang, biographical and geographical names.

WORD TREATMENT: Pronunciation clearly shown, good definitions, verbal illustrations of use, synonyms, and 535 pictorial illustrations.

Others in this series are *Webster's Intermediate Dictionary*, for middle schools, and *Webster's New Elementary Dictionary*, for elementary schools.

Also very useful in school libraries and media centers is *World Book Dictionary* (discussed earlier). It is intended as a companion to *World Book Encyclopedia*.

Etymological Dictionaries

General dictionaries, notably the *Oxford English Dictionary*, give some attention to word origins, but curiosity about word origins among persons who agree with Ernest Klein's belief, that "to know the origin of words is to know the cultural history of mankind," often leads them to dictionaries devoted exclusively to etymology. Names that come to mind, then, are Skeat, Onions, Partridge, and (more recently) Klein. Skeat's *An Etymological Dictionary of the English Language* has long been considered the standard scholarly work, whose histories of 14,000 words have been greatly revised and expanded to about 38,000 in Onions' *Oxford Dictionary of English Etymology*, which has fewer literary allusions than Skeat. Usage is given by century and semantic change is indicated. Less comprehensive is Partridge's *Origins: A Short Etymological Dictionary of Modern English*, though it may be of more general interest since he groups words that are etymologically related to each other. Also engaging is his enthusiasm, reflected in *Name into Word*, which gives discussions of proper names that have passed into common use in the English language. His foreword concludes: "He who despises the history of words despises the history of mankind; and he who ignores the history of words ignores that one part of himself which can lastingly affect the world outside himself, the sole part that merits a posterity. By the words of others shall we, using intelligence, know them; by our own words do we, if we strive, know ourselves" (p.xiv). This is a stout retort to the question "Who uses an etymological dictionary?" —from a man who was a powerful influence in the field until his death in 1979. (As he said at 80, "I'm one of those bloody fools who don't know when they're beaten" (Shenker, p.120).

Ernest Klein's *A Comprehensive Etymological Dictionary of the English Language* has more entries than the *Oxford Dictionary of English Etymology*. Its subtitle, "dealing with the origin of words and their sense development, thus illustrating the history of civilization and culture," reflects Klein's central purpose. Like Onions, he embodies the findings of modern philological scholarship and gives, for the first time, full reference to Tocharian, the extinct language rediscovered at the end of the nineteenth century. Included among the nearly 50,000 entries are etymologies of proper and mythological names.

→ Klein, Ernest. A comprehensive etymological dictionary of the English language, dealing with the origin of words and their sense development, thus illustrating the history of civiliation and culture. Amsterdam, [etc.], Elsevier, 1966–67. 2v. Unabridged 1v. ed., 1971. 844p.

→ Oxford dictionary of English etymology. Ed. by C. T. Onions with the assistance of G. W. S. Friedrichsen and R. W. Burchfield. Oxford, Clarendon Pr., 1966. 1024p.

→ Partridge, Eric. Name into word: proper names that have become common property. A discursive dictionary. 2nd ed. rev. and enl. N.Y., Macmillan, 1950. 648p.

→ _____. Origins: a short etymological dictionary of modern English. [4th ed.] London, Routledge & Paul, [1966]. 972p.

→ Skeat, Walter William. An etymological dictionary of the English language. New ed., rev. and enl. [4th ed.] Oxford, Clarendon Pr., 1910. 780p.

The development of etymological scholarship is briefly treated in general encyclopedias, and in a more lively fashion by James R. Hulbert, *Dictionaries, British and American*.

Usage

Since good dictionaries record the usage of words, why is it necessary to consult other sources on the subject? This question is well answered in the introductory chapter of Wilson Follett's *Modern American Usage:*

> The first and obvious reply is that a dictionary does not give reasons even when it gives examples of varying usage in one or two brief quotations. Often, what makes a word preferable is its relation to others in a passage. The narrow context of a dictionary sentence gives too few clues to the force and versatility of a particular word. Definitions must be supplemented with discussion. This discussion draws its authority from the principle that good usage is what the people who think and care about words believe good usage to be. . . . The fact that those who attend to language disagree on many points does not alter the nature and force of good usage, any more than the diverse judgments of critics about fine art or of courts about the law alter the nature and force of art and of law [p.6].

The same guide also sets forth the two related purposes of a book on usage:

> By analyzing structural errors and ambiguities it reminds writers and speakers of grammatical norms that are frequently flouted; and by discussing words and idioms it provides a list of distinctions and suggestions in the realm of tact. In neither department can it be complete; it does not pretend to be a grammar book, nor does it profess to discuss every failure of judgment or subtlety in the use of words. It concentrates on the prevailing faults of current speech and prose. And the most useful service it can render is to make its readers think for themselves on these matters. To become sensibly self-conscious about words is more important than to memorize and act on this or that suggestion without thought [p.5].

Books on usage vary widely in contents and reflect the views of their individual compilers to a greater extent than unabridged dictionaries. Thus it is desirable to have a number of them in a well-stocked reference collection, selected with great attention to the authority of the compilers. One of the best known in H. W. Fowler, author of *A Dictionary of Modern English Usage*, published in 1926 and revised in 1965 by Ernest Gowers. Margaret Nicholson, author of *A Dictionary of American-English Usage*, based on Fowler, considers his dictionary indispensable: "Fowler not only teaches you how to write; he is a demon on your shoulder, teaching you how not to write, pointing out and exhibiting, with terrifying clarity, your most cherished foibles: Love of the Long Word, Elegant Variation, Genteelism, Pedantry, Battered Ornaments." Her dictionary is intended as an adaptation of Fowler, not a replacement, with American variations. Longer articles were shortened, and more academic articles and those less pertinent to usage today were omitted, to make room for new entries and illustrations.

Eric Partridge's *Usage and Abusage*, distinguished for its exuberance and wit, supplements Fowler and Nicholson with fuller treatment of battered similes, clichés, and woolliness. Though primarily English in emphasis, it contains some comment on American usage by Professor W. Cabell Greet.

Follett, whose *Modern American Usage* was mentioned earlier, has been ranked by Edward Weeks as one of the two liveliest champions of good English usage in our time, the other being H. W. Fowler. Follett died before he completed his guide and Jacques Barzun finished the work, submitting it to a small group of writers and teachers of English for criticism. The authority of its compilers recommends it. Its positive tone challenges readers to think for themselves, a point that must be remembered. Here is an example: "*exciting*. This by now intolerable word needs no illustration from current sources: it is ubiquitous and nearly meaningless in all contexts" (p.147).

Margaret Bryant, in *Current American Usage*, gives emphasis to frequently debated points of usage, noting regional differences. Based on a cooperative effort of members of the National Council of Teachers of English, her handbook cites dictionaries, current periodical articles, and special investigations of council members as sources.

Bergen and Cornelia Evans, in *A Dictionary of Contemporary American Usage*, admit in their preface that they are prejudiced in favor of literary forms, though they "have tried to present the facts about current usage fairly and accurately." The relative recency of their book and the popularity of its authors have contributed to its use, though it has been the subject of much controversy in supporting contemporary usage more than older ideas of "correctness."

Lighter in tone and of less reference value is the *Harper Dictionary of Contemporary Usage*, whose editors solicited the opinions of "experts" on the use of certain words. The text lacks the conviction of earlier works but its emphasis on contemporary slang, regionalism, and disputed pronunciations lends some interest.

Roy Copperud's *American Usage: The Consensus* gives a readable comparison of seven usage dictionaries and some general dictionaries in their treatments of some problems of usage.

→ Bryant, Margaret M. Current American usage. N.Y., Funk &Wagnalls, [1962]; distributed by Crowell. 290p.

→ Copperud, Roy H. American usage: the consensus. N.Y., Van Nostrand–Reinhold, 1970. 292p.

→ Evans, Bergen, and Evans, Cornelia. A dictionary of contemporary American usage. N.Y., Random, 1957. 567p.

→ Follett, Wilson. Modern American usage; a guide. Ed. and completed by Jacques Barzun (and others). N.Y., Hill & Wang, 1966. 448p.

→ Fowler, Henry Watson. Dictionary of modern English usage. 2nd ed., rev. by Sir Ernest Gowers. Oxford, Oxford Univ. Pr., 1965. 725p.

→ Morris, William, and Morris, Mary. Harper dictionary of contemporary usage. N.Y., Harper & Row, 1975. 650p.

→ Nicholson, Margaret. A dictionary of American-English usage, based on Fowler's Modern English usage. N.Y., Oxford Univ. Pr., 1957. 671p.

→ Partridge, Eric. Usage and abusage; a guide to good English. 6th ed. rev. and slightly enl. London, Hamish Hamilton, 1965; N.Y., British Book Centre, 1965. 392p.

A computer-produced index to notes and articles in *American Notes and Queries* (1962–67), *American Speech* (1925–66), *Britannica Book of the Year* (1945–67), and *Notes and Queries* (1925–66), which is a convenient source for meaning and use of words and phrases, is C. Edward Wall and Edward Przebienda, *Words and Phrases Index* (Ann Arbor, Mich.: Pierian Pr., 1969–70; 4v.).

Synonyms and Antonyms

General dictionaries, both abridged and unabridged, usually treat synonyms and antonyms in their word entries, but many dictionaries are devoted entirely to these forms. Like books on usage, they attempt to give more discussion and examples than a general dictionary. But they must be used with proper caution, as Partridge warns in his *Usage and Abusage:*

> The educated person does not need to be told that, in the desire for variety, to consult a dictionary of synonyms (so called) and take haphazard an apparent synonym is to expose himself to the risk—almost to a certainty—of making himself ridiculous. . . . Sound advice is this:—If you are in doubt as to which of two (or more) synonyms to use, consult a good dictionary that gives abundant examples. And this:—If you want to use two or more synonyms as a stylistic device, make sure that the choice fulfills your purpose [p.327, 1942 ed.].

Margaret Nicholson, in *A Dictionary of American-English Usage*, also notes that "misapprehension of the degree in which words are synonymous is responsible for much bad writing of the less educated kind" (p.566).

Following Partridge's sound advice, experienced writers may turn to Roget's *International Thesaurus*, whose arrangement and comprehensiveness have made it an excellent companion to a good dictionary. Roget set out to make "a collection of words . . . arranged not in alphabetical order, as they are in a Dictionary, but according to the ideas they express." His six primary classes of categories, still observed in the new edition, are: (1) Abstract relations, (2) Space, (3) Matter, (4) Intellect, (5) Volition, and (6) Affections. His stated object was, "the idea being given, to find the word or words by which that idea may be most fitly and aptly described." Dutch, in his preface to the revised 1965 edition, notes that this is the opposite of a dictionary's function, which is, "the word being given, to find its signification or the idea it is intended to convey." Dutch further differentiates between the two functions:

> A thesaurus (in the sense it acquired after Roget used it in the title of his work) does not seek, like a dictionary, to define a word in all its meanings and in one place. Its business is with contexts, not with definitions. It discourses rather than analyzes. It starts with a meaning, not with a word, and sets the words which symbolize some aspect of that meaning in a context, rather like sentences in a book. A valid context exhibits the related aspect of the component words, throwing into relief, by a kind of mutual reflection, those elements of meaning which each individual word can contribute to the governing idea, and suppressing senses which are ambiguous, irrelevant, or incompatible [p.vii–viii].

Careful reading of the preface and study of the six classes and their subdivisions are necessary to any discriminating use of the thesaurus. Many new entries and cross-references have been added to the 1965 edition. As might be expected, the index is longer than the classified section. Its very comprehensiveness makes it a dangerous tool in the hands of those who are not proficient in the English language, especially since it is lacking in discriminations found in *Webster's* and *Funk & Wagnalls*.

Webster's New Dictionary of Synonyms, unlike Roget, is arranged alphabetically, but is quite comprehensive, with copious cross-referenced word clusters of synonyms and with appended antonyms. Meanings are carefully discriminated and illustrations of use are drawn from classical and contemporary writers, using the resources assembled for *Webster's Third*. It was prepared by two associate editors of the Merriam-Webster editorial staff.

Also alphabetically arranged is *Webster's Collegiate Thesaurus,* whose more than 100,000 synonyms, antonyms, idiomatic phrases, and related and contrasted words have been drawn primarily from *Webster's Third*. Although it includes unusual words a bit too freely (giving *whigmaleerie* as a synonym for *caprice*), it is distinguished for the "meaning cores" and verbal illustrations for each main entry, for the use of double bars when necessary to warn the user to consult a dictionary, and for the separation of synonyms from related and contrasted words.

Fewer unusual words will be found in the *Reader's Digest Family Word Finder*. Each main entry is followed by an illustrative sentence or sentences, usually supplied by the editors, and a list of synonyms, arranged in decreasing order of use, with technical, foreign, slang, and informal terms given last. Word origins, usage notes, and notes on pronunciation are supplied for some of the 10,000 alphabetically arranged main entries.

The Synonym Finder, unlike *Webster's Collegiate Thesaurus* does not discriminate between synonyms and related words, or include contrasting words or antonyms, but it is useful for its comprehensiveness (1 million words claimed by the publisher), representing a wide range of usage, both formal and informal, general and technical.

One other example may be cited to illustrate how books on synonyms may vary greatly in content and arrangement. *Funk & Wagnalls Modern Guide to Synonyms* is limited to 6,000 synonyms and related words, fully discussed in about 1,000 essays on clusters of related words, with antonyms listed at the end of those essays to which they apply. Alphabetical arrangement, under headword, is augmented by an index to all the words discussed in the essays. It is distinguished for well-selected and carefully discriminated meanings, for its illustrative quotations (supplied by the staff), and for its emphasis on words in current use.

These are only a few among many such handbooks, selected as well-known examples of classified or alphabetical arrangement.

→ Hayakawa, S. I., ed. Funk & Wagnalls modern guide to synonyms and related words; lists of antonyms, copious cross-references, a complete and legible index. N.Y., Funk & Wagnalls, [1968]. 726p.

→ Reader's Digest family word finder: a new thesaurus of synonyms and antonyms in dictionary form. Pleasantville, N.Y., Reader's Digest Assn., 1975. 896p.

→ Rodale, Jerome Irving. The Synonym finder. Completely rev. by Laurence Urdang and Nancy LaRoche. Emmaus, Pa., Rodale Pr., 1978. 1361p.

→ Roget, Peter Mark. Roget's international thesaurus. Robert L. Chapman, ed. 4th ed. N.Y., Crowell, 1977. 1455p.

→ _____. The original Roget's thesaurus of English words and phrases. New ed. completely revised and modernized by Robert A. Dutch. N.Y., St. Martin's Pr., 1965. Repr. 1978. 1405p.

→ Webster's Collegiate thesaurus. A Merriam-Webster. Springfield, Mass., Merriam, 1976. 944p.

→ Webster's New dictionary of synonyms. Springfield, Mass., Merriam, rev. ed. 1973. 909p.

Pronunciation

A good general dictionary always gives pronunciation and is adequate in most cases. But pronouncing dictionaries, those giving only pronunciation, are often convenient to use when only pronunciation is sought, saving wear and tear on larger dictionaries. Their characteristics include:

1. Emphasis on difficult words in selection of vocabulary
2. Indication of variant pronunciations in different regions, as in *Kenyon and Knott*
3. Inclusion of proper names not always found in general dictionaries, as in *NBC Handbook*
4. No definitions.

Two examples are briefly described below:

→ Kenyon, John Samuel, and Knott, Thomas Albert. A pronuncing dictionary of American English. 2nd ed. Springfield, Mass., Merriam, 1953. 484p.

> Uses the International Phonetic Alphabet to give pronunciation of the colloquial speech of cultivated Americans, noting regional differences; includes proper names—with emphasis on American, some British, and a few foreign—and names in literature and history.

→ NBC handbook of pronunciation. 3rd ed. Originally comp. by James F. Bender for the National Broadcasting Co.; rev. by Thomas Lee Crowell, Jr. N.Y., Crowell, 1964. 418p.

> Uses respelling and phonetic alphabet to give pronunciation of about 20,000 entries, with emphasis on proper names and common words often mispronounced. Aimed at broadcasters.

Since these dictionaries contain fewer entries than unabridged dictionaries, and since many biographical and geographical dictionaries give pronunciation of so many more names, these additional sources must often be used for pronunciation of words not found in pronouncing dictionaries. Also, news magazines and encyclopedias, especially *Encyclopedia Americana*, often give pronunciation of difficult proper names (e.g. the given name of Pope John Paul II).

Slang

"Slang, being the quintessence of colloquial speech, must always be related to convenience rather than to scientific laws, grammatical rules and philosophical ideals. As it originates, so it flourishes best, in colloquial speech." Thus Eric Partridge begins his discussion of the origin, uses, and reasons for use of slang, in his *Slang, Today and Yesterday* (3rd ed. rev.; New York: Macmillan, 1950), p.4.

Though slang is increasingly included in general dictionaries, books on usage, and dictionaries of synonyms, recourse to dictionaries devoted entirely to slang often produces:

1. Definitions of more recent slang
2. Derogatory or taboo words not always found in standard dictionaries
3. More detailed information on the historical origins of slang expressions
4. More illustrative quotations.

For an extended history of slang and dialect, consult Henry Louis Mencken, *The American Language* (4th ed., corr., enl., and rewritten; New York: Knopf, 1936; 769p.; supps. 1–2, 1945–48). Brief observations on the nature of slang and slang dictionaries are given in James R. Hulbert, *Dictionaries, British and American* (p.89–95), which contains the outdated statement that no serious attempt at a dictionary of American slang has been made. This is no longer true, since the first publication (1960) of *Dictionary of American Slang* by Wentworth and Flexner.

Dictionary of American Slang is a good example of a compilation that includes recent slang words and many taboo words not found in general dictionaries. Though it covers all periods of American history in its 22,000 entries, modern slang is emphasized, and the second supplemented edition updates the original by adding the important new slang words and definitions that have become popular since 1960. Its brief definitions are often (but not always) illustrated with quotations and citations to their sources. Words considered taboo are so indicated, as are those used by one group or culture (e.g. drug, student, prison, hot rod). Cant, jargon, and argot, as words and expressions peculiar to special segments of the population, are included when used or understood by the general public and thus become slang. Flexner has added comment on the characteristics of slang and on the sociological factors that influence the creation of a slang vocabulary, as well as the linguistic processes involved in the formation of new slang terms. The large number of periodical articles in the appended bibliography serves as a reminder that current periodical indexes should be consulted, especially for recent terms.

Partridge's *Dictionary of Slang and Unconventional English*, which emphasizes English slang, has been frequently revised since its original 1937 publication, giving further evidence of the rapidly changing nature of slang, with older words passing out of use and new words coming in at an ever increasing rate. Drawn chiefly from printed sources, it is particularly valuable for its quotations, with citation to sources. It is considered the most scholarly of the slang dictionaries, particularly because of its historical approach. As noted earlier, many of the words have been incorporated in the supplement to the *Oxford English Dictionary* (4v.).

Quite different in arrangement and word treatment is the somewhat dated Berry and Van den Bark's *American Thesaurus of Slang*, whose more than 100,000 words are listed under dominant ideas, classes, and occupations, including underworld, sports, military, and western. Entries are given in standard English, with their slang equivalents. Unlike the *Dictionary of American Slang*, it does not give origins or dates of usage, but acknowledges the assistance of a number of consultants in various fields.

→ Berry, Lester V., and Van den Bark, Melvin. American thesaurus of slang. 2nd ed. A complete reference book of colloquial speech. N.Y., Crowell, 1953. 1272p.

→ Partridge, Eric. A dictionary of slang and unconventional English. 7th ed. N.Y., Macmillan, [1970]. 1528p.

→ Wentworth, Harold, and Flexner, Stuart Berg. Dictionary of American slang. 2nd supplemented ed. N.Y., Crowell, 1975. 766p.

These dictionaries are updated in part by *Current Slang: A Quarterly of Slang Expressions Presently in Use* (v.1, no.1, Spring 1966). Each issue of this mimeographed quarterly is devoted to a particular kind of slang—Air Academy, for example—giving meaning, place found, and information about the user for each term. The editors are Stephen H. Dill and Clyde Burkholder, Department of English, University of South Dakota, Vermillion, South Dakota.

Dialect

No attempt will be made here to review the controversies in matters of definition, limits, and acceptability of dialect that exist at the present time. Some consider the concept of dialect as a form of language spoken in a particular area as only relative, but general dictionaries continue to label words as dialect, for example, *Webster's New Collegiate Dictionary*. Perhaps Fowler's definition, in his *Modern English Usage*, will serve: "Dialect is essentially local; a dialect is the variety of a language that prevails in a district, with local peculiarities of vocabulary, pronunciation, and phrase." This agrees substantially with the definition in *Webster's*. We have had dialect dictionaries for a long time, with promise of more to come, employing more recent methods of compilation.

Little has been said to this point about newer processes in the preparation of dictionaries, except that *Random House Dictionary of the English Language* was the first general dictionary to use electronic data processing equipment in its production and that *The American Heritage Dictionary* was produced from data stored on magnetic tapes. But under way for some time is a project in "regional English" that utilizes recent developments in dictionary compilation. It has been described in detail in R. L. Venezky, "Storage, Retrieval, and Editing of Information for a Dictionary" (in *American Documentation* 19:71–79 [Jan. 1968]), with the accompanying abstract:

A computer system has been designed for storing, retrieving, and editing data for the Dictionary of American Regional English (D.A.R.E.). This dictionary, in contrast to most commercial dictionaries, will consist of words which have regional rather than national currency and will derive its entries from data collected by its own fieldworkers, readers, and researchers. Entries, consisting of a headword or phrase, plus descriptors for such items as the user, meaning, pronunciation, and collection technique for this word or phrase are stored in a central file. Interrogations on this file can be made on the value of any headword or description, or any logical combination of such values.

Any portion of an entry which satisfies an interrogation may be designated for retrieval. An experimental editing system employing an on-line CRT (cathrode ray tube) terminal has been developed for the editing process, although a more flexible system will be needed for the actual editing which is scheduled to begin in approximately three years.

Such methods were unknown to Joseph Wright, whose dialect dictionary is described below:

→ Wright, Joseph. English dialect dictionary; being the complete vocabulary of all dialect words still in use, or known to have been in use during the last 200 years; founded on the publications of the English Dialect Society. London, Frowde, 1898–1905. 6v.

SCOPE: English dialect words in use from 1700–1900 in England, Ireland, Scotland, and Wales in both literary and spoken language.
WORD TREATMENT: Gives definition and explanations, geographical area, pronunciation, etymology, and illustrative quotations.

This work has been hailed by Logan Pearsall Smith in his essay on popular speech, in which he says, "Of all the various forms of non-literary English, the local dialects have been most carefully documented and studied; glossaries of all, and grammars of some of them have been published, and the material in these has been put together, with that collected by the Dialect Society, in six volumes of Dr. Wright's immense *Dialect Dictionary*, which is not only one of the greatest lexicographical achievements ever performed by one scholar, but a work for the lover of words of inexhaustible fascination, enabling him, as it does, to explore at ease the wide regions which lie around the streets and suburbs of our polite vernacular." This is quoted in Eric Partridge's *Slang, Today and Yesterday* (p.133–34), which contains an entertaining chapter on the affiliations of slang with dialect, cant, and vulgarisms.

Abbreviations

Thus far we have considered special dictionaries that are primarily concerned with usage, since not only dictionaries of usage but also those of synonyms and slang help a user select the right word for the right time. Also, etymological dictionaries add to the understanding of the true meanings of words. Other special dictionaries are less related to usage but nevertheless supply information that may not be found in a general dictionary. One well-known type is the dictionary of abbreviations.

If slang is increasing, due to our society's becoming fragmented into more and more cultural subgroups, each adding to the general slang vocabulary, certainly the use of abbreviations and acronyms is increasing, and dictionaries of abbreviations and acronyms are hard pressed to keep up with them. Furthermore, the fact that one set of initials may stand for so many different things makes us realize that it is necessary to know their setting to discover the correct equivalent. Thus "ALA" may bring to mind the American Library Association to librarians, but the American Landrace Association to a farmer who raises hogs. And since abbreviations and acronyms are added daily, dictionaries of these forms must be updated by consulting the periodical literature in individual fields, through such indexes as *Education Index, Public Affairs Information Service*, and *Applied Science and Technology Index*, to name only a few.

In selecting dictionaries of this kind, comprehensiveness and currency are of prime importance, especially since good unabridged and desk dictionaries include some abbreviations. Dictionaries in special fields also give attention to abbreviations and acronyms pertinent to the field. Only two recent titles are listed below:

→ Acronyms, initialisms, & abbreviations dictionary: a guide to alphabetic designations, contractions, acronyms, initialisms, abbreviations, and similar condensed appellations. Covering aerospace, associations, biochemistry, business and trade, domestic and internal affairs, education, electronics, genetics, government, labor, medicine, military, pharmacy, physiology, politics, religion, science, societies, sports, technical drawings and specifications, transportation, and other fields. v.1. Ed. by Ellen T. Crowley. 1st ed.– , Detroit, Gale Research, 1960– . Supplemented by v.2, New Acronyms, initialisms, and abbreviations, 1971– , and v.3, Reverse acronyms, initialisms, and abbreviations dictionary. 1st ed.–, 1972– .

> Since its first edition in 1960, this frequently revised and updated guide has increased from 12,000 entries to 130,000, with each annual supplement (v.2), adding about 12,000 more. V.3 rearranges contents of v.1 under complete words or phrases. The introduction should be read for editorial policies; for example, if an acronym is found in several forms, all are included. The large number of entries under one contraction (a full column of AD's) requires care in searching. For an assessment of its strong and weak points, see *Booklist* (Feb. 15, 1977), p.918.

→ DeSola, Ralph. Abbreviations dictionary. 1st ed.– . N.Y., Elsevier North–Holland, 1958– . Latest, 5th ed., 1978.

> Contains over 40,000 abbreviations, acronyms, anonyms, contractions, initials and nicknames, short forms and slang shortcuts, signs and symbols, some of them not found in *Acronyms, Initialisms . . .* (listed above), which in turn has many entries not found in DeSola. Revised at intervals.

One type of abbreviation which must be singled out for special mention is that of periodical titles. These abbreviations often present real problems of identification, especially in the field of science and technology. Here the *World List of Scientific Periodicals Published in the Years 1900–1960* (4th ed., ed. by Peter Brown and George Burder Stratton; 3v.; London: Butterworths, 1963–65) is particularly helpful since it supplies the standard abbreviations for 60,000 titles of periodicals concerned with the natural sciences and technology. It has been kept up to date by the *British Union–Catalogue of Periodicals*. (The value of national library catalogs as a source of abbreviations has been noted earlier.) Also useful are periodical indexes, which usually include a list of periodicals indexed, together with the abbreviations used.

Special Fields

The increasing specialization of our age has naturally led to increasingly specialized vocabularies, which in turn require an increasing number of dictionaries in subject fields. They take various forms, including:

1. Encyclopedic dictionaries (giving not only definitions of terms but other descriptive information, brief biographies of persons prominent in the field, and agencies active in the field)
2. Monolingual dictionaries (restricted largely to definitions of terms)
3. Bilingual dictionaries (restricted largely to pertinent words in one language with their equivalents in another language)
4. Polyglot dictionaries (giving equivalents in two or more languages).

Only the monolingual dictionary in a subject field is considered here, and a good one should meet the following criteria:

1. It should be sponsored by an active association in the field, concerned with standardizing the vocabulary of the field or, at least, with recording the existing vocabulary as used by specialists.
2. It should have an informed editorial board, concerned with setting sound criteria for selection and treatment of terms.
3. Its vocabulary should be selected from a wide range of books and current journals in the field.

A carefully compiled dictionary in a subject field should supplement a general dictionary by providing:

1. More new words and trade names in the field
2. More highly specialized terms in the field
3. Accurate difinitions in terms of the subject, more fully treated, and with added descriptive matter when pertinent, including diagrams and other illustrations as needed
4. Illustrative quotations from cited authorities in the field, when pertinent
5. Balanced and unbiased treatment of abstract terms on which there is a difference of opinion
6. Revised editions when necessary to keep up with expanding vocabulary.

Barratt Wilkins has compared twelve subject dictionaries (six from the sciences and six from the social sciences) with *Webster's Third New International Dictionary*. Based on a check of 180 terms, he justifies the usefulness of subject dictionaries because of the number of terms not found in the unabridged dictionary and because of the quality of their definitions (*RQ* 9:234–36 [Spring 1970]).

The demand for specialized dictionaries has led some publishers to issue hastily prepared volumes, which add little to what may be found in a good, up-to-date unabridged dictionary, though Hulbert says:

> It is, however, only fair to the general lexicographer, whether commercial or historical, to point out that his main function is to explain the whole vocabulary of the language, and that if one wants sure definition of technical words and uses one should consult a more specialized lexicon, e.g. of philosophy, social sciences, medicine, etc. Heaven help the maker of a specialized dictionary if his definitions are not accurate! It is his job to make them so [p.76].

It should also be noted that special dictionaries often are not concerned with etymology, syllabication, or pronunciation. Thus special dictionaries must be selected with care, after determining whether they augment the general dictionary sufficiently to warrant purchase, especially in a general library.

Since only a few special dictionaries are discussed here, some of the most useful sources for dictionaries in other fields must be reviewed. Many can be located in the index to *Sheehy*, where they are cited under subject, as *Biological sciences—dictionaries*. Additional titles will be found in guides to the literature of subject fields (as noted in the earlier chapter on bibliography). Also useful for detailed commentary are encyclopedias in special subject fields, an excellent example being the article on dictionaries in the *Encyclopedia of Philosophy*.

A very exhaustive list of subject dictionaries in the Library of Congress is found in *Dictionaries, Encyclopedias and Other Word-Related Books* (Detroit: Gale, 1975–). This includes titles catalogued since 1966.

Examples from the fields of librarianship and publishing, with which librarians should be familiar, are:

→ American Library Association. Committee on Library Terminology. A.L.A. glossary of library terms, with a selection of terms in related fields, prep. by Elizabeth H. Thompson. Chicago, ALA, 1943. 159.

→ Bookman's glossary. 5th ed., ed. by Jean Peters. N.Y., Bowker, 1975. 169p.

→ Harrod, Leonard M. The librarian's glossary of terms used in librarianship, documentation and the book crafts, and reference books. 4th rev. ed. Boulder, Colo., Westview Pr., 1977. 903p.

→ Orne, Jerrold. The language of the foreign book trade; abbreviations, terms, phrases. 3rd ed. Chicago, ALA, 1976. 333p.

→ Thompson, Anthony. Vocabularium bibliothecarii. 2nd ed. English, French, German, Spanish, Russian. Paris, UNESCO, 1962. 627p.

Social Sciences

The large number of dictionaries in the social sciences may be explained not only by the increasing vocabulary but by the need to standardize the existing vocabulary. Titles listed below are intended to demonstrate how they have proliferated in recent decades, most of them having been published since 1970.

→ Ammer, Christine, and Ammer, Dean S. Dictionary of business and economics. N.Y., Free Press, 1977. 461p.

→ Banki, Ivan S. Dictionary of administration and supervision. Los Angeles, Systems Research, 1971. 131p.

→ _____. Dictionary of supervision and management. Los Angeles, Systems Research, 1976. 276p.

→ Encyclopedia of anthropology. Ed. by David F. Hunter and Phillip Whitten. N.Y., Harper & Row, 1976. 411p.

→ Encyclopedia of computer science. Anthony Ralston, ed. N.Y., Petrocelli/Charter, 1976. 1523p.

→ English, Horace, and English, Ava C. A comprehensive dictionary of psychology and psychological terms. N.Y., Longmans, 1958. 594p.

→ Good, Carter V. Dictionary of education. 3rd ed. N.Y., McGraw-Hill, 1973. 681p.

→ Gould, Julius, and Kolb, William L., eds. A dictionary of the social sciences. N.Y., Free Pr. of Glencoe, 1964. 761p.

→ Greenwald, Douglas, and others, eds. The McGraw-Hill Dictionary of modern economics. 2nd ed. N.Y., McGraw-Hill, 1973. 792p.

→ Hinsie, Leland E., and Campbell, R. J., Psychiatric dictionary. 4th ed. N.Y., Oxford Univ. Pr., 1970. 928p.

→ Johannsen, Hans, and Page, G. Terry. International dictionary of management. Boston, Houghton Mifflin, 1975. 416p.

→ Kohler, Eric L. A dictionary for accountants. 5th ed. Englewood Cliffs, N.J., Prentice-Hall, [1975]. 497p.

→ Mitchell, Geoffrey D. A dictionary of sociology. Chicago, Aldine, 1968. 224p.

→ Moore, Norman D. Dictionary of business, finance, and investment. N.Y., Drake, 1976. 542p.

→ Roberts, Harold S. Roberts' dictionary of industrial relations. rev. ed. Wash., Bur. of Nat. Affairs, 1971. 599p.

→ Sloan, Harold S., and Zurcher, Arnold J. Dictionary of economics. 5th ed. N.Y., Barnes & Noble, 1971. 520p.

→ Wolman, Benjamin B., ed. Dictionary of behavioral science. N.Y., Van Nostrand–Reinhold, 1973. 478p.

→ Wortman, Leon A. A deskbook of business management terms. N.Y., AMACON, 1979. 640p.

Foreign-Language Dictionaries

Monolingual dictionaries of languages other than English follow the same patterns and have the same general purposes as English-language dictionaries. The same criteria may be applied in evaluating their adequacy. They require that the user have some familiarity with the language represented and are thus not as often consulted by beginning students as the bilingual dictionary, whose characteristics must be considered separately. Compared with general monolingual dictionaries, bilingual dictionaries

1. Have a more limited vocabulary
2. Give little or no historical information
3. Give less attention to etymologies
4. Give pronunciation and stress
5. Give parts of speech and genders
6. Give equivalents in another language
7. Indicate levels and fields of usage, e.g. slang
8. Give illustrative phrases
9. Often include proper names
10. Often include sections on grammar
11. Often consider the nationality of the intended user.

Polyglot dictionaries, those which give equivalents in three or more languages, are most often found in scientific and technical fields and are not considered here.

Foreign-language dictionaries are generously represented in Sheehy's *Guide*, both in the section on general dictionaries and under special subjects, like chemistry and physics. Further commentary or additional titles may be found in guides by Collison and Walford, as noted below:

→ Collison, Robert Lewis. Dictionaries of English and foreign languages, a bibliographical guide to both general and technical dictionaries, with historical and explanatory notes and references. 2nd ed. N.Y., Hafner, 1971. 303p.

> Early and modern English-language dictionaries, Celtic languages, and comparative philology have been added to the updated sections on the languages of Europe, Asia, and Africa, and dialect dictionaries for a number of European countries, found in the first edition. Many titles are critically annotated.

→ Walford, A. J., and Screen, J. E. O. A guide to foreign language courses and dictionaries. 3rd ed. rev. and enl. London, Lib. Assn.; Westport, Conn., Greenwood, 1977. 343p.

> Annotates dictionaries in most of the main European languages, plus Arabic, Chinese, and Japanese. Also includes courses and audiovisual aids.

Guides to individual subject fields (examples are found in the chapter on bibliography) are also good sources for bilingual and polyglot dictionaries in a particular field.

All of these sources are of help in determining what is available or which are more suitable for various types of libraries or users. But since new editions of established titles, as well as newly compiled dictionaries, are published with increasing frequency, current trade bibliographies should be consulted for more recent publications. Also useful is the catalog issued at intervals by Stechert-Macmillan, Inc., *The World's Languages Catalog*, a listing by some 300 languages of about 4,000 general dictionaries and grammars, and by subject for more than 100 specialized dictionaries.

Listed below are a few examples of general monolingual and bilingual dictionaries for languages most frequently studied in the United States. Their scope and word treatment are noted briefly, with occasional commentary quoted from other sources.

First, however, are a few general sources of foreign words and phrases often found in English texts or spoken English. Two of the better known are

C. O. Sylvester Mawson, *Dictionary of Foreign Terms* (2nd ed. rev. and updated by Charles Berlitz; New York: Crowell, 1975; 368p.), and Mario Pei and Salvatore Ramondino, *Dictionary of Foreign Terms* (New York: Delacorte, 1974; 366p). These contain both classical and modern terms and phrases, their pronunciation, and English equivalents, many of them not found in general English-language dictionaries.

French

→ Littré, Émile. Dictionnaire de la langue française. Éd. intégrale. Paris, Jean-Jacques Pauvert, 1956–58. 7v.

> SCOPE: About 70,000 entries.
> WORD TREATMENT: Includes syllabication, etymology, history, definitions, and illustrative quotations with exact citation to sources. According to Walford, it is "particularly rich in examples, ranging from the 9th to the 17th centuries . . . on the etymological side, the work needs supplementing by more recently compiled dictionaries."

→ Robert, Paul. Dictionnaire alphabétique et analogique de la langue française; les mots et les associations d'idées . . . Paris, Société du Nouveau Littré, 1970. 6v.; supp., 1970, 514p. Distributed in the U.S. by Paris Publications, Port Washington, N.Y.

> SCOPE: Historical dictionary, including words from the literary language and current, technical, scientific, and regional terms. Highly recommended as a dictionary and a thesaurus.
> WORD TREATMENT: Gives pronunciation, etymology, part of speech, gender, history of word from date of first-known usage, definitions, synonyms, antonyms, cross-references to words and quotations with related meaning, and 120,000 quotations from French writers, including recent ones, with citation to sources.

> *Le Petit Robert* (10th ed., 1972), a 1v. abridgment, retains a great part of the original, but gives fewer quotations, uses a different pronunciation key, and treats etymologies more briefly.

→ Harrap's new standard French and English dictionary, ed. by J. E. Mansion. Completely rev. and enl. Ed. by R. P. L. and Margaret Ledésert. N.Y., Scribner, [1971–72]. Pt. 1 in 2v.

> SCOPE: Contains about 100,000 main entries, with 60 percent more material than in earlier edition, larger scientific and technical vocabulary, and more French-Canadian and slang.

WORD TREATMENT: Pronunciation (International Phonetic Alphabet), part of speech, translation, variant and specialized meanings, labels for archaic, obsolete, literary, vulgar, slang and colloquial words, and field labels (e.g. Bot.).

→ Larousse modern French-English (English-French) dictionary by Marguerite-Marie Dubois (and others). N.Y., McGraw-Hill, c1960. 2v. in 1. Later printings.

SCOPE: Modern, including colloquial and slang terms, Americanisms, scientific and technical terms, and geographical names.

WORD TREATMENT: Gives part of speech, gender, pronunciation (International Phonetic Alphabet), equivalents, and usage labels.

→ New Cassell's French dictionary: French-English, English-French, Compl. rev. by Denis Girard (and others). N.Y., Funk & Wagnalls, [1962]. 762p., 655p. Later printings.

SCOPE: Modern, including technical, scientific, slang and French-Canadian words in current use, and obsolete words in literature.

WORD TREATMENT: Indicates some plurals, irregular verbs, gender, part of speech, some compound and derivative words, translations of phrases and expressions, illustrative examples, and pronunciation (International Phonetic Alphabet).

German

→ Grimm, Jacob, and Grimm, Wilhelm. Deutsches Wörterbuch. Im Auftrage des Deutschen Reiches und Preussens mit Unterstützung des Reichministeriums des Innern, des Preussischen Ministeriums für Wissenschaft, Kunst und Volksbildung, und der Notgemeinschaft der deutschen Wissenschaft hrsg. von der Preussischen Akademie der Wissenschaften. Leipzig, Hirzel, 1854–1960. 16v. New ed. in progress. Bd. 1– . 1965– .

SCOPE: Words of the literary language from about the end of the 15th century, omitting obsolete words.

WORD TREATMENT: Compiled on historical principles, resembles *Oxford English Dictionary*. Gives etymology, history, use in different regions, and many illustrative quotations. The standard German dictionary.

→ Der Sprach-Brockhaus. Deutsches Bildwörterbuch für Jedermann. 7. durchgesehene Aufl. Wiesbaden, Brockhaus, 1958. 800p.

SCOPE: About 30,000 entries, including technical terms, colloquialisms, abbreviations, and geographical names.

→ Harrap's Standard German and English dictionary. Ed. by Trevor Jones. London, Harrap, 1963– . v.1– (In progress)

SCOPE: Covers 19th century to present, with emphasis on literary, historical, political, and scientific terms. Includes proverbs and proper names. V.3 (1974) covers *L* to *R*.

WORD TREATMENT: German-English volume gives part of speech, pronunciation (International Phonetic Alphabet), English equivalents (American English given only when British English is unsatisfactory), and examples of usage. Self-evident compounds are omitted and each word is treated separately.

→ Langenscheidt's New Muret-Sanders encyclopedic dictionary of the English and German languages. Compl. rev. 1962. Ed. by Otto Springer. London, Methuen; N.Y., Barnes & Noble, 1962–75. 2 pts. in 4v.

SCOPE: About 180,000 entries, including scientific and technical terms, idiomatic phrases, colloquialisms, geographical and biographical names.

WORD TREATMENT: English-German part gives pronunciation (International Phonetic Alphabet), syllabication, etymology, part of speech, illustrative phrases, idiomatic expressions, synonyms, field and geographical labels, with equal treatment of American English and British English in pronunciation, spelling, and vocabulary. Outstanding bilingual dictionary.

→ New Cassell's German dictionary: German-English, English-German, based on the editions by Karl Breul, compl. rev. and re-edited by Harold T. Betteridge. N.Y., Funk & Wagnalls, [1958]. 629p., 619p. Frequently reprinted.

SCOPE: Modern, with some attention to literary, scientific, colloquial, and slang terms. Appendixes of geographical and personal names, and abbreviations.

WORD TREATMENT: Indicates gender, part of speech, equivalents, illustrative phrases, synonyms, levels of usage, and pronunciation (English words only). A favorite of students.

→ Wildhagen, Karl, and Héraucourt, Will. The new Wildhagen German dictionary; German-English, English-German. Chicago, Follett, 1965. 1296p., 1061p.

SCOPE: Modern, with emphasis on present-day language, including poetic, colloquial, dialect, and slang terms.

WORD TREATMENT: Gives part of speech, gender, pronunciation (International Phonetic Alphabet), "with special regard to syntax, style, and idiomatic usage" (according to its subtitle).

Greek

→ Kykkōtēs, Hierotheos. English-modern Greek and modern Greek-English dictionary; including English and Greek grammar, geographical and proper names, and abbreviations. 3rd ed. London, P. Lund, 1957. 2v. in 1 (644p.)

SCOPE: About 45,000 entries. "This work was never intended to be an example of scientific lexicography" (Pref.).

WORD TREATMENT: Gives part of speech, gender, pronunciation, equivalents, and examples of usage. Valuable combination.

→ Liddell, Henry George, and Scott, Robert. Greek-English lexicon . . . A new ed. rev. and aug. throughout by Henry Stuart Jones . . . with the assistance of Roderick McKenzie . . . and with the cooperation of many scholars . . . [9th ed.]. Oxford, Clarendon Pr., 1925–40. 2111p; supp., 1968.

SCOPE: About 10,000 entries for classical Greek to A.D. 600, omitting Patristic and Byzantine Greek, including some scientific and technical terms, Latin and Semitic words, and proper names.

WORD TREATMENT: Gives part of speech, pronunciation, little etymology, and many illustrative quotations with citation to source. Indispensable.

Italian

→ Battaglia, Salvatore. Grande dizionario della lingua italiana. Turin, Unione Tipografico-Editrice Torinese, 1961– . v.1–. (In progress; v.9, Lib–Med, 1975)

SCOPE: A scholarly historical dictionary, resembling *Oxford English Dictionary*.

WORD TREATMENT: Gives etymology, gender, part of speech, full definitions in historical order, and illustrative quotations with citation to sources.

A good, up-to-date illustrated dictionary with an extensive vocabulary is:

→ Devoto, Giacomo, and Oli, Gian Carlo. Vocabolario illustrato della lingua italiana. N.Y., Funk & Wagnalls, [1968]. 2v.

→ Hazon, Mario. Garzanti comprehensive Italian-English, English-Italian dictionary. N.Y., McGraw-Hill, 1963. 2090p.

> SCOPE: About 120,000 entries for words in current use, including literary, scientific, commercial, slang, and colloquial terms.
>
> WORD TREATMENT: Gives gender, part of speech, field label, illustrative phrases, and pronunciation, using accent marks for Italian, International Phonetic Alphabet for English. Coverage is excellent.

→ Reynolds, Barbara. The Cambridge Italian dictionary. Cambridge, Cambridge Univ. Pr., 1962– . v.1– . (In progress)

> SCOPE: About 50,000 entries, including little-used and obsolete words as well as those in current use and scientific and technical terms. From the point of view of the English-speaking user (Intro.).
>
> WORD TREATMENT: Gives equivalent (with definition when necessary), part of speech, and labels for obsolete and specialized words, with limited attention to etymology and pronunciation.

→ _____. The concise Cambridge Italian dictionary. Cambridge, Cambridge Univ. Pr., 1975.

> Based on the incomplete *Cambridge Italian Dictionary*. Gives both Italian-English and English-Italian.

Latin

→ Harper's Latin dictionary. A new Latin dictionary founded on the translation of Freund's Latin-German lexicon, ed. by E. A. Andrews. Rev., enl., and in great part rewritten by Charlton T. Lewis and Charles Short. N.Y., Cincinnati, Amer. Book Co., 1907. Repr.: Oxford, Clarendon Pr., 1955. 2019p.

> SCOPE: Classical, to A.D. 600, with about 60,000 entries, including geographical and biographical names.
>
> WORD TREATMENT: Gives pronunciation (using accents), gender, part of speech, declension, conjugation, equivalents, and many illustrative quotations with exact citation to sources.

> The standard bilingual dictionary.

→ Cassell's New Latin-English, English-Latin dictionary, by D. P. Simpson. London, Cassell; N.Y., Macmillan, 1977 [c1959]. 883p.

> SCOPE: About 30,000 entries. Latin vocabulary covers most of the words used by classical authors from about 200 B.C. to A.D. 100. Includes proper names.
>
> WORD TREATMENT: Gives indication of vowel length, gender, part of speech, declension, conjugation, equivalents, and illustrative quotations with citation to author only.

Russian

→ Akademiia Nauk SSSR. Institut Russkogo IAzyka. Slovar' sovremennogo russkogo literaturnogo iazyka. Moskva, 1950–65. 17v.

> SCOPE: Literary, artistic, social, political, and general scientific vocabulary of the 19th and 20th centuries, including many loan words from other languages. About 15,000 entries in each volume.
>
> WORD TREATMENT: Gives field labels, variant meanings and forms, derivations, references to other dictionaries, and many illustrative quotations with citation to sources.

> "This exhaustive dictionary will doubtless rank as one of the world's greatest lexicographical achievements. Indispensable for advanced studies" (Rosemary Neiswender, *Guide to Russian Reference and Language Aids* [N.Y., Special Libraries Assn., 1962], p.22).

→ Miuller (Müller), Vladimir Karlovich, comp. English-Russian dictionary. 14th ed., N.Y., Dutton, [1973]. 912p.

> SCOPE: Modern, containing about 70,000 words, including scientific, technical, socio-political, and specialized terms. Appended list of personal and geographic names.
>
> WORD TREATMENT: Gives pronunciation according to International Phonetic Alphabet, part of speech, commonest meaning first, with illustrative quotations.

> "Addressed primarily to Russian students of English but still the best in its field for the English-speaking reader" (Neiswender, p.27). Considered inferior to *New English-Russian Dictionary*, ed. by I. R. Galperin [Moscow, 1972], by reviewer in *Choice* (10:1848 [Feb. 1974]).

→ Wheeler, Marcus. The Oxford Russian-English dictionary. B. O. Unbegaun, gen. ed. Oxford, Clarendon Pr., 1972. 918p.

scope: About 50,000 entries. "This work is intended as a general-purpose dictionary of Russian as it is written and spoken. It is designed primarily, though not exclusively, for the use of those whose native language is English" (Intro.).

Spanish

→ Academia Española, Madrid. Diccionario histórico de la lengua española. Seminario de Lexicografía: Director, Julio Casares . . . Madrid, 1960– . Pt.1– . (In progress)

scope: Major historical dictionary, resembling *Oxford English Dictionary*.

word treatment: Gives gender, part of speech, etymology, meanings in historical order, and many illustrative quotations with citation to sources.

→ Crowell's Spanish-English and English-Spanish dictionary by Gerd A. Gillhoff. N.Y., Crowell, 1966. 1261p.

scope: Strong in Spanish-American vocabulary, including scientific, slang, technical, commercial, colloquial, and idiomatic terms. Appended outline of Spanish grammar.

word treatment: Gives gender, part of speech, equivalents, some examples of usage, and indication of use in individual Spanish-American countries.

→ Cuyás, Arturo. Appleton's New Cuyás English-Spanish and Spanish-English dictionary. Rev. and enl. by Lewis E. Brett (Pt. I) and Helen S. Eaton (Pt. II). Revision ed., Catherine B. Avery. 5th ed. N.Y., Appleton, 1972. 698p., 589p.

scope: More than 130,000 entries. Modern, including technical terms and words in use in Spanish America and Philippine Islands. Appended lists of geographical and personal names.

word treatment: Gives gender, pronunciation for English and difficult Spanish words, equivalents, major different applications of terms, and usage labels.

One of the better bilingual dictionaries.

→ Simon and Schuster's International dictionary. Diccionario international Simon and Schuster. English/Spanish, Spanish/English. Tana de Gámez, ed. in chief. N.Y., Simon and Schuster, [1973]. 1605p.

SCOPE: More than 200,000 entries, including scientific and technical terms, vulgarisms, proper and place names, and abbreviations.

WORD TREATMENT: International Phoentic Alphabet used to indicate English words. Both British and American pronunciation shown, if they differ; also British and American usage. Many illustrative phrases augment the definitions.

→ Velázquez de la Cadena, Mariano [and others]. New revised Velázquez Spanish and English dictionary. Newly revised by Ida Navarro Hinojosa, Manuel Blanco-González, and Richard John Wiezell. Chicago, Follett [1974]. 698p., 788p. 2v. in 1.

SCOPE: About 151,000 entries. Modern, with particular attention to terms and idioms used in Spanish America and United States. Appended lists of geographical and personal names.

WORD TREATMENT: Gives pronunciation, gender, part of speech, various meanings, illustrative phrases, and usage labels.

The second-best bilingual dictionary.

→ ———. A new pronouncing dictionary of the Spanish and English languages. Comp. . . . with Edward Gray and Juan Iribas. Rev. ed. N.Y., Appleton-Century-Crofts. 1973. 2v. in 1.

First published in 1852, frequently revised. Authoritative.

A useful dictionary, available in paperback, is Edwin B. Williams, *Bantam New College Spanish and English Dictionary* (Bantam, 1968, and later printings).

Summary

In summary, libraries have a responsibility for providing a well-selected range of dictionaries for their users, and their librarians must provide informed instruction, based on thorough knowledge of a dictionary's purpose, for (as Confucius said long ago) "When words lose their meaning, the people will lose their liberty."

This chapter has tried to explain how and why dictionaries are made; the differences between unabridged and abridged dictionaries; dictionaries concerned with etymologies, usage, synonyms and antonyms, pronunciation, slang and dialect, abbreviations; dictionaries restricted to special fields; and monolingual and bilingual foreign dictionaries—with brief descriptions of some in current use.

5

Encyclopedias

*It is wise to refer to encyclopedias for first
guidance; it is priggish to disregard them;
it is foolish to depend too much on them.*

—GEORGE SARTON
GUIDE TO THE HISTORY OF SCIENCE

How does one begin to discuss those monumental syntheses of knowledge, encyclopedias, so often maligned? Perhaps these attempts of mankind through the ages to bring order to the circle of knowledge should be approached first as reflections of the eras in which they were compiled—an important fact to remember in viewing their assets and limitations.

The era in which they were produced reflects not only the state of knowledge at that time but also their underlying purposes. As Warren E. Preece has observed, "Encyclopedias may be undertaken, as in classical Greece, to 'make a man whole,' as in Medieval Europe, to 'make a man Christian,' as in 18th-Century France, to 'make a man free'" ("The Organization of Knowledge and the Planning of Encyclopedias," *Journal of World History* 9, no.3:798–818 [1966]). Challenging Raymond Queneau's statement that encyclopedias are the product of culminating civilizations, he suggests "that encyclopaedias have enjoyed their greatest successes, have seemed to attain their greatest vitality, in those periods of history of which it might be said—at least in retrospect—that the world was held in an uneasy balance between the death of one age and the birth of another. It is possible to conjecture that it is in the midst of the tensions created by the imminent decline of one intellectual tradition and the imminent evolution of another that the function of the encyclopaedist and the support accorded him have assumed their greatest proportions." And Preece cites examples to prove his point.

Others, in reviewing the history of encyclopedias, have noted the spirit of the age, as in the eighteenth century, the classic age of encyclopedias, when Diderot's great French *Encyclopédie* was said to incorporate the basic philosophy of eighteenth-century French rationalism. This has been recently documented in Robert Darton's *The Business of Enlightenment: A Published History of the Encyclopédie, 1775–1800* (Cambridge, Mass.: Belknap Pr. of Harvard Univ. Pr., 1979). In the twentieth century, nationalism, sectarianism, political trends, and new educational theory have been important factors in the production of hundreds of encyclopedias.

Certainly the growth of education has affected the making of encyclopedias, and the earlier compilations of information intended for the intellectual élite were gradually replaced by those addressed to the general reader, as in the nineteenth century, when Brockhaus chose *Konversations-Lexikon* as the title for his simply written, popular encyclopedia to intimate to his readers, largely members of the middle class, that his work contained the polite learning that could provide the means of acceptance into good society.

More recently, the expansion of public education has stimulated the publication of encyclopedias for children and young people, whose contents and style of writing are directed to this particular audience.

Most important has been the growth of knowledge, as well as its accessibility. Preece emphasizes the necessity that the encyclopedist have access to this body of extant knowledge. "It must be pointed out that in practical terms this today is equivalent to saying that he must have access to the scholar, the authority, the specialist whose particular work it is, and has been, to husband knowledge . . . . When the encyclopaedist talks today of access to the body of knowledge, he means, therefore, the world of those whose business knowledge is" (p.803).

The encyclopedist must view this body of knowledge with a clear sense of purpose. Much has been written on the purpose of encyclopedias, some of it repetitious and some of it representing conflicting points of view. Many will agree with Preece, who attributes the existence of encyclopedias to a desire to bring order to existing knowledge (p.799). Among other writers of this century, we find Charles Van Doren endorsing the opinion of Lucien Febvre, editor of the *Encyclopédie Française*, that the primary aim should be to teach, and only secondarily to inform ("The Idea of an Encyclopedia," *The American Behavioral Scientist* 6:23 [Sept. 1962]). On the other hand, Jacques Barzun, in the same journal, views an encyclopedia as first and foremost a work of reference, used only indirectly for undersanding ("Notes on Making a World Encyclopedia," p.7–14). Harry S. Ashmore, writing as editor in chief of the *Encyclopaedia Britannica* in the same issue, describes the encyclopedia "as a countinuing link between the academic and lay worlds, a work of factual reference, certainly, but also a major instrument of popular education. . . . . It will not, of course, repeat all the expert knows, or needs to know. An encyclopedia is not, and should not be, a textbook—a fact which seems to elude the single-minded who fault the work for its failure to include esoteric matter of their specialized interest" ("Editing the Universal Encyclopedia," p.15–18).

These are all men of the twentieth century, who must inevitably view the encyclopedia in terms of this century. Whether they face a more difficult task than their predecessors cannot be finally stated, but the increasing proliferation and complexity of knowledge, together with the responsibility of bringing it into some order and awareness of the changing audience for whom it is intended, present problems. Will it be possible for them to produce a set of volumes that will meet the needs of the scholar as well as those of the vaguely defined general reader? Certainly scholars have become more highly specialized in their scholarly interests, but are they not also men with intellectual curiosity about subjects outside their specialities? And if this be true, do they not share this in common with the general reader? Alas, this does not seem to be the case, for their realization of the complexity of knowledge makes scholars suspicious of syntheses, contemptuous of generalizations, narrowly snobbish about the encyclopedia as a form. Yet editors of encyclopedias are increasingly dependent on scholars as contributors, though often hard put to translate their articles into a language that is comprehensible to the general reader.

Warren Preece, editor of the *Britannica*, believes that the 15th edition of this respected encyclopedia has answered, at least in part, the needs of the times. In "The New Britannica" (reprinted from *Scholarly Publishing*, January and April 1974), he describes the planning and the efforts which went into the edition, saying, "It is reasonable and probably not too flippant to submit that by the twentieth century general eneyclopaedias had become almost neurotic in their ambivalence. Although their limited size and scale and necessarily broad scope made them unsuitable sources of knowledge for the specialist in his own field, they were written by specialists on the basis of advice provided by specialists and edited by persons who had begun to acquire editorial skills only after they had first become specialists" (p.101).

Revision of contents is a very sensitive point with editors, for encyclopedias may be revised in a number of different ways:

In arrangement, e.g. *Book of Knowledge*, which changed in 1966 from topical to alphabetical arrangement. *By continuous revision*, favored by American encyclopedia publishers, who develop various kinds of programs, e.g. *Americana*, with revision of areas requiring "urgent" attention and revision volume-by-volume, with all articles in the volume being reviewed, with some dropped, new ones added, and others updated or rewritten. *Compton's Encyclopedia* has a program which involves updating population statistics, noting deaths and revision of certain areas rather than single volumes. Both add new illustrations and drop old ones when necessary. *By new editions. New Columbia Encyclopedia*, 1975 edition, is a thorough revision of the earlier edition.

These revisions require editorial decisions. Also, in their efforts to keep the size within bounds, editors must determine the amount of space devoted to various subject fields, and to illustrations, bibliographies, and indexes. They must deal with how the contents should be arranged and with how to avoid accusations of bias. And these are not all the problems to be faced.

What man would undertake this task alone? No one. Thus the modern encyclopedia has become the product of many men. What are their qualifications? What specific problems do they face? It seems appropriate to outline these points in the making of a good general encyclopedia, as we did in the preceding chapter on dictionaries. (For guidelines for reviewing general English-language encyclopedias, see the appendix.)

The Making of Encyclopedias

I. Staff
   A. The editor, his qualities and capacities. According to Otto White-lock in his "On the Making and Survival of Encyclopedias" (*Choice* 4:381–89 [June 1967]), the requirements are:
      1. A universal mind (in the sense that the editor is not wedded to a single discipline to the exclusion of all others), able to grasp the significance of new developments and integrate them into existing material
      2. Thorough familarity with the encyclopedia for whose balance and progress he is responsible
      3. Faith in his or her capacities and willingness to enlist the assistance of men and women of equal caliber, without fear of being overshadowed by those more expert in a given field
      4. Ability to serve as a competent catalyst.

      More practical considerations, mentioned by Robert Collison in *Encyclopedias: Their History throughout the Ages* (p.13–14), are:

      1. He has a strict publication schedule to observe.
      2. He must keep his eye on his rivals' efforts.
      3. He must watch his own staff and his outside contributors to ensure that wittingly or unwittingly they do not plagiarize material already published elsewhere.
      4. He must cooperate with editors' offices in other countries, and with the demands of the sales force who know that scholarship

must be tempered with popularity and a due regard for current interests however ephemeral, if the sets of the encyclopedia are not to lie unused on the warehouse shelves. [Ashmore would not agree with the latter, having "never heard of any of my editorial contemporaries on major encyclopedias complain of pressures toward corruption of editorial content in the name of sales promotion," p.16.]

5. He must keep up-to-date with modern scholarship, with political trends and controversies, and with the new topics and names that spring into fame overnight.
6. Unprejudiced himself, he must be cognizant of prejudices in others, and temper his contributors' opinions to safeguard his readers' susceptibilities.
7. All this must be done without lowering his own standards.

B. Board of editors
   1. Selected for their breadth of interests and their concern for the organization of knowledge
   2. Responsible for suggesting long-range improvements
   3. Responsible for advising editors on broad problems, just as the editorial board of a good dictionary functions.

   Wallace S. Murray, in "Editorial Policies and Procedures of Grolier Incorporated," has described some concerns of conscientious editors, including revision (*Booklist* 73:207–8 [Sept. 15, 1976.])

C. Consultants and contributors.
   1. Selected for their thorough knowledge of the subject fields for which they are responsible—not necessarily "big names," to be used in advertising the encyclopedia
   2. "The scholar as writer demands the right to be precise and he is aware that technical precision may involve the necessity of using the vocabulary of his own field of authority. He is likely to want the justifiable right to express his own position on matters in which his professional competence entitles his position to serious consideration. He is likely to be suspicious of persons who handle his contribution but who do not share his own eminence in his field, he may regard as 'dangerous oversimplification' any effort to express ideas in languages more likely to be understood by those who are not his peers, and, as his correspondence frequently indicates, he has quite often a proprietary feeling toward the encyclopedia which for nearly 200 years has enjoyed a reputation as being the repository of statements by world-famous scholars of their times" (Preece, p.815).

3. "Scholarly advisers are still, apparently, glad to be associated with the project and invitations to contributors are still accepted far more often than they are rejected. . . . Editorial suggestions are for the most part accepted when reasons for them are made clear" (Preece, p.816).

D. Central editorial staff
   1. Reseachers and reference librarians who check facts and figures for accuracy
   2. Those who check on readability of articles
   3. Indexers
   4. Proofreaders
   5. Layout artists and photograph editors (more numerous with the increased use of illustrations).
   All of these staff members must be highly proficient in their several skills, and a permanent staff is maintained by major encyclopedias.

The making of an encyclopedia is presented in *Random House Encyclopedia* under "Colorpedia" (New York: Random House, 1977; p.1781). Nine color photographs illustrate the steps, from an author in the publisher's office to the final proof.

II. Scope
   General characteristics, which also reveal the use that may be made of the encyclopedia's contents, are best approached by broad subject fields, as noted below:
   A. Science and technology. Reputable publishers go to great lengths in selecting qualified scientists as consultants and contributors, recognizing the ever expanding body of scientific knowledge as well as the high esteem in which it is held. But rapid advances in this broad area make it impossible for encyclopedias to be more than relatively current; they must often be augmented and up-dated by special encyclopedias, such as the *McGraw-Hill Encyclopedia of Science and Technology* and its yearbooks and by articles that are located through special indexing and abstracting services. However, they are useful for broad overviews. General encyclopedias are also useful for biographies of important scientists, especially those no longer living, although these are more fully covered in *Dictionary of Scientific Biography*. Encyclopedias designed primarily for family use contain how-to-do-it information and career opportunities in science and technology.
   Young people's encyclopedias with good coverage of scientific subjects are *World Book, Compton's, Merit Students Encyclopedia, Britannica Junior*, and *The New Book of Knowledge*. Written

in a simple, readable style and copiously illustrated, they are often preferred by adults with a limited knowlege of science and the language of science.

Science and technology are more fully treated in adult encyclopedias, especially *Encyclopedia Americana, New Encyclopaedia Britannica*, and *New Columbia Encyclopedia*. Some articles may not be comprehensible to those with no background in the field. *Random House Encyclopedia* is distinguished for the well-captioned illustrations that accompany its scientific articles.

All major encyclopedia publishers, conscious of this highly sensitive area, attempt to update topics through continuous revision and special articles on timely subjects in encyclopedia yearbooks.

B. History. In the broadest sense of the term, encyclopedias are all history, especially in the sense of a record of events, including histories of countries, subjects, and biographies of historically important persons. They may be consulted with a fair degree of confidence by those seeking condensed accounts of kingdoms and battles long ago. But can they be expected to include the latest interpretations of historical periods? Because of the historical research constantly being carried out and changing interests, it is often necessary to consult fuller and more recent sources.

To check an encyclopedia's coverage of recent history, look at articles on various countries to determine whether current political and economic conditions have been adequately reported.

C. Geography. Geographical information has been included since the beginning of encyclopedias, and early ones are interesting reflections of what was known about the world at that time. The increased amount of information on geographic areas is strikingly illustrated by comparing the article on Florida in the first edition of *Britannica* with the one in the most recent edition.

Certain generalizations applicable to twentieth-century encyclopedias are:

1. Treatment of individual countries, states, and cities varies greatly, according to the "nationality" of an encyclopedia. Compared with others, American encyclopedias have more entries for small American cities and towns, and longer articles on individual states (the *Americana* is an outstanding example). Articles on states vary in emphasis. For example, articles written by American historians are apt to give fuller attention to the history of states. Increasingly, a "state article" is written by more than one contributor, as in *World Book*, in which a historian, a journalist, and a professor of geography or geology

are jointly responsible. *Compton's* also contains long, well-illustrated articles on countries and states.

2. In spite of the emphasis on an encyclopedia's country of origin, American editors are sensitive to the current interest in newer nations and tend to treat them more fully than in the past. They give more attention to recent developments in older countries, though, in both cases, yearbooks and periodical indexes must be used for recent events and statistics. The rise of new nations makes it difficult for general encyclopedias to incorporate current information in sufficient depth. In such cases, other reference sources, such as *Encyclopedia of the Third World* by George Thomas Kurian (New York: Facts on File, 1978; 2v.), are helpful.

3. Maps are an important feature, and most encyclopedia publishers employ cartographers and map publishers who supply maps which accompany the articles, as in *Britannica, Random House*, and *Collier's*, with maps by Rand McNally. Among foreign encyclopedias, *Enciclopedia Universal Ilustrada Europeo-Americana* (usually cited as *Espasa*) is noted for its many geological, geographical, and historical maps, including some for cities and towns; maps in the *Grand Larousse Encyclopédique* are distinguished for their quality. But encyclopedias should be augmented by world atlases, which have more maps on a larger scale and give more detail. (These are discussed in chapter 7.)

4. The extent of other illustrative material varies widely and is greatest in encyclopedias for young people. Complaints that illustrations of a foreign country do not always give an accurate picture of life in that country have made editors more sensitive in selection of photographs for other than their "colorful" aspects. Also, the increasing use of illustrations, both in color and black and white, has resulted in many more photographs of countries and the people who live in them, as in *Random House Encyclopedia* and the *New Britannica*.

D. Political science and economics. Again, the "national origin" of an encyclopedia affects the treatment of political science and economics. Americans are usually more sensitive to national biases in foreign encyclopedias than to biases in those published in the United States. For example, Patricia Kennedy Grimsted, in her thorough analysis of the *Great Soviet Encyclopedia* (in English), refers to the omission of biographies of disgraced personalities and the "frequent substitution of propagandistic overtones for precise statistics and comprehensive factual background"

("Detente on the Reference Shelves?" *Wilson Library Bulletin* 49:728–40 [June 1975]).

However, most encyclopedias in democratic countries strive for objectivity in reporting on political and economic topics, and in most cases they succeed. *Encyclopedia Americana* and *Encyclopedia International* have been noted for their objectivity and up-to-date coverage of important political changes and election data. *Collier's* and *Compton's* give more emphasis to American political figures and events, and less to the international scene, bearing in mind their American audience. *New Columbia Encyclopedia* has a good representation of important American political figures and (to a lesser extent) others throughout the world, both living and dead. *Lincoln Library* devotes separate sections to Government and Politics and to Economics and Useful Arts, stressing the history of these subjects.

Compton's "occasionally engages in subtle political bias, promoting a nationalistic attitude toward the United States and Western democracies while concurrently disparaging other systems" (Kenneth Kister's *Encyclopedia Buying Guide* . . . [New York: Bowker, 1978], p.93); and the *New Encyclopaedia Britannica*, in spite of its stated aim to avoid expressions of bias or prejudice, has been accused by some critics of a pro-Soviet bias, for emphasizing growth and progress in foreign countries, while slighting negative factors, and for treating political and social problems cautiously. However, on the whole it is recognized for its excellence.

William Katz, in *Introduction to Reference Work*, recognizes the problem of presenting issues and ideas in his discussion of viewpoint (3rd ed.; v.1, p.144), raising the question: "How is the encyclopedia to be objective when such controversial issues are involved as capitalism and communism, civil rights and segregation, conservatism or liberalism?" The problem may be solved, according to Katz, by adopting a chronological historical approach, ignoring the differences entirely, or making an effort to balance an article by presenting two or more sides.

Bearing this in mind, we may consult encyclopedias for:

1. Political and economic theories (though more fully covered in *International Encyclopedia of the Social Sciences*)
2. Political and economic history, often treated in articles on individual countries
3. Political and economic conditions in individual countries, usually treated in articles on those countries. This information must be updated by yearbooks and even more current sources, such as *Facts on File* and *Keesing's Contemporary Archives*, as

well as by current statistical sources (discussed in a later chapter)

4. Biographies of important political figures, living and dead. These are usually well covered.

E. Education. Much that has been noted in political science and economics will apply to coverage of education. The same kinds of educational information will be found (though more fully treated in *Encyclopedia of Education* [Macmillan/Free Press]), for:

1. Educational theories and methods
2. History of education
3. Educational conditions in individual countries (usually treated in articles on those countries and updated in yearbooks)
4. Biographies of great educators
5. Accounts of great universities (sometimes with photographs of campuses).

F. Biography. The use of encyclopedias in biographical reference has been noted in an earlier chapter; it is well to remember, however, that if the nationality of a biographee is known, an encyclopedia that is published in that country is most apt to contain an evaluative account of his or her life. (For example, Spaniards and Spanish-Americans are well represented in *Espasa*.) Also, it is often surprising to note the varying selections of biographees, even in comparing encyclopedias which are similar in scope and purpose. For example, comparison of biographical entries in *Random House Encyclopedia* and *University Desk Encyclopedia* reveals that while both include persons prominent in all fields (including jazz musicians, baseball players, and movie stars), a number of names are found in only one of these recently published volumes. *Random House* usually gives fuller treatment—more personal details, more works of authors, etc. Since this is often the case, it is wise to consult several encyclopedias in searching for biographical information.

Reflecting the times, encyclopedias tend to include more persons from the sports and entertainment fields than formerly, as well as living persons—though this often gives them qualms, as William D. Halsey observed in his "Remarks on the Maintenance and Continuing Revision of General-Purpose Encyclopedias and Dictionaries" (*Booklist* 73:209–10 [Sept. 15, 1976]). He says, "Surely if one can see fame in a person who has died, one should be able to recognize it in one who is still alive. The passage of years has taught me that it isn't this easy. Reference books do not confer immortality, and the price we pay for entering what no one wants or needs is very predictably the elimination of information that is both wanted and needed. And the line between simple notoriety and lasting fame may not be as clear about a particular individual at any given moment as one might wish. (An editor with whom I once worked used the term 'bobtail' to describe any person included in any reference book who was not yet dead, and therefore necessarily a source of some insecurity to the editors.)"

Other generalizations are:

1. Appended bibliographies often include the best full-length biographies of persons and, in the case of writers, the definitive editions of their works.
2. Encyclopedias usually give fuller treatment to biographies of important persons than do one-volume universal biographical dictionaries (such as *Webster's Biographical Dictionary*).
3. Well-indexed encyclopedias include references to persons in other articles which often augment information supplied in the biographical account. Some also index persons under vocation and name of country.
4. Family encyclopedias often append lists of important persons in their articles on individual states.
5. Young people's encyclopedias often contain interesting illustrations for a biographee, in addition to more conventional portraits, which often accompany the biographical sketches in adult encyclopedias.
6. Yearbooks contain obituaries and sketches on persons recently prominent.

G. Philosophy. It is to the Greek philosophers that we owe the foundations of the classifications of knowledge used in encyclopedias. Now, in an age where there is a great gulf between the concerns of academic philosophers (who tend to consider the average person philosophically illiterate) and the layman's "philosophy of life," the importance of the general encyclopedia as a source of philosophic thought must be considered. This is particularly true for users of school and public libraries, especially since these libraries usually have weak collections in philosophy.

Though no adequate substitute for *Encyclopedia of Philosophy*, a general encyclopedia has certain advantages. For example, encyclopedias for young people contain simple explanations of philosophical concepts that may be easily understood by persons without formal philosophical training. More difficult to comprehend, adult encyclopedias attempt to cover the field in an orderly fashion, though not always reflecting currently active schools.

A good analysis of the treatment of philosophy in older general encyclopedias, together with names of outstanding contributors, is included in the *Encyclopedia of Philosophy* (New York: Macmillan and Free Pr., 1967; v.6, p.170–74). This article (by William Gerber) covers both English-language and foreign philosophers and, though somewhat dated, provides a kind of synthesis that is extremely useful to reference librarians.

While recognizing that philosophy, as a discipline, may not receive the same emphasis or continuous or frequent revision as that given to science in twentieth-century encyclopedias, we may consult them profitably for:

1. General articles on philosophy, covering history and methodology, with attention to contributions of major philosophers and schools of thought
2. Articles on various disciplines of philosophy, e.g. metaphysics
3. Biographies of philosophers
4. Analyses of philosophical treatises in summary form
5. Important conferences and recent important books, found in yearbooks.

More extensive articles, with long bibliographies, on ideas which have shaped philosophic thought must be sought in Philip P. Wiener, ed., *Dictionary of the History of Ideas* (New York: Scribner, 1973–74; 5v.).

H. Religion. Again, we may reflect that religion has been important in the history of the encyclopedia, as in medieval Europe, when (as noted earlier) it was intended to "make man Christian."

Louis Shores, discussing objectivity in an encyclopedia, in a 1960 address to Drexel Institute students and faculty, told them that "at least two American encyclopedias have no biography of Jesus because they have despaired of reconciling the faiths involved. . . . What the encyclopedist knows he must do is submit every article in religion to his 'faiths' advisers" (in his *Reference as the Promotion of Free Inquiry* [Littleton, Colo.: Libraries Unlimited, 1976], p.182–83). Of course, editors of encyclopedias seek the counsel of qualified advisers in their efforts to provide impartial treatment of religious subjects.

Today, in the so-called age of ecumenism, we may expect a more balanced coverage of the world's great religions. Thus a general encyclopedia may be consulted for:

1. Articles on the nature and history of religions
2. Biographies of saints, prophets, biblical characters, and religious thinkers, past and present
3. Predominant religions in various countries (usually in articles on these countries)
4. Synopses of the sacred writings of various religions
5. Current concerns, in the yearbooks.

As might be expected, some of these topics are more fully covered in special reference works in the field, such as Bible dictionaries or denominational encyclopedias. For example, the *New Catholic Encyclopedia* devotes a great deal of space to biographies of the saints, to accounts of the progress of Catholicism in all parts of the world, and to reinterpretations of controversial figures such as Martin Luther. In addition, its articles on labor, education, argiculture, and marriage (to name only a few) reflect contemporary theology. Also noteworthy, in spite of its shortcomings, is *Encyclopaedia Judaica*. Its biographies of those who have contributed to nearly 6,000 years of Jewish history and its accounts of Jewish events augment those in general encyclopedias. The *New Catholic Encyclopedia* issues supplements at intervals; *Encyclopedia Judaica Yearbook* contains new and updated articles on subjects covered in the basic set, a number of feature articles on current topics, and a regular feature on Jewish-Christian relations.

I. Literature. It is obvious that editors, in their efforts to achieve balance, must give fuller attention to literature of the past than to that of the present, but encyclopedias may be used as starting points for the following types of information:

1. Biographies of authors, with emphasis on older writers, who have stood the test of time, and less emphasis on current writers, unless they have achieved wide popularity or received literary awards. Encyclopedias for young people are strong in accounts of writers for children, especially winners of prizes such as Newbery and Caldecott. Foreign encyclopedias give emphasis to biographies of their national authors, such as *Espasa* to Spanish and Latin American writers or *Larousse* to French. They are also a good source for translations of authors of the English-speaking world and for foreign criticism of these authors, both being found in their appended bibliographies.
2. Histories of literature in various countries, with emphasis on the Western world and on the national literature of the ency-

clopedia's country of origin, though attention to some of the newer nations will be found in recent revisions of American encyclopedias.

3. Characteristics of literary forms (e.g. poetry, drama, fiction, essays, biography, and children's literature, though the latter is more fully treated in young people's encyclopedias)

4. Synopses of literary works, such as those found in *Americana* and in foreign encyclopedias, such as the famous, but still useful, nineteenth-century Larousse, *Grand Dictionnaire Universal*, which has many articles on individual works of literature.

5. Recent best sellers, awards, etc., found in the yearbooks.

Encyclopedias are not intended as substitutes for multivolume histories of national literature, such as the *Literary History of the United States* or the *Cambridge History of English Literature*. Nor will their bibliographies be as exhaustive as those in the *Cambridge Bibliography of English Literature* or the *Critical Bibliography of French Literature*. Moreover, these national compilations are updated by many serial bibliographies, such as those described in Richard Gray's *Serial Bibliographies in the Humanities and Social Sciences* (cited earlier).

Nor should we expect as many recent critical reevaluations of authors whose work has been reassessed by newer critics. These must be sought in literary quarterlies. Nor are literary quotations as easily identified as they are in quotation books, whose single purpose is identification.

But encyclopedias may not be safely ignored in the field of literature, especially since their contributors are often recognized literary critics.

J. Art and music. Although encyclopedias have been criticized for not reflecting recent movements in art and music, they are justified in giving more attention to the past—again, to achieve proper balance: current enthusiasms may fade into ephemera in a few decades. Their useful features include:

1. Biographies of artists and composers

2. Histories of art and music, sometimes with separate articles on individual countries. However, one-volume encyclopedias cover art and music so sketchily that they are useful only for identification.

3. Descriptions of musical instruments, orchestras, musical forms and notation, often illustrated, though these are more fully

treated in sources such as Grove's *Dictionary of Music and Musicians*

4. Characteristics of various schools and movements in art
5. Reproductions of works of art. *Enciclopedia Italiana* is often cited for its excellent reproductions, though they cannot substitute for those in the *Encyclopedia of World Art*. The *New Catholic Encyclopedia* is a good source for religious art
6. Words and music of songs, as in the nineteenth-century *Larousse* (cited under literature), which gives words and music (melody only) of about 600 songs.

K. Libraries and related subjects. General encyclopedias are sources of information on libraries, professional library associations, biographies of famous librarians, and histories of famous libraries, as well as on the history and characteristics of reference books, such as dictionaries and encyclopedias, bibliographies, and atlases.

Fuller information on these topics will be found in *Encyclopedia of Library and Information Science* (New York: Dekker), which deserves special mention because of its importance to librarians. Begun in 1968, with 26 volumes published by 1979 and covering through *Sci*, it contains an impressive array of signed articles by qualified contributors, ranging in length from a few paragraphs to long monographs. There are clear descriptions of activities (notably one on abstracting), types of libraries (notably art libraries), with an accompanying article on the literature of the field; library service in individual countries; and biographies of distinguished persons in library and related fields (such as Aldus Manutius). Its international scope and treatment of information science provide a sound basis for closer cooperation among various types of libraries and for a better understanding of their services.

This admittedly superficial analysis of the coverage of various subject fields suffers from too many generalizations, most of them widely known. Also it suffers from random (rather than systematic) statements on the coverage in individual encyclopedias, which must be sought in more comprehensive sources. A number of such sources of information, on the evaluation of individual titles and on the history of encyclopedias, are noted below.

Kenneth Kister's *Encyclopedia Buying Guide: A Consumer Guide to General Encyclopedias in Print* (New York: Bowker, 1978; 389p.) is the most valuable source of detailed, recent information on 36 currently published English-language encyclopedias. Scheduled to appear every three years, it covers the following points for each set: Facts in Brief (including number of volumes and words, user classification, and price); Purpose and Scope; History and Authority; Treatment (Reliability, Objectivity, Recency); Clarity and Reader Suitability; Arrangement and Accessibility; Bibliographies; Graphics; Physical Format; Special Features; Sales Information; Summary (concluding with valuable comparisons of similar sets); and Other Critical Opinions (citations to reviews).

Based on careful examination by the author, assisted by five academic and library consultants, it illustrates its comment with specific examples from recent editions of individual encyclopedias, for both children and adults. The methodology is explained in a prefatory section, "How to Use This Book." Specialized works in specific subject fields are covered in Bowker's forthcoming *Encyclopedias & Dictionaries for Specialists*.

Three appendixes list, with brief comment: (1) Discontinued Encyclopedias, 1960–1978, (2) Almanacs and Yearbooks, and (3) Encyclopedia Bibliography. The latter includes books, articles, and sources which regularly review encyclopedias, such as *Booklist* and *American Reference Books Annual*. The latter reviewed Kister in its 1979 volume (p.35).

The section on reference and subscription books in *Booklist* includes lengthy, detailed analyses of new British and American encyclopedias, as well as comparisons of the extent of revision of later issues or editions of older encyclopedias, usually at five-year intervals. These are prepared by the Reference and Subscription Books Review Committee of the American Library Association. Also useful are the evaluations of twenty English-language encyclopedias by the committee, in "Encyclopedias: A Survey and Buying Guide" (*Booklist*, 75:632–41 [Dec. 1, 1978]; 75:708–15 [Dec. 15, 1978]; 75:767–72 [Jan. 1, 1979]; 75:830–33 [Jan. 15, 1979]; and 75:882–91 [Feb. 1, 1979]). In addition to assessing the authority, arrangement, accuracy, objectivity, recency, quality, style, bibliographies, illustrations, physical features, and special attributes of individual encyclopedias, it briefly discusses each of these factors as "points to be considered before purchase." All of the titles (except *Chambers's Encyclopedia*) are also reviewed in Kister, sometimes in more recent editions.

Brief, signed reviews of encyclopedias available in the United States appear rather promptly in *American Reference Books Annual* (Littleton, Colo.: Libraries Unlimited, 1970–). The five-year cumulative index of subjects, authors, and titles adds to ease of location of particular titles. Reviews, though shorter than those in *Booklist*, are usually discerning.

Textbooks on reference materials always include encyclopedias, a notable example being William Katz's *Introduction to Reference Work*, volume 1, *Basic Information Sources*. It gives little attention to history, but contains an excellent account of the four publishers "who control approximately 95 percent of the general encyclopedis published for all age groups in the

United States" (3rd ed., p.137). Also discussed are major foreign encyclopedias and outstanding examples of special encyclopedias in art, history, and science. It can be recommended further for its readable style, recency, and good list of suggested readings.

Much has been written on the history of encyclopedias, but perhaps best known is Robert L. Collison's *Encyclopedias: Their History throughout the Ages* (2nd ed.; New York: Hafner Publishing Co., 1966), subtitled "a bibliographical guide with extensive historical notes to the general encyclopaedias issued throughout the world from 350 B.C. to the present day." Its bibliographies append well-written chapters on the beginnings, the Middle Ages, Diderot to the Encyclopédistes, the *Encyclopaedia Britannica*, *Brockhaus*, the nineteenth century, and the twentieth century, prefaced by a chronology. Appendix I, General Bibliography, begins with the note, "The articles under the heading *encyclopaedia* in most encyclopaedias are disappointing, with some notable exceptions listed below. Nevertheless, these articles are well worth examining since they often throw light on the particular encyclopaedia being handled, and they sometimes record contemporary circumstances of publication, etc., long since forgotten" (p.229).

Collison's article on encyclopedias in *The New Encyclopaedia Britannica—Macropaedia* (Chicago: Encyclopaedia Britannica, 1975; v.6, p.779–99) is the best article on the subject in any encyclopedia, and the *Micropaedia* entry in the *New Britannica* is only a brief description: "The text article [Collison] covers general and specialized encyclopaedias from the Middle Ages until modern times. It examines the role of encyclopaedias, the types of material included in them, and the levels of presentation. It reviews the kinds of encyclopedias available during various periods and in various regions, surveying the history of encyclopaedias in both the Eastern and Western worlds from classical times to the present" (v.3, p.889). This illustrates the difference in treatment of the same subject in the *Macropaedia* and *Micropaedia*. Collison reminds us that "even today, a modern encyclopaedia still may be called a dictionary, but no good dictionary has ever been called an encyclopaedia."

Padraig Walsh, in his *Anglo-American General Encyclopedias: A Historical Bibliography, 1703–1967* (New York: Bowker, 1968; 270p.), thanks Collison in his introduction "for his invaluable advice, and also for blazing the trail for me with his important *Encyclopaedias: Their History throughout the Ages*" (p.xix). He includes publishing histories and brief biographical notes on outstanding editors of 419 alphabetically listed works; an index to compilers, editors, and others associated with the works; an index of publishers and distributors; a chronology covering 1703–1967; and a general bibliography, which recommends Collison as "a primary source of information" and cites a number of periodical articles. Appended is a forum on encyclopedias, with remarks by Louis Shores, Lowell Martin, William D. Halsey, William H. Nault, and Walsh at a symposium on July 6, 1965, reprinted from *RQ* (5:3+ [Winter 1965]).

Additional books and articles on individual encyclopedias may be located through such sources as *Library Literature* and *National Union Catalog*.

The Circle of Knowledge: Encyclopaedias Past and Present (Chicago: Newberry Library, 1968; 56p.), prepared as a catalog of an exhibition commemorating the 200th anniversary of the *Encyclopaedia Britannica*, is distinguished for its large number of facsimile pages from early encyclopedias and for the well-written introduction by James M. Wells, which concludes with a quotation from the first edition of *Britannica*:

> With regard to errors in general, whether falling under the denomination of mental, typographical or accidental, we are conscious of being able to point out a greater number than any critic whatever. Men who are acquainted with the innumerable difficulties of attending the execution of a work of such an extensive nature will make proper allowances. To these we appeal, and shall rest satisfied with the judgment they pronounce.

Since the encyclopedia articles only spottily list examples of encyclopedias in special fields, those who seek fuller information must look elsewhere. As noted in the earlier chapter on bibliography, guides to the literature of individual fields are useful, as well as *Walford, Sheehy*, and Kister's *Encyclopedias & Dictionaries for Specialists*. Conveniently, the index to *Sheehy* lists encyclopedias under specific subject fields. Also not to be overlooked are articles in special encyclopedias, such as the one noted earlier in *Encyclopedia of Philosophy*.

Since knowledge of the indexes to encyclopedias is fundamental to using them efficiently, articles on the indexing of individual encyclopedias are valuable sources of information. A number are included in *Indexers on Indexing*, edited by L. M. Harrod for the Society of Indexers (New York: Bowker, 1978; 430p.). For a full description of the indexing of *Britannica 3*, see Rosa Cassas' article in *American Society of Indexers Newsletter* (no.15, p.5–6 [Sept. 1974]). (Other articles from the *Indexer* have already been noted, in the bibliography chapter under "Indexes").

It is apparent that there is no dearth of information on encyclopedias for those who are willing to read it. And librarians *must* read it, since not only are they expected to be knowledgeable about these circles of knowledge, they are also sometimes associated with individual works. As Louis Shores points out in his article "Judging an Encyclopedia" (*RQ* 4:3–5 [Sept. 1964]): "Certainly encyclopedias today have drawn more heavily from library science than at any time in the history of these great works. The authority lists of all major American encyclopedias today will reveal librarians serving as contributors, advisers, editors and even as editorial directors. Librarians sit on policy boards and interpret patrons' needs as well as the best practices in such technical matters as subject headings, indexing, cross-referencing, bibliographies and even more fundamentally, scope and balance of content." None should know better than he—remembering his long connection with *Collier's Encyclopedia.* (Another well-known library educator is Lowell Martin, who for a number of years was editorial director of Grolier Incorporated.)

Reference librarians and others concerned with teaching the use of the encyclopedia to beginning users will find a number of audiovisual aids listed in guides to these materials. They can be used profitably, especially with large groups.

Multivolume Adult Encyclopedias

It is hardly possible to store in the memory the special features, strengths, and weaknesses of individual encyclopedias, though some of them may be learned by continuous use, especially by those who have total recall. Even then, knowledge of particulars must be revised from time to time because good encyclopedias are in a state of continuous revision.

Although modern multivolume encyclopedias, having the same general purpose, are subject to certain generalizations, differences in treatment and kinds of information in individual articles almost always occur.

Familiarity with individual encyclopedias, developed only through extended use, is often conditioned by the critical reception they have received, as reflected in the reviewing media. The rest of this section on English-language encyclopedias is devoted to an outline of the strengths and weaknesses of five multivolume adult sets, five one- to three-volume sets, and seven sets intended for children and young adults. All are currently available in the United States and are, with a few exceptions, found in most American libraries. Reader suitability, as noted after each title is that assigned by Kenneth Kister in *Encyclopedia Buying Guide* (1978 ed.).

→ The new encyclopaedia Britannica in 30 volumes. Ed. Warren E. Preece. Chicago, Encyclopaedia Britannica, Inc. 1979. 30v. *Age 15 through advanced adult.*

In 1974, *The New Encyclopaedia Britannica*, generally known as *Britannica 3*, was issued in its 15th edition, the first entirely new edition in 45 years. It differs in arrangement from the 14th edition (and from any other encyclopedia) by being in three parts: *Propaedia, Micropaedia*, and *Macropaedia* (coined words which put some people off).

When a new edition of an encyclopedia is published in the United States, it is duly reviewed in the Reference and Subscription Books section of *Booklist*, in *American Reference Books Annual*, and in *Library Journal*, but not in many other journals. Indeed, these three sources of reviews of reference books took proper notice of *Britannica 3* when it appeared—and so did many other journals which usually don't "tackle" encyclopedias. One important reason for the widespread critical attention it received was its new approach to the circle of knowledge, although it resembles in part the French *Encyclopaedia Universalis* (discussed later in this chapter).

In more detail, the contents may be described as follows: *Propaedia*, subtitled *Outline of Knowledge and Guide to the Britannica*, is a topical guide to the *Macropaedia*, arranged in ten parts (which are further subdivided): Matter and Energy, The Earth, Life on Earth, Human Life, Human Society, Art, Technology, Religion, The History of Mankind, and The Branches of Knowledge (logic, mathematics, science, history, the humanities, philosophy). According to the editor, "this outline, consisting of 10 parts, 42 divisions, and 189 sections, became for the editorial staff a table of intents, and a planning tool of extreme importance. At a later stage and in a slightly rewritten form, it became the one-volume topical index or table of contents . . . of the new set." The editors were then required to draw up a list of articles to cover the outlined topics.

The ten volumes of the *Micropaedia* contain over 100,000 unsigned articles (750 words or less), serving as both a source of quick reference and an index to the *Macropaedia*. The articles include brief summaries of those in the *Macropaedia*, as well as other subjects. Its text is on computer tape, to allow for frequent revision. In 19 volumes, the *Macropaedia* contains over 4,200 lengthy, scholarly articles by international authorities. They range in length from about 1,500 words to over 30 pages, and a few are as long as 100 pages.

Thus, according to the editors' intent, the *Micropaedia* is designed for "the curious, intelligent layman," seeking quick answers to reference questions or a guide to the long articles in the *Macropaedia*. The *Propaedia* may be used "for guidance in synthesizing systematically reading programs over the wide areas of knowledge." Also, according to the editors, *Britannica 3* "is to achieve a minimum of fragmentation and maximum control of duplication."

Critical opinion is varied as to how successfully *Britannica 3* has achieved its goals. Richard Gray (cited below) considers the *Micropaedia's* indexing failures "decidedly minor." After testing it, he concluded that it "serves its indexing function extremely well except when pressed to the outer limit of discrete term retrieval." However, he regrets that the *Micropaedia* does not refer to the *Propaedia*, "for it could so easily have cited *Propaedia* rubric numbers and thus have validated the claim that Britannica's trinity is truly a unity." He feels that the *Propaedia* "urgently needs a discrete subject index" and that it should cite references to the *Micropaedia* as well as to the *Macropaedia*.

He also points out that many rubric references in the *Propaedia* lead nowhere. But he concludes that the weaknesses, "which are decidedly minor given the magnitude of the achievement, do not critically hamper its use," and he recommends it for all libraries except those serving elementary and middle-school clinteles.

Kister, in his *Encyclopedia Buying Guide, 1978*, believes that *Britannica 3* needs a detailed general index, one which would likely "encompass two volumes and run upwards of a million analytical entries." He also examines the matter of objectivity and summarizes the attacks of several critics who have accused the set of bias, although he concludes that "in most controversial areas, *Britannica 3* is free from blatant bias."

That the articles in the *Macropaedia* are not as "readable" as those in other American encyclopedias is generally agreed, but its many strong points assure its wide usefulness. Its strengths are:

1. Distinguished international authorities among contributors and consultants, including many university professors
2. Strong international coverage
3. Newly written articles throughout, with only about 15 percent of material retained from the 14th edition.
4. Broad coverage of various subject fields, excelling in biography, the humanities, and the sciences
5. High degree of accuracy
6. Depth of treatment of subjects in *Macropaedia*
7. Well illustrated
8. Well-selected, lengthy, annotated bibliographies in the *Macropaedia*.

Weaknesses:

1. Inadequately indexed
2. Although some entries have been updated in later printings, more revision is desirable.
3. Evidence of bias (in treatment of political science and economics).

Further references:

Booklist 71: 1021–28 (June 1, 1975); 75:889–91 (Feb. 1, 1979).
Cole, Dorothy Ethlyn. "*Britannica 3* as a Reference Tool; a Review," *Wilson Library Bulletin* (June 1974), p.1–3.
Davis, Robert Gorham. "Subject: The Universe," *New York Times Book Review*, Dec. 1, 1974, p.98, 100.
Einbinder, Harvey. "Politics and the New *Britannica*," *Nation*, Mar. 22, 1975, p.342–44.

Evans, G. Edward. *American Reference Books Annual* (1979), p.37–39. (1978 printing).

Gray, Richard A. *American Reference Books Annual* (1975), p.34–37.

Josel, Nat. *RQ* (Summer 1974), p.352–54.

Shields, Gerald. *Library Journal* (Apr. 15, 1974), p. 1101–3.

Wolff, Geoffrey. *Atlantic* (June 1974), p.37–47; (Nov. 1976), p.107–10.

→ The Encyclopedia Americana. Bernard S. Cayne, ed. in chief. Danbury, Conn., Americana Corp. (a subsidiary of Grolier, Inc.), 1979. 30v. *Age 15 through advanced adult.*

Unlike the *New Encyclopedia Britannica*, the *Americana* is arranged in one alphabet under about 55,000 entries. It has long been recognized for its strong coverage of American history, biography, and geography, although it maintains a well-balanced international coverage as well. The method of revision differs in part from that used by other encyclopedias, since, in addition to updating articles throughout the set and inserting new articles on topics of current interest, there is an ongoing program of thorough revision of individual volumes. According to the publisher, between 1976 and 1979 "two volumes have been completely restructured, rewritten, or revised and have been reset from first page to last." Some critics, including Kenneth Kister, feel that this is not enough, and in his evaluation of the 1977 volume he suggested that *Americana* would benefit from complete revision (in his *Encyclopedia Buying Guide*, p.111). The publisher claims that the 1979 edition has 1,400 new and revised articles, including 320 new subject entries and about 400 new illustrations. All critics agree that *Americana* has many noteworthy features, and it has been widely recommended for homes and libraries.

Strengths:

1. Well-qualified editorial staff
2. Some distinguished contributors
3. Excellent coverage of American history, biography, and geography
4. Articles for each century (unique to *Americana*)
5. Very objective in its treatment of controversial subjects
6. Clearly written, logically arranged articles, with glossaries for 40 of them and tables of contents for some larger ones
7. Authoritative
8. Well-selected, up-to-date bibliographies

9. Illustrations (though often in black and white) well integrated with the text
10. Excellent detailed index of over 350,000 entries.

Weaknesses:

1. More revision needed
2. Some fragmentation of descriptions (because of specific approach to subject matter).

Further references:

Booklist 72:1541–44 (July 1, 1976) (1975 ed.); 75: 886–89 (Feb. 1, 1979).

Wynar, Bohdan S. American Reference Books Annual (1977), p.40–44 (1976 ed.).

→ Chambers's encyclopaedia. London, International Learning Systems Corp., Ltd., 1966. Reprinted with corrections, 1973. 15v. Age 15 through adult.

Arranged under broad and specific entries, this encyclopedia augments those of American origin by its more thorough coverage of British geography and biography. Its contributors include persons of international reputation, and it is noted for its well-written, scholarly articles, but its publishers deliberately have not adopted the policy of continuous revision.

Strengths:

1. Strong coverage of Britain, Europe, and Asia
2. Detailed index.

Weaknesses:

1. Lack of revision
2. Illustrations poor and too few
3. Bibliographies out of date.

Further references:

Booklist 75:882–84 (Feb. 1, 1979) (1973 ed.).

→ Collier's encyclopedia with bibliography and index. William D. Halsey, ed. dir.; Louis Shores, ed. in chief; Emanuel Friedman, ed. N.Y., Macmillan Educational Corp., 1979. 24v. Age 15 through advanced adult.

First published between 1949 and 1951, Collier's reflects the advice and assistance of notable librarians, among them Louis Shores, who was active in its planning from 1946. Its 25,000 articles, many by well-known contributors, are reliable, although intentionally they are not always covered in as much depth as those in *Britannica* and *Americana*. Only 1,400 of its 17,000 illustrations are in color, but, with few exceptions, all are well related to the text. *Collier's* is noted for its scrupulous continuous revision, with nearly 600 new articles added between 1974 and 1976. Among the new articles in the 1979 edition are those on skateboarding, farm machinery, mahjongg, and science fiction, as well as those on the role of blacks in nineteenth-century American history, biographies of writers (such as John Cheever), and a number in the sciences. It is generally found in all types of American libraries.

Strengths:

1. Consistently objective in its articles
2. Well-balanced coverage, including practical information
3. Effective graphics, including excellent maps
4. Useful bibliographies in v.24, listing 11,500 books in English addressed to the average reader and easily available
5. Up to date
6. Superior index.

Weaknesses:

1. Some users prefer bibliographies at the end of articles rather than in separate volume.

Further references:

> *Booklist* 69:913–16 (June 1, 1973) (1972 ed.); 75:884–86 (Feb. 1, 1979) (1975) ed.).
> Wynar, Bohdan S. *American Reference Books Annual* (1972), p.74–75 (1971 ed.); (1979), p.33–34 (1978 ed.).

→ Funk and Wagnalls new encyclopedia. N.Y., Funk & Wagnalls, 1977. 27v. *Age 12 through general adult.*

The low cost of this general encyclopedia recommends it for budget-minded families, although it will not replace the sets mentioned earlier for library use. Its 25,000 factual, straightforward articles, accompanied by more than 7,500 illustrations (1,800 in color), do not have the depth of articles in *Britannica, Americana*, and *Collier's*. But it has been recognized by qualified critics as the best of the sets which are available in supermarkets because of the quality and comprehensiveness of its contents.

Strengths:

1. Strong biographical, geographical, and scientific/technical coverage
2. Up to date
3. Well-selected bibliographies (v.27)
4. Well indexed, including references to illustrations (v.27)
5. Controversial articles factual and unbiased.

Weaknesses:

1. Quality of some illustrations inferior.

Further references:

Booklist 71:512–15 (Jan. 15, 1975) (1973 ed.); 75:830–32 (Jan. 15, 1979) (1975 ed.).

Wynar, Bohdan S. American Reference Books Annual (1974), p.22–24.

Encyclopedia Supplements

It is generally agreed that encyclopedia supplements (annuals or year-books) are more successful in recording the preceding year's events than in updating the parent sets. While publishers emphasize in their advertising that their supplements or yearbooks serve to keep the basic set current, they do not systematically update articles in the encyclopedias. Thus they are less closely related to the parent sets than is usually claimed. There is considerable variation in their arrangement, quality and quantity of illustrations, extent of indexing, and special features, but on the whole they have a better format than the less expensive independent annuals, such as World Almanac and Information Please Almanac, which contain similar information (as noted in chapter 7).

It is well to remember that much of the material in the annuals is not incorporated in later revised editions of the encyclopedias. Also, in searching for an event, remember that they usually cover the last three months of one year and the first nine months of the next. They also contain feature articles and special reports, often by well-known authorities, which will not be found elsewhere. For example, Isaac Asimov's "Is There Life in Outer Space?" appears in Collier's Yearbook for the year 1978. Americana Annual, for the year 1976, has a report on the U.S. presidential election by Marquis Childs. In its 1978 publication for the year 1977, Britannica Book of the Year expanded the number of feature articles and special reports, among them one by Martin Marty on religious persecution, titled "The Modern Martyrs." It also reprints two revised articles from Britannica 3, one in part, one entirely.

All five encyclopedias mentioned above have yearbooks: *Britannica Book of the Year*, published continuously since 1938; *The Americana Annual*, published continuously since 1923; *Chambers's Encyclopaedia Yearbook*, published since 1968, superseding Chambers's *Encyclopaedia World Survey* (1952–65); *Collier's Encyclopedia Year Book*, published since 1939 and also issued as the *Merit Students Year Book*; and *Funk & Wagnalls New Encyclopedia Yearbook*.

While their contents vary, certain generalizations hold, and the following patterns indicate the reference use which can be made of them:

1. Brief biographies of persons who have died or become prominent during the year. The obituaries, giving date of death, serve as a guide in the location of longer newspaper accounts
2. Chronologies of major events
3. Recent socio-economic statistical data, usually for large areas and not always with citation to source
4. Brief reports of activities in various fields, often noting important conferences and publications
5. Recent developments in countries over the world
6. Special sections containing long, signed articles on topics of current interest, usually by well-known authorities
7. Photographs and other illustrative material (e.g. cartoons).

One- to Three-Volume Encyclopedias

Libraries with a number of reputable multivolume encyclopedias still find many reference uses for one–three-volume encyclopedias and usually keep them close at hand for quick reference. They are especially useful for identification of persons and places and for brief overviews of a subject. When responsibly edited and well arranged, they provide an admirable starting point in a search. They are also desirable for home use where cost and space are factors.

Until recently, these condensations have saved space by leaving out almost all pictorial illustrations as in the case of the *New Columbia Encyclopedia*, which squeezes more than 40,000 articles, 66,000 cross-references and about 400 illustrations and maps into a little more than 3,000 pages. Nor is the *Lincoln Library of Essential Information* distinguished for the 1,200 illustrations which accompany its 25,000 topics. Nor are *Cadillac Modern Encyclopedia's* noteworthy. But with publication of *The Random House Encyclopedia* in 1977, things have changed. Over 11,000 of its nearly 14,000 pictures are in color, and geared in with the 896 long articles in its Colorpedia section. About four black-and-white photographs on every other page accompany the 25,000 short articles in the Alphapedia section. Also filled with illustrations is *The University Desk Encyclopedia*, first published in

1977. Thus these encyclopedias can no longer be overlooked as pictorial sources.

The strengths and weaknesses of these five titles, as reflected in the reviewing media, are further detailed below. The encyclopedias were selected because of their recognized excellence, as in the case of the *New Columbia Encyclopedia*, or because they have features which make them suitable for home use, e.g. *Cadillac Modern Encyclopedia*.

→ The new Columbia encyclopedia. William H. Harris and Judith S. Levey, editors. 4th ed. N.Y., Columbia Univ. Pr., 1975; 3,068p. Distributed by J. B. Lippincott. *Age 15 through advanced adult.*

Strengths:

1. Widely known consultants
2. Excellent biographical and geographial coverage, including newly emergent nations
3. Lucid, concise style of writing in unsigned articles, with text proceeding from easy to difficult
4. Current, well-selected, ample bibliographies, more than 40,000 in all
5. High degree of accuracy
6. Clear, well-placed illustrations
7. Thoroughly revised from the earlier edition, giving greater coverage of non-Western countries and peoples; more advanced and detailed coverage of the sciences; metric equivalents where pertinent; and pronunciation of unfamiliar entries, e.g. scientific and foreign.

Weaknesses:

1. Index is needed.

For a description of the compilation of the 1975 edition, together with its being set by computer, see Judith S. Levey, "The Making of a General Encyclopedia" (*Booklist* 73:208–9 [Sept. 15, 1976]).

Further references:

Booklist 73:628–29 [Dec. 15, 1976]; 75:769–71 [Jan. 1, 1979].
Gray, Richard A. *American Reference Books Annual* (1976), p.59.

→ Random House encyclopedia. N.Y., Random House, 1977. 2856p. (Special school and library edition distributed by Encyclopaedia Britannica Educational Corp., 1977. 2v. Also published in other editions in Europe, Asia, and Africa.) *Age 12 through general adult.*

Quite different from *The New Columbia Encyclopedia* is the profusely illustrated *Random House Encyclopedia*, which was widely reviewed at the time of its publication. Compare the treatment of several subjects in both encyclopedias and it is obvious that they complement each other. Much material in *Random House* will be intelligible to younger readers, not only because of the extensive use of captioned illustrations but because its text is less scholarly in tone than that of *The New Columbia Encyclopedia*.

Random House also differs from *Columbia* in arrangement, its Colorpedia section being classified under seven categories: The Universe, Earth, Life on Earth, Man, History and Culture, Man and Science, and Man and Machines, each introduced by a brief essay by a well-known scholar. The content is further arranged under 896 topics, each treated in about 1,400 words of commentary, and there are detailed captions for the small, highly colored illustrations (which often seem crowded, though occupying more space than the text on the two-page spread devoted to each topic). Some topics lend themselves readily to pictorial treatment (e.g. *Spiders and scorpions*); less satisfactory is *What is philosophy?* and its see-also references, where the many illustrations are less useful. The Alphapedia section contains 25,000 very briefly treated entries for concepts, people, and places, and references to the Colorpedia (serving as the only index to the Colorpedia). Entries are much more briefly treated than in the *Columbia*. There is also a time chart of 23 two-page spreads, giving a chronological approach by broad areas, e.g. literature, religion and philosophy, and science and technology.

Hugh Kenner, in a trenchant review of *Random House* in *Harper's* (Dec. 1977, p.102–7), points out a number of errors he discovered, concluding, "If you say 'So what?' you don't want an encyclopedia. You want a great big polychromed gee-whiz pacifier sputtering facts and unfacts like a wobbly Roman candle, and this is just your book if you're willing to lift it. It has at least 1,000 good pages too." Other reviews have been less acerbic, but in pointing out errors in fact, Kenner serves to remind us of the importance of careful verification when using a secondary source such as an encyclopedia.

Strengths:

1. Good coverage in biography, geography, fine arts, science and technology
2. Colored illustrations well integrated with the text and usually well captioned
3. Metric equivalents where pertinent
4. Useful time chart
5. Controversial subjects objectively covered
6. Clearly and simply written.

Weaknesses:

1. The Alphapedia, intended to serve as an index to the Colorpedia, is not an adequate substitute for a separate, detailed index. For example, many illustrations (with their captions) are not noted in related articles
2. Some critics have noted the omission of persons whom they consider worthy of inclusion or inadequate treatment of other biographical entries (a criticism often made of other encyclopedias as well)
3. Suffers the inevitable results of compression: extreme brevity and superficiality
4. Pictorial treatment less suited to such subjects as literature, philosophy, and religion than to science and technology.
5. Appended bibliography of about 1,500 relatively recent English-language titles not well selected
6. Attempt to reduce all subjects to a two-page spread of words and pictures (in the Colorpedia) is the major conceptual difficulty.
7. Coverage of topics within a given subject in some cases arbitrary and misleading.

Further references:

George, Mary. *Library Journal* (Nov. 1, 1977), p.2252–53.
Cheney, Frances Neel. *American Reference Books Annual* (1978), p.41.
Kenner, Hugh. "Images at Random," *Harper's* 225:102–7 (Dec. 1977).

→ The university desk encyclopedia. Lausanne, Elsevier, 1977; trade ed.: N.Y., Dutton. 1056p. *Age 12 through general adult.*

This recent one-volume encyclopedia has less than half as many entries as *Columbia*, nor are its illustrations as numerous as those in *Random House*, but its alphabetical arrangement and simply written text make it suitable for younger readers and for home use.

Strengths:

1. Current, reliable, objective, and authoritative, with some exceptions
2. 25,000 briefly treated entries and 46 longer articles; profusely illustrated, often in color, including maps, charts, photographs, art reproductions, and line drawings.
3. Adequate cross-references, with many *see* and *see also* references, except for the 46 special articles (which are not always referred to in entries on related subjects).

Weaknesses:

1. Lack of balance in treatment of some subjects, e.g. more space devoted to *Cheeses* than to *Christianity*, more to *Match* than *Materialism*, and almost as much to *Microscope* as to *Middle Ages*
2. Subjects superficially treated
3. No bibliographies.

Further references:

Campbell, John D. *Library Journal* (June 1, 1977), p.1267.

Cheney, Frances Neel. *American Reference Books Annual* (1978), p.42–43.

→ The Cadillac modern encyclopedia: the world of knowledge in one volume. Max S. Shapiro, ed. St. Louis, Cadillac Publishing Co., 1973. 1954p. *Age 12 through general adult.*

Columbia, Random House, and *University Desk* encyclopedias are superior to *Cadillac* in a number of ways, but, as a relatively recent and inexpensive volume for homes and small libraries, it has several points to recommend it. Although it contains only 18,000 entries, it has a special reference section of 300 pages with more than 200 documents, charts, and tables, covering a wide range of subjects. It has been recognized as a handy source for ready reference.

Strengths:

1. Science, mathematics, and law well represented
2. Business and economics adequately covered
3. Problems, examples, and solutions supplied for some topics
4. Controversial subjects dealt with objectively
5. Clear, matter-of-fact style of writing, comprehensible to junior high students
6. Usually reliable.

Weaknesses:

1. Short, often dated bibliographies for less than half the entries
2. Undistinguished illustrations
3. Humanities, recent social and political topics, and biography less fully treated than science
4. Special Reference Supplement not sufficiently cross-referenced in main body of the text.

Further references:

American Reference Books Annual (1975), p.31–32. (Unsigned)
Booklist 71:623–24 (Feb. 15, 1975); 75:767–68 (Jan. 1, 1979).
Hirsch, Annette. *Library Journal* (Mar. 1, 1974), p.642–43.

→ The New Lincoln library encyclopedia. Rev. with each new printing. 39th ed. Columbus, Ohio, Frontier Pr. Co., 1978. 3v. *Age 12 through general adult.*

In 1978 the *Lincoln Library of Essential Information* changed its title to *The New Lincoln Library Encyclopedia*. First published in 1924, it is arranged under 12 major areas of knowledge. The order was rearranged in the 1978 edition, as follows: Geography, Economics, History, Government, Education, English Language, Literature, Fine Arts, Mathematics, Science, Biography, and Miscellany (each is subdivided under 6 to 30 topics). Fine Arts has been expanded from 4 to 15 topics, adding crafts, dance, environmental design, sculpture, and other related subjects. The Miscellany section has dropped a number of subjects, but some are incorporated in other sections. The other 10 areas follow substantially the same pattern as earlier editions. More than 50 subject dictionaries or glossaries are incorporated under appropriate major areas (e.g. for abbreviations, animals, literary plots, etc.). Much information is presented in tabular form. Dale-Chall vocabulary lists and readability index formulas have been used to ensure that the reading level is suitable for its intended audience.

While its classified arrangement makes it less convenient for ready reference, there is a complete index of 25,000 entries in each volume. It is superior to *The Volume Library* (Nashville, Tenn.: Southwestern Co.), which is also classified in its arrangement but suffers from unevenness and insufficient revision.

Strengths:

1. Broad subject coverage
2. Readable style
3. Useful subject dictionaries and tabulations
4. Objective
5. Well indexed
6. Test or review questions for major areas.

Weaknesses:

1. Unevenly revised
2. Bibliographies not uniformly updated
3. Undistinguished illustrations.

Further references:

Booklist 68:865–66 (June 15, 1972) (1971 ed.); 75:768–69 (Jan. 1, 1979), (1974 ed.).
Wynar, Bohdan S. *American Reference Books Annual* (1973), p.106 (1972 ed.).

Children's and Young Adults' Encyclopedias

Encyclopedias for children and young people have come a long way since the old *Book of Knowledge*, begun in 1912 and so dear to children of several generations ago. Now, good sets are compiled with rather scrupulous attention to the school curriculum, e.g. *World Book*, with its continuing use of the Nault-Caswell-Brain Curriculum Analysis. This analysis of courses of study in schools in the United States and Canada provides up-to-date information on topics in typical school systems from kindergarten through grade 12.

Also important is the style of writing, which must be readable, interesting, and geared to the age group for which it is intended. Editors try to organize articles in pyramid style, proceeding from the simple to the more complex, as in *Merit* and *World Book*. Also employed are vocabulary lists, such as the 44,000 words developed for *World Book* by Edgar Dale, who serves as chief readability consultant for *World Book*. Some encyclopedias try to match the vocabulary of certain articles to the reading skills of children most apt to consult those articles. *Merit*, for example, is usually successful in its stated purpose to include individual articles "designed and written at the grade level at which they are taught." Most of the encyclopedias aimed at the younger age groups also define difficult or technical words when they are used in the text.

Good illustrations, including photographs, diagrams, and maps, are essential, not for decoration but to complement the text. *Compton's* and *World Book* are generally superior to *Merit* in this respect. *Britannica Junior's* colorful illustrations and effective maps are designed to attract the attention of young children.

Bibliographies are sometimes provided for major articles, as in *World Book*, which augments them with 200 reading and study guides, with titles listed separately for younger and more advanced users. *Compton's* reading guides are organized by subject area. Only about 10 percent of the articles in *Encyclopedia International* have bibliographies, and some are badly outdated, as are some of those for major articles in *Merit*. *Britannica Junior* has been criticized for having none at all, nor does *The New Book of Knowledge*, which compensates in part by its *Home and School Study and Reading Guides* (well-selected lists of 6,000 titles keyed to articles in the encyclopedia).

These sets must be well arranged for ease of use and well indexed. *Compton's* and *World Book* are outstanding in this respect. For a detailed description of finding devices (index, cross-references, etc.) and visual aids in *World Book*, see A. Richard Harmet's remarks in "The Making of a General Encyclopedia" (*Booklist* 73:206–7 [Sept. 15, 1976]). *Encyclopedia International* is easy to use because of its entries and good index. *Merit* also has a good index, which cites illustrations as well as text among its entries.

Britannica Junior, New Book of Knowledge, and *Young Students Encyclopedia* also have indexes which can be easily used by young people.

Like adult encyclopedias, some of the encyclopedias for children and young adults have yearbooks, which are more important as a record of what happened during the previous year than as an updating of subjects in the encyclopedia. Often profusely illustrated, they have special articles on subjects of current interest. *The World Book Year Book* also reprints a few new and revised articles from the latest edition of *World Book*, as well as signed articles on important developments that are usually related to articles in the main set. It includes lists of new words and phrases and a three-year cumulative index which covers the two previous editions of the *Year Book*. *Compton's Yearbook* is well illustrated and contains see-references to the main set. *Encyclopedia International* has an annual supplement, *Encyclopedia Yearbook*, which is less satisfactory, being less related to the basic set than those of *World Book* and *Compton's*. The same can be said for *Merit Students Year Book* and *Young Students Encyclopedia Yearbook*, although they are useful for a record of events. *Britannica Junior* has no annual supplement.

The encyclopedias mentioned above may be approached in terms of their strengths and weaknesses, as reflected in critical comment on recent editions. Their reader suitability (noted after each title) is that assigned by Kenneth Kister in *Encyclopedia Buying Guide* (1978 ed.).

→ The world book encyclopedia. William H. Nault, ed. dir. Chicago, World Book–Childcraft International, Inc. 1979. 22 v. *Ages 9 through 18.*

Strengths:

1. Distinguished advisory board and expert consultant committees
2. Updated annually (172 new articles and 2,323 articles completely or partially revised in 1978 edition; 79 new articles and 1,573 revised in 1979). Special attention to current political and social issues
3. Well organized
4. Outstanding coverage of history and social sciences, biography and geography, and other subjects in the school curriculum
5. Tested in more than 400 classrooms in the U.S. and Canada to determine whether students find needed information
6. Highly accurate
7. Balanced treatment of controversial subjects
8. Clear, direct style, using controlled vocabulary, with articles written in pyramid style, from simple to more complex. Technical and advanced terms defined
9. Research Guide/Index and bibliographies for major articles

10. Metric equivalents where pertinent
11. More than 29,000 illustrations, about half in color, including good reproductions of original art, portraits of biographees, and photographs of places. Full-time cartographic staff responsible for producing maps integral to the set
12. Considered by some to be the best encyclopedia for children and young adults and for families in need of a general reference set.

Weaknesses:

1. Some biographies not treated in sufficient depth
2. Not all illustrations entirely successful.

Further references:

Booklist 75:1383–85. (May 1, 1979). Detailed comparison of 1973 and 1978 editions of *World Book*, recommending it for school and public libraries and as a general-purpose encyclopedia for the home. *Booklist* 75:714–15 (Dec. 15, 1978).

Depp, Roberta J. *American Reference Books Annual* (1978), p.43–44 (1977 ed.).

→ Compton's encyclopedia and fact index. Chicago, F. E. Compton Co. (a division of Encyclopaedia Britannica), 1979. 26v. *Ages 9 through 18.*

As popular and highly esteemed as *World Book* by some users, *Compton's* differs from *World Book* in using a broad (rather than specific) subject approach in its contents. However, *Compton's* complements this approach by providing a Fact-Index in each volume which includes not only references to the long articles in the set but also a number of brief articles, together with many illustrations in color. Nearly 500 consultants and contributors, among them eminent scholars, librarians, and educational specialists, assist the editors and lend authority to the volumes.

A review of the 1974 edition in *Booklist* (71:466–67 [Jan. 1, 1975]) reflects the generally held opinion, as well as being a succinct statement of the purpose of such encyclopedias: "A children's encyclopedia has to be visually attractive, physically sturdy and easy to handle, enticing and motivational in all its aspects, and geared to a child's ability to find references in the index and locate materials throughout the set. In all these aspects *Compton's* passes the test. A children's encyclopedia must also meet the educational, cultural, and recreational needs of children. *Compton's* continues to meet these needs also."

Although recent editions have been criticized for insufficient revision, the publisher announced that the 1979 edition was the most complete revision in five years, with updating of most of the bibliographies, updated articles on the 50 states and emerging countries, and new articles on people and places.

(The same publisher is responsible for *Compton's Precyclopedia*, which is intended for children beginning to read. As expected, it is very simply written and heavily illustrated.)

Strengths:

1. Authoritative contributors
2. Broad coverage, with topics treated in greater depth than in most other sets for the same audience, due in part to the use of broad rather than specific subjects
3. High degree of accuracy
4. Controversial subjects treated objectively
5. Clearly and interestingly written, with vocabulary progressing from simple to complex and many articles graded according to the level at which they are apt to be used. Difficult terms defined in the text
6. Fact summaries for articles on major countries, 50 states, and Canadian provinces; reference-outlines for 80 core articles
7. Reading guide in each volume organized by subject area
8. More than 30,000 well-selected illustrations and maps, well integrated with the text.

Weaknesses:

1. Difficult words not always defined
2. Some biographies too briefly treated in Fact-Index
3. Some bibliographies lacking
4. Some outdated illustrations.

Further references:

Booklist 71:466–67 (Jan. 1, 1975) (1974 ed.); 75:708–9 (Dec. 15, 1978).

Wynkoop, Sally. *American Reference Books Annual* (1975), p.32–33 (1973 ed.).

→ Merit students encyclopedia. William D. Halsey, ed. dir.; Emanuel Friedman, ed. N.Y., Macmillan Educational Corp., 1979. 20v. *Ages 9 through 18.*

This well-designed, well-edited encyclopedia is arranged under specific subjects (about 21,000 articles), selected with the needs of students in mind and based on an analysis of public school curricula in the United States and Canada. It has fewer illustrations than *Compton's* and *World Book*, but these have been commended for their suitability. Over 5,000 of the 19,200 illustrations are in color. Although not preferred to

Compton's and *World Book*, *Merit* has much to recommend it for schools and homes.

Strengths:

1. Experienced editorial staff and distinguished board of special editors
2. Signed articles by qualified contributors
3. Balanced coverage of subject matter
4. High degree of accuracy
5. Improved index, which includes references to the illustrations
6. Frequently revised, with over 1,300 articles added, rewritten, or updated in the 1979 edition, reflecting current interests (e.g. *Legionnaire's Disease, skateboarding*, and *"test-tube" baby*)
7. Clearly written, proceeding from the simple to the complex, with definitions of difficult words and dictionary definition for each entry. Vocabulary matches reading level at which appropriate subjects are taught in school
8. Intelligent use of illustrations and outstanding maps
9. Major articles, beginning with summaries, and references to related subjects.

Weaknesses:

1. Some bibliographies dated or lacking
2. Inadequate cross-references.

Further references:

Booklist 75:711–12 (Dec. 15, 1978).
Wynar, Bohdan S. *American Reference Books Annual* (1979), p.35–36 (1978 ed.).

→ Encyclopedia international. Edward Humphrey, ed. in chief. Danbury, Conn., Lexicon Publications (a subsidiary of Grolier, Inc.) 1977. 20v. *Ages 9 through 18.*

Like *World Book*, this encyclopedia is organized under specific subjects and is easy to use.

Strengths:

1. Many notable contributors
2. Reflects needs of high school students
3. American history, social sciences, consumer education, home management, and current social problems given most attention, with adequate coverage of science and many biographical and geographical entries

4. Index arranged in effective hierarchy of topics and subtopics
5. High degree of accuracy
6. Objective treatment of controversial subjects
7. Simply and clearly written
8. About 13,000 well-captioned illustrations, in proximity to text, and over 1,000 maps
9. Convenient access to contents, with many cross-references
10. Study guides, career guides, and glossaries for some articles.

Weaknesses

1. Insufficient revision
2. Humanities, literature, and the arts less fully represented than other subjects
3. Bibliographies either dated or lacking; only about 10 percent of the articles have appended bibliographies.

Further references:

Booklist 75:709–11 (Dec. 15, 1978).
Wynar, Christine L. *American Reference Books Annual* (1977), p.44–47 (1976 ed.).

→ The new book of knowledge. Martha Glauber Shapp, ed. in chief; Wallace S. Murray, ed. dir. Danbury, Conn., Grolier Educational Corp., 1979. 21v. plus separate index for schools and libraries and paperbound Home and School Study Reading Guides. *Ages 7–14.*

Encyclopedias for elementary school children, with their simple vocabulary and uncomplicated articles, are often suitable for older students with reading difficulties or slow learners. Outstanding among these is *The New Book of Knowledge*, which includes over 9,000 articles, arranged under broad subjects that are directly related to the school curriculum or reflect the recreational activities of children.

Strengths:

1. Experienced Curriculum Advisory and Library Adivisory boards
2. Well-qualified contributors
3. Broad subject coverage, geared to the needs of elementary school children and including literary excerpts, games, and projects. Biographical and geographical articles abundant
4. Accurate
5. Controversial subjects treated objectively
6. Home and School Study and Reading Guides, with over 1,000 well-selected up-to-date bibliographies

7. Readable style of writing; the Dale-Chall Readability Formula is used to determine the reading level of individual articles
8. Well illustrated with 22,400 illustrations (13,700 in color) and over 1,000 detailed maps
9. Index in back of each volume plus a cumulation in one volume (90,000 entries); adequate cross-references
10. Kept up to date by continuous revision.

Weaknesses:

1. Illustrations not fully indexed

Further references:

Booklist 75:637–39 (Dec. 1, 1978).
Wynar, Christine L. *American Reference Books Annual* (1977), p.47–51 (1976 ed.).

→ Britannica junior encyclopaedia for boys and girls. Marvin Martin, ed. Chicago, Encyclopaedia Britannica Educational Corp., 1979. 15v. *Ages 7 through 14.*

Also directed to elementary school children, *Britannica Junior Encyclopaedia* contains over 4,000 articles—less than half the number in *The New Book of Knowledge.* Unlike *The New Book of Knowledge*, it has no bibliographies (except one for *Children's literature*) but it has other attractive features.

Strengths:

1. Experienced Editorial Advisory Committee
2. Generally well balanced, with special attention to science and nature study, history, geography, biography, and sports (1979 edition gives results of the 1978 World Series)
3. Generally reliable
4. Controversial subjects objectively treated
5. Illustrations complement text
6. Added brief, factual information on about 20,000 topics in Ready Reference Index in volume 1
7. Easy to use.

Weaknesses:

1. Revision in recent years not adequate (lack of attention to current topics)
2. Brevity of infc.mation in Ready Reference Index
3. No bibliographies
4. Reading level in some articles too difficult.

Further references:

> *Booklist* 75:634–35 (Dec. 1, 1978).
> Wynar, Christine L. *American Reference Books Annual* (1978),
> p.37–39 (1977 ed.).

→ Young students encyclopedia. Rev. ed. Laurence Urdang, ed. in chief.
Middletown, Conn., Xerox Education Publications. 1977. 21v. plus 1v.
World Atlas and 2v. *Xerox Intermediate Dictionary* (earlier ed. 1972,
Funk & Wagnals. 20v.) *Ages 7 through 14.*

Young Students Encyclopedia is less impressive and less expensive
than either *Britannica Junior* or the *New Book of Knowledge* and is
included here because its 1972 edition was recommended for home
purchase by the Reference and Subscription Books Review Committee, which concluded its lengthy review with: "As clearly stated in the
Foreword this encyclopedia is for home purchase and is intended to be
used with parental guidance. *Young Students Encyclopedia* has an
advantage over other encyclopedias sold in the supermarket at this
price in that the information though brief is reliable, reasonably up to
date, skillfully written, and attractively presented on quality paper with
colorful drawings and photographs. While *Young Students Encyclopedia* will not replace more comprehensive standard encyclopedias
for children, it can supplement them when inexpensive additional sets
are needed. With this understanding *Young Students Encyclopedia* is
recommended for purchase for home, elementary school, and public
library children's departments" (*Booklist* 71:551–55 [Feb. 1, 1974]).
   This review, published in 1974, was based on careful examination of
a new encyclopedia, but important to the reputation of any encyclopedia is the extent of its revision. Thus far, there has been a limited
revision, and this must be borne in mind in evaluating the set.

Strengths (in addition to those noted above):

1. Outstanding use of graphics
2. Suggested activities for children
3. Controversial subjects treated objectively.

Weaknesses:

1. Needs more active revision policy
2. No bibliographies
3. Maps lack clarity and detail
4. Some articles are too brief.

Further references:

> *Booklist* 71:551–55 (Feb. 1, 1974); 75:640–41 (Dec. 1, 1978) (1973 ed.).
> Wynar, Christine L. *American Reference Books Annual* (1974), p.26–27.

Foreign-Language Encyclopedias

English-language encyclopedias will naturally be used most often in American libraries, but no good reference librarian can afford to overlook the great encyclopedias of other countries (some of which have been briefly mentioned earlier in this chapter). Not only should they be part of college and university reference collections and in public libraries serving foreign-born constituents, but also part of good school libraries, where children's encyclopedias, such as *Encyclopédie Larousse des Enfants*, are useful in foreign-language teaching.

Sheehy's *Guide to Reference Books* gives a good, brief introduction to foreign-language encyclopedias, pointing out strong features such as quality and number of illustrations, the history and literature of a particular country, and other information not found in English-language encyclopedias (p. 102). Also outlined are three main purposes that require their use: (1) to find an article in a foreign language for a reader who does not use English readily; (2) to find a foreign article that is better than the corresponding article in English; (3) to find something on topics omitted altogether in English encyclopedias (usually in biography, topography, history, or literature of the country of origin of the encyclopedia). Librarians with limited knowledge of foreign languages are advised to keep in mind the alphabet of the language and variations in forms of proper, personal, and geographic names.

Maxwell Scientific International has issued a pamphlet, *An Extensive Library Guide to English and Foreign Encyclopedias, 1974–1978* (64p.), which lists the major standard reference sources in many languages, arranged alphabetically by language, with facsimiles of title pages and brief descriptions of each.

In the following notes on outstanding contemporary multivolume French, German, Italian, Russian, and Spanish encyclopedias, their use in American libraries will be emphasized. Appreciation of their history may be gained from Robert Collison's *Encyclopedias: Their History throughout the Ages*. Particularly interesting are his accounts of Diderot and the Encyclopedists, and the history of the Brockhaus family and its famous work, described in the eleventh edition of *Encyclopaedia Britannica*: "No work of reference has been more useful and successful, or more frequently copied, imitated, and translated." Collison's brief commentary on Larousse is augmented by Herbert R. Lottman's "Larousse: French Publishing's Giant" (*Publishers Weekly* [Sept. 9, 1968], p.31–35), which attributes to founder Pierre Larousse (1817–75) the concept of the encyclopedic dictionary. Today, Bull computers cope with the problem of continuous revision of 500,000 entries. "The '*Grand Larousse*' itself contains 150,000 articles. The cards and their keepers are to be found in a large room, looking something like a daily newspaper's editorial office. . . . More than 500 technical magazines are scrutinized regularly to keep the files up to date. Much of the writing of articles is done by outside contributors, but then is gone over, reduced in size and above all revised '*a la sauce Larousse*,' as one employee has it—the point being that Larousse publications are for the general reader, not the specialist" (p.32).

French

→ Encyclopaedia universalis. Paris, Encyclopaedia Universalis France (a division of Encyclopaedia Britannica), 1968–75. 20v.; supp., 1977– . (Titled *Universalia*)

The first 16 volumes contain about 10,000 long, signed articles on broad subjects by such eminent French scholars as Etiemble and Bastide, as well as by authorities from other countries. Also, a few translations of extracts from *Encyclopaedia Britannica*, which it resembles in some ways. Volume 17, *Organum*, shows the interrelationships between the major subject areas of knowledge in a series of signed essays, tables, and bibliographies. Volumes 18–20, the *Thesaurus-Index*, contain about 25,000 additional short articles, including biographies and historical events. France and French Canada receive special attention. Its colored illustrations are chiefly limited to art reproductions; also has good maps and charts. Supplements cover events of the preceding year and are well illustrated. Because it attempts to cover the whole range of human knowledge, it is a valuable reference source.

→ La grande encyclopédie. Paris, Librairie Larousse, 1971–78. 20v. and index

Unlike *Encyclopaedia Universalis, La Grande Encyclopédie* emphasizes the 20th century, especially in the social sciences, science and technology, with less emphasis on the humanities. It is more "popular" in treatment and makes wider use of illustrations in color. Its bibliographies are not as lengthy and it employs a more easily read style, making it more comprehensible to a user with a limited knowledge of French. Utilizing the best features of the dictionary and classified arrangements, it contains signed articles on general concepts, historical periods, biographies, philosophies, and literary and artistic movements, as well as complicated technical processes. A detailed index to the text and the handsome illustrations is given in the last volume. Periodic updating is planned.

German

→ Brockhaus Enzyklopädie in zwanzig Bänden. 17 völlig neubearb. Aufl. des Grossen Brockhaus. Wiesbaden, Brockhaus, 1966–76. 24v. v.1–20, A–Z; v.21, Karten; v.22–23, Ergänzungen, A–Z; v.24, Bildwörterbuch der deutschen Sprache.

This new edition of the famous German encyclopedia contains 225,000 articles, 25,000 illustrations (2,000 in full color), and 800 maps. Arranged under short topics, with excellent cross-references, it includes many new entries for places and living persons, plus many expanded ones (e.g. Indian literature). International in scope, but with emphasis on German subjects, it retains its clear and simple style in its unsigned articles, addressed to the general reader. These are the work of about 1,000 international contributors. Combining the features of dictionary and encyclopedia, it is a useful source of abbreviations (e.g. ENIAC [Electronic Numerical Integrator and Computer]), giving its German equivalent as well as a brief description. While the updated bibliographies include numerous non-German works (such as the one appending the article on English literature, which gives principally English titles), they are also useful for German translations of non-German authors (e.g. Poe). Also facsimiles of autographs of distinguished persons (e.g. Franz Kafka). Numerous illustrations, many of them new to this edition, range from small, somewhat muddy black-and-white reproductions of works of art to small, but very clear maps of cities (e.g. Aachen) and clear photographs of persons. Color reproductions of works of art and photographs illustrating life in various countries are excellent. Large color maps of countries are conveniently indexed on verso of maps. Each volume gives a list of maps in that volume, and volume 1 appends pronunciation tables and abbreviations used in the text. All illustrations are close to the text they illustrate. *The Times Literary Supplement* (Aug. 3, 1967, p.716), in its review of the first two volumes, gives examples of new and extended articles and notes the greatly improved format.

The extent of revision in this (seventeenth) edition is not surprising to those familiar with the history of the house of Brockhaus. Its founder, Friedrich Arnold Brockhaus, was a dedicated believer in frequent revisions, and "in 1817 and 1818, volumes of the second, third and fourth editions were appearing concurrently—a curiosity in bibliography, in the history of the encyclopaedia, and in publishing history in general" (Collison, *Encyclopaedias*, p.159). That it retains the features for which it has long been noted assures its usefulness in American libraries.

Italian

→ Enciclopedia italiana de scienze, lettere ed arti. Roma, Istituto della Enciclopedia Italiana, fondata da Giovanni Treccani, 1929–30. 36v. Appendice I: 1938; Appendice II: 1938–1948, pub. 1948–49, 2v.; Appendice III; 1949–1960, pub. 1961, 2v.

Each volume gives the editorial staff and identifies contributors and their contributions, which are signed with initials in the text. Contributors are chiefly European scholars and professors, with Italians in the majority. Strong in the humanities and in biography, but representing the "circle of knowledge" of the 1930s, it is of value in American libraries chiefly for its large number of well-reproduced illustrations, especially those in dark sepia. Katz notes the nearly 200 photogravure plates accompanying the article on Rome (p. 163). Florence (Firenze) is less fully treated but a number of plates on the city's architecture are included. Colored illustrations are not equal to the reproductions in *Encyclopedia of World Art*, though ranging more widely in subject matter. The small black-and-white ones lack the clarity of those in *Larousse* and *Brockhaus*. The maps, many of them foldouts, produced by the Touring Club of Italy, are clear but not indexed on verso, as in *Brockhaus*. The bibliographies which append the longer articles are very good, emphasizing European and English language titles, but most of them have not been updated in the appendixes. Thus the profusely illustrated 28-column article on St. Augustine (found under "Agostino") lists no work later than 1928 in its appended bibliography.

Hailed by Collison as "one of the most important encyclopedias of the 20th century . . . one of the finest examples of the national encyclopaedia ever produced . . . and the standard of reproduction of illustrations has never been surpassed in a work of similar nature" (*Encyclopedias*, p. 207).

In spite of its appendixes, a new edition is needed if *Italiana* is to maintain its very high reputation. Further evidence of the need of a new edition is found in Livio C. Stecchini's "On Encyclopedias in Time and Space" (*The American Behavioral Scientist* 6:5 [Sept. 1962]), in which he notes the lack of treatment of contemporary issues in this "outstanding achievement of learning, (which) was made possible by the unique cirumstance that in that generation almost all Italian intellectuals, from the Communists to the Fascists, including the radical democrats and the liberals, were under the influence of Hegelian philosophy. The *Enciclopedia Italiana* realized Hegel's program for a universal knowledge. Because of the Hegelian notion that the truth of an idea is in its history, it has approached better than any other encyclopedia the idea of providing complete and objective information; topics are treated historically with a full review of the several opinions on the subject.

Therefore, even though the work was written under Fascist auspices, all points of view succeeded in finding some expression in it. Because of the historical method and because of the political circumstances, the *Enciclopedia Italiana* falls short in the treatment of truly contemporary issues."

Russian

→ Bol'shaia sovetskaia entsiklopediia. 3rd ed. Moskva, Sovetskaia Entsiklopediia, 1970–79. 30v.

→ Great Soviet encyclopedia: a translation of the third edition. A. M. Prokhorov, ed. in chief. N.Y., Macmillan, 1973– . In progress. To be completed in 30v. plus index.

The English translation of the *Great Soviet Encyclopedia* differs from the original in omitting brief articles which, according to the editors, total less than 1 percent of the Russian text (these are indicated in the list of contents in each volume). Also not included are many illustrations from the original—maps, photographs, etc. The editors of the English edition have updated some statistics, dates, and name changes, but not consistently.

The purpose of the translation, as stated in the publisher's foreword, aptly describes its use in Amerian libraries: "to convey the scope and point of view of the *Great Soviet Encyclopedia* and to bring to scholars and others with a serious professional interest in Soviet affairs a primary source through which they can gain a richer knowledge and understanding of the contemporary Soviet Union. The major value . . . lies in the wealth of information about the USSR and its peoples that has been previously unavailable in English. Although the Encyclopedia is general in scope, it naturally concentrates on the Soviet Union. . . . Another value . . . is its consistent statement of the Soviet point of view. . . . The Encyclopedia also reflects the state of the art in Soviet science and technology . . . and serves as a guide to current Soviet thinking and research."

Patricia Kennedy Grimsted, whose review of the first five volumes provoked sharp reply from the editors, made a number of severe criticisms of the English edition, but she did agree that "it will be helpful for many libraries to have available in English many BSE articles for both their factual content and their presentation of the Soviet point of view. The lengthy coverage of many of the lesser-known areas or peoples of the USSR would certainly not be duplicated in any general or even specialized Western encyclopedia. Many of the BSE articles are signed by the most distinguished Soviet scholars, and their availability in smooth English translation to many non-Russan readers is a tremendous advantage for specialists and non-specialists alike" ("Detente on the Reference Shelves?" in *Wilson Library Bulletin* 49:728–40 [June 1975]).

Others have found the translation smooth and easily to read. And for those who wish to compare the text of an article with the original, exact citation to the original is given for every article.

The publishers, in compiling statistics on number of articles in each subject field, give 19,500 for geography; 10,800 for biology; 10,000 for technology; 10,000 for world history; 6,200 for literature; 5,800 for USSR history; 4,200 for fine arts and architecture; 4,000 for music, theater, films, 4,000 for economics; and fewer for other fields, from 200 in logic to 3,200 in physics. While the number of articles does not necessarily indicate the amount of space devoted to a subject, it is a fairly good indication of relative emphasis.

Many of the over 100,000 articles have appended bibliographies, including all found in the original set, but they are presented in a form which can be checked through the *National Union Catalog*. Thus works in languages that do not use the Latin alphabet are given in the Library of Congress transliteration system for that language, or, if there is no Library of Congress system, in the transliteration system used throughout the translation. Names of authors whose works are translated into Russian appear in the original language, not in the Russian transliteration. The bibliographies of articles on people are divided into works by and works about, with the latter arranged first by publications in Russian, then foreign works in Russian translation, and then the original and other languages. Other bibliographies usually reflect the structure and content of the articles.

The English translation, arranged by the Latin (not the Cyrillic) alphabet, *must* be used with the Index (published at five-volume intervals and cumulating with each, e.g. v.1–5, v.1–10, v.1–15, with a final cumulation covering v.1–30). Prepared by computer, it is detailed and accurate, and it is estimated that, when complete, it will contain approximately 500,000 entries. Clear instructions for its use are given.

Transliterating volume by volume from the Cyrillic to the Latin alphabet results in some volumes of the English translation having articles that begin with most of the letters of the Latin alphabet. For example, v.20, published in 1979, contains articles from *Absolute Ceiling* to *Zone Time*. Among the entries are *Katherine Prichard* (1884–1969), "member of the Communist Party of Australia since 1920"; *Road Traffic Rules*, compulsory for all participants in road traffic; and *Rule of Inference*.

A detailed review of the first volume of *Great Soviet Encyclopedia* will be found in *Booklist* (July 15, 1974), p.1211–12, and a note on volumes 2–5 was published May 1, 1976 (p.704). The editors' reply to

Grimsted's review (cited above) is in *Wilson Library Bulletin* (Sept. 1975), p.20–21. See also *Choice* (July/Aug. 1974), p.736, for a brief review, and for a more lengthy one, Theodore Shebad, "Aalen Stage to Zulu War," in *The New York Times* (Jan. 14, 1974, p.25).

Spanish

→ Enciclopedia universal ilustrada europeo-americana. Barcelona, Espasa; Madrid, Espasa-Calpe, 1905–33. 80v. in 81. Suplemento anual, 1934– . 1935– . Irregular.

One of the world's most extensive encyclopedias, it is generally known as *Espasa*. V.1-70 and Apéndice v.1-10 (A–Z) are arranged alphabetically by short topic, with many cross-references. Supplements are arranged under broad topics, e.g. *Geografía e Historia*, further subdivided by countries. It has dictionary and encyclopedic features. Dictionary entries give etymology and French, Italian, English, German, Portuguese, Catalan, and Esperanto equivalents, but no quotations for illustrations of use. Encyclopedic features include its broad international coverage, though it is especially strong for Spain and Latin America and in biographical and geographical entries. Bibliographies for longer articles have been well selected (though now dated) and do not appear to include Spanish translations from original works of non-Spanish writers. It is noted for its large number of geographical, geological, historical, and statistical maps, including a number of small cities; and for its many full-color reproductions of paintings (though these are excelled by the *Encyclopedia of World Art*). It is a fine source of Spanish and Spanish-American biography.

The supplements, which have appeared biennially since 1953–54, usually are published several years later, e.g. 1971–72 was published in 1978. In spite of this lag, they are valuable for their large number of brief biographies, often with accompanying photographs, found in the *Biografía y Necrologia* section, and for the more than 400 pages covering socio-economic conditions by countries, with emphasis on Spain, in the *Georgrafía e Historia* section, illustrated with many fuzzy news photos and a few colored plates. Sports are well covered under *Deportes*, with a separate section on bullfighting (*Tauromaquia*). They are also useful for statistics of tourism (*Turismo*) and for world coverage of theater, dance, and film (profusely illustrated with stills, and with lists of award-winning films and a good appended bibliography). Unlike those in the basic set, articles in the supplements are signed with initials. The list of contributors with their affiliations, found in front of each volume, reveals that all are Spanish and chiefly writers or members of academic professions.

In using the basic set it may be well to remember the comment of Livio C. Stecchini in his article "On Encyclopedias in Time and Space." He brands it "remarkable for its lack of concern with the reliability of the information and for the casualness of the editing, by which two entries may be dedicated to the same person under different names" (p.3).

In summary, foreign encyclopedias are useful in American libraries for:
1. Viewpoints other than American
2. Biographies of nationals of the countries of publication
3. Excellent illustrations (in some cases)
4. Plots of novels, dramas, and films
5. Facsimiles of autographs of distinguished people
6. Abbreviations
7. Subjects of national interest
8. Maps of cities
9. Bibliographies that emphasize the language of the country of publication.

General Reference Features of Encyclopedias

One great strength of the modern general encyclopedia is that it incorporates the features of many other types of reference sources:
1. Like an unabridged monolingual dictionary, it defines words, and sometimes gives their pronunciation.
2. Like a bibliography, it cites sources of further information, (though not always as comprehensively as required by certain users).
3. Like a universal biographical dictionary, it devotes generous amounts of space to biographies of individuals, both living and dead.
4. Like a gazetteer, it supplies pertinent information on large and small geographic areas, more often than not with accompanying maps.

That it will continue to retain these features seems more than likely; and, as noted, its inadequacies must be filled by additional forms of reference sources, such as:
1. Special encyclopedias for fuller or more highly technical information
2. Bibliographies, indexes, and abstracts designed to meet the need for fuller and more-up-to-date information
3. Unabridged dictionaries for further information on words and their usage
4. Statistical sources that provide more detailed and up-to-date data, especially on socio-economic conditions
5. Atlases, which provide maps on a larger scale and in more detail, especially for smaller areas.

Sources of Statistics

You can prove a fact conclusively,
Regardless of the fact you want to get.
Treat a young statistic kindly
And he's always answered kindly until yet.
—ANONYMOUS

This chapter acknowledges the widespread production and uses of statistics in today's world—with no reason to doubt that they will multiply—and suggests that reference librarians can and should improve their understanding of statistics. It concludes with an annotated, representative list of statistical sources.

It is a truism to speak of the pervasiveness of statistics in modern society. So obsessed are we with numbers (though the written or spoken word may be highly suspect, numerical information suggests precision, great accuracy) that we use them to "prove" practically anything. From all sides (government agencies, research organizations, colleges and universities, corporations, etc.), we are bombarded with statistics on the stock market, public opinion polls, TV ratings, sports, population trends, socio-economic and political conditions, and on and on. Important decisions in our national and personal lives are made on the basis of statistics. Alas, however, statistics and the interpretation of statistics do not constitute an exact science; they are, rather, partly an art and partly a science. Librarians should therefore appreciate this wisdom from the authors of an introductory statistics text:

Those who accept statistics indiscriminately will be duped unnecessarily; those who distrust statistics indiscriminately will often be ignorant unnecessarily; recognize, therefore, that there is an alternative between gullibility and blind distrust (in W. Allen Wallis and Harry V. Roberts, *Statistics: A New Approach* [Glencoe, Ill.: Free Pr., 1956], p.17).

It should not go unnoticed that the revolution in statistical work, wrought by the computer, in both the speed of publication and the multiplication of detail available (whether published or unpublished), continues unrelentingly. Consider, for instance, the experience of the U.S. Bureau of the Census before and after the advent of the computer. The mechanical tabulating system it developed for the 1890 census counted 250 items a minute; by 1950 it had increased to 2,000 items per minute. The next major speedup of data processing came in 1951, with the first large-scale electronic computer, UNIVAC I, designed and built specifically for the Bureau. This machine was able to tabulate 4,000 items per minute, but subsequent generations of computers have increased the speed to nearly 1 million items per minute.

To take advantage of these computers, there had to be advances in getting data ready for processing. Punching cards, though far faster than writing, is still basically a hand operation that is subject to human error and creates quantities of perishable records. During the 1950s, the National Bureau of Standards and the Census Bureau developed a system called FOSDIC (Film Optical Sensing Device for Input to Computers). Questionnaires that were completed by using a pencil to blacken dots opposite the appropriate answers were permanently photographed onto microfilm with automatic cameras. FOSDIC then "read" the blackened dots and transferred the data to magnetic tape for the computer at speeds that ranged from 3,000 items a minute, with the earliest models, to 70,000 items a minute in the 1970 version. In 1980, FOSDIC will transmit the data over long distances to the computers at Bureau headquarters as well.

FOSDIC also performs simple checks and tabulations so that discrepancies can be reviewed before the computer begins its work. Other equipment was obtained so that data from survey or Census report forms could be keyed directly from the computer tape and checked for acceptability at the same time.

At the other end of the computer process, high-speed electronic printers were utilized, beginning in the 1950s, that produced tabulations in forms that required only the addition of headings to be published by offset processes. Later, the Bureau took advantage of a new high-speed composer that converted the data on the computer tape to words and numbers on offset negative film. A variety of electronic data plotters came into use to produce maps, charts, and graphs from the computerized data (U.S. Bureau of the Census, *Fact Finder for the Nation: History and Organization* [CFF no.4, rev.], Washington, May 1979, p.10–11).

Statistical Reference Service and Evaluation of Statistical Sources

It is a fair question to ask why reference librarians should grasp the fundamentals of statistics. In answer, at least three substantial reasons may be given. First, as facilitators or intermediaries between users and information they are increasingly called upon to do much more than merely locate and collect statistics—they are expected to provide informed interpretation of these materials, as they have traditionally done for other parts of library collections. Awareness of statistical methodology and principles improves their ability to perform intelligently in this role.

Second, the literature of virtually every discipline, including the humanistic, reflects increasing use and sophistication of quantitative methods of research. The impact of this trend on librarians' requisite skills is obvious.

Third, it appears that reference librarians and others will increasingly be expected to undertake "research" (which may very well include statistical analyses) of their own, either as individual investigators or in collaboration with others, and that the presence or absence of such activity may spell the difference between advancement and standing still in a position.

In addition to helping others with their projects, reference librarians will undoubtedly, more and more, apply their expertise to their own research, which, as suggested above, might include a solid statistical component. Clearly, then, librarians will need a good grasp of the most frequently used statistical terms and techniques. The paragraphs that follow suggest a few fundamental elements of statistical analysis.

We begin by recognizing that there are two large classes of statistics, descriptive and inferential. *Descriptive* statistics deal with the condensation and summarization of a body of data—ages, heights, salaries, test scores, and so on. *Inferential* (or inductive) statistics permit the drawing of broad conclusions or generalizations about a *population* or *universe* (the *whole* number of people, incomes, test scores, or other characteristics being considered) on the basis of information on only a part—a *sample*—of the population. Statistical data, then, consist of numbers that represent measurement of some characteristic or phenomenon.

Turning to descriptive statistics, let us suppose that, for a group of 11 hotel employees, the years of service are 6, 9, 12, 10, 12, 12, 14, 7, 8, 11, 9. Merely by looking at these figures of so small a group we can easily get an idea of how the group as a whole fared. If, however, we had the years of service of 1,099 employees, the task would not be easy, unless we organized the data in some way. One way is a *frequency distribution*, which lists the values in numerical order, from largest to smallest, or vice versa, and the frequency of occurrence (designated by *f*) of each value. In the interest of simplicity, let us illustrate with reference to the smaller group:

Years of Service	Frequency (f)	Years of Service	Frequency (f)
14	1	9	2
13	0	8	1
12	3	7	1
12	3	7	1
11	1	6	1
10	1		Total 11

Such data may be graphed, permitting the researcher (or reader) to "see" what the distribution looks like, in a *frequency polygon* (fig. 1), one of several useful graphic devices.

Building upon the organization of data in a frequency distribution, statisticians may summarize data by calculating the average or most typical value. These values, called *measures of central tendency* (central points in the frequency distribution around which the values tend to cluster), are of three kinds. The *mean* (more properly, in this case, *arithmetic mean* [symbol $\bar{X}$]) is the arithmetic average of all the values. In the example shown in figure 1, the sum of the years of service (110), divided by 11 (the number of employees) produces a mean of 10. The *median* is the midpoint of the values—in the example, 10 (five persons are above and five are below 10 years). The *mode* is the most frequently occurring value, or 12—the number of years of each of three persons in the example.

Statisticians also employ measures of *variability* (or dispersion), as shown in figure 2. The simplest such measure is the *range*, the span of values in a distribution (14-5, or 9, in figure 1). More complicated, but very useful, is the *standard deviation* (symbol s), which indicates the extent to which values cluster about the mean. The formula is:

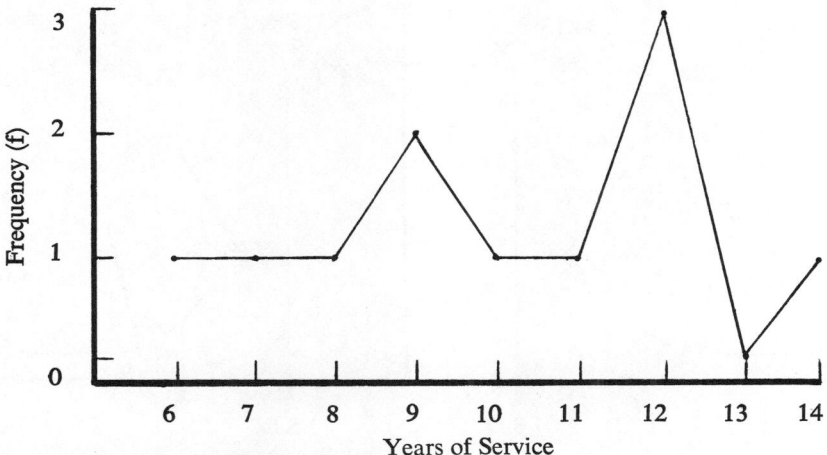

Figure 1. Frequency Polygon

Years of Service X	Variation from Mean (X) (X-X̄)	Variation Squared (X-X̄)²
6	-4	16
9	-1	1
12	2	4
10	0	0
12	2	4
12	2	4
14	4	16
7	-3	9
8	-2	4
11	1	1
9	-1	1
		60

Figure 2. Measures of Variability

$s = \sqrt{\dfrac{\Sigma(X - \bar{X})^2}{n}}$, and because $n = 11$, $\bar{X} = 10$, and $\Sigma(X - \bar{X})^2 = 60$,

$s = \sqrt{\dfrac{60}{11}} = \sqrt{5.45} = 2.33$

Mention of the standard deviation leads to a brief examination of a *normal distribution*, which is pictorially a bell-shaped or normal curve (fig. 3).

In this distribution the mean, median, and mode are identical, and half of the values lie to the right (i.e. above) and half to the left of (below) the

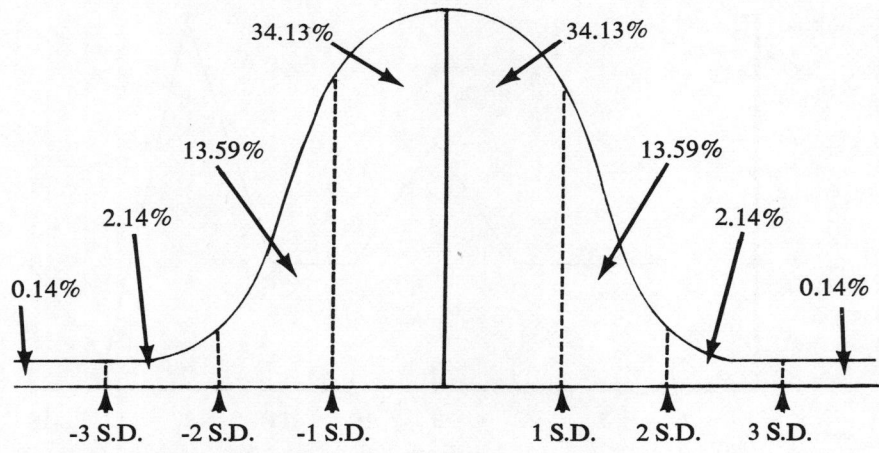

Figure 3. Normal Distribution

mean. It is also true that one standard deviation above the mean (1 S.D.) includes 34.13 percent of the values in the distribution, and so does one standard deviation below the mean (− 1 S.D.). In other words, slightly more than two-thirds of the values (68.26%) fall between 1 S.D. and − 1 S.D. The mean plus and minus 2 and 3 standard deviations accounts for 95.44 and 99 + percent of the values. Note that the tails of the curve never quite touch the baseline and that the exact number of standard deviations required to reach 100 percent varies from situation to situation. Not all distributions are normal and these are said to be *skewed*—negatively, if the mean and median are lower (smaller) than the mode; positively, if they are higher (greater) than the mode (figs. 4a and 4b).

Directing attention to *inferential statistics*, we remind ourselves that descriptive statistics describe characteristics of the entire group (which statisticians call the *population* or *universe*) being considered, such as test scores, ages, college students, welfare recipients, automobile accidents. A population may be very large or very small; usually, however, it is not possible or practical (too costly or too time consuming) to measure populations. Instead, statisticians take a small number of measurements or observations, termed a *probability sample*, and on that basis make generalizations (inferences) about the characteristics of the population. (Note: Characteristics of the population [means, medians, standard deviations, etc.] are *parameters*; characteristics of a sample are *statistics*.) To be effective, the sample must be *representative* of the population. For this reason, members of the population are selected in some *random* manner, so that every element from which the sample is drawn has a known probability of being included in the sample. (Three types of probability sampling may be distinguished: *simple random*, in which each member of the population is as likely as any other to be included in the sample; *systematic*, in which the first member is randomly selected and all others are selected at a fixed interval, say, every 15th instance; and *stratified*, in which the population is divided into similar groups and a random sample is taken from each group; e.g., in order to estimate the average income in an area, divide the population into occupational groups.) Still, it must be recognized that no matter how carefully the sample may be selected it is not *exactly* representative of the larger body. To put it another

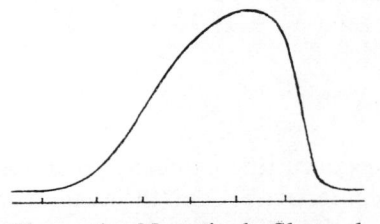

Figure 4a. Negatively Skewed

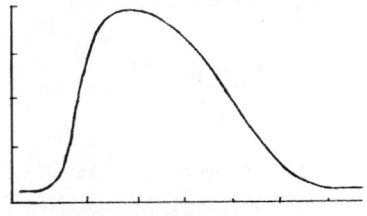

Figure 4b. Positively Skewed

way, inferential statistics, based on the mathematics of probability, provide techniques for making inferences about a population based on sample data and for evaluating the risks involved. In lay language, "probably," "likely," "odds," and "maybe" are examples of synonyms for probability.

Having selected a sample and having computed a statistic/statistics, we are prepared to make a statement (a *hypothesis*) about the population. More specifically, the hypothesis to be tested is a *null* or statistical hypothesis, meaning one with a probability of rejection at some level of significance. For example, suppose the null hypothesis is that a given population should have a mean of 50 ($\mu = 50$)—any difference between that mean and the sample mean is due to chance. To test this hypothesis, a sample of 25 is drawn from the population; its mean ($\bar{X}$) is 51. Let us say that the probability value selected—to represent the risk the researcher will accept of wrongly rejecting the null hypothesis (i.e. wrongly regarding results as valid which in fact were due to chance [a Type I error] or wrongly accepting the hypothesis [ascribing chance to valid results, a Type II error])—is .01 ($p = .01$), the 1 percent level of significance. This is to say that the results could have happened by chance 1 out of 100 times; in this example we may reject the hypothesis at that level. In passing, it may be noted that .05 (5%) and .001 (.1%) also are frequently used by researchers.

To illustrate another technique of statistical inference, let us consider the sampling distribution of sample means. Inasmuch as the sampling distribution is approximately normal if the number of cases (N) in the sample is over 30 (and for which a z test is used), we can turn our attention to the "Student t distribution" ("Student" was the pen name of a statistician, W. S. Gosset) for under-30 situations, where the distribution is not close to normal, changing with the number of cases in the sample.

Example: A sample of 18 coal miners shows a mean income of $72 per week, compared with an average of $66 for all industrial workers in a census of a certain area. The standard deviation (s) of income for coal miners is $4 per week. Is the mean income of coal miners higher than the mean income of all industrial workers? To recapitulate, we have: $\mu = 6$, $\bar{X} = 72$, $s = 4$, $N = 18$.

Next comes the computation of standard score:

$$\sigma_{\bar{x}} \text{ (standard error of means)} = \frac{s}{\sqrt{N-1}} = \frac{4}{\sqrt{17}} = \frac{4}{4.12} = .97$$

$$t = \frac{\bar{X} - \mu}{\sigma_{\bar{x}}} = \frac{72-66}{.97} = \frac{6}{.97} = 6.2$$

The probability of so unusual a sample's occurring by chance requires calculating t (from a special table) for 17 degrees of freedom (the number of observations free to vary; i.e. $N - 1 = 18 - 1 = 17$) at the chosen level of significance (.05): $t = 2.11$. The value of $t = 6.2$ (in the computation above) is larger than 2.11, so that samples this unusual would occur by chance less than 5 percent of the time. Decision: Reject the null hypothesis. Coal miners, on the average, tend to receive higher wages than industrial workers generally (Sanford M. Dornbusch and Calvin F. Schmid, *A Primer of Social Statistics* [New York: McGraw-Hill, 1955], p.157–64, 239).

To determine whether the values in one sample are more variable than those in another sample, an *F test*, using the *variance* (the square of the standard deviation) and a table of *F* values, reveals whether the variability in one set of data is significantly larger than in another. The *analysis of variance* technique, also using the *F* test, may be used for analyzing differences among any number of samples and/or differences among groups within samples.

Where we wish to know whether there is a relationship between the values for one measure (say, swimming speed) and those for another measure (say, weight) for each individual in a group, *correlation* is the appropriate statistical technique. Symbolically, simple correlation is represented by a coefficient of correlation. An example is the *Pearson product-moment correlation*, from $r = -1.00$ for perfect negative correlation (the values of one variable increase proportionally to the decrease of the values of the other variable; fig. 5a) to $r = 1.00$ for perfect positive correlation (the values of one variable increase proportionally to those of the other variable; fig. 5b). No degree of correlation (zero correlation) is $r = .00$.

Regression analysis, closely allied with correlation, allows statisticians to predict one variable from another whose value is known. For the mathematics involved, using a library example, see Ray L. Carpenter and Ellen Storey Vasu, *Statistical Methods for Librarians* (Chicago: ALA, 1978), pages 72–75.

The techniques discussed thus far have been concerned with the value of a population parameter. *Parametric statistics* assume that the measured variable is normally distributed in the population (or, as a minimum, that the form of the distribution is known) and that the data represent an interval (e.g. 30–35, 36–41) or a ratio (60 minutes is six times as long as 10 minutes)

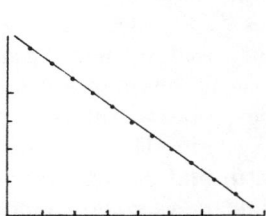 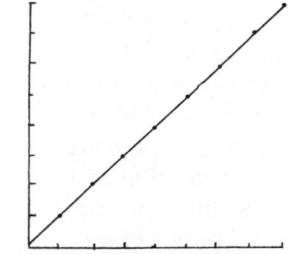

Figure 5a. Perfect Negative Correlation   Figure 5b. Perfect Positive Correlation

scale of measurement. But in some cases it is not feasible (or possible) to make rigid statistical assumptions about the shape of the population being sampled. *Nonparametric* or distribution-free tests fill this void, and the most important nonparametric method is the *chi-square* (x^2) test. It is used to determine the probability that the frequencies observed in a study differ from some theoretical hypothesized frequencies.

Let us suppose that in a survey 40 people preferred Brand C toothpaste and 60 preferred Brand D. The null hypothesis is that there is no difference between the number of people who prefer Brand C and those who prefer Brand D. If the hypothesis is correct, we would expect half the people (50) to prefer Brand C and half to prefer Brand D. In the chi-square test, these are the *expected* frequencies, i.e. those expected to occur by chance. In fact, however, the *observed* frequencies were 40 and 60. The question, then, is are the observed frequencies (*fo*) sufficiently different to justify rejection of the null hypothesis? The calculation is:

$$x^2 = \sum \frac{(fo - fe)^2}{fe} = \sum \frac{fo^2}{fe} - n = \sum 104 - 100 = 4$$

fo	fe	fo²	fo²/fe
40	50	1600	32
60	50	3600	72
			104

Reading the chi-square table (found in many standard texts) at the .05 level, with 1 degree of freedom if the variables are indeed independent, we see that the chi-square value would be no larger than 3.841. Therefore we reject the null hypothesis that there is no difference between the number of people selecting Brand C and those choosing Brand D. We would not, however, reject it at the .01 or .001 levels.

Reference librarians may next address themselves to considering some reasons for the difficulty of statistical questions and suggestions for evaluating statistical sources. Statistical questions may be difficult because the answers are in a form which is hard to obtain, understand, identify, and evaluate. Often the material that is needed to answer a single question is scattered, so that one part will be found in one publication and others in other publications, and the parts do not always fit together because of differences in bases of coverage or units of measurement, even in the same series. For example, "in trying to find statistics on the monetary value of production of some commodity in various countries, [one] will find different units of value on account of the various monetary systems. Then, the sources of current statistical information are often hard to find because they are either in serial publications, unindexed periodicals, newspapers, and government bulletins or are of the kind known as 'fugitive materials,' mimeographed press releases and services" (Margaret Hutchins, *Introduction to Reference Work* [Chicago: ALA, 1944], p. 70).

Experienced librarians well know that some users want more up-to-date statistics than have been published, or they want them arranged differently from the way the compilers have published them—by, say, age and county when they have been published by sex and state, or consumption statistics when only production and export statistics are available. Such requests may require librarians to think of extramural sources; for example, it is possible that the agency which collected and published the statistics on the subject has the needed figures on file and would make them available to the researcher.

Still, it must be recognized that there are instances where certain statistics have not been collected or made available—even though the requester's position may be that surely—somewhere—there are the data on the desired topic. It is hard to convince this person that the statistics may not have been collected because of protests from certain groups, as in the case of the 1970 *Census of Population*, when the Census Bureau was not permitted to include a question on church membership.

Another aspect may be the confidentiality of records—not whether the data have been collected.

> In order to protect the confidentiality promised respondents and required by law, it is necessary for the Census Bureau to make sure that its published data, in print or on tape, do not disclose information about particular individuals. Therefore the Bureau withholds, or suppresses, tabulations of characteristics of very small groups of people or housing units, but in such a way that it is still possible to show those characteristics at higher levels of aggregation. . . . Persons unable to obtain a birth certificate and needing a proof of age are able to request a search of old census records by the Census Bureau, for a fee. . . . This service is available to the person enumerated and not to someone else wanting to find out about him or her. [U.S. Bureau of the Census, *Reference Manual on Population and Housing Statistics from the Census Bureau* (Washington: the Bureau, 1977), p.3, 92]

Other data are not available because of the nature of the subject, e.g. rape, for which only widely ranging estimates have been made by different groups. Also, persons often ask for comparable statistics on such subjects as marriage and divorce, or juvenile deliquency, for earlier periods than they are available.

It is also appropriate to stress the importance of the preliminary interview with the inquirer to determine, for example, (1) how accurate the information must be (will a rough estimate do?), (2) exactly what is wanted (ambiguous terms must be defined; for instance, if statistics of the twenty-five largest reference departments are requested, what standard of size is meant—the community, the library, the reference staff, the collection, or the number of questions answered daily?), (3) how the statistics are to be broken down or classified (e.g. by year, month; dollars; tons; country, state, county; age, sex, race). (Cf. Hutchins, p.70–72.)

Evaluation of statistical sources accents the importance of primary (i.e. original) sources in statistical reference work. They are more accurate, since in any reproduction, other than photoreproduction, typographical errors may be introduced. They may be more detailed and more complete than in a secondary source; for example, from the original table of United States population, by decades 1790–1970 and for each state, the secondary source might show only the 1960 and 1970 figures for but five states. Primary sources may be far superior to secondary ones in providing notes explaining how (and even why) the statistics were prepared and any limitations— recognition of bias in data compilation, change in agency responsible for collection of data, change of classification (such as that reflected in a re-definition of urban and rural population or standard metropolitan statistical areas), etc.—to be remembered in using the data.

One type of note that is not included in the above paragraph is singled out for additional comment. The statistical measure involved here is the index number, or index, to measure relative changes over time. Suppose that the tons of wheat consumed in 1967 are stated as 100 percent (the base). If consumption in, say 1970, was 6 percent greater than in 1967, this fact would be shown as 106. If statisticians convert to a different base, it follows that this change must be duly noticed. In passing, it should be observed that index numbers are equally useful for showing relative change in such variables as production, prices, and employment. It is also to be remembered that, at any given time, one may encounter the use of several different indexes—a reminder that while a base of 100 for a given time period (e.g. 1967 = 100) may be the one most frequently seen, it is by no means the only one used. For instance, in the September 1977 issue of *Survey of Current Business* (a title discussed more fully later in this chapter), besides 1967 = 100, the following were used: 1972 = 100, 1910–14 = 100, Dec. 1975 = 100, 1968 = 100, 1913 = 100, 1947–49 = 100, 1941–43 = 10, Dec. 31, 1965 = 50, 1969 = 100 (p.S-2, -3, -8, -9, -10, -11, -21, -22, -25, respectively).

Since the quality of the notes in all statistical sources (secondary as well as primary) is so critical in judging the value of the sources, let us sample their variety from a superior secondary source, *Statistical Abstract of the United States, 1977*. Following each example is an indication of the type of note being illustrated.

p.5, table 1, note 3: "The official 1970 resident population count is 203,235,298; the difference of 23,372 is due to errors found after tabulations were completed." (Data collection procedure note)

p.5, no. 2 headnote (part): "Total population includes Armed Forces abroad; resident population excludes them." (Statement of universe note) p.9, no. 6 headnote: "Center of population is that point . . ." (Definition)

p.14, no. 12 headnote: "In thousands, except percent. . . . For explanation of methodology, see source . . ." (The source is "U.S. Bureau of the Census, *Current Population Reports*, series P-25, Nos. 460 and 642, and unpublished data.") (Unit indicator, cross-reference source)

p.94, no. 134 headnote: "In millions of dollars, except percent. For years ending June 30 . . ." (Unit indicator, time restrictor)

p.95, no. 136 headnote: "Data differ from those in table 134 which are for fiscal years . . ." (Comparability, time restrictor)

p.148, no. 240 headnote: "As of spring of year. Based on sample and subject to sampling variability" (Time restrictor, data collection procedure)

n.1: "For definition of median, see p. xii." (Cross-reference)

p.242, no. 401 n.1: "Data not entirely comparable because of changes in classifications." (Comparability)

p.358 (in general explanation to the tables that follow in the section "National Defense and Veterans Affairs"): "VA estimates of veterans cover all persons with service during periods of war or armed conflict and include those living outside the United States. . . . Similar data from the Bureau of the Census relate to civilian males 16 years old and over, who live in the United States and who have served in the Armed Forces, whether in war or peacetime." (Comparability)

p.464, no. 752: "Source: 1922–1956, Robert J. Lampman . . .; 1958, James D. Smith and Staunton K. Calvert . . .; 1962–1972, James D. Smith . . ." (Source)

p.479, no. 771 headnote: "1967 = 100, except as noted. See headnote, p. 439" n.9: "January 1972 = 100." (Index, cross-reference, index)

p.684, no. 1152 n.2: "Comparable data not available." (Comparability)

p.685, no. 1155 n.2: "Beginning 1965, excludes horses and mules." (Time restrictor, change of universe)

p.714, no. 1219 n.1: "Data are for farms having sales of $2,500 and over." (Universe)

p.715, no.1221 footnote: "D withheld to avoid disclosure." (Nondisclosure)

p.770, no. 1319 headnote: "Based on a probability sample of about 167,000 construction establishments with payroll . . ." (Data collection procedure)

Awareness of these notes is essential for careful statistical reference work, especially since inexperienced users are apt to overlook them. It should also be noted that prefaces to statistical compilations (e.g. U.S. Bureau of the Census, *Historical Statistics*) and articles that discuss problems of data analysis (e.g. Howard V. Stambler, "Problems in Analyzing Urban Employment Survey Data," *Monthly Labor Review* 92:51–54 [Nov. 1969]) may likewise be valuable in evaluating sources.

While most of the remainder of this chapter is devoted to annotating a representative list of statistical reference sources, it may be useful at this point to suggest a short list of the most frequently consulted titles, along with page references to their annotations.

Almanacs, 257–58
American Statistics Index, 244
Freund & Williams. Dictionary/Outline of Basic Statistics, 239
International Encyclopedia of Statistics, 239–40
Kendall & Buckland. A Dictionary of Statistical Terms, 240
State (and local, if any) statistical abstract, 260–61 (see comment on *Statistical Abstract*)
Statistical Abstract (and supplements), 260–61
Statistical Reference Index, 243
Statistics Sources, 243
Survey of Current Business, 263
U.N. Statistical Yearbook, 260
U.S. Bureau of the Census. Bureau of the Census Catalog, 244

Work with statistical sources brings to light a most valuable skill of good reference librarians: the ability to pigeonhole or categorize sources rapidly—a bit of mental gymnastics, so to speak—in order to try to connect types of sources and types of questions. A review of the more general types of sources thus seems in order.

1. Bibliographies and indexes
    a. National library catalogs are a source of books on statistical methods and for location of compilations of statistics on broad subjects, e.g. agriculture, labor, and population.
    b. Guides to the literature of subject fields supply pertinent sources of statistics (discussed further in this chapter).
    c. Indexes, such as *Public Affairs Information Service*, are often a source of current statistics (to be discussed further).
2. Biographical sources. These are useful only for such specific vital statistics as birth and death dates, sex, age, place of residence, and occupation of individuals.
3. Dictionaries. These are useful only for population statistics of larger geographical areas, for statistics on colleges and universities, and, to a certain extent, for definitions of statistical terms.
4. Encyclopedias
    a. General encyclopedias contain (usually for larger geographical areas) socio-economic statistics such as area, population, education, production, etc., which must be updated by their yearbooks and other sources (to be discussed further).
    b. They also contain general articles on statistical theories and methods, such as the brief but clear article in *Compton's Encyc-*

lopedia. Special encyclopedias in appropriate subject fields are even better sources on theories and methods, e.g. *International Encyclopedia of the Social Sciences* and *International Encyclopedia of Statistics*. (The latter title is described later in this chapter.)

While this chapter's emphasis is clearly on sources of statistics, rather than statistical methods and theories, we may indicate a bibliographic route to statistical theory and methodology:

→ Kendall, Maurice George, and Doig, Alison G. Bibliography of statistical literature. N.Y., Hafner, 1962–68. 3v.

    CONTENTS: V.1, 1950–58; v.2, 1940–49; v.3, pre-1940, and supplements to v.1–2. Lists papers but no books, chiefly in Western languages, on statistical theory and method from the 16th century to the end of 1958. Augments Oscar Buros, *Statistical Methodology Reviews, 1933/38–1941/50* (N.Y., Wiley, 1938–51; 3v.; titles and imprint vary), which includes only books, with abstracts from their reviews.

Nor will we consider the forms in which statistical data may be presented, such as tables, graphs, and charts, though librarians may be asked for information on such subjects. In this connection, Mary Eleanor Spear's *Practical Charting Techniques* (New York: McGraw-Hill, 1969; 394p.), A. J. Cameron's *A Guide to Graphs* (New York: Pergamon, 1970; 158p.), and A. J. MacGregor's *Graphics Simplified* (Toronto: Univ. of Toronto Pr., 1979; 64p.) are satisfactory introductions.

Terminology

Statistical reference service cannot fail (as has been suggested) to recognize the problem of terminology. Not unique to the collection and interpretation of statistics, it is faced by all disciplines, especially in the social and behavioral sciences, with a rapidly changing vocabulary, and has resulted in a continuing effort on the part of those responsible for statistical activities to bring about some uniformity in definitions of terms—some standardization that will result in relative reliability for the data being collected. Evidence of this concern is found in special dictionaries and encyclopedias:

→ Freund, John E., and Williams, Frank J. Dictionary/outline of basic statistics. N.Y., McGraw-Hill, 1966. 195p.

    Contains over 1,000 statistical terms and an outline of statistical formulas.

→ International encyclopedia of statistics. Ed. by William H. Kruskal and Judith M. Tanur. N.Y., Free Press, 1978. 2v.

Extensive alphabetically arranged articles on statistics proper and on social science topics with special relevance to statistics, to which are appended selected bibliographies. Articles reprinted from *International Encyclopedia of the Social Sciences* have been revised, corrected, and updated.

→ Kendall, Maurice George, and Buckland, William R. A dictionary of statistical terms; prep. for the International Statistical Institute. 3rd ed. Edinburgh, Oliver & Boyd, 1971. 166p.

About 2,500 terms well defined, with evaluations of controversial usage. Deletes glossaries of French, German, Italian, and Spanish equivalent terms, a feature of the 1st (1957) and 2nd (1960) eds.

An outstanding example of a federal agency concerned with definitions of terms is the U.S. Bureau of the Census, and no user of its statistical array should ignore the prefatory definitions that accompany many of its collections of data, such as the decennial *Census of Population*. They are particularly significant in constructing comparative tables of data, as terminology has been changed and refined since the early censuses.

The recent demands of some government programs for interrelating data from a number of government agencies further increase the need for greater uniformity in terminology. Federal agencies, other than the Census Bureau, are responsible for compilation of the following dictionaries and manuals, which have a wider use outside these agencies.

→ U.S. Employment Service. Dictionary of occupational titles. 4th ed. Wash., Govt. Prt. Off., 1977. 1371p.

Information on approximately 20,000 occupations in the U.S. economy. Widely used by business and industry where uniform descriptions of occupations are necessary, in government contracts and government-subsidized job-training programs. Deletes sex and age references in previous editions.

→ U.S. Office of Management and Budget. Standard industrial classification manual, 1972. Wash., Govt. Prt. Off., 1972. 649p.

"The Standard Industrial Classification was developed for use in the classification of establishments by type of activity in which engaged; for purposes of facilitating the collection, tabulation, presentation, and analysis of data relating to establishments; and for promoting uniformity and comparability in the presentation of statistical data collected by various agencies of the United States government, State agencies, trade associations, and private research organizations" (Intro.). Includes manufacturing and nonmanufacturing industries.

→ U.S. Social and Economics Statistics Administration. Dictionary of economic and statistical terms. Wash., Govt. Prt. Off., 1973. 84p.

Divided into 5 sections: national income and product accounts; balance of payments accounts; economic and statistical indicators; demographic and social terms; economic and statistical terms. Index. 1st ed., 1969.

Professional associations, as well as government agencies, are concerned with this problem of terminology, and those who have struggled with inadequate and inaccurate statistics for libraries were hopeful that they would be improved as a result of the ALA Statistics Coordinating Project's *Library Statistics: A Handbook of Concepts, Definitions, and Terminology* (Chicago: ALA, 1966; 160p.). (The National Center for Education [formerly Educational] Statistics is currently updating and expanding the handbook.) The problem was also faced by those who attended the National Conference on Library Statistics, a conference cosponsored by the Library Administration Division of the American Library Association and the NCES in June 1966 and reported in *National Conference on Library Statistics* (Chicago: ALA, 1967; 100p.). The report of a LAD project, prepared under contract with NCES, was published as *Planning for a Nationwide System of Library Statistics* (Washington: Govt. Prt. Off., 1970; 117p.). NCES also negotiated with state agencies to collect and report data to meet the needs of planners and policymakers for all types of libraries. The outcome, in 1974, was a unified data collection program, known as LIBGIS/Library General Information Survey, designed to acquire data over a 5–6 year period on staff, collections and holdings, services, cooperative interlibrary arrangements, facilities, and expenditures for the various types of libraries. (Cf. U.S. National Center for Education Statistics, *The Condition of Education* (1978 ed.), Pt.2: NCES Programs and Plans, Fiscal Years 1978 and 1979 [Washington: Govt. Prt. Off., 1978; p.9] and Boyd Ladd's *National Inventory of Library Needs, 1975: Resources Needed for Public and Academic Libraries and Public School Library/Media Centers; A Study Submitted . . . to National Commission on Libraries and Information Science* [Washington: Govt. Prt. Off., 1977; 277p.], which briefly refers to the problem in two appendixes: methodology of the inventory and standards and indicators of needs within the changing context of library service.)

Another aspect of the question of what is being measured is geographic area. It is important to be aware, for instance, that some counties in the United States have changed in size since their establishment, sometimes through the creation of several counties from an earlier one, less often by the merging of two counties.

It is a problem to locate statistical data for a small area, since broad areas such as countries, states, and provinces are usually the units for which statistics are reported in almanacs and statistical yearbooks. A useful directory of current sources is:

→ U.S. Bureau of the Census. Directory of federal statistics for local areas; a guide to sources, 1976. Wash., Govt. Prt. Off., 1978. 359p.

> Updates and considerably enlarges the 1966 vol. of the same title, abstracting 361 publications (182 in 1966 ed.) and indexing 2,300 (versus 900) subjects. Directs user to more than 100 kinds of areas smaller than states (cities, counties, census tracts, blocks, school districts, etc.). Arranges descriptions of the statistics under 16 large topics, e.g. agriculture, crime and law enforcement, environment and climate. Appendixes have article on unpublished data for local areas (microform, data files, special tabulations) and an annotated list of guides to federal and municipal statistics, published and unpublished.

Bibliographies

The access route to the desired statistics is frequently through the guides, bibliographies, indexes and abstracts to the statistical literature, as well as to those in individual subject fields. Listed below are some examples of these works that alert the user to the existence of specific statistical data. They include (1) General Sources, those not limited by subject or type of collecting agency; (2) Government Sources—United States, including indexes to and general descriptions of federal statistical activities; (3) Government Sources—Foreign; and (4) Subjects, including a few representative titles. The large number of titles under sources of government statistics, while certainly far from exhaustive, serves to remind us of the importance of national governments as collectors and publishers of statistics.

General Sources

→ Burrington, Gilliam A. How to find out about statistics. Oxford, etc., Pergamon, 1972. 153p.

> Introductory manual emphasizing British sources of statistics: careers, education, statistical organizations, books, guides, and general sources.

→ Current index to statistics: applications, methods, and theory. v.1– , 1975– . Wash., American Statistical Assn. Annual.

Computerized index to the statistical literature, listing annually over 2,000 articles from more than 50 journals. Indexed by author and important words in titles plus key words where available. (Cf. *Journal of the American Statistical Assn*. [June 1976], cover II.)

→ Harvey, Joan M. Sources of statistics. Rev. ed. Hamden, Conn., Linnet Books; London, Bingley, 1971. 126p.

Describes the main statistical publications of the United Kingdom and some of the more important U.S. and international organizations, considered to be reliable by the compiler. Chapters devoted to general sources; population, vital statistics, and migration; social statistics; education; labor; production; trade; finance; prices; transport and communications; and tourism. Full content notes on individual titles. Index must be used with care by Americans because of some differences in terminology (e.g. hire purchase). Note: Harvey has edited *Statistics—Africa* (1970–), *Statistics—America (North, Central & South America)* (1973–), *Statistics—Europe* (1968–), and *Statistics—Asia and Australasia* (1974–), all distributed by Gale Research.

→ Statistical theory and method abstracts. v.1– , July 1959– . Edinburgh, Longman Group, etc., for International Statistical Institute. 4 issues per yr. plus index supp.

International coverage, topically arranged. Abstracts are in English and titles are translated into English. Cumulative author index appears in the annual index supplement.

→ Statistics sources. 1st– ed. Detroit, Gale Research, 1962– .

In the 5th (1977, 976p.) ed., some 11,800 specific subjects, with citation to periodicals, yearbooks, directories, and other compilations issued by state, federal, and foreign agencies, associations, companies, universities, etc., are covered. Identifies principal statistical compilations by country. Its alphabetical arrangement, as well as its broader coverage of American series, make it more useful in American libraries than *Harvey*. Contains annotated list of dictionaries, bibliographies, guides, yearbooks, and periodicals.

Congressional Information Service, publisher of *American Statistics Index* (below), began publication in January 1980 of a complementary service, *Statistical Reference Index*, as a selective guide to current American statistical publications from sources other than the U.S. government.

Government Sources

UNITED STATES

→ American statistics index. 1973– . Wash., Congressional Information Service, 1973– . Annual with monthly supps.

Subtitled "A comprehensive guide and index to the statistical publications of the U.S. Government," this service provides a variety of ways of locating statistics, invaluable notes on series, lists of tables, and detailed descriptions of individual publications. The base edition, *1974 Annual and Retrospective Edition*, covers statistical publications in print as of Jan. 1, 1974, and those of importance published in the 1960s. The 1974 ed. fully supersedes *ASI 1973*

→ U.S. Bureau of the Census. Bureau of the Census catalog, 1946– . Wash., Govt. Prt. Off., 1947– . Quarterly and cumulative to annual with monthly supps.

Useful for contents notes on individual titles and, since 1964, for unpublished material available on tape, microform, or cards. For the period 1790–1972, consult *Bureau of the Census Catalog of Publications: 1790–1972* (Wash., 1974; 320p., 591p.).

→ _____. Directory of federal statistics for states; a guide to sources, 1967. Wash., Govt. Prt. Off., 1967. 372p.

"A comprehensive finding guide to available published sources of Federal statistics on social, political, and economic subjects" (Intro.). Companion to the Bureau's *Directory of Federal Statistics for Local Areas; a Guide to Sources, 1976* (above).

→ U.S. Office of Management and Budget. Statistical Policy Division. Statistical services of the United States Government. Rev. ed. Wash., Govt. Prt. Off., 1975. 234p.

Describes the federal statistical system and principal socio-economic statistical series. Provides a statement of statistical responsibilities of each agency and a list of its principal statistical publications. *Statistical Reporter* (July 31, 1940–) is a monthly summary of current federal statistical programs. Issued since Oct. 1977 by Office of Federal Statistical Policy and Standards, Dept. of Commerce.

FOREIGN

→ Ball, Joyce, ed. Foreign statistical documents; a bibliography of general, international trade, and agricultural statistics. Stanford, Calif., Hoover Institution on War, Revolution, and Peace (Stanford Univ.), 1967. 173p.

Emphasis "mainly on publications using a Western European language either as the first or second language," with current and defunct sources listed under name of country.

→ Great Britain. Central Statistical Office. Guide to official statistics. 1976– . London, H.M.S.O., 1976– . Biennial.

Covers 12 broad areas (general sources of statistics; area, climate, environment; population and vital statistics; etc.). Describes about 2,500 sources published during last 10 years. Alphabetical index. Bibliography. See also Gloria Westfall, "British Statistical Information," *Government Publications Review* 3:123–32 (1976).

→ Mitchell, Brian R. European historical statistics, 1750–1970. N.Y., Columbia Univ. Pr., 1975. 827p.

Main sources were the official publications of 24 European governments, including Russia. Bibliographical references.

→ U.S. Library of Congress. Census Library Project. General censuses and vital statistics of the Americas. Wash., Govt. Prt. Off., 1943. 151p.

Though old, this annotated record of 21 American republics and American colonies and territories is still useful, since it includes many serial sources still being published.

→ _____. _____. National censuses and vital statistics in Europe, 1918–1939; an annotated bibliography. Wash., Govt. Prt. Off., 1948. 215p. 1940–48 supp. 1948. 48p.

Good for historical statistics found in national censuses and official statistical publications.

→ _____. _____. Statistical bulletins; an annotated bibliography of the general statistical bulletins of major political subdivisions of the world, prep. by Phyllis G. Carter. Wash., 1954. 93p.

Gives beginning date, frequency, categories of statistical data, holdings in Washington libraries, etc., for periodicals issued more frequently than annually. Notes those that include bibliographies.

→ _____. _____. Statistical yearbooks; an annotated bibliography of the general statistical yearbooks of major political subdivisions of the world. Prep. by Phyllis G. Carter . . . Wash., 1953. 123p.

Gives beginning date, frequency, types of statistics covered, and holdings in Washington libraries for yearbooks from about 200 countries and areas.

→ Urquhart, M. C., and Buckley, Kenneth A. H., eds. Historical statistics of Canada. Cambridge, Cambridge Univ. Pr.; Toronto, Macmillan, 1965. 672p.

> Covers period 1867–1960, with explanatory notes and citation to sources. Well indexed.

Subjects

AGRICULTURE
→ Blanchard, Joy Richard, and Ostvold, Harold. Literature of agricultural research. Berkeley, Univ. of California Pr., 1958. 231p. (Univ. of California bibliographic guides, 1)

> Section F, Social Sciences, comments on selected statistics sources. See also specific index entries, e.g. lumber trade—statistics.

→ U.S. Dept. of Agriculture. Agricultural statistics, 1936– . Wash., Govt. Prt. Off., 1936– . Annual.

> Covers "agricultural production, supplies, consumption, facilities, costs, and returns." For earlier statistics, consult the department's *Yearbook of Agriculture*, 1894–1935. Since 1936, the yearbook has been devoted to specific subjects, one each year, such as food and life, trees, grass, insects, seeds, climate, and outdoors U.S.A. These individual volumes are important reference sources, though detailed statistics are not emphasized. *Agricultural Situation*, issued monthly, gives current statistics on crops, livestock, and prices.

CRIME AND CRIMINALS
→ U.S. Federal Bureau of Investigation. Uniform crime reports for the United States and its possessions. v.1– . Wash., Govt. Prt. Off., Aug. 1930– . Annual.

> Gives state, metropolitan area, and city statistics of offenses, arrests by age group, and police employment statistics, based on returns from local law-enforcement agencies using uniform definitions of offenses. Quarterly update entitled *Uniform Crime Reports*.

ECONOMICS AND BUSINESS
→ Commodity year book. v.1, 1939– . N.Y., Commodity Research Bureau, 1939– . Annual (suspended 1943–47).

> About 100 raw commodities and semifinished products are arranged alphabetically, giving supply and demand, consumption, prices, and exports. Updated by *Statistical Abstract Service*, issued 3 times a year.

→ Daniells, Lorna M. Business information sources. Berkeley, Univ. of California Pr., 1976. 439p.

This guide, successor to the classic *Sources of Business Information*, by Edwin T. Coman (Berkeley: Univ. of California Pr., 1964; 330p.), includes 6 pertinent chapters: 4, Basic U.S. statistical sources; 5, Industry statistics; 6, Foreign statistics and economic trends; 7, Investment sources; 8, U.S. business and economic trends; 17, Management science and statistical methods.

→ Editor & Publisher. Market guide. v.1– . 1924– . New York. Annual.

For U.S. and Canadian cities and towns gives data on transportation, population, housing, savings banks, auto registration, gas meters, telephones, retail outlets, heaviest buying days, etc. Helpful to those planning plant relocation and to those moving to another city.

→ Federal reserve bulletin. v.1– . 1915– . Wash., U.S. Board of Governors of the Federal Reserve System. 1915– . Monthly.

Best source of banking and monetary statistics, including Federal Reserve banks, department store trade, consumer credit, production indexes, and international finance.

→ Maltby, Arthur. Economics and commerce: the sources of information and their organisation. London, Bingley; Hamden, Conn., Archon Books, 1968. 239p.

Chapter 9, "Sources of Information on Economic Statistics," describes chiefly British and international sources, with a concluding section on using statistical material.

→ Sales & Marketing Management. Survey of buying power. 1930– . New York, Bill Pubs. Annual (July 10 [or other] issue date).

Population, effective buying income, and retail sales estimates of U.S. markets. Since Oct. 1973, pt. II of the *Survey* provides (in one issue) projections of U.S. and Canadian metropolitan markets and an annual survey of TV, newspaper, and radio markets. In prior years the *Survey* had been supplemented by "Marketing on the Move" issue, which featured projections of metropolitan markets, and an annual "Survey of Media Markets" (newspaper, TV, radio) issue.

→ U.S. Bureau of the Census. Current industrial reports. Wash., U.S. Bureau of the Census. Monthly, quarterly, annually.

Textiles, apparel, pulp and paper, primary metals, machinery, etc., are covered. This series supplements the product data collected in the annual survey of manufactures and the census of manufactures. While specific product detail varies in each report series, data are generally presented on commodity products, shipments, consumption, and/or inventories.

→ _____. [Economic censuses]. Wash.

The 1977 Economic Censuses comprise the censuses of retail trade, wholesale trade, service industries, construction industries, manufactures, mineral industries, and transportation; the censuses of outlying areas; the Enterprise Statistics Program; the Survey of Minority-owned Business Enterprises and the Survey of Women-owned Businesses. . . . The economic censuses constitute comprehensive and periodic canvasses of the Nation's industrial and business activities. The first economic census of the United States was conducted as part of the 1810 decennial census, when inquiries on manufacturing were included with the census of population. Mineral data were first collected in 1840. The first censuses of construction and business were taken in 1929. An integrated economic census program was begun for 1954. In that year, the censuses covered the retail and wholesale trades, selected service industries, manufactures, and mineral industries. The basic procedures developed for these censuses have been used in all subsequent economic censuses.

The economic censuses are required by law under title 13 of the United States Code, sections 131, 191, and 224, which requires that they be taken at 5-year intervals covering years ending in 2 and 7. (U.S. Bureau of the Census, *Mini-Guide to the 1977 Economic Censuses* [Wash., 1978], p. 1–2.)

→ _____. Guide to foreign trade statistics. Wash., Govt. Prt. Off., 1967–. Annual.

"Sample illustrations of the content and arrangement of data on imports, exports, and shipping" (U.S. Bureau of the Census, *Directory of Federal Statistics for Local Areas: A Guide to Sources, 1976*, p.326).

→ Wasserman, Paul, and Kemmerling, Diane. Commodity prices. Detroit, Gale Research, 1974. 200p.

Distinguished for its specific subject index to more than 5,000 agricultural, commercial, industrial, and consumer products, with sources of prices appearing regularly in more than 150 U.S. and Canadian periodicals, chiefly trade journals. Updates and revises *Sources of Commodity Prices* (N.Y., Special Libraries Assn., 1959; 170p.).

→ Woytinsky, Emma S. Profile of the U.S. economy: a survey of growth and change. N.Y., Praeger, 1967. 601p.

Useful for its broad historical approach and for its statistical tables augmented by charts, graphs, and maps. Well indexed.

Though expensive, and seldom found in small public and college libraries, financial services must be mentioned because of their importance in business and finance. They are particularly important for data on individual companies, and because they are kept up to date by looseleaf services, with periodic cumulations. Noted here are only two examples which are usually found in any public library offering business information service.

→ Moody's Investor's Service. Moody's Manual of investments, American and foreign. N.Y., Service, 1929– . 6v. Annual, with semiweekly bulletins.

Covers governments and municipals; banks, insurance, real estate, investment trusts; industrials; public utilities; and transportation, giving brief history of the company or government, plants, officers, income, and earnings and value of stock over a 15-year period for industries and a 10-year period for security prices. The service also issues *Moody's Handbook of Common Stocks*, a quarterly, covering about 1,000 of the best-known American stocks.

→ Standard and Poor's Corp. Corporation records. N.Y., Standard and Poor's, May 1914– . 7v. looseleaf.

Data on balance sheets, earnings, and market prices given for major American and Canadian corporations.

Also important for stock and bond quotations are newspapers, such as the *New York Times* or the more highly specialized *Wall Street Journal*. Other newspapers, together with business periodicals, are described in Daniells' *Business Information Sources* (above). Daniells' remarks about services, of which *Moody's* and *Standard and Poor's* are well-known examples, are cogent. The standard directory of services is Mary Grant and Norma Cote, *Directory of Business and Financial Services* (7th ed.; New York: Special Libraries Assn., 1976), listing more than 1,000 services and with subject index.

EDUCATION

→ Standard education almanac, 1968– . Chicago, etc., Marquis, etc., 1968– . Annual.

Statistical data, including enrollments, expenditures and instructional staff for all levels, plus related statistics, such as education and the federal government, using *Statistical Abstract of the United States* and U.S. Office of Education publications as the principal sources. Some tables give comparable data for earlier periods. Subject index.

→ U.S. National Center for Education Statistics. Digest of educational statistics, 1962– . Wash., Govt. Prt. Off., 1962– . Annual. (Author and title vary slightly)

Data from both governmental and nongovernmental sources covering the entire field of American education, from kindergarten through graduate schools. Series of data on enrollments, staff, finances, libraries, etc., some extending as far back as 1870, are given for historical perspective. Expanded coverage of library statistics began in 1968. For projections of enrollment, instructional staff, expenditures, and student charges, see *Projections of Educational Statistics*, also issued by NCES, with an appended section on general methodology.

→ Woodbury, Marda. A guide to sources of educational information. Wash., Information Resources Pr., 1976. 371p.

Chapter 6, Statistical Sources, identifies organizations (National Center for Education Statistics, National Education Assn. Research Division, etc.) and selected titles (*Statistical Abstract of the United States, Fact Book on Higher Education*, etc.).

GOVERNMENT ACTIVITIES, INCLUDING ELECTION STATISTICS

→ America votes; a handbook of contemporary American election statistics. v.1– . [1954/55–]. Biennial. Wash., etc., Elections Research Center, Congressional Quarterly, etc., 1956– .

Gives, alphabetically by state, election returns since 1945 for president, governor, senator, and congressmen; by county and ward, for most recent returns, for president, governor, and U.S. senator.

→ Book of the states, 1935– . Lexington, Ky., Council of State Governments, 1935– . Biennial.

Gives statistical and directory information on constitutions and elections, legislatures and legislation, the judiciary, administrative organization, finance, intergovernmental relations, state services. Issued biennially in even-number years, with supplements in odd-number years updating directory information on elected officials and legislators. Augmented to some extent by individual state manuals (legislative "blue" or "red" books), many of which are entered in *Public Affairs Information Service Bulletin* and/or *Monthly Checklist of State Publications*.

→ Governmental Affairs Institute, Washington, D.C. America at the polls; a handbook of American presidential election statistics, 1920–1964. Comp. and ed. by Richard M. Scammon. Pittsburgh, Univ. of Pittsburgh Pr., 1965. 520p.

State and county election returns for president since 1920, following the pattern of *America Votes*.

→ Municipal year book, 1934– . Wash., International City Management Assn., 1934– . Annual.

Statistics and surveys of activities of city governments, including finance, public welfare, etc. Contains directory of city officials.

HEALTH AND WELFARE
→ U.S. Social Security Administration. Social security bulletin, v.1– . March 1938– . Wash., Administration, 1938– . Monthly.

Reports current data on the operations of the Social Security Administration; cumulated in an annual statistical supplement.

→ World Health Organization. World health statistics annual, 1962– . Geneva, W.H.O., 1965– .

Includes vital statistics and causes of death; infectious diseases, causes, deaths, and vaccinations; health personnel and hospital establishments. Previously issued as *Annual Epidemiological and Vital Statistics*.

INSURANCE
→ Ferguson, Elizabeth, ed. Sources of insurance statistics. N.Y., Special Libraries Assoc., 1965. 191p.

Valuable for detailed subject approach to current serial publications.

LIBRARIES
→ The Bowker annual of library and book trade information, ed. 1– , 1956– . Sponsored by the Council of National Library Associations. N.Y., Bowker, 1956– . Annual.

Statistics of school, public, college and university, and special libraries, augmented by surveys of the status of state and national library statistics. Book-trade statistics include production and sales in the United States, international book production, import and export figures. Other valuable features are calendar of book-trade and promotional events, library standards, pertinent legislation, grants, library prizes and awards, recent publications in the field, basic books for librarians and the book trade, library education, and a directory of national, state, regional, provincial, and international associations.

→ Rather, John Carson. Statistics of libraries; an annotated bibliography of recurring surveys. Wash., Off. of Ed., 1961. 50p.

Its 156 recurring surveys are arranged by type of library or alphabetically by state, with description of kinds of data included in each. Well indexed.

OCCUPATIONS
→ U.S. Bureau of Labor Statistics. Occupational outlook handbook; employment information on major occupations for use in guidance. 1st ed.– . Wash., Govt. Prt. Off., 1949– . Biennial.

Useful in vocational counseling for its statistics on present and estimated number of future employees in more than 700 occupations. Also describes nature of the work, earnings, and working conditions, together with qualifications and training required. Update with the Bureau's *Occupational Outlook Quarterly*, 1957– .

POPULATION AND HOUSING
→ Population index. v.1, 1935– . Princeton, N.J., Office of Population Research, Princeton Univ. and the Population Assn. of America, 1935– . v.1– . Quarterly.

Best index to sources of demographic statistics, both United States and foreign, with abstracts of books and journal articles arranged under 18 categories, such as fertility, marriage and divorce, regional population studies. Includes articles on current demographic subjects, with apppended bibliographies. Quarterly and annual geographic indexes. Cumulative list of sources in *Population Index Bibliography, 1935–68* (Boston, G. K. Hall, 1971; 9v.).

→ U.S. Bureau of the Census. Census of population. Place and publisher varies, 1790– .

→ _____. Census of housing. Wash., Govt. Prt. Off., 1940– .

→ _____. Joint population and housing reports. Wash., Govt. Prt. Off. Var. dates.

In light of the seemingly endless variety of information to be found in the published and unpublished materials (computer tapes, microforms, special tabulations) of, say, the 1970 decennial censuses, one is hard pressed to imagine that the 1790 census asked only five questions. That early census, incidentally, made the United States the first country to provide for the regular enumeration of its inhabitants. Then the count was made by marshals of the judicial districts for the purpose of allocating representation in Congress. Information on sex and color of free persons and on free males of 16 years and upward indicated the numbers available for military service. The original purpose—to furnish a basis for apportionment of congressional seats and state legislative districts—still holds. Its effect partly explains the wave of protests from cities whose officials questioned the reliability of the preliminary population figures released in mid-1970. An added cause for their concern was the probable reduction in state and federal aid distributed on a per capita basis.

But the state and local governments are only a small segment of those who use census data; they are used by other federal government agencies, such as the Bureau of Labor Statistics; by trade publishers who compile statistical yearbooks, atlases, and encyclopedias; by social agencies; by community planners; and by those engaged in business and industry. The decennial census provides a wealth of information on the composition and characteristics of the population: age, sex, race, marital status, education, income, occupation, housing, and ethnic identification, which is available in both published and unpublished form and described in the *Bureau of the Census Catalog* or the more specialized volume, *Reference Manual on Population and Housing Statistics from the Census Bureau* (Washington: U.S. Bureau of the Census, 1977; 146p.). The latter is a comprehensive introduction to demographic data from the Bureau, providing "an appropriate and up-to-date starting point for the new or prospective user, and a handy reference for the experienced data user" (Pref.).

There is nothing static about the work of the Census Bureau, and to meet the needs of users for post-census data and/or data on subjects not asked in the census, one needs to be aware of the reports of the Current Population Survey and the Annual Housing Survey (*Reference Manual*, esp. p.99–107). Attention is directed also to *Data User News* (Jan. 1975–), the Bureau's monthly news letter: "Its articles cover a wide range including reports just issued, new data programs being developed, available computerized data files and programs, planning for upcoming censuses, announcement of seminars and exhibits, and answers to user questions. Significant reports, programs or applications related to census data but developed by data users are also occasionally described in a 'Reader's Exchange' section. A regular monthly feature is 'Selected New Publications' providing titles for reports just off the presses. (Before 1975 this publication was entitled *Small Area Data Notes*)" (*Reference Manual*, p.118). An occasional supplement to *Data User News*, "1980 Census Update" (Jan. 1977–), describes developments in planning for the next decennial census.

There are other valuable sources of population statistics, but two, not issued by the Bureau of the Census, deserve special mention:

→ United Nations. Statistical Office. Demographic yearbook; Annuaire démographique, 1948– . N.Y., 1949– . Annual.

Emphasizes characteristics of the population, giving official statistics for about 250 geographic areas of the world on nationality, births and deaths, marriage and divorce, etc. Cumulative subject index in 1963 issue.

→ U.S. National Center for Health Statistics. Vital statistics of the United States. 1937– . Wash., Govt. Prt. Off., 1939– . Annual.

Good source for statistics on births and deaths, marriage and divorce, for states, metropolitan areas, and other geographical areas of the United States, Puerto Rico, and the Virgin Islands. Supersedes *Mortality Statistics* and *Birth, Stillbirth and Infant Mortality Statistics*. For more current statistics, use *Monthly Vital Statistics* and *Vital and Health Statistics*.

RELIGION
→ Yearbook of American and Canadian churches, 1916– . Pub. by National Council of Churches of Christ in the U.S.A. N.Y., 1916– . Annual.

Statistics on church membership, financial support, etc., which are more detailed than those in the U.S. Bureau of the Census, *Population Characteristics*, P20, no.79. They also update the Bureau's *Religious Bodies: 1936*, of which no later editions have been published.

Religious statistics must be used with caution, as pointed out by Frank Wilson Price in "World Christian Statistics—Some Warnings, and Discussion on Their Future Collection" (in H. Wakelin Coxill and Kenneth Grubb, eds., *World Christian Handbook* [Nashville: Abingdon, 1967], p.48–52). Among the difficulties in collecting worldwide church statistics, Price lists the lack of uniform terminology, the failure of some churches to keep adequate records, the variety of sources which must be consulted, and the discrepancies in these sources. He recommends that a worldwide cooperative agency be established to collect and publish pertinent data.

SOCIAL CONDITIONS
→ U.S. Office of Federal Statistical Policy and Standards. Social indicators, 1976. Wash., Govt. Prt. Off., 1977. 646p.

The Commerce Department edition considerably expands *Social Indicators, 1973* (U.S. Office of Management and Budget; 272p.), from 8 to 11 chapters and from 165 to 374 charts. The contents of each chapter (e.g., 1, Population; 3, Housing; 7, Education and Training; 10, Culture, Leisure, and Use of Time) are in three parts: text and charts, statistical tables, and technical notes.

WEATHER
→ U.S. Environmental Data and Information Service. Daily weather maps, weekly series. 1968– . Wash., Govt. Prt. Off. Weekly.

"Features for each day of the weekly period, Monday through Sunday, a surface weather map of the U.S. showing weather conditions observed daily at 7 a.m. EST throughout the country. Three other smaller maps on each page show the pattern of winds and temperatures near the 18,000-foot level at 7 a.m. EST; the highest and lowest temperatures for the previous day at selected stations in the U.S.; and the areas over which precipitation was reported in the preceding 24 hours. . . . A complete explanation of the maps and the weather symbols used are included" (U.S. Supt. of Documents, *Government Periodicals and Subscription Services* [Price List 36], May 1978 issue).

→ U.S. National Meteorological Center, Suitland, Md. Long Range Prediction Group. Average monthly weather outlook. 1946– . Wash., Govt. Prt. Off. Semimonthly.

"Gives resume of average rainfall and temperature for the preceding month and the weather outlook for the following month" (ibid.).

Periodicals Indexes

Certain indexes to periodicals (in appropriate fields) are useful in establishing the existence of statistics, especially in current sources. Among them, the following may be noted:

→ Business periodicals index. N.Y., Wilson, 1958– . v.1– . Monthly, with quarterly and annual cumulations.

Subject index to periodicals, chiefly American, in accounting, advertising, banking and finance, insurance, public administration, etc.

→ Public Affairs Information Service. Bulletin of the Public Affairs Information Service. 1st– , annual cumulations. N.Y., Service, 1915– . v.1– . Frequency varies.

> Excellent source for current statistics, since it is a selective subject list of the latest books, pamphlets, government publications, reports of public and private agencies, and periodical articles relating to economic and social conditions, public administration, and international relations. Statistics are indexed under subject, with subheading *Statistics*.

Other Types of Statistical Sources

Emphasis thus far has been given to works which refer the user to other sources to be consulted, though several, such as *Statistical Abstract* and *Stateman's Yearbook*, also contain statistical tables. But what types of reference materials may be singled out because of the actual statistical data in their contents? The following have been generally recognized for their usefulness:

1. Dictionaries of statistics, as distinguished from dictionaries of statistical terms
2. Almanacs
3. Statistical yearbooks
4. Atlases
5. Periodicals.

Included here are representative examples of each, together with their general characteristics. Many more will be found in Sheehy's *Guide to Reference Books*, especially statistical yearbooks of foreign countries and on special subjects, the latter conveniently located through the index under subject, "Agriculture—Statistics," for example. General sources are covered in section CG. Also useful is v.2 of A. J. Walford's *Guide to Reference Materials*, especially sections 31, Statistics, and 33, Economic Statistics.

Though not as recently published as *Sheehy* or *Walford*, Peter R. Lewis's *The Literature of the Social Sciences* (London: Library Assn., 1960) has an excellent chapter on statistics, distinguished for its organization and informed commentary on the relative usefulness of various types. Other sources, such as some of the titles mentioned earlier, must be used for more recent statistical publications.

Dictionaries of Statistics

Dictionaries of statistics, as distinguished from dictionaries of statistical terms, are the least useful, the least used, and, therefore, the least often published of all statistical sources. This can be explained in part by the proliferation of statistics during the last two centuries, which were more conveniently issued earlier in other types of publications. Dictionaries of statistics are occasionally consulted for historical statistics, but in careful work they must be augmented by other sources, such as guides to statistics in various fields. The two included here are distinguished chiefly for the long time span covered in their contents.

→ Mulhall, Michael George. Dictionary of statistics. 4th ed. rev. London, Routledge, 1899. 853p.

A source for statistics from the 3rd century to 1898, arranged alphabetically by subject in two parts, the latter covering 1890–98. Authorities for statistics are not always cited, though a list of sources is appended.

→ Webb, Augustus Duncan. New dictionary of statistics. London, Routledge; N.Y., Dutton, 1911. 682p.

Supplements *Mulhall*, covering 1899–1909; citing sources for all statistics; and separately listing 325 sources used.

Almanacs

Almanacs are frequently used as ready-reference sources of statistics, since they make extensive use of government statistical publications in their tables, giving citation to source. The wide range of subjects covered and the adequate indexes to their random arrangement recommend them for questions involving broad geographic areas, where the most recent statistics are not required. Emphasis is given to the country of publication, which makes it advisable for libraries to acquire some almanacs published outside the United States. Several of these are included here.

→ Canadian almanac and directory for the year 1847– . Toronto, Copp Clark Co., 1847– . Annual.

Reliable source for Canadian socio-economic statistics, as well as for its list of Cabinet officers and members of the House of Commons.

→ The Hammond almanac. 1979– . Maplewood, N.J., Hammond, 1978– . Annual.

Grouped under large subjects are statistics on taxes and expenditures, finance, industry, labor, transportation, social services, crime, military affairs, education, communications, and miscellaneous facts and figures, with sources generally cited. Well indexed. Successor to *New York Times Encyclopedic Almanac*, 1969–71, *The Official Associated Press Almanac*, 1972–75, and *CBS News Almanac*, 1976–78.

→ Information please almanac, atlas and yearbook, 1947– . N.Y., Viking, etc., 1947– . Annual.

More nearly resembles encyclopedia yearbooks in its articles on topics of current interest and in its review of the year in sports, theater and film, literature, etc. Contains statistics on all countries, with emphasis on the United States.

→ Reader's Digest almanac and yearbook. Ed. 1– . 1966– . Pleasantville, N.Y., Reader's Digest Assn., 1966– . Annual.

Resembles encyclopedia yearbooks in its emphasis on news highlights of the year. Arranged in 20 broad sections, covering the world in review, the United States, American home and family (including hobbies and recipes), education, medicine and public health, religion, communications, travel and transportation, international affairs, sports, etc. Illustrated with many news photos. Statistics, scattered throughout, may be located through the index.

→ Whitaker, Joseph. Almanack; 1869– . London, Whitaker, 1869– . v.1– . Annual.

Well-indexed source for worldwide statistics, but with greatest emphasis on British Commonwealth. Good companion to American almanacs.

→ World almanac and book of facts, 1868– . N.Y., Newspaper Enterprise Assn., etc., 1868– . v.1 . Annual.

Cited by Sheehy as "the most comprehensive and most frequently useful of the American almanacs of miscellaneous information. Contains statistics on social, industrial, political, financial, religious, educational, and other subjects; political organizations; societies; historical lists of famous events, etc. Well up to date and, in general, reliable; sources for many of the statistics are given. A useful handbook, and one with which the reference worker should familiarize himself thoroughly. Alphabetical index at the front of each volume. Each issue before 1915 had also a short index of notable articles in preceding volumes" (p.485).

Statistical Yearbooks

More useful than almanacs in statistical reference work are statistical yearbooks, since they concentrate on statistical data, often omitting the directory and miscellaneous information found in almanacs. They usually contain statistics covering a longer period of time, useful for comparative purposes by those seeking to establish trends in population, the economy, education, etc. These comparative tables are convenient since they make it unnecessary to consult so many individual annual volumes. This type of publication is well covered in both *Sheehy* and *Walford*, and given below are only a few examples of frequently used annuals covering a wide range of subjects.

→ Europa year book, 1959– . 1st ed.– . London, Europa Publs., 1959– . Annual.

V.1 covers United Nations, its agencies, other international organizations, and Europe (arranged by country), giving general statistics and information on the government, constitution, religion, press, publishers, radio and television, finance, trade and industry, transport and tourism, etc. V.2 covers Africa, the Americas, Asia, and Australia in the same fashion.

→ Great Britain. Central Statistical Office. Annual abstract of statistics, v.1– . 1840/53- . London, H.M.S.O., 1854– . Annual.

Useful for index to sources as well as for its wide coverage of British statistics for 10-year periods, including area and climate, population and vital statistics, social conditions, education, labor, production, retail distribution, and miscellaneous services, transport and communications, external trade, national income and expenditure, home finance, banking and prices. Supplemented in part by *Monthly Digest of Statistics*, which includes only tables for which monthly and quarterly statistics are available. For earlier period, see B. R. Mitchell and Phyllis Deane, *Abstract of British Historical Statistics* (Cambridge, Cambridge Univ. Pr., 1962; 531p.), and B. R. Mitchell and H. G. Jones, *Second Abstract of British Historical Statistics* (Cambridge, Cambridge Univ. Pr., 1971; 227p.).

→ International statistical yearbook of large towns. V.1– . 1961– . La Haye, International Statistical Institute, 1961– . Biennial.

Includes data collected by International Statistical Institute on population, births and deaths, unemployment, economic conditions, dwellings and construction, public services and transportation, libraries, etc. European cities of more than 100,000 population and non-European cities of more than 750,000 are covered.

→ Statesman's year-book; statistical and historical annual of the states of the world, 1864– . London and N.Y., Macmillan, 1864– .

In addition to statistics on governments of the world, there is an appended bibliography for each country, which emphasizes statistical and other reference works.

→ Statistical abstract of Latin America. 1955– . Los Angeles, Univ. of California at Los Angeles, Center of Latin American Studies, 1956– . Annual (irreg.).

Current and comparative data (population, social, economic, political topics) on the American nations and dependencies south of the United States.

→ United Nations. Statistical Office. Statistical yearbook; Annuaire statistique, 1948– . N.Y., 1949– . Annual. Supplement. 1967– .

Gives official statistics with citation to sources on population, manpower, agriculture, manufacturing, trade, transportation, finance, housing, education, culture for more than 150 geographic areas. Updated by *Monthly Bulletin of Statistics*. Should be used with the *Supplement* (1967–) to both publications, which supplies more detailed definitions and explanatory notes for the statistical series than those in the yearbooks and bulletins. *World Statistics in Brief: United Nations Statistical Pocketbook* (N.Y., United Nations, 1976–) is an annual compilation of basic international statistics selected from the wealth of statistics compiled regularly by the UN Statistical Office and the statistical services of UN specialized agencies.

Lewis has noted that collections of international statistics, such as these, serve three purposes: "They give an overall picture of world or regional conditions, they enable comparisons on a common basis to be made between different countries, and they provide accessible statistics for countries which either do not publish their own or publish them very late" (p.66). They have added usefulness in libraries without extensive collections of official statistical publications of foreign countries. The aim of *Current National Statistical Compendiums* (Westport, Conn.: Greenwood, 1974–) is to issue on microfiche, beginning with 1970, all statistical yearbooks published by governments of the world. (See reviews in *Reference Services Review* 4:8 [Oct./Dec. 1976] and *Microform Review* 4:279–80 [Oct. 1975].)

→ U.S. Bureau of the Census. Statistical abstract of the United States, 1878– . Wash., Govt. Prt. Off., 1879– . Annual.

Most frequently used source of socio-economic statistics (in summary form under broad sections, such as population, education), drawn principally from U.S. government publications, but including some private and international sources. Note especially the following appendix material: guide to sources of statistics, guide to state statistical abstracts, and (since 1976) statistical methodology and reliability, i.e. brief, fairly nontechnical descriptions of the sample surveys and censuses of government statistical agencies (Census of Agriculture, National Crime Survey, Higher Education General Information Survey, etc.). The *Abstract* is reprinted by Grosset and Dunlap as *U.S. Fact Book: The American Almanac;* supplements to the Abstract appear irregularly. Three are included here because they are important for statistics of smaller areas. (See also Nathalie D. Frank, "After the Statistical Abstract, What?" *RQ* 14:204–10 [Spring 1975], a bibliographical essay on 64 titles, mostly governmental.)

→ _____. Congressional district data book. (Districts of the 87th– . Congress) [1961/62–]. Wash., Govt. Prt. Off., 1961– . Biennial. (A Statistical Abstract supp.)

Supplements *Statistical Abstract* by giving, for each congessional district, data on population and housing, vital statistics, banking, agriculture, manufactures, trade, votes for president and representative, etc., prefaced by source notes and explanation of terms in tables.

→ _____. County and city data book, 1949– . Wash., Govt. Prt. Off., 1952– . Irregular. (A Statistical Abstract supp.)

Presents, in addition to the areas indicated in the title, statistics for geographic regions and divisions, states, and standard metropolitan statistical areas. Source notes, explanations.

→ _____. Historical statistics of the United States. Wash., Govt. Prt. Off., 1949– . Irregular.

Contains historical statistics on the same subjects covered in *Statistical Abstract*, citing governmental and nongovernmental sources. Good for determining when statistics were first collected on various subjects. Citation to source, definitions of concepts, reference to more detailed sources, and methodological and historical information for each series should be read for intelligent use of the data.

Atlases

Atlases are chiefly useful for economic statistics, and a number of economic atlases have appeared in recent years, among them the *Oxford Economic Atlas of the World*, Oxford's regional economic atlases, and others described in *Sheehy* and *Walford*. But by far the most often used in American libraries is:

→ Rand McNally and Co. Rand McNally commercial atlas and marketing guide. N.Y., Rand McNally, 1876– . Annual.

Excellent source of statistics on small geographical areas, giving population, business and manufactures, retail trade, communications, agriculture, etc., for U.S. cities and counties.

For additional titles, see chapter 7, "Thematic Maps and Atlases."

Periodicals

Periodicals, often published by governments or trade or professional associations, such as those indexed in *Commodity Prices*, are an excellent source of current socio-economic statistics, and their statistical information may be located in part through such indexes as *Public Affairs Information Service* (noted earlier). Examples are numerous, as will be seen by consulting *Ulrich's International Periodicals Directory* or *Statistics Sources*. A few examples are given below.

→ Across the board. v.13, no.10, Oct. 1976– . N.Y., Conference Board. Monthly. Continues *Conference Board Record*.

The Conference Board, an economic and business research organization, supports its reports with statistics, graphics, and documentation.

→ Broadcasting. v.1– . Nov. 26, 1945– . Wash., Broadcasting Pubs. Weekly.

Comprehensive coverage of radio and television broadcasting: statistics, recent trends, developments.

→ Business week. no.1– . Sept. 7, 1929– . Hightstown, N.J. Weekly.

Probably the general business magazine with which most libraries would begin. Objective, conservative, clear articles are appropriately accompanied by charts, graphs, statistical tables.

→ CPI detailed report. Aug. 1974– . Wash., U.S. Bureau of Labor Statistics. Monthly, Continues *Consumer Price Index*.

Index numbers for changes in prices of consumer goods and services.

→ Fortune. v.1– . Feb. 1930– . Chicago, Time, Inc. Monthly.

Fairly objective, carefully researched material. Easy-to-read graphs and charts, often in color.

→ Monthly labor review. v.1– . July 1915– . Wash., U.S. Bureau of Labor Statistics. Monthly.

Articles on employment, labor force, wages, prices, productivity, etc., are scholarly and may include illustrative material. One large regular feature of every issue: Current labor statistics.

→ Producer prices and price indexes. Mar. 1978– . Wash., U.S. Bureau of Labor Statistics. Monthly. Continues *Wholesale Prices and Price Indexes*.

Cf. *CPI Detailed Report* comment (above).

→ Pulp and paper. v.1– . Feb. 1927– . San Francisco, etc., Miller Freeman Pubs.

News items and several articles, frequently accompanied with graphic materials.

→ Survey of current business. v.1– . Aug. 1, 1921– . Wash., U.S. Bureau of Economic Analysis. Monthly.

Articles (in first half of each issue) give information trends in industry and the business situation. "Current Business Statistics" (the second half) includes general business indicators, commodity prices, construction and real estate, domestic trade, labor force, finance, foreign trade, transportation and communication, and index numbers for various commodities, e.g. food, lumber, etc. These series update *Business Statistics*, a biennial statistical supplement to *Survey of Current Business*. *Weekly Business Statistics* updates selected data published monthly in the *Survey*.

7

Sources of Geographical Information

Neither a purely natural nor a purely social science, geography has studied—from its development as an organized field of knowledge in classical Greece—human societies in their spatial and ecological environment. To be sure, geography is not alone in its concern for people and their environment:

Many fields in the natural and social sciences study a particular category of phenomena, not excluding its distribution and variations over the earth. What geography, and geography alone, studies is the areal character of the earth in which man lives—the form, the content, and the function of each areal part, region, or place and the pattern of and interconnections between the areal parts. If the total diversity of places and their interrelations were simply the sum of areal variations and connections of physical, biological, and social phenomena, the subject could readily be divided into distinct fields: physical geography, biogeography, and human, or social, geography; or possibly two parts, the geography of nature and the geography of man. In reality, however, the phenomena of these several abstract categories are in many cases very closely interrelated in their areal variations and connections from place to place. Indeed, what the geographer observes as individual features—i.e., a soil, river water, a farm, a transport route—are element complexes in which factors of physical, animate, and social origin are so intricately interwoven as to require study within a single field. Places, or areas, large or small, may be studied either specifically or generically. The Human interest in individual places is indicated by the practice from earliest times of giving each area a proper name—"Hudson River," "Pennsylvania," or "the South." Geography, like history, is ultimately concerned with attaining maximum comprehension of individual cases. An essential step in the description as well as the understanding of the individual areas is the determination of its generic characteristics. When we speak of places as "deserts," "canyons," "cities," "farms," or "culture areas," we limit the criteria in each case to a few closely interrelated features, overlooking aspects in which places of the same type may be radically different. Comparative study of the characteristics of places by kind may reveal indications of significant correspondence, leading to hypotheses of generic relationships [Richard Hartshorne, "Geography," in *International Encyclopedia of the Social Sciences* v.6 p.115–16].

Readers with an interest in additional overviews of the field of geography will be impressed with Chauncy D. Harris's chapter (p. 139–80) in Carl M. White et al., *Sources of Information in the Social Sciences* (2nd ed.; Chicago: ALA, 1973), Norton Ginsburg's chapter (p.293–318) in *A Reader's Guide to the Social Sciences* (rev. ed. edited by Bert F. Hoselitz [New York: Free Pr., 1970]), and the scholarly but readable overview by Preston E. James, *All Possible Worlds: A History of Geographical Ideas* (Indianapolis: Odyssey Press/Bobbs-Merrill, 1972; 622p.).

Geographers, like members of other professions, do not want for organizations they may join. In the United States, the two principal geographical organizations are the Association of American Geographers (Washington, D.C.) and the American Geographical Society (New York). (Their publications are discussed later in this chapter.) The International Geographical Union, founded in 1923, seeks to promote, through academies of science, research councils, or similar bodies, in more than 80 countries, international cooperation in geographic research and to organize international geographical congresses.

To serve the needs of geographers and others, large academic and research libraries are developing extensive collections of maps and other geographical information. Their interests are seen in the activities of such organizations as the Geography and Map Division of the Special Libraries Association (its *Bulletin* commenced in 1947), the Western Association of Map Libraries (*Information Bulletin*, Sept. 1969–), and the Geography and Map Libraries Section of the Division for Special Libraries of the International Federation of Library Associations and Institutions (IFLA) (*Inspel: International Journal of Special Libraries*, 1966–). The great collections of the Library of Congress and the American Geographical Society are evidence of the wealth of information being acquired and systematically organized.

Of interest to library school students is "A Survey of the Usage of a Large Map Library" by C. B. Hagen (Special Libraries Assn. Geography and Map

Division, *Bulletin* 80:27–31 [June 1970]). Based on a survey from 1967 to 1969, it revealed that the Map Library at the University of California at Los Angeles was used by practically everyone on campus, but

> rather distressing statistics showing low usage concerns the School of Library Service. During the period of the survey, only 3% of the student body had used the Map Library and these have been students who came to school already showing an interest in maps. . . . Despite the fact that ours is the largest map library in the West, attracting a continuous stream of outside visitors, practically no library students—unless required to do so—have shown an interest to visit our facility [p.29].

Two studies of the circulation records of the Map Room, Southern Illinois University at Carbondale (June–Dec. 1972 and June 1972–June 1975), reported lending materials for outside use to only 1 or 2 percent of the potential borrowers in the university (3 or 4 percent among graduate students, the heaviest users) (Jean M. Ray, "Who Borrows Maps from a University Library Map Collection—And Why? [Report I and] Report II," *Special Libraries* 65:104–9 [Mar. 1974]), 69:13–20 [Jan. 1978]). Certainly prospective librarians must be aware of map resources.

School libraries or media centers are also faced with the problem of supplying materials needed in the teaching of geography. In this they are helped by such agencies as the National Council for Geographic Education, which is deeply concerned with the use of newer media, as a cursory glance at its official journal, *Journal of Geography*, will reveal. An excellent article, "Maps in the Classrooms," by Barbara S. Bartz, appears in its January 1970 issue (p. 18–24). It is not enough for the school library to have a good atlas and a few years of the *National Geographic* to augment the geographical information in school encyclopedias. Films, filmstrips, globes, and other sources are needed, and guides to their location are noted later. "Using Road Maps in the Junior High School," by Jack Ferguson (*Journal of Geography* 75:570–74 [Dec. 1976], is another article that exemplifies the usefulness of this periodical, which, it should be remembered, is equally valuable for the teachers in colleges and universities.

But between the research worker and the elementary school student is the general reader, whose demands or needs for geographic information will inevitably change as research activities and methods in teaching geography in schools and colleges change. As a case in point, the Travel Geography Program of Long Beach (Calif.) City College is enthusiastically described in "Field Trips, Catalysts of Senior Citizen Education," by Adolf Stone (*Journal of Geography* 75:276–79 [May 1976]).

To conclude this introductory section, a few remarks pertaining to the pervasive role of governments in geography and cartography are in order. For this purpose the long and extensive involvement of the U.S. government affords a good example. (It is acknowledged that the contributions of state and local governments have been considerable.)

No less a person than General George Washington was responsible for perhaps the first official mapping and map-collecting agency in the federal government. Apparently because of Washington's complaints to the Continental Congress about the army's lack of accurate maps, Robert Erskine was appointed geographer and surveyor to the army in 1778 (Walter Thiele, *Official Map Publications* [Chicago: ALA, 1938] p. 104).

In the pre–Civil War years, the surveys conducted by the national government were chiefly exploratory in character and were usually confined to the area west of the Mississippi. The most important of the early surveys was the expedition (1804–6) of Captains Meriwether Lewis and William Clark, who ascended the Missouri River to its source and then descended the Columbia River to the Pacific. The expeditions of Zebulon Pike in 1805 and 1807 to the Mississippi and the Arkansas rivers were also important. So too were the 1820 expedition in Upper Michigan, Wisconsin, and Minnesota conducted by General Lewis Cass, then superintendent of Indian affairs, and an expedition in 1832 to one of the sources of the Mississippi by Henry Rowe Schoolcraft, the student of Indian life, while traveling in behalf of the Bureau of Indian Affairs.

In the period from 1835 to 1850 the surveys and exploration in the western territories under army auspices were many. Of these perhaps the most noteworthy were those of John C. Fremont of the Oregon country and Upper California. Of the civilian surveys of the period, those by David Dale Owen, beginning in 1839, under the auspices of the General Land Office, were important, embracing the geology of the region that is now Illinois, Iowa, Wisconsin, and Minnesota.

During 1853–61, the War Department made surveys for a railroad from the Mississippi River to the Pacific Ocean. Apparently no government survey of note was undertaken during the Civil War, but with the close of the war the surveying and mapping of the West was resumed with renewed vigor. Between 1867 and 1879 four surveying expeditions were put in the field, two by the War Department and two by the Department of the Interior. These surveys have become known more popularly as the King, Hayden, Powell, and Wheeler Surveys, after the geologists in charge of them.

The King Survey (more officially known as the Geological Exploration of the Fortieth Parallel) was authorized by Congress in 1867. Its main purpose was "to examine and describe the geological structure, geographical condition, and natural resources of a belt of country extending from the one hundred and twentieth meridian eastward to the one hundred and fifth meridian of longitude, along the fortieth parallel of latitude." Its director, Clarence King, was a civilian, as were all his scientific assistants.

The second survey (Geological and Geographical Survey of the Territories), also authorized by Congress in 1867, called for "a geological survey of Nebraska, said survey to be prosecuted under the direction of the Commissioner of the General Land Office." F. V. Hayden was assigned to this survey, which was eventually extended over all the territories, and work was done in Wyoming, Idaho, Montana, New Mexico, and Colorado. Although it was primarily geological, this survey included work on topography, geology, paleontology, ethnology, philology, botany, and related sciences.

The third survey, Geographical and Geological Survey of the Rocky Mountain Region, began in 1867 (under the aegis of the Smithsonian Institution) as an exploration of the Colorado River. In 1868 it was recognized by Congress in a joint resolution authorizing the secretary of war "to issue rations for twenty-five men of the expedition engaged in the exploration of the river Colorado under direction of Professor [John Wesley] Powell." This expedition remained under the control of the Smithsonian Institution. After its completion, Congress (1874) authorized Powell to continue the survey in Utah, under the direction of the secretary of the interior; subsequent appropriation acts extended the survey to the "Rocky Mountain region." The survey covered southern Wyoming, central and southern Utah, southeastern Nevada, and northern Arizona. Although primarily geographical, it established geodetic points and included work in topography, ethnology, geology, botany, paleontology, and related sciences.

The fourth survey was under the direction of Lt. George M. Wheeler of the War Department's Corps of Engineers. Entitled Geographical Survey West of the One Hundredth Meridian, it extended over the western parts of the Dakotas, Nebraska, Kansas, and Texas and the Rocky Mountain and Pacific Coast states. Although mainly geographical or topographical, this survey was made to obtain "at the same time and as far as practicable without greatly increasing the cost, all the information necessary before the settlement of the country, concerning the branches of mineralogy and mining, geology, paleontology, zoology, botany, archaeology, ethnology, philology, and ruins."

It is thus clear that in the early 1870s four surveys (two under the Interior Department and two under the War Department) were simultaneously in progress under specific congressional appropriations, each employing its own methodology and, in several places, duplicating coverage of the same areas.

In addition, the Coast and Geodetic Survey (begun in 1807 as the Survey of the Coast and renamed the U.S. Coast Survey in 1836, the Coast and Geodetic Survey in 1878, and the National Ocean Survey in 1970) had by congressional authority (1871) extended its work into the interior of the country.

As a result, Congress in 1878 called upon the National Academy of Sciences for the formulation of a less wasteful plan to carry on these activities. In its report to the House of Representatives, the academy recommended the termination of these conflicting surveys and their consolidation into an agency in the Department of the Interior, to be known as the United States Geological Survey. Congress acted upon these recommendations on March 3, 1879, creating what has become the major land surveying and mapping service of the federal government. The first 100 years of the USGS are modestly set forth in Morris M. Thompson, *Maps for America: Cartographic Products of the U.S. Geological Survey and Others* (Washington: Govt. Print. Off., 1979).

(The above paragraphs on the federal government's cartographic/geographic activities to the landmark date 1879 have relied heavily on Anne M. Boyd, *United States Government Publications* [3rd ed. rev. by Rae E. Rips; New York: Wilson, 1952), p.238–46]; Brookings Institution, Washington, D.C., Institute for Government Research, *The U.S. Geological Survey: Its History, Activities and Organization* [Service Monographs of the United States Government, no.1; New York and London: D. Appleton and Co., 1918 (c1919), p.1–13], Walter Thiele *Official Map Publications* [Chicago: ALA, 1938; p.104–15]; and Thompson [cited above]).

To meet the needs of various federal agencies to supply accurate and consistent place names (including their spelling) in the United States for use in maps, charts, and other federal publications, President Harrison created in 1890 the U.S. Board on Geographic Names (Alan E. Schorr, "A Brief History of the United States Board on Geographic Names," Special Libraries Assn., Geography and Map Division, *Bulletin* 96:18–20 [June 1974]). Its decisions are accepted as the standard authority for both governmental and nongovernmental use.

The twentieth century has witnessed dramatic increases in the nation's needs for and uses of geographical/cartographical materials. In many instances existing federal agencies (with or without name changes) have assumed responsibility for appropriate materials; in others, new agencies have appeared, such as the Department of Transportation and the Tennessee Valley Authority. Inasmuch as Thompson's work is both current and sufficiently comprehensive in its overview, it seems appropriate merely to alert readers to two of its chapters: "8: Maps from Other Agencies" (i.e. other than the U.S. Geological Survey) and "9: Cartographic Information Sources."

Emphasis in this chapter is given to bibliographic sources, not only because of the development of library systems, which demand that librarians become increasingly aware of what may be found outside their own limited collections, but also because of the ever increasing amount and diversity in geographical sources.

Attention also is given to atlases, the most important source, and to a lesser degree to gazetteers and travel guides, particularly those often found in general collections and whose contents must be mastered for efficient reference service. Guidelines for reviewing atlases will be found in the appendix.

Since familiarity with the geographical information in general reference books will result in wiser selection of geographical sources by avoiding those which merely duplicate the information in general sources, an overview of those already discussed is in order. Outlined briefly, as in previous chapters, are the types of information that may be located in bibliographies and indexes, biographical sources, encyclopedias, dictionaries, and statistical sources.

1. Bibliographies and indexes
    a. Trade bibliographies and national library catalogs, useful for locating titles of atlases, handbooks, and travel guides for individual countries and cities, such as books listed under name of country with the subdivision *Description and travel*. For description of 29 national bibliographies containing references to maps and atlases, see Donald A. Wise, "Cartographic Sources and Procurement Problems: Appendix F, A List of National Bibliographies Containing References to Atlases and Maps" (Special Libraries Assn. Geography and Map Division, *Bulletin* 115:35–38 [Mar. 1979]).
    b. Bibliographic guides (to be discussed further)
    c. Indexes to periodicals, useful for locating articles on cities, resorts, travel, and recreation, such as *Readers' Guide*; to one periodical, such as the cumulated index to *National Geographic Magazine*; and to one type of source, such as *Bibliographic Index*, which includes books, parts of books, and articles containing bibliographies from a wide range of sources.
2. Biographical sources. Useful for biographies of geographers and cartographers, as well as for information on place names (special sources include the Association of American Geographers, *Directory* [Washington, AAG, 1949– ; title varies], discussed below)
3. Encyclopedias. As pointed out, these are useful sources of geographical information. Together with their yearbooks, they contain descriptions of countries, states and cities, city plans, and maps, the latter often found in atlas volumes as well as in the body of the encyclopedia. Less useful for small areas and for thematic maps than more specialized sources, but useful for articles on maps and charts, photogrammetry, surveying, etc.
4. Dictionaries. Useful only for brief identification of larger places and for definitions of geographic terms. Must be augmented with dictionaries of geographical terms.
5. Statistical sources. These are extremely useful (as indicated), not only for data in tabular form but increasingly for thematic maps such as

those of the Bureau of the Census, whose Geography Division is responsible for a series of distributional maps of the United States. The *Rand McNally Commercial Atlas* (mentioned for its statistics) will be discussed further, as will the interrelated activities of government agencies.

General Reference Works

Bibliographies

The bibliography of geography and cartography is wide and varied, as even a brief survey of its current state will reveal. The highly selected list by Chauncy D. Harris of about 120 bibliographic entries in White's *Sources of Information in the Social Sciences* (2nd ed., 1973; p. 155–80), directed to librarians and to students in the social sciences, emphasizes works in English. Note too that this bibliography is preceded by Harris's list of outstanding works in the chief fields of geography (p.139–55).

For a second view of the literature, with copious appended references, consult Nora T. Corley, "Geographical Literature" (in *Encyclopedia of Library and Information Science* v.9, p.266–82). Articles in the same volume of related interest are "Geological Libraries and Collections" and "Geological Literature"; the latter gives an overview of the development of geological literature over the world.

Bibliographic guides, catalogs of collections, bibliographies and indexes, special guides to government publications, and other sources are briefly described below.

To proceed from the general to the more specific, the familiar guides to reference books offer a good beginning. In Walford's *Guide to Reference Material* (3rd ed.), the section on geography, exploration, and travel contains well-annotated lists of bibliographies, manuals, encyclopedias, dictionaries, periodicals, directories, and gazetteers, with citations to reviews. A separate section on area studies reflects the great expansion of the literature in recent years. Section CL, Geography, and section D, History and Area Studies, in *Sheehy* are most useful in American libraries as sources of general works, gazetteers, dictionaries, encyclopedias, handbooks, and guidebooks.

Another general source, more restricted in number of titles but recommended for its well-organized, interestingly written chapter on geographical sources, is William Katz, *Introduction to Reference Work,* volume I, *Basic Information Sources* (3rd ed., 1978).

Increased emphasis on area studies has been responsible for recent bibliographies of regions and individual countries, such as:

→ Bederman, Sanford H. Africa: A bibliography of geography and related disciplines; a selected listing of recent literature published in the English language. 3rd ed. Atlanta, Publishing Services Div., School of Bus. Adm., Georgia State Univ., 1974. 334p.

> 1st–2nd editions (1970, 1972) had title: A bibliographic aid to the study of the geography of Africa: a selective listing of recent literature published in the English language. Author arranged under individual countries with topical indexes by country. 3,629 citations in 3rd ed.— more than 1,600 more than in 1st ed.

→ Hall, Robert B., and Noh, Toshio. Japanese geography: a guide to Japanese reference and research materials. Rev. ed. Ann Arbor, Univ. of Michigan Pr., 1970. 233p.

> Titles of reference sources are translated. Covers bibliographies, dictionaries and encyclopedias, gazetteers, travel guides, atlases and maps, and major fields of geography. Well annotated.

→ Harris, Chauncy D. Guide to geographical bibliographies and reference works in Russian or on the Soviet Union. Chicago, Univ. of Chicago, Dept. of Geography, 1975. 478p. (Research paper no.164)

> Annotated list of 2,660 entries covering primarily 1946–73, earlier periods selectively.

→ Herman, Theodore, ed. The geography of China; a selected and annotated bibliography. N.Y., State Educ. Dept., 1967. 44p. (Foreign Area Materials Center, Univ. of the State of New York. Occasional publication no.7)

> English-language material on reference materials, human and physical geography, with author index.

→ Sukhwal, B. L. South Asia: A systematic geographic bibliography. Metuchen, N.J., Scarecrow, 1974. 827p.

> More than 10,000 titles, unannotated, mostly in English and mostly post-1947. Sections on South Asia in general and individual countries (India, Pakistan, Bangladesh, Sri Lanka [Ceylon] etc.) subdivided by fields of geography—agricultural, economic, political, etc. Titles include books, articles, pamphlets, atlases, theses and dissertations.

A good annotated list of specialized bibliographies in geography (historical, population, manufacturing, transportation, economic regions, statistical geography and cartography, military, travel, etc.) is found in White's *Sources of Information in the Social Sciences* (p.161–206).

Literature Guides

Guides to the literature of the field have increased in recent years. They include:

→ Brewer, J. Gordon. The literature of geography: a guide to its organisation and use. 2nd ed. London, Bingley; Hamden, Conn., Linnet Books 1978. 264p.

A practical and useful guide. Appraisal of general reference sources precedes sections on specialized branches (e.g. history of geography and geographical thought, geographical techniques and methodology, physical geography, human geography), with emphasis on current works in English. Unlike the 1973 ed., this edition includes a chapter on cartobibliography.

→ Harris, Chauncy D. Bibliography of geography: Part I, Introduction to general aids. Chicago, Dept. of Geography, Univ. of Chicago, 1976. 276p. (Research paper, no.179)

By concentrating its 585 main entries on the post-1945 period, this first-rate work is a true update to *Wright and Platt* (below). Entries in the 16 chapters (1, Bibliographies of bibliographies; 4, Specialized bibliographies of geography; 5, Books; 6, Serials; 10, Maps and atlases; 15, Statistics, etc.) are carefully annotated and are bibliographically complete. Note its appendix 2, "A Small Geographical Reference Collection."

→ Lock, C. B. Muriel. Geography and cartography: a reference handbook. 3rd ed. rev. and enl. London, Bingley; Hamden, Conn., Linnet Books, 1976. 762p.

Despite its claim to be a combination of the 2nd ed. of the author's *Geography: A Reference Handbook* (1972) and *Modern Maps and Atlases* (1969), this volume is mostly a new edition of the 1972 work; few pages are from *Modern Maps* (below). Is valuable however, for its information on geographical societies and their publications and on prominent deceased geographers. International in scope, ranging from ancient times to the present, but with British emphasis.

→ Wright, John Kirtland, and Platt, Elizabeth T. Aids to geographical research; bibliographies, periodicals, atlases, gazetteers, and other reference books. 2nd ed. compl. rev. N.Y., pub. for the American Geographical Society by Columbia Univ. Pr., 1947. 331p.

Because it provides comprehensive, international coverage up to about 1945, Wright and Platt is still useful for its bibliographies and other reference works. Its sections on topical aids and regional aids are updated in part by Harris (above) and by *A Geographical Bibliography for American College Libraries* (below). Its list of geographical periodicals is updated by *International List of Geographical Serials* (also noted below). New geographical periodicals and other serials have been reviewed annually in an issue of *Geographical Review*, v.42 (1952) to date.

Selection Aids

Recommended lists are useful not only as buying guides but also as selective bibliographies, by identifying significant titles in individual areas. A recent one displays the growing interest of professional associations in adequate library collections for teaching purposes.

→ Lewthwaite, Gordon R.; Price, Edward T.; and Winters, Harold A. A geographical bibliography for American college libraries. Rev. ed. Wash., Assn. of American Geographers, 1970. 214p. (Assn. of American Geographers. Commission on College Geography. Pubn. no.9)

Library Catalogs

Library catalogs of rich special collections are a valuable source of research materials. An outstanding example is:

→ American Geographical Society. Research catalogue. Boston, G. K. Hall, 1962. 15v. and map supp. Supplement 1972– .

Books, periodical articles, pamphlets, and government publications in one of the largest geographical libraries in the world, arranged by systematic and regional classifications. Is kept up to date by:

→ _____. Current geographical publications; additions to the research catalogue of the American Geographical Society. v.1– , 1938– . N.Y., The Society, 1938– . v.1– . Monthly, except July and Aug.

Since Nov. 1964, contains separate section on maps. Its classified arrangement is supplemented by annual indexes to subjects, authors, and regions. Beginning with v.41 no.3 (Mar. 1978), published by Univ. of Wisconsin–Milwaukee Library in cooperation with American Geographical Society, which remains in New York.

The increased use of various teaching aids in schools, as well as their proliferation, has resulted in a growing number of aids to their selection and use. The examples listed below are intended only to indicate the types of publications in which they may appear: separate publication, yearbook, periodical.

→ Kingsbury, Robert C. Sources of information and materials: maps and aerial photographs. Provisional ed. Boulder, Colo., High School Geography Project, 1970. 159p.

> Geographers, cartographers, high school teachers, and others assisted in this project of the Assn. of American Geographers. Lists agencies and dealers useful in acquiring maps, atlases, aerial photographs, filmstrips, slides, films, globes, transparencies, raised relief models, and other equipment for classroom teaching. Also included are annotated bibliography of nontechnical literature on maps, aerial photography, and remote sensing; list of atlases suitable for classroom use; and description of pertinent government agencies.

→ National Council for Geographic Education. Pacesetter series. 1970– . Oak Park, Ill. (Formerly National Council for Geographic Education Yearbook)

> Each annual is a series of articles by authorities discussing a central theme.

→ Shores, Louis. Instructional materials: an introduction for teachers. N.Y., Ronald. 1960.

> P.155–87 describes gazetteers, guidebooks, atlases, maps and globes, with instructions for their selection and use. Appended bibliography lists films and filmstrips. Cited because of Shores's pioneering advocacy of multimedia approach.

The monthly *Journal of Geography*, official organ of the National Council for Geographic Education, should be used regularly for information on all aspects of geographic media.

Government Publications

All governments produce and distribute a wide variety of pertinent publications, some of which are extremely important to the field of geography. For example, during World War II the United States government made and printed more maps than had been made throughout the previous history of the world. Useful adjuncts to government indexes and catalogs, such as *Monthly Catalog of United States Government Publications* and *Monthly Checklist of State Publications*, are:

→ Guide to U.S. government maps. McLean, Va., Documents Index, 1975– .

A series of bibliographies of government-published maps. First volume listed about 5,000 U.S. Geological Survey maps from 1879 to mid-1970s and provided area, subject, and coordinate indexes.

→ Low, Jane Grant-Mackay. The acquisition of maps and charts published by the United States government. Champaign, Univ. of Illinois School of Library Science, 1976. 36p. (Occasional papers, no.125)

A most satisfactory overview for new and experienced map librarians. Bibliography appended.

→ Morehead, Joe. Introduction to United States public documents. 2nd ed. Littleton, Colo., Libraries Unlimited, 1978.

"Federal Mapping and Charting Activities," in appendix A (p.295–308), is a current, succinct account that ends with a list of references.

→ Schmeckebier, Laurence Frederick, and Eastin, Roy B. Government publications and their use. 2nd rev. ed. Wash., Brookings Inst., 1969.

Chapter 16, Maps (p. 406–40), describes bibliographic sources, important atlases (such as the *National Atlas of the United States*), county and state maps, and thematic, historical, and world maps, together with the agencies responsible for their production.

Maps and Atlases

The types of information conveyed by maps and atlases (volumes of maps) seem almost limitless. The following list is intended merely to illustrate their variety: bodies of water (oceans, rivers, lakes, etc.), mountains, deserts, highways, streets, railroads, airports, dams, canals, soils, forests, agriculture, minerals, political entities (boundaries between continents, nations, states, counties, capital cities, county seats, school districts, parks), fire insurance maps, weather.

Maps and atlases, so important a part of any general reference collection, must be selected with care, as will be noted later. A good source for those in print is:

→ International maps and atlases in print. 2nd ed. Kenneth L. Winch, ed. N.Y., Bowker, 1976. 866p.

More than 15,000 maps and atlases from about 1,000 official and commercial publishers, listed by Universal Decimal classification, with map index diagrams and geographical name index. Includes roads, localities, town plans, official surveys, political and administrative areas, physical and geological features, earth resources, biogeography, climate, human geography, and economic, historical, and mathematical maps and atlases. Excludes aeronautical and nautical charts. Gives information on language, size, and often scale. Invaluable source for world, space, moon, planet, and star atlases.

Also useful is:

→ Alexander, Gerard L. Guide to atlases: world, regional, national, thematic; an international listing of atlases published since 1950. Metuchen, N.J.: Scarecrow, 1971. 671p. Supplement. 1977. 362p.

Includes 1,786 world atlases, chronologically arranged; 393 regional, 1,809 national, and 1,568 thematic atlases, with indexes to language, authors, cartographers, and editors. Supplement adds 2,993 entries. No annotations or title indexes.

→ Lock, C. B. Muriel. Modern maps and atlases, an outline guide to twentieth century production. Hamden, Conn., Archon Books; London, Bingley, 1969. 619p.

Exhaustive list of international maps and atlases, national and regional; thematic maps and atlases, with introduction on the techniques of modern cartography. Augments the usefulness of more general sources by attention to cartographic methods employed and to the activities of national governments and private agencies.

→ Walsh, James P. General world atlases in print, 1972–1973; a comparative analysis. 4th ed. N.Y., Bowker, 1973. 211p.

Analyzes 40 major atlases published or available in the United States and 100 inexpensive English-language atlases. Includes criteria for atlas evaluation and selection. Provides for each atlas full bibliographic information, strengths and weaknesses, age suitability, graded recommendation.

Further information on sources of maps and atlases is found in Donald A. Wise's "Cartographic Sources and Procurement Problems" (*Special Libraries* 68:198–205 [May/June 1977) and its 11 appendixes in the *Bulletin* of the Geography and Map Division of Special Libraries Association. The appendixes are as follows: (A) Selected Serials Containing Lists and/or Reviews of Current Maps and Atlases and (B) Selected Map and Atlas Accession Lists (112:19–22, 23–26 [June 1978]); (C) Selected List of International Dealers in

Out-of-Print Maps and Atlases (113:65–68 [Sept. 1978]); (D) Selected List of United States Dealers in Out-of-Print Maps and Atlases (expands the list which appeared in the aforementioned issue of *Special Libraries*); (E) Selected Special Subject or Area Bibliographies Relating to Maps and Atlases (114:40–42, 43–44 [Dec. 1978]). (F) A List of National Bibliographies Containing References to Atlases and Maps; (G) United States Official Mapping Agencies; (H) Library of Congress Cartographic Acquisitions by Federal Agency; (I) Sources of Official State Maps; (J) Selected United States Private and Commercial Map Publishers; (K) Selected Sources for Maps Published by International Organizations (115:35–38, 39–40, 41, 41–46, 46–49, 49–50 [Mar. 1979]).

In recent years the *Bulletin* has regularly included notes concerning maps, reviews of outstanding atlases, and an extensive list of new maps. To single out but one article, "Maps and Atlases: Basic Reference Bibliography," by Mai Treude (map librarian, University of Minnesota), is worthy of close attention (*Bulletin* 111:32–37 [Mar. 1978]).

For fascinating articles on rare old maps, accompanied by facsimile reproductions, the *Quarterly Journal* of the Library of Congress is valuable.

Another useful acquisition aid was found in the journal *Surveying and Mapping*, which carried a regular column "Distinctive Recent Maps," prepared from 1948 through 1968 by Walter W. Ristow and from 1969 by Richard W. Stephenson. With Stephenson as compiler, this column was transferred to another publication of the American Congress on Surveying and Mapping, *ACSM Bulletin*, beginning with the latter's May 1974 issue.

More limited, but a useful free source, is the pamphlet compiled by the U.S. National Ocean Survey, *List of Frequently Used Federal Government World, United States, and Historical Maps*. It lists not only the Survey's maps but also those issued by various federal agencies.

The growing emphasis on thematic atlases is described by Jack A. Clarke in "State and Local Atlases" (*RQ* 9:232–34 [Spring 1970]).

Examples of varied sources on maps and atlases could be extended indefinitely, but must be concluded with four titles:

→ American Geographical Society. Map Dept. Index to maps in books and periodicals. Boston, G. K. Hall, 1968. 10v. Supps. 1971– .

Though this invaluable guide will be found only in larger libraries, its existence should be known to all librarians. Its subject and geographical-political division entries include many hard-to-locate and little-known maps in the society's large holdings of geographical periodicals and books from all over the world.

→ New York Public Library. Dictionary catalog of the Map Division. Boston, G. K. Hall, 1971. 10v.

This catalog displays the extremely rich holdings of a large research library: 280,000 sheet maps, 6,000 atlases, 11,000 reference volumes. Includes entries from other divisions of NYPL (Manuscript, Rare Books and Prints).

→ Stommel, Henry M., and Fieux, Michele. Oceanographic atlases: a guide to their geographic coverage and contents. 1st ed. Woods Hole, Mass., Woods Hole Pr., 1978. 97p.

→ U.S. Library of Congress. Geography and Map Division. The bibliography of cartography. Boston, G. K. Hall, 1973. 5v.

About 90,000 cards are reproduced. Unquestionably the most comprehensive published bibliography on cartography.

Serial Publications

The importance of serial publications in the field of geography is widely recognized. The following titles are examples of lists, an abstracting service, and periodical indexes. Also useful for popular articles is *Readers' Guide* and, for those in more specialized journals, the already mentioned *Current Geographical Publications*.

→ Geo abstracts. 1966– . Norwich, Univ. of East Anglia. 7 ser. (A–G) with 6 no. a year. (1966–71: Geographical abstracts)

Covers (A) Landforms, (B) Climatology and Hydrology, (C) Economic Geography, (D) Social Geography, (E) Sedimentology, (F) Regional and Community Planning, and (G) Remote Sensing, Photogrammetry and Cartography. Comprehensive annual subject and author indexes.

→ Harris, Chauncy D., and Fellmann, Jerome D. International list of geographical serials. Chicago, 1971. 267p. (Univ. of Chicago, Dept. of Geography. Research paper no.138)

Includes current and discontinued titles, listed with full bibliographic details under name of country. More than 300 serials from 64 countries (121 serials in English from 37 countries), selected on basis of quality of geographic material, are described in Harris's *Annotated World List of Selected Current Geographical Serials in English, French, and German, Including Serials in Other Languages with Supplementary Use of English or Other International Languages*. 3rd ed. Chicago, 1971. 77p. (Univ. of Chicago, Dept. of Geography. Research paper no.137)

→ National Geographic Magazine. Cumulative index. v.1– . 1952– . Wash., National Geog. Soc., 1952– .

   V.1, 1899–1946; v.2, 1947– . Articles are indexed by author, subject, and title, with maps indexed separately. Good source for maps and color photographs, which profusely illustrate the articles.

→ Royal Geographical Society. New geographical literature and maps. n.s. v.1– , 1951– . London, The Society. Semiannual.

   Based on a selection of additions to the library, listed primarily by region. Includes British theses.

→ Van Balen, John. Geography and earth sciences publications, 1968/1972– . An author, title and subject guide to books reviewed and an index to the reviews. Ann Arbor, Mich., Pierian Pr., 1978– .

   V.1 (covering 1968–72) indexed from 21 periodicals from the United States, Canada, and Western Europe; v.2 (1973–75) indexed 38.

Dissertations

The increased number of graduate departments in geography and the research being conducted are shown in the following:

→ Browning, Clyde E. Bibliography of dissertations in geography, 1901 to 1969: American and Canadian universities. Chapel Hill, Univ. of North Carolina Dept. of Geography, 1970. 96p. (Studies in Geography, no.1).

   Gives author, title, university, and date for each of 1,582 titles arranged under 23 subject categories, e.g. agricultural geography, association of man and environment, climatology, cultural geography, urban geography. A regional index is appended.

Place Names

Increased interest in place names accounts for the second edition of a well-known guide for those interested in toponymy.

→ Sealock, Richard Burl, and Seely, Pauline Augusta. Bibliography of place-name literature; United States and Canada. 2nd ed. Chicago, ALA, 1967. 352p.

   Contains 3,599 numbered entries for books, articles, and some manuscript compilations in two sections: by states under United States, and by province under Canada. Annotated throughout, with some citations to book reviews. Appended author and subject entries, the latter principally place names. Much of the new material in this edition is taken from the regular bibliographic feature in *Names*, a quarterly publication of American Name Society, whose recent issues serve to update this exhaustive bibliography.

Cartographic History and Map Librarianship

The history of maps is fascinating and the study of them engages not only cartographers but also amateur collectors, who search for them in second-hand dealers' shops. The brief accounts of maps and mapmakers in encyclopedias are readily available, and provide good introductions to the subject, but for those seeking more information, there are books which give one a fuller appreciation of the art, such as:

→ Bricker, Charles. Landmarks of mapmaking: an illustrated survey of maps and mapmakers. Amsterdam, Elsevier, 1968. 276p., 200 maps, 150 illus.

Fine example of superb bookmaking, rich in reproductions of rare maps, often from the best available copies. Deals only with European cartography from the 15th to the 19th century and is enlivened with delightful descriptions.

→ Brown, Lloyd A. The story of maps. Boston, Little, Brown, 1944. 397p.

Interesting, readable account of the men who made maps and how they made them, including the Egyptian astronomer, geographer, and mathematician Ptolemy, who faced the continuing problem of balanced coverage of the world by deciding: "We will make ten maps for Europe; we will make four maps for Africa; for Asia we will make twelve maps to include the whole, and we will state to which continent each map belongs, and how many and how great are the regions of each."

→ Lister, Raymond. Antique maps and their cartographers. Hamden, Conn., Archon Books, 1970. 128p. 58 maps.

Chapters, with appended bibliographies, cover the history of mapmaking to the late 19th century; profusely illustrated with facsimiles of early maps.

→ _____. How to identify old maps and globes; with a list of cartographers, engravers, publishers and printers concerned with printed maps and globes from c.1500 to c.1850. Hamden, Conn., Archon Books, 1965. 256p.

Also a readable outline history of maps and charts, methods of early map production, description of decoration and conventional signs, and terrestrial and celestial globes and armillary spheres, illustrated with facsimiles of old maps.

→ Lynam, Edward. The mapmaker's art: essays on the history of maps. London, Batchworth Pr., 1953. 140p.

The author, once superintendent of maps for the British Museum, drew on this collection, one of the richest and most interesting collections of printed maps in the world, for his material. Devoted to English mapmakers, from the famous Benedictine, Matthew Paris of St. Albans Abbey (who about the year 1250 had a map of Great Britain drawn, probably to illustrate his *History of the English People*), to those of the 18th century. Illustrated with many facsimiles of famous old maps.

→ Skelton, Raleigh A. Maps: a historical survey of their study and collecting. Chicago, Univ. of Chicago Pr., 1972. 138p.

A well-written, informative overview of the study and collecting of maps by a leading authority on the history of cartography.

→ Thrower, Norman J. W. Maps and man: an examination of cartography in relation to culture and civilization. Englewood Cliffs, N.J., Prentice-Hall, 1972. 184p.

Especially good for its attention to thematic mapping.

→ Woodward, David, ed. Five centuries of map printing. Chicago, Univ. of Chicago Pr., 1975. 177p.

Scholarly examination of printing techniques, accompanied by superior reproductions.

Reproductions of old maps and atlases are being made more readily available to those who can afford them through the publishing program of Theatrum Orbis Terrarum Ltd. in Amsterdam, which for several years has been reproducing a series of rare and important atlases in facsimile, beginning with Ptolemy's *Cosmographia* and including such famous works as the *Theatrum Orbis Terrarum* of Ortelius and Blaeu's *Light of Navigation*. The same company is also issuing *Acta Cartographica*, a series of unabridged reprints of monographs and studies dealing with the history of cartography, drawn from over 150 of the foremost European and American historical journals from the first half of the eighteenth century, when interest in the history of cartography began to emerge.

But for every person interested in old maps there are thousands who use modern maps and atlases, the products of cartographers and draftsmen who draw on what has been learned about the world from surveying, aerial photographs, and (increasingly) remote sensing. Thus a thorough knowledge of atlases and their use is essential for librarians, who can only learn their value by examining their contents and noting their special features. Useful orientation is given in:

→ Greenhood, David, and Alexander, Gerard L. Mapping. Rev. ed. Chicago, Univ. of Chicago Pr., 1964. 289p.

Designed for the amateur, whether user, maker, or collector. Part I, on getting the most out of maps, contains readable information on coordinates, distance, content, and projections. Part II gives instructions and describes methods and materials for mapmaking. (Cf. *Wilson Library Bulletin* 40:93 [Sept. 1965].)

→ Larsgaard, Mary. Map librarianship: an introduction. Littleton, Colo., Libraries Unlimited, 1978. 330p.

The first textbook in the field oriented toward American librarians. Much practical information, extensive current bibliography, 15 appendixes.

→ "Map Collections." In *Illinois Libraries*, 56:342–430 [May 1974].

A recent source of acquisition tools, books on map reading and appreciation, on maps in libraries, and an annotated bibliography on geography and map use, it will help the reference librarian become acquainted with the bibliographic control necessary for effective reference service. The papers were written for a map workshop in Macomb, Ill. (Sept. 21, 1973), and the principal speakers were experienced map librarians.

→ Monkhouse, F. J., and Wilkinson, H. R. Maps and diagrams: their compilation and construction. 3rd ed. London, Methuen, 1971. 522p.

Detailed analysis of many types of maps. Monkhouse is also the compiler of *A Dictionary of Geography*.

→ Post, J. B., ed. "Map Librarianship." In *Drexel Library Quarterly* 9:4 [Oct. 1973]. 90p.

Though intended for beginning map librarians, its articles on the selection and acquisition of materials, cataloging and classification, preservation and maintenance, and brief descriptions of some collections using a computer-produced map catalog, will be of interest to those who give reference service. As the editor points out, "All reference work can be broken down into ascertaining what the questioner really wants . . . and knowing the collection. . . . Such knowledge can come only from actually working with a collection. To some extent, the map librarian should be like the alcoholic bartender—his or her own best customer."

→ Raisz, Erwin J. General cartography. N.Y., McGraw-Hill, 1948. (1st ed., 1938)

This was the text that introduced cartography to American colleges and universities.

→ Robinson, Arthur H. Elements of cartography. 4th ed. N.Y., Wiley, 1978.

The standard text, successfully combining fundamental principles with contemporary concepts and methods (1st ed., 1953). For its contribution to a theory of cartography, see Arthur H. Robinson and Barbara Bartz Petchenik, *The Nature of Maps: Essays toward Understanding Maps and Mapping* (Chicago: Univ. of Chicago Pr., 1976).

→ Tyner, Judith. The world of maps and mapping: a creative learning aid. New York, McGraw-Hill, 1973. 49p.

A concise and colorful survey of all types of maps.

Journals with frequent articles on maps and map use which are found in most academic libraries include *American Cartographer, Annals of the Association of American Geographers, Geographical Review, Journal of Geography*, and *Professional Geographer*. Also, the Association of Canadian Map Libraries has published annual proceedings since 1968.

What to Look For

In looking at an atlas, one should be most aware of the maps themselves and not unduly impressed with photographs of countries and other extraneous material. Some American atlases have been criticized for including too much of the latter, using space that might better have been devoted to maps.

Note also the balance of coverage, for most authorities agree that a fair allocation of space to maps on a worldwide basis is the most important criterion in judging a world atlas. One of those authorities is Richard Edes Harrison, who, in "Atlases Revisited" (*Saturday Review* 45:37–40 [Mar. 24, 1962]), helps to explain the problem: "In Europe, where most nations are of medium or small size, this fair allocation offers no great disadvantage but in the United States we tend to cover our own land at such favorable scales that the rest of the world is seriously underemphasized. This can only lead to grave misconceptions of geography" (p.37).

There is also general agreement that a good world atlas should consist of maps of all parts of the world, reproduced on a reasonably large scale, with a large number of place names and a good index. These should be accompanied by an adequate table of contents, instructions in the use of the atlas—including an explanation of map symbols, projections, and abbreviations—and sources used in its compilation. Careful reading of all these parts is as necessary for efficient use as reading the introductions of unabridged dictionaries, since, like the dictionary, the atlas conforms to set rules.

In looking at individual maps, note whether the copyright date is shown, for not all maps in an atlas are equally up to date. Note how relief is shown, whether by layer coloring to indicate different elevations above sea level, or by shading, or by hachures. Note the selection and application of the colors, bearing in mind that "maps should have harmony within themselves. An ugly map, with crude colors, careless line work, and disagreeable poorly arranged lettering may be intrinsically as accurate as a beautiful map, but it is less likely to inspire confidence" (John K. Wright, "Map Makers Are Human," *Geographical Review* 32:542 [1942]). In the past, few American atlases have been distinguished for their coloring, being excelled by the work of European cartographers. However, there has been much improvement in this respect in recent years.

Note the projections used, remembering that "a projection is a systematic compromise with accuracy of area or with true shape. The larger the area shown on the map, the greater is the distortion. The maximum difficulty is encountered in attempting to show the entire world on one flat map, and to meet this problem, mapmakers have, through the centuries, utilized a number of different projections. . . . A good reference atlas should use different projections, each best suited to the desired objective" (Walter W. Ristow, "World Reference Atlases," *Special Libraries* 38:71 [Mar. 1974]).

Note the scales used, for "a well designed atlas needs a carefully chosen sequence of map scales. The most successful ones employ a minimum of scales, which are multiples of one another. They use the same scale for all the sectional maps covering a given continent. The aim, of course, is to have maps of different areas easily comparable. This means large pages. For a serious research atlas, 1:10,000,000 is probably the smallest permissible scale except for continental or world maps" (Daniel Gómez-Ibáñez, "World Atlases for General Reference," *Choice* 6:626 [July–Aug. 1969]).

Note the treatment of place names. Recent English-language atlases tend to follow the rulings of the U.S. Board on Geographic Names (often cited as BGN) or, the Permanent Committee on Geographical Names in London (PCGN). These rulings are based on the local spelling of a name. For places that have distinctive English names, the English form is often given under the official form, and both forms will appear in the index. Atlases of the future will further reflect the efforts of the group of experts on geographical names appointed in 1960 by the secretary general of the United Nations, whose report stressed the need for standardization of geographical names.

Publishers of good world atlases are concerned with all these aspects and, in this highly competitive field of publishing, are continuously revising their works to meet the demand for well-balanced, handsome, accurate, and up-to-date atlases. Some have established reputations over the years, among them the distinguished John Bartholomew and Son in Edinburgh, responsible for the maps in the *Times Atlas*. Also widely recognized is the Cartographic Department of the Oxford University Press, publishers of the *Oxford Atlas of the World*. Muriel Lock has praised its cartography as "of the highest quality, in the van of new techniques" (*Modern Maps and Atlases*, p.87). She also commends the Cartographical Institute of Bertelsmann Verlag, in Gütersloh, Germany, which sponsored *Der Grosse Bertelsmann Weltatlas*, published simultaneously in a number of European countries, and revised and updated in 1964 as the *McGraw-Hill International World Atlas*. In the United States, the most widely recognized publishers are Hammond, Rand McNally, and the National Geographic Society.

To cite but one instance of a foreign government agency that has produced notable world atlases in recent years, we mention the USSR Chief Directorate of Geodesy and Cartography, which issues *Atlas Mira*.

The average librarian needs some assistance in selection of atlases, such as that provided by reviews in the Reference and Subscription Books Review section of *Booklist* and in geographical journals.

Lock, in *Modern Maps and Atlases*, considers three world atlases "preeminent by general consent": the *Times Atlas of the World*, the *Soviet World Atlas*, and the *Atlante Internazionale del Touring Club Italiano* (p.82). Daniel A. Gómez-Ibáñez agrees in his highly critical "World Atlases for General Reference" (p.630), believing these are the only three of the eleven works he reviews which "contend seriously as top quality world atlases for general use."

While there is considerable agreement among experts on which world atlases are superior, it is interesting to compare extended reviews which vary greatly in particulars. Thus even the famous *Times Atlas of the World* (comprehensive ed.) was criticized by Roman Drazniowsky, map curator of the American Geographical Society, for its spelling of foreign place names and for its cartography (which he found no improvement over that in the previous five-volume edition), closing with: "The reviewer would like to add that some corrections of political divisions, changes in place-names, and the addition of some pipelines do not make this edition a superb atlas, as compared to the Mid-Century edition. It is hoped that this statement is not too harsh, but one sets and expects a high standard from the professional atlas makers and cartographers, and a high standard was achieved in the previous editions of the *Times Atlas*, particularly the superb Mid-Century edition" (Special Libraries Assn. Geography and Map Division, *Bulletin* 73:26–28 [Sept. 1968]).

On the other hand, we find this edition hailed in *Booklist and Subscription Books Bulletin* (July 15, 1968) as "another landmark in cartography." And Daniel A. Gómez-Ibáñez, in his "World Atlases for General Reference," described it as "by far the best English atlas, perhaps even the best in the world."

All of which only serves to remind us that authorities do not always agree and that the art of atlas reviewing is not easily acquired, and seldom by the general reference librarian, who must depend on critical evaluations of authorities. It is wise to be aware of the year in which a review was written.

It is also wise to bear in mind the qualifications of the reviewer, for an atlas condemned by a cartographer or geographer for its lack of balance in world coverage, might be less severely criticized by a lay reviewer, who is pleased with the large-scale maps of a particular country. And individual maps, praised for their "uncluttered" appearance by reviewers who are aware that users not proficient in map reading find them easy to use, may be severely criticized by sophisticated reviewers, demanding the maximum of detail, who label them flat and dull.

Librarians, knowing the kinds of people who use their atlases, will acquire the best and most recent atlases, whose maps may be detailed or "uncluttered," as well as those with balanced world coverage and those with emphasis on the country of origin.

To demonstrate that reviewers do not always agree in their evaluation of individual world atlases, the titles below are accompanied by outlines of favorable and unfavorable comment, drawn chiefly from sources already mentioned and, in some cases, using almost the exact wording of the original reviewer. The section on English and American publications is followed by a much briefer section on foreign publications, since the average American user is apt to experience difficulty in using foreign atlases. They cannot be overlooked, however, because of some of their distinguished features, which are noted below.

English and American World Atlases

Most authorities agree that the *Times Atlas* is the best world atlas published in recent years, essential in all libraries which can afford it. For this reason, it is described first.

→ Bartholomew, John, ed. Times atlas of the world: mid-century edition. London, Times Pub. Co., 1955–59. 5v.

Descriptive and favorable comment:
1. Balanced coverage
2. More detailed than any other atlas, since (except for Central America) no part of the world is shown in a scale smaller than 1:5,000,000, with the most significant areas on the scale of 1:1,000,000
3. Projections and cartographic techniques best suited to each map area
4. Good paper, spacious layout, legible lettering, and good color, with layer coloring to show relief
5. Final maps printed by deep-etch photo offset, achieving sharp outlines and excellent registration
6. Many double-page thematic world maps, showing population, climate, food production, vegetation, languages, religions, time zones, etc.
7. Plans for major cities
8. Detailed index to each volume, using official local forms of place names, with *see* references from variations. For each entry, gives country, latitude and longtitude, map plate number, and cross key reference.

These features are also found in the one-volume Comprehensive edition, which is based on the Mid-Century edition.

→ Bartholomew, John, and Son, Ltd. The Times atlas of the world. Comprehensive ed. London, Times Newspapers Ltd.; distributed by Times Books, etc., N.Y., etc., 1967– .

Descriptive and favorable comment:
1. Many thematic maps
2. Added introductory articles covering world minerals, energy, food, and extraterrestrial subjects, e.g. artificial satellites (22p.)
3. Added glossary of geographical terms (9p.)
4. Clear and legible star charts
5. Updating, with revised editions to be published at intervals
6. Single index to more than 200,000 place names, more convenient than the separate indexes to the 5-volume edition.

Unfavorable comment: See page 286.

The *New York Times Atlas of the World* (N.Y., Times Books, 1972–) is a concise version of this atlas.

→ Rand McNally and Co. The International atlas. Chicago, Rand McNally, 1969– .

Descriptive and favorable comment:
1. Compiled with the assistance of 115 cartographers from 14 foreign countries
2. Balanced coverage, with 65 map pages for Canada and United States, 47 for Europe, 50 for Asia, and 26 for Africa
3. Maps generally more attractive than earlier Rand McNally products, most of them in 4 colors.
4. Only 6 proportionate scales
5. Local forms of names used as far as possible, with English forms employed for major water bodies, mountain ranges, and features extending beyond national boundaries
6. Textual matter given in English, German, Spanish, and French (Portuguese added in 1979 ed.)
7. Detailed maps of urbanized regions at 1:1,000,000 scale and more than 60 of the world's major metropolitan areas at 1:3,000,000 scale, the latter conveniently grouped to avoid use of insets in regional maps.
8. Master glossary, giving translations of geographic terms from 52 languages
9. Comprehensive, computer-produced index of more than 160,000 place names, giving latitude and longitude as well as page reference, and including historical names no longer in official use
10. A major production that deserves the attention of cartographers and librarians.

Unfavorable comment:
1. Introduction omits explanation of the map projections
2. Metropolitan area maps somewhat disproportionately represented, with United States and Canada allocated 11 of 29 pages to depict 14 of 60 cities
3. Relief depiction too dark in places
4. No thematic or special-purpose maps in the body of the atlas
5. Tight binding obscures the continuity of the double-page spreads (corrected with 1974 ed.)
6. Not every country represented in a reasonably large scale on a single page or pair of pages (e.g. Yugoslavia).
NOTE: The essay "Patterns and Imprints of Mankind," by Marvin Mikesell, appeared in the 1969 ed. only; a new section, "World Scene," was substituted in the 1974 and 1979 eds.

The *Britannica Atlas* (Chicago: Encyclopaedia Britannica Educational Corp., 1942–) superseded *Encyclopaedia Britannica World Atlas* and *Encyclopaedia World Atlas International*. Produced for Britannica by Rand McNally. Its most thorough revision, making it a truly international atlas, occurred in 1969, when it and Rand McNally's *International Atlas* (above) were published as a joint project. Except for revisions and minor differences the atlases are the same.

→ Goode's World atlas. Chicago, Rand McNally, 1922– (1922–49 editions had title *Goode's School Atlas*.)

Descriptive and favorable comment:
1. Outstanding school-size atlas, on all approved lists
2. Well-balanced coverage
3. Uniform scale, mostly 1:4,000,000
4. More than 100 special-purpose maps on population, world economics, etc.
5. Physical-political maps exceptionally good, easily read, with clear contour lines, light and pleasant layering, and clearly defined political boundaries.
6. Clear and legible lettering, with place names in native and often English forms.
7. Maps of cities and their environs, on scale of 1:1,000,000
8. Excellent section on mapmaking and map projections
9. Index of more than 30,000 entries, giving pronunciation, longitude and latitude, and location on maps.

Unfavorable comment (earlier editions):
1. Not well printed, making it almost impossible to trace the course of a river
2. Inaccurate relief only weakness (corrected in recent editions).

→ Soviet world atlas in English. 2nd ed. Moscow, 1967. 250p. Index gazetteer. Moscow, 1968. 1021p. (English-language ed. of *Atlas Mira*).

Descriptive and favorable comment:
1. Best-balanced atlas in print
2. Superbly drafted maps
3. Numerous city plans
4. Entire world shown at least at 1:7,500,000, most of Europe at 1:2,500,000, Asia at 1:3,000,000 or 1:5,000,000, United States at 1:5,000,000
5. Careful layer coloring and contours depicting relief
6. Extensive range of symbols for physical and cultural features

7. Unconventional framing giving fresh insights into geographical relationships
8. Separate index gazetteer.

Unfavorable comment:
1. Its usefulness to non-Russian readers is limited because of the confusing treatment of non-Western place names.

An interesting item in a *New York Times* article (Jan. 18, 1970), reporting the discovery by American and European cartographers of the apparent adoption by Soviet authorities of a systematic plan to misrepresent locational information on new USSR maps, is given by Harry Steward in "Soviet Map Distortions" (Special Libraries Assn. Geography and Map Division, *Bulletin* 79:45 [Mar. 1970]). Examples in the *Times* article refer specifically to the 1954 and 1967 editions of *Atlas Mira*. Steward concludes: "The changes are attributed in the *Times* article to current Soviet policies in national security and defense. However, their comparatively easy detection by visual observation and comparison, let alone the growing ability of sophisticated orbiting surveillance systems to gather locational information, makes them a little puzzling to explain. Consequently, the report goes on to suggest that the distortions may be aimed at the Chinese, whose repertoire of cartographic information and technological ancillaries is more limited than that of the U.S.A."

→ National Geographic Society, Washington, D.C. Cartographic Division. National Geographic atlas of the world. Wash., the Society, 1963– .

Prepared from revised and updated single maps which first appeared in the *National Geographic*, with new ones added.

Descriptive and favorable comment:
1. Comprehensive, informative, accurate, and attractive, employing most modern cartographic techniques
2. Well-balanced coverage
3. Coverage of obscure and lesser-known areas
4. Inset maps of major cities and metropolitan areas
5. Useful historical maps
6. Informative profiles of countries, states, and territories, updated from earlier editions
7. Clear and easily read maps, beautifully executed, pleasing in color
8. Projections vary according to the purpose and extent of individual maps and reflect new techniques of mapping
9. Section on Africa considerably updated from first edition, and physical maps have more sharply delineated topographic features
10. Maps of the oceans especially well done and informative

11. Only atlas drafted in the United States systematically showing roads and railroads.
12. Index of more than 139,000 entries
13. Revisions, updating, and corrections evident throughout the volume.

Unfavorable comment:
1. Lush prose employed in descriptive text
2. Not stoutly bound
3. Maps bled to all edges of the pages, making rebinding difficult without trimming of map material
4. Binding prevents atlas from lying flat when opened
5. Mishmash of scales.

→ Hammond, Inc. Hammond medallion world atlas. Maplewood, N.J., Hammond, 1966– .

Descriptive and favorable comment:
1. Logical and convenient arrangement of maps and text on facing and adjoining pages for every continent, country, state, and province, including political, physical, and special-purpose maps, statistical data, and index of cities, towns, villages, physical features, and political divisions.
2. Large, clear, well-detailed, extremely accurate maps, with effective use of color
3. Each political map has an inset map that shows physical features, economy, and population density
4. Comprehensive index of more than 100,000 entries, cumulating indexes to individual areas.

Unfavorable comment:
1. Many maps are small relief maps or thematic maps of uncertain value in a general reference atlas, leaving little room for large-scale world maps
2. Foreign regional maps do not show roads or railroads or relief
3. Balance of coverage is poor.

Other Hammond atlases are *Hammond Ambassador World Atlas* (1954–), less expensive than the *Medallion* but with the same maps, gazetteer-index, and world statistical tables, but without the historical and environmental sections; *Hammond Citation World Atlas* (1966–), identical with *Ambassador* but reduced 20 percent in size; *Hammond International World Atlas* (1966–), same as *Citation*, but U.S. state maps and general index omitted. (See *Booklist* 68:729–33 [May 1, 1972] for full description of these atlases.)

School Atlases

Goode's World Atlas, formerly *Goode's School Atlas*, has already been described. It is to be remembered as a first purchase for school media centers, having been noted in White's *Sources of Information in the Social Sciences* (1964 ed.) as "the most widely used, and generally the best, American world atlas for school, home, or office" (p.172). Here, one additional title and an article on school atlases are noted.

→ World book atlas. Chicago, World Book–Childcraft, 1964– .

> "*The World Book Atlas* has been designed to complement and supplement the World Book Encyclopedia with a collection of thematic, historic and general reference maps" (Pref.). Its maps are notable for clarity of detail and pleasing use of color. Index has more than 80,000 entries.

Charles E. Current gives a good overview of school atlases in his "The Acquisition of Maps for School (and Other Small) Libraries" in *Wilson Library Bulletin* 45:578–83 (Feb. 1971).

Foreign-Language Atlases

French

→ Larousse, *firm, publishers*, Paris. Atlas international Larousse politique et économique. Paris, Larousse, 1950– . Maps in portfolio, with index and statistical tables.

Descriptive and favorable comment:
1. Stresses the unifying physical and economic factors of world geography
2. Descriptive text in French, English, and Spanish.
3. Generally attractive and readable maps
4. Contains about 75 maps, mostly folded, including helpful thematic maps covering agriculture, industries, and communications
5. Political maps designed to show propinquity of neighboring countries
6. Much of the statistical data is recent
7. Local form of place names on maps
8. Index includes place names in local form and French, English, and Spanish versions, all with map numbers.

Unfavorable comment:
1. Some countries not shown in their entirety except on a very small scale in political maps
2. Some maps too dark in color to be easily legible, with some over-crowding.
3. Maps on unbound sheets may present problems in shelving and preservation.

Italian

→ Touring Club Italiano. Atlante internazionale. Milano, Touring Club Italiano, 1968.

Descriptive and favorable comment:
1. One of the finest European atlases
2. 173 pages of beautiful maps, printed by the most modern lithographic techniques, illustrating atlas mapmaking at its most skillful
3. Hand-drawn and hand-lettered maps, showing a profusion of places, yet very legible.
4. Particularly useful for location purposes
5. Excellent thematic maps
6. Maps showing intranational boundaries, roads and railroads, and many other features
7. Exemplary treatment of place names, conforming to BGN/PCGN recommendations
8. Only atlas that systematically lists cartographic, statistical, and linguistic sources used in compiling each place
9. Useful notes and glossaries
10. Separate index volume of more than 250,000 entries.

Unfavorable comment:
1. Somewhat unbalanced coverage; Europe has 39 percent of the maps, Asia 19 percent.
2. Suffers from almost too much detail.

Russian

→ USSR. Glavnoe Upravlenie Geodezii i Kartografii. Atlas mira. 2. izd. [Redaktsionnaia kollegiia: A. N. Baranov i dr.] Moskva, 1967.

See *Soviet World Atlas in English*, p. 290–91.

It is obvious from the descriptions of these world atlases that in using them for geographical reference:

1. Maps of a particular area are best represented in atlases published in that area.
2. Arrangement varies, and this should be remembered in choosing the one whose arrangement best answers a particular question.
3. Table of contents lists large geographic areas and should be consulted first when large area is sought.
4. Indexes vary in indicating location and should be clearly understood.

For a list of more than 8,500 world, regional, national, and thematic atlases published from 1950 through 1975, see Gerard L. Alexander, *Guide to Atlases: World, Regional, National, Thematic; an International Listing of Atlases Published since 1950* (Metuchen, N.J.: Scarecrow, 1971; 671p.) and *Supplement* (1977; 362p.).

National Maps and Atlases

Most countries have an established national cartographic agency, and their activities are well described in Lock's *Modern Maps and Atlases*. But not all areas are mapped at medium or large scale, nor is there the uniformity desired by certain international agencies, such as the United Nations Commission on National Atlases, which since 1956 has encouraged creation of national and regional atlases in individual countries and the unification and standardization of the contents of the principal maps. Also active is the International Geographical Union Commission on National Atlases, which offers assistance to organizations engaged in the preparation of integrated national and regional atlases.

National atlases are often fine examples of cartography, portraying the geographical, economic, and social aspects of the country, and sometimes include historical maps. They require careful planning, and years of effort are spent in their compilation, as in the case of the *National Atlas*, prepared under the direction of the U.S. Geological Survey's chief cartographer.

→ The national atlas of the United States of America. Wash., Govt. Prt. Off., 1970. 417p.

> Representing a great deal of research and experimentation and involving 84 federal agencies, commercial firms, universities, and individuals, it is chiefly a thematic atlas, showing the country's physical characteristics—geology, climate, soils, and vegetation; its history—discovery, exploration and growth; battlefields and scientific expeditions; economic and social conditions; and the United States and world affairs. Brief text and detailed index of 41,000 names, with population, map

location, latitude and longitude. Will be widely used because of the high quality of its 756 maps.

Other publications of the U.S. Geological Survey are also of primary importance, and their topographic maps, familiarly known as "quads," are widely used. Representing a quadrangular area bounded by lines of latitude and longitude, and taking their names from a town or natural feature in the area represented, they are published on sheets about 17 by 21 inches, except for the 1:24,000 scale maps, which are 22 by 27 inches. As an example of their efficiency in data storage, it has been estimated that the average quadrangle contains over 100 million bits of information. Even the smallest library should have at least the sheet of the area in which it is located, since these topographic maps show relief, drainage, and culture (towns, roads, railroads, and other works of man). Separate index maps for each state, showing the extent to which the state is mapped, are available free from the U.S. Geological Survey.

The U.S. Geological Survey also publishes two series of base maps of states, showing counties, cities, towns, railroads, streams, public-land lines, highways, relief, and other features on a scale of either 1:500,000 (approximately 8 miles to an inch) or 1:1,000,000 (approximately 16 miles to an inch).

Other important government agencies are the Bureau of Land Management, for its wall map of the United States, showing national parks, forests and wildlife refuges, Indian reservations, and reclamation projects; the Soil Conservation Service of the U.S. Department of Agriculture, for its extensive series of county soil survey maps; and the National Ocean Survey, for its nautical charts. The U.S. Lake Survey publishes navigational charts of the Great Lakes and their connecting waters.

Although often neglected in small libraries, government publications should not be overlooked as reliable and modestly priced sources which are especially valuable for small areas. In addition to the more exhaustive lists and indexes (some of them noted earlier), they are often listed in subject bibliographies, available free from the Superintendent of Documents, including numbers 32, Oceanography; 102, Maps; 160, Earth Sciences; 183, Surveying and Mapping—to name only a few. Free pamphlets from individual agenies are also useful, such as *Topographic Maps* and *Types of Maps Published by Government Agencies*, available from the U.S. Geological Survey. The Survey operates the National Cartographic Information Center (successor, with broadened responsibilities, to its Map Information Office), which collects, processes, and disseminates information concerning maps, aerial photography, geodetic positions, and elevations.

Clara E. Le Gear gives good coverage of atlases in *United States Atlases: A List of National, State, County, City, and Regional Atlases in the Library of*

Congress (Washington: Govt. Prt. Off., 1950–53; 2v.; repr.: New York, Arno Pr., 1971 [Library of Congress Reprint Series]).

Thematic Maps and Atlases

Thematic maps are often simply defined as maps on a specific subject, and are so described in glossaries of geographical terms in most world atlases. The same atlases also contain many thematic maps (as already shown). But recent years have seen great developments in this field, due in part to the growing recognition of their efficiency for certain types of data storage. As Lock points out in the introduction to her extensive section on thematic maps and atlases:

> Much of the work being done in thematic mapping is still in its experimental stages; new combinations of colouring and symbols are being tried out in economic and population mapping. In the mapping of climate and oceanographic data, the work of numerous scientists is only now coming into maximum usage through international co-ordination. In the use and interpretation of all such maps also much remains to be learned and methods of reproduction are constantly under review [*Modern Maps and Atlases*, p.404].

The use of thematic maps for problem analysis has greatly increased in recent years, and new technical developments have improved their production, such as greater precision of photographic and copying equipment and the computerization of certain aspects of cartography. Data gathered by remote sensing (the term applied to collecting data about objects or phenomena that are not in contact with the data-gathering device) have greatly increased because of the wide use of aerial photography since World War II, along with new types of advanced remote sensors, better aircraft and satellites, and more elaborate systems for transmission, storage, and display of data.

All of these factors result in wider and more varied sources of thematic maps, which will be reflected in library collections. Here we can only consider several examples of thematic atlases that have been used for many years to supplement the thematic maps in general atlases, among them, the historical, economic, and several other special-purpose atlases to be found in most general reference collections.

Biblical Atlases

→ Grollenberg, L. H. Atlas of the Bible. N.Y., Nelson, 1965 (c1956). 165p.

Reflecting recent discoveries of archaeologists, and using expert cartographers, the maps show all biblical places which can be identified with any certainty. Photographs of Palestine and its neighbors are linked by a 60,000-world commentary. Fully indexed.

Historical Atlases

The importance of maps in teaching history has long been recognized and historical atlases have been published to provide a fuller coverage than that usually found in historical writing. Not all of them bear the word *atlas* in their titles, though they usually do. A notable exception is:

→ Miller, Theodore R. Graphic history of the Americas. N.Y., Wiley, 1969. 59p. maps, text.

Andrew H. Clark, reviewing this title in Special Libraries Association, Geography and Map Division, *Bulletin* 79:55–56 (Mar. 1970), says: "This is a sort of atlas (indeed, I would rate it as the most useful atlas of American geographical history, or historical geography, that I have yet encountered) but its title is, nevertheless, very apt, for a vast amount of chronological and locational information is contained on each of its pages. . . . Nothing exists that compares with it as a student aid for checking on location, distribution and movements of people, or changing political or military control. Moreover there is a good deal of variety in the demographic, economic and cultural (e.g. linguistic and religious) detail given. Certainly no library serving historians or geographers (from the eighth grade on) should be without it." About half of the pages cover the Western Hemisphere, the rest the United States or Canada. Clark notes some errors in names, dates, or other facts.

Other volumes, devoted to world history, are:

→ Shepherd, William Robert. Historical atlas. 9th ed. N.Y., Barnes & Noble, 1964. 226p. of col. maps (part fold). 115p.

Considered one of the best in English, chronologically arranged from 1450 B.C. to A.D. 1964, with maps for the period since 1929 prepared by Hammond. Well indexed. This edition is revised and updated by the publisher from time to time. Supplemented by:

→ Gilbert, Martin. Recent history atlas: 1870 to the present day. Cartography by John R. Flower. N.Y., Macmillan, 1969. 121p. maps.

Contains 120 black-and-white maps with brief accompanying text, giving detailed coverage of World Wars I and II, Korean conflict, and Vietnam.

→ Rand McNally and Co. Atlas of world history, ed. by R. R. Palmer. Chicago, Rand McNally, 1965. 216p. maps (part col.).

Emphasizes North American and European history, particularly the 19th and 20th centuries, but some maps for the rest of the world; all well made, with brief commentary on the significance of each. Fewer maps and index entries than in *Shepherd*, but both are acquired by most libraries.

→ The Times atlas of world history, by the Times of London. Ed. by Geoffrey Barraclough. Maplewood, N.J., Hammond, 1978. 360p.

Impressive blending of illustrative material (plates, maps, illustrations), text, glossary, index. In 7 sections: (1) the world of early man, (2) the first civilizations, (3) the classical civilizations of Eurasia, (4) the world of divided regions, (5) the world of the emerging West, (6) the age of European dominance, (7) the age of global civilization. The broad sweeps of historical movements (religions, great civilizations, etc.) are accented much more than histories of nations, particular events, and the like.

→ Van Der Heyden, A. A. M., and Scullard, H. H., eds. Atlas of the Classical world. N.Y., Nelson, 1959. 221p.

Resembles Grollenberg's *Atlas of the Bible* in format, devoting space not only to maps but to artifacts and photographs of works of art. Beautifully edited.

If we turn our attention to atlases of American history, several titles may be cited:

→ American Heritage. The American Heritage pictorial atlas of United States history, by the editors of American Heritage. N.Y., American Heritage, [1966]. 424p.

Differs from *Jackson* and *Lord*, not only in contents but also in its color maps and "pictorial maps" of major battles of the Revolutionary and Civil wars and national parks.

→ Atlas of early American history: The Revolutionary era, 1760–1790. Lester J. Cappon, ed. in chief; Barbara Bartz Petchenik, cartographic ed.; John Hamilton Lang, assist. ed. . . . Princeton, pub. for the Newberry Library and the Institute of Early American History and Culture by the Princeton Univ. Pr., 1976. 157p.

Nearly 300 superb maps and supporting text portray the significant cultural, economic, military, and political aspects of the 30-year period, divided into 3 time frames: pre-1776, the war period, postwar years to 1790. Many maps are accompanied by brief text, in addition to the text pages following the maps section. Index.

→ Gilbert, Martin. American history atlas. Cartography by Arthur Banks. N.Y., Macmillan, 1969. 114p. maps.

Emphasizes social and economic conditions in its 112 maps, covering the period from the discovery of America to 1968.

→ Jackson, Kenneth T. Atlas of American history. Kenneth T. Jackson, ed.; James Truslow Adams, ed. in chief, orig. ed. Rev. ed. N.Y., Scribner, c1978. 294p.

Revised ed. has 198 black-and-white maps (143 in 1943 ed.), of which 51 are new and others have been updated. Designed to accompany *Dictionary of American History*. Does not duplicate the maps in *Paullin* and *Wright*. Traces the growth of America from its discovery to the present. Indexed by names appearing on the maps and under such subjects as roads, boundaries, etc.

→ Lord, Clifford L., and Lord, Elizabeth H. Historical atlas of the United States. Rev. ed. N.Y., Holt, 1953. 238p. Repr. Johnson Reprint, 1969.

Covers colonial period to 1950 in 312 outline maps, mostly black and white, which supplement *Jackson* and *Paullin*. Useful not only for maps covering population, education, transportation, military campaigns, etc., but also appended statistical tables. Indexed by place and subjects.

→ National Geographic Society. Picture atlas of our fifty states. Wash., The Society, 1978. 304p.

Appropriate for middle graders and others. Extensive use of full-color photographs, charts, maps, and illustrations. Textual information for each state is uniform, including a map indicating principal cities, physical features; statistics, pictures of state bird, state tree, state flag; and 2 page spread of representative photographs.

→ Paullin, Charles Oscar. Atlas of the historical geography of the United States, ed. by John K. Wright. [Wash., N.Y.], pub. jointly by Carnegie Inst. of Washington and the Amer. Geographical Soc., 1932. 162p. 688 maps. [Carnegie Inst. publ. 401]

The first major historical atlas of the United States, notable for its 688 maps, some of them reproductions of early maps, whose broad coverage includes: Natural environment; Cartography, 1492–1867; Indians, 1567–1930; Explorations; Settlement, population and towns, 1650–1790; States, territories and cities, 1790–1930; Population, 1790–1930; Colleges, universities and churches, 1773–1890; Boundaries, 1607–

1927; Political parties and opinion, 1788–1930; Political, social and educational reforms, 1775–1931; Industries and transportation, 1620–1931; Foreign commerce, 1701–1929; Distribution of wealth, 1799–1928; Plans of Cities, 1775–1803; Military history, 1689–1919, etc. Accompanied by excellent descriptive text.

Agricultural Atlas

→ World atlas of agriculture: under the aegis of the International Association of Agricultural Economists. Novara, Italy: Instituto Geographico de Agostini, 1969– .

Atlas sheets and monographs. Land utilization and relief maps arranged by major world regions, with source indicated for each map.

Economic Atlases

Though thematic maps, showing contemporary economic conditions, will be found in general world atlases and earlier conditions are included in historical atlases, the detailed and broader coverage in economic atlases makes them more useful to economists, businessmen, geographers, and students interested in world economics. A few outstanding examples, some notable for their frequent revision, are:

→ The Bartholomew/Scribner atlas of Europe: a profile of Western Europe. N.Y., Scribner, 1974. 128p.

Uncluttered, pleasingly colored maps, graphs, and diagrams give a clear picture of many facets of the economic and social life in 18 countries of Western Europe: European unity and cooperation, press and TV, population, languages, weather, farming and industry, transportation, travel, trade, housing, health, education, constitutions. Supervised by John Bartholomew, with the best cartographic techniques. Selectively indexed and exact citation to sources of information.

→ Oxford economic atlas of the world. Prep. by the Cartographic Dept. of the Clarendon Pr. 4th ed. [N.Y.], Oxford Univ. Pr., 1972. 239p.

An improvement over the 1965 (3rd) edition by reason of its larger size and added information. Maps giving world distribution patterns are accompanied by statistical tables and economic commentary. Clear commodity maps show major trade flows. New maps for disease, medical care, education, foreign aid and trade, employment, birth control, and nutrition. Also added is a gazetteer of 8,000 names, chiefly urban, and for economically important sites. 1st ed., 1954.

Oxford also issues a series of Oxford Regional Economic Atlases, based on the *Oxford Economic Atlas of the World*, with separate volumes for the USSR and Eastern Europe; the Middle East and North Africa; Africa; the United States and Canada; Western Europe; Latin America; India, China, and Japan; and Southeast Asia, Australia, and New Zealand.

Distinguished for its currency and detailed statistical information, and found in every library that can afford the annual subscription price, is:

→ Rand McNally and Co. Rand McNally commercial atlas and marketing guide. N.Y., Rand McNally, 1876– . Annual.

> Extremely useful for its state maps, which vary in scale from 1:342,000 for Connecticut to 1:1,580,000 for Texas, emphasizing marketing areas and accompanied by statistics. Less often consulted for its small-scale maps of foreign countries, which make up about a tenth of the volume and are separately indexed.

Space Atlas

→ Moore, Patrick. The Rand McNally new concise atlas of the universe. Chicago, Rand McNally, 1978. 190p.

> Produced with the collaboration of NASA, the U.S. Geological Survey, and astronomer Sir Bernard Lovell. About 1,000 illustrations, 400 in full color. Four sections: Atlas of the earth from space, Atlas of the moon, Atlas of the solar system, Atlas of the stars.

Wildlife Atlas

→ Rand McNally atlas of world wildlife. Martyn Bramwell, ed. Chicago, Rand McNally; London, Mitchell Beazley Ltd., 1973. 208p.

> Maps, charts, photographs, and other illustrations show the evolution, environment and interrelationships of wildlife, using a thematic approach. About 180 maps of all sizes show the distribution and emigration of plants and animals. Brief accompanying text.

General guides to reference materials, such as *Sheehy* and *Walford*, contain many other examples of thematic atlases, easily located through their indexes under both subject—Bible, for example—and atlases. Subheadings in *Sheehy* under "atlases" give a good idea of their variety, including agricultural, anthropological, astronomical, biblical, Catholic church, Christian world, climatic, congressional districts, economic, historical, Islamic, linguistic, literary, and maritime.

That thematic maps will multiply greatly in the future is evident in:

→ Kingsbury, Robert C. Creative cartography: an introduction to effective thematic design. (Occasional Publication, no.4. Dept. of Geography, Indiana Univ., 1969)

> Designed for students of thematic cartography and others who would include thematic maps in research papers, dissertations, journal articles, and books. Contains instructional materials not generally available in published form.

Finally, quite a different sort of special-purpose atlas is of interest to librarians who work with the visually handicapped:

→ Large Type Hammond-Jennison World Atlas. N.Y., Watts, 1969. 144p.

> Though the United States is emphasized in its 115 pages of maps, most of them large scale and double spread, this is an admirable effort to produce uncluttered maps, in clear colors, with boundaries indicated by broad red lines. Appropriately, the index to about 2,000 names is in large type also. Can be used with elementary school students as well as the partially sighted.

Advances in making maps for blind students have been reported by Paul A. Groves and Joseph W. Wiedell in "New Development in Educational Cartography" (*Journal of Geography* (69:204–12 [Apr. 1970]). After describing some of the problems encountered in designing a tactual map, they conclude, "A great many blind people find maps fascinating. . . . The maps which are proposed for use by the blind are intended to be read, not looked at. They are as clear as we, the cartographers, can make them, but they are not simple."

For that matter, maps intended for the sighted are seldom simple, and skills in map reading, essential for all who want to understand the world, must be mastered.

Much easier to use are gazetteers, which are usually defined as a geographical dictionary or index. As noted, many atlases have index-gazetteers or gazetteer-indexes, often containing many more place names than appear in separately published gazetteers, which are chiefly used for quick location questions. These (and several others which are very exhaustive) are briefly discussed here.

Gazetteers

Ideally, a gazetteer should give the officially standardized form of spelling of place names, with cross-references to variant spellings; should give exact latitude and longitude, based on the latest information; and should give pronunciation. Emphasis should be on inclusiveness of entries rather than amount of historical and socio-economic information for individual entries, for other sources, such as general encyclopedias, supply more information of this sort than will be found in a gazetteer.

Two gazetteers that most nearly meet these criteria are the multivolume work of the U.S. Board on Geographic Names and the *Times Index-Gazetteer of the World*, both distinguished for their inclusiveness. Less inclusive, but useful for pronunciation, are the *Columbia Lippincott Gazetteer, International Geographic Encyclopedia and Atlas*, and *Webster's Geographical Dictionary* (listed below with a postal guide that may be used to verify the spelling of a name). The latter are convenient for ready reference.

→ Columbia Lippincott gazetteer of the world, ed. by Leon Seltzer with the Geographical Research Staff of Columbia University Press and with the cooperation of the American Geographical Society, with 1961 supp. N.Y., Columbia Univ. Pr., 1962. 2148 p., 23p.

Gives location, pronunciation, and considerable socio-economic information for about 130,000 names, much of it substantially the same as in the original printing in 1952, but with new nations and 1960 U.S. census figures added. Was severely criticized by Richard Edes Harrison for failing to follow international standardization of spelling of place names, though he described it as exhaustive and "loaded with prestige" in "Geography at Home" (*Saturday Review* 42:43 [Mar. 21, 1959]).

→ International geographic encyclopedia and atlas. Boston, Houghton, 1979. 1024p.

Published with the cooperation of the editors of the *New Columbia Encyclopedia*. More than 25,000 entries give location, pronunciation, history, economic importance, educational and cultural institutions, etc., for place names and provide definitions of geographical terms. 200 b&w, 64 full-color maps.

→ Times, London. Index-gazetteer of the world. Boston, Houghton, 1966. 996p.

Gives official spelling, cross-references from variants, and latitude and longitude for about 345,000 geographical names. Map references to the *Times Atlas* are given for about 198,000, but others may be located on large-scale maps since latitude and longitude are given for each entry. Pronunciation and socio-economic information not given.

→ Webster's New geographical dictionary; a dictionary of names of places with geographical and historical information and pronunciations. Rev. ed. Springfield, Mass., Merriam, 1972. 1370p.

> Gives location, pronunciation, but less socio-economic data than *Lippincott* for about 47,000 entries. Up-to-dateness indicated by use of 1970 U.S. census figures and the attention to new nations. Glossary of geographical terms with foreign equivalents, and appended maps by Hammond.

→ U.S. Board on Geographic Names. Gazetteer. no.1– . Wash., Govt. Prt. Off., 1955– . Irregular (In progress)

> Each number covers a single country; recent ones include Ghana, Argentina, Syria, Liberia, Gambia, and a 2nd ed. (1968) for Mainland China. Gives official standard names, with cross-references from variants, latitude and longitude, and location on specified official maps. No.83, France, contains 100,000 entries, compared with *Lippincott's* 130,000 for the whole world. Pronunciation and socio-economic information not given.

→ U.S. Postal Service. National zip code and post office directory. 1979– . Wash., Govt. Prt. Off., 1979– .

> Combines *Directory of Post Offices* and *National Zip Code Directory*. Contents arranged in 12 sections: 3, Mail services (classes, special postal services); 6, Special zip code lists (3-digit zip codes, zip codes for military installations, etc.); 7, State list of post offices, stations and branches; 8, Post offices with city listings; 10, Alphabetical list of post offices; 11, Numerical list of post offices; 12, Names of discontinued postal units.

In summary, the smaller gazetteers may be used for pronunciation of place names and for longitude and latitude of geographical features of the world. The larger ones are most useful for verification of the official spelling of a name and for locating obscure places whose names do not appear even in large world atlases. For most inquiries, the index to a good world atlas will supply the answers.

Encyclopedias, Directories, Handbooks

→ Association of American Geographers. Directory. Wash., the Assn., 1949– . (Title varies)

> Gives birthplace, date of birth, education and degrees, chief fields of professional interest and research, occupation, home address.

→ _____. Guide to graduate departments of geography in the United States and Canada. 1968/1969– . Wash., the Assn., 1968– .

Information provided: addresses, telephone numbers, degrees offered, programs and research facilities, list of staff with degrees and specializations. Alphabetical staff directory and geographical index of institutions by state and province.

→ Carrington, David K., and Stephenson, Richard W. Map collections in the United States and Canada. 3rd ed. N.Y., Special Libraries Assn., 1978. 230p.

Covers 743 collections, giving information on staff, collection size, area specializations, special cartographic collections, depository arrangements, reproduction facilities, etc. Alphabetical by states and, within states, alphabetically by city.

→ Geographers: Biobibliographical Studies. v.1– , 1977– . London, Mansell. Annual.

"Brief sketches, alphabetically arranged, of individuals who have made significant contributions to the development of geographical thought and of geography as a scientific subject and academic discipline. It includes both famous and lesser known figures from all over the world, primarily from the 19th and 20th centuries. Each study describes its subject's education, life and work, scientific ideas and geographical thought, and the influence of those ideas" (Intro.).

→ Harder, Kelsie B., ed. Illustrated dictionary of place names, United States and Canada. N.Y., Van Nostrand Reinhold, 1976. 631p.

Lists over 15,000 named places, natural features, and historic sites, emphasizing name derivations and changes. See *Stewart* (below).

→ Lands and peoples. N.Y., etc., Grolier, 1929/30– . 7v.

Particularly useful in elementary and secondary school libraries for its good overview of the history, geography, culture, and economics of the country. About 1,700 photographs in full color and appended bibliography. Text is aimed at 5th grade reading level and contents reflect the current social studies curriculum.

→ Showers, Victor. World facts and figures. N.Y., Wiley, 1979. 757p.

The Guinness book for geography, this volume features tables on such matters as the longest rivers or highest mountains by continent, the countries with highest and lowest birth rates, the largest, oldest, wettest cities, the world's largest libraries, etc. Country gazetteer section includes area and population, birth and death rates; city gazetteer section provides date of settlement, location, elevation, highest and lowest and average temperatures. Bibliography of 260 titles, topically arranged. (1st ed., 1973, entitled *The World in Figures.*)

→ Stewart, George R. American place names: a concise and selective dictionary for the continental United States of America. N.Y., Oxford Univ. Pr., 1970. 550p.

Some 12,000 entries, A–Z order, briefly explaining name origins. Bibliography appended. See *Harder* (above).

→ World directory of map collections. Comp. by the Geography and Map Libraries Subsection. Ed. by Walter W. Ristow. Munich, Verlag Dokumentation, 1976. 326p. (IFLA Pubns., 8); distributed Unipub, New York.

Lists for each of about 285 collections in some 45 countries name and address of the collection, date of establishment, director's name, number of professional staff members, collection policies, reproduction facilities, etc. Countries for which directories already exist are selectively represented.

Dictionaries of Geographical Terms

Not to be confused with geographical dictionaries (such as those already described), these supplement unabridged dictionaries by giving fuller information on individual terms, with definitions restricted to geography. The following are considered the most useful:

→ Monkhouse, Francis J., and Small, John. A dictionary of the natural environment. N.Y., Wiley, 1978. 320p.

Based in part on Monkhouse's *A Dictionary of Geography* (1965, 1970), with more than 4,000 clearly defined terms, particularly in physical geography. Appendix of analytical list of terms by field.

→ Stamp, L. Dudley, ed. A glossary of geographical terms. London, Longmans, 1961– .

The most comprehensive definitions and origins of modern geographical terms, with Greek and Latin roots appended.

→ _____., ed. Longmans dictionary of geography. London, Longmans, 1966.

> Its definitions of geographical terms are based on fuller information in Stamp's *Glossary* (above) Includes entries for individual geographers, geographical societies, and journals.

Travel Guides

It has long been recognized that travel guides are a useful source of geographical and historical information, often augmenting gazetteers, with fuller descriptions of towns and historic sites, and often more local maps and plans of cities than in atlases. They grow more popular each year.

Modern travel guides—intended to make it easier, more comfortable, and more pleasant to see the world—have multiplied so greatly, along with our mobility, that librarians may wish for the early nineteenth century, when the firm of Baedeker was the principal publisher of guides for most of the countries to which travelers went. The excellence of its guides, their accuracy and detail, and the quality of its maps may explain why they are still being updated and published today, and why *Baedeker* has so long been synonymous with *travel guide*.

Few of the guides today resemble Augustus Hare's (1834–1903) *Walks in Rome*, which, like his walking books on other European cities, was intended for travelers who had time for leisurely strolls and who were interested in the history of what they saw along the way. Now there are many special-purpose guides, including those for scholars who study abroad, for those who want to stay healthy while traveling, for those who must see Europe from a wheelchair, and for those who have limited budgets. Since most libraries cannot acquire even a small percentage of these guides but still need to know of their existence, a recent and much-needed bibliography is very useful:

Bibliographies

→ Heise, Jon O., and others, eds. Travel guidebooks in review. 3rd ed., rev. Syracuse, N.Y., Gaylord, 1978. 187p.

> Somewhat oriented to students and other low-budget travelers. Basic arrangement is in 5 parts—Europe, Asia, Africa, South America, worldwide. Valuable appendixes: a list of all travel books in English, names and addresses of publishers of titles reviewed, guidebooks published in series, a basic travel library, basic international employment sources, and a basic study-abroad library.

For a period when traveling was more fraught with hardship, there was another valuable bibliographical source:

→ Cox, Edward Godfrey. A reference guide to the literature of travel, including voyages, geographical descriptions, adventures, shipwrecks and expeditions. Seattle, Univ. of Washington Pr., 1935–49. 3v. (Univ. of Washington. Publ. in language and literature, v.9–10, 12)

> V.1, The Old World; v.2, The New World; v.3, Great Britain. Lists "in chronological order, from earliest date ascertainable down to and including the year 1800, all the books on foreign travels, voyages and descriptions printed in Great Britain, together with translations from foreign tongues and continental renderings of English works" (Pref.). Well indexed and annotated; describes Hakluyt's *Voyages* as "among the various collections of voyages made and printed in England, the highest rank must be awarded. . . . To compile a collection of voyages . . . back nearly three centuries . . . was no easy task."

This bibliography is of interest to historians as well as geographers. Other examples, limited to the United States and distinguished for descriptive and critical comments on titles selected by specialists, are:

→ Clark, Thomas D. Travels in the Old South; a bibliography. Norman, Univ. of Oklahoma Pr., 1956–59. 3v. (American exploration and travel ser., no.19)

> Covers period 1527 to 1860.

→ _____. Travels in the new South; a bibliography. Norman, Univ. of Oklahoma Pr., 1962. 2v. (American exploration and travel ser., no.36)

> Covers period 1865 to 1955.

→ Coulter, E. Merton. Travels in the Confederate states; a bibliography. Norman, Univ. of Oklahoma Pr., 1948. 289p. (American exploration and travel ser., [no.11])

> Covers period 1861 to 1865.

While most of the titles in *Clark* and *Coulter* are not travel guides in the strict sense of the word, they are of great reference value for those seeking contemporary accounts of what places looked like at an earlier period. In a rapidly changing world, they provide historical perspective. For those who know Cape Kennedy as it is today, it is interesting to learn that John K.

Wright described it in 1911 as "uninhabited, dark treeless lowlands . . . the one place in the world where everybody is contented with his lot and wants nothing changed" (quoted in Nordis Felland, "Obituary: John K. Wright," Special Libraries Assn. Geography and Map Division, *Bulletin* 77:29–30 [Sept. 1969]).

Travel guides of earlier periods are usually kept by libraries for this same purpose, and reprints, such as the 1969 Johnson reprint of Carl David Arfwedson, *The United States and Canada in 1832, 1833 and 1834*, supply information not easily located elsewhere. Another title is:

→ The Pacific tourist; an illustrated guide to Pacific R.R., California, and pleasure resorts across the continent. F. E. Shearer, ed. N.Y., Adams & Bishop, 1884. 379p. Repr. by Bounty Books, a division of Crown Publishers, 1970.

> A facsimile edition of the most popular rail tourist guide to the American West of the 1870s, profusely illustrated. Notable for contributions by F. V. Hayden and Clarence King, known for their early surveys of the West.

But for current information, the series of travel guides kept up to date by reputable publishers are most often sought. Among them are:

→ American Automobile Association. Tour book. Wash., AAA. Annual.

> Gives temperatures, recreational facilities, minimum age for drivers, maps of downtown areas of major cities, and tourist attractions. Covers the United States, Mexico and Central America, and Canada.

→ American guide series, comp. by Federal Writers' Project (later called Writers' Program). [Pub. variously by different publishers], 1937– .

> Separate volumes for each state contain chapters on history, geology, art, agriculture, and industry, as well as descriptions of small towns and villages. Recent editions, currently published in Houghton Mifflin's New American Guide series, are available for some states and are more accurate and better illustrated than the original editions.

→ Baedeker handbook(s) for travelers. London, Allen & Unwin, 1828– .

> Cover countries, regions, and cities of Europe and parts of North and South America, the Near East, and Egypt. Valuable for wide range of descriptive information and for maps, city plans, and diagrams.

→ Fielding, Temple. Fielding's travel guide to Europe. N.Y., Sloane, 1948– . Annual.

Up-to-date information; a practical guide for the American tourist.

→ Fodor's travel guides, ed. by Eugene Fodor. N.Y., McKay, 1953– .

Revised annually, with area guides covering Europe, India, Japan and East Asia, Caribbean, Bahamas and Bermuda. Also annual guides to about 20 individual countries, including Holland, Israel, Turkey, and Yugoslavia.

→ Frommer, Arthur. _____(country, region, city) on _____dollars a day. N.Y., Simon and Schuster. Frequently revised.

Examples: Europe, South America, Spain, Boston. Popular with students and indigent travelers.

→ Let's go: The budget guide to _____. Written by Harvard Student Agencies. N.Y., Dutton. (Subtitle varies) Frequently revised.

The volume on Europe—to illustrate the series—covers Eastern as well as Western European countries plus North Africa and Israel. Information is wide ranging: sightseeing, food, lodging, visas, passports, etc.

→ Lynch, Michael, ed. All Asia guide. 10th ed. Rutland, Vt., Tuttle, 1978.

This comprehensive, authoritative guide for some 25 Asian countries covers basic information for each country: passports, lists of hotels and holidays, climate, foods, street maps, etc.

→ Michelin travel guide(s). Roslyn Heights, N.Y. Frequently revised.

Highly regarded by seasoned travelers, with whom these guides are the favorites. Many countries covered, and now available in English translation. The "green guides" furnish detailed descriptions of places of interest, suggested itineraries, places to stay, plans of towns; the "red guides" provide background information on a country's political and cultural history, currency conversion, lexicons of needed phrases.

→ Mobil travel guides. Chicago, Rand McNally. 7v. Frequently revised.

Contain road maps, points of interest, food and lodging, tipping, liquor regulations. Volumes: Northeastern states, Middle Atlantic states, Southeastern states, Great Lakes area, Southwest and South Central area, California and the West, and Northwest and Great Plains states.

→ Muirhead's Blue guides. London, Benn, 1918– . Distributed in the U.S. by Rand McNally.

Preferred by some seasoned travelers to *Baedeker*, though similar in style and coverage.

→ Nagel's Travel guide(s). Geneva, Paris, Nagel.

Cover many of the same countries and cities as *Baedeker* and *Muirhead* and, like them, are strictly factual, as stated on jacket of the 1956 English-language edition for Europe: "A travel guide is not a collection of anecdotes and amusing experiences. It is a handbook of practical information, reliable and up to date."

→ Weiss, Louise. Access to the world: A travel guide for the handicapped. N.Y., Chatham Square Pr., 1977; distributed by Contemporary Books, Chicago. 178p.

Useful compilation of lists of hotels, airport facilities, private and public organizations that can help travelers, etc. High reference value.

Librarians, selecting travel guides for libraries, should remember Nagel's description and stay away from those which try to be amusing or are too personal in tone. They should also check on the adequacy of indexing, since even some of the good guides are lacking in this respect. They and their clientele will be most appreciative of the quality of the "Travel Guides" section in *American Reference Books Annual*.

Other Travel Information

Information on transportation and accommodations is found in current directories, such as:

→ Hotel and motel red book, 1886– . N.Y., American Hotel Assn. Directory Corp., 1886– . Annual.

Gives prices and other information (but not ratings) for hotels, motels, and resorts in the U.S. and other countries for members of the association only. The annual official guide of the British Travel Association, *Hotels and Restaurants in Britain*, provides much fuller information for Britain, including touring guide, town plans, transportation, recreation, etc.

→ Official airline guide, 1943– . Oak Brook, Ill., etc., Reuben H. Donnelley etc., 1943– . Monthly. Publisher varies. Various editions.

Guide to airline routes and schedules.

This chapter has tried to give a brief overview of geography: its methodology, organizations, principal sources of information retrieval from journals, bibliographic guides, government and serial publications, maps and atlases, and how to assess their worth, as well as thematic atlases, gazetteers, and sources of travel information. The chapter must be augmented with more exhaustive guides.

Appendix
Guidelines for Particular Types of Reference Works

84. ATLASES

I. *Atlas as a Whole*
   A. Authority of the Publisher, Editorial Staff, and Special Contributors
      1. What is the previous cartographic experience of the publisher? What comparable works has the publisher produced?
      2. What is the experience and professional competence of the editorial staff and the special contributors? Do certain individuals have major responsibility for the publication? If so, what are their qualifications and reputations in the field?
   B. Scope, Purpose, Objectives
      1. Are they stated, and to what extent are they accomplished?
      2. To what levels of readership is the atlas directed? Is the atlas intended to meet the needs of a particular group, such as students, families, or business people? Is it all-purpose? To what extent does it meet the needs of its intended readership?
   C. Currency
      1. How up to date is the material as a whole? Does the copyright date accurately reflect the work's currency?

Reprinted from the *Reference and Subscription Books Review Committee Manual* (Chicago: ALA, 1979).

2. If revised, how thorough has revision been? Reviewers are reminded that map revisions necessitate index changes. It is also important to compare the new edition carefully with the previous edition.
3. Are there any indications that the atlas will be revised when necessary or on a regular schedule?

D. Arrangement and Organization of the Maps and Text
1. How are the contents of the atlas arranged?
2. Does the preliminary material address the question of map projections, scale, symbols and other important data?
3. What kind of supportive text is included? Is it logically placed with reference to the maps?

II. *Range and Quality of Individual Maps*

A. Authority
1. What is the experience of the cartographer if he or she is not the same as the publisher or not part of the editorial staff?
2. Are there bibliographical and other references to indicate the sources and authority of the maps?

B. Date of Publication
1. Do the maps provide current, accurate, and reliable information? Reviewers should examine closely those maps where recent significant changes in political boundaries, dams, canals, and names have been made. A detailed study should be made of an area with which the reviewer is familiar.
2. Are the maps dated? An atlas should not be criticized for not dating individual maps, but when dates are provided, attention should be called to this feature.

C. Number of Maps and Adequacy of Coverage
1. Is there adequate representation of important areas and regions? Which regions of the world are emphasized in terms of numbers of maps? Does the atlas provide balanced coverage, e.g., does it cover all areas of the world or does it place too much emphasis on country of origin?
2. Are insets used? Are they adequate in size? Number? Quality?

D. Types of Maps Provided
1. How would the atlas be categorized with respect to the kind of maps included? Are they political, physical, historical, resource or a combination of two or more? Maps are political if they emphasize political boundaries and the locations of (a large number of) towns, cities, and administrative divisions. They are physical if they ignore or minimize boundaries and manmade features and emphasize natural features.
2. Is there a sufficient variety for the purpose of the atlas?

E. Projection
1. What types are used? Are they clearly identified? Does the atlas provide assistance in interpreting them?
2. Is comparison of maps facilitated through consistency in projection?

F. Size and Placement of Maps
 1. Are maps of sufficient size?
 2. Are they displayed so all parts are clearly visible? (Reviews should particularly note double-page maps.)
G. Scale
 1. Are scales plainly indicated? Is scale indicated as a fractional representation (1:63,360) and/or as the number of miles to the inch (or kilometers to the centimeter)? Are distances given in the British system of units or the metric system?
 2. Is there a reasonable consistency in scales to facilitate comparisons of countries and regions?
H. Method of Showing Relief, e.g., Hachuring, Contour Lines, Shading, Layer Tints
 1. Is the method effectively used and attractive?
 2. Is there adequate explanation of the method?
I. Use of Colors
 1. Are the colors sufficiently differentiated to be meaningful?
 2. Do they add to the attractiveness of the atlas or do they appear garish or inappropriate?
 3. Are colored backgrounds such that lettering and symbols are legible?
 4. Is there a key which indicates the meaning of the colors? Is the color key located on each map or on a separate page centrally located in the atlas?
J. Details
 1. Are details well differentiated, e.g., are elevations, rivers, highways, and other features clearly indicated?
 2. Is the lettering distinct and easily read? Is there overcrowding?
 3. Are geographical names given in the vernacular or translated? Do names consistently follow the style of a recognized body such as the U.S. Board on Geographic Names or the Permanent Committee on Geographical Names (United Kingdom)?

III. *Index Gazetteer*
A. Is there a general index for the whole atlas? Are there individual map indexes?
B. Approximately how many entries does the index contain? (Do not accept publisher's claim of the number of index entries without checking. Take names at random from a sampling of maps and check to see if they appear in the index.)
C. Does the index include all political names and physical names shown on the maps, or is it selective? In what way? Are index entries accurate? (Check a sampling of entries against the maps.)
D. How does the index refer to the location of places on a given map? (Cross-reference grid? Latitude and longitude?)
E. Does the index include population figures, area, or other additional information, e.g., pronunciation, latitude and longitude? Are the statistics up to date and accurate? Based on reputable sources?

IV. *Supplementary Material, e.g., Bibliographies, Descriptive Text, Charts, Tables, and Other Features*
   A. What kinds of supplementary information are provided?
   B. Does supplementary material contribute to or detract from the primary purpose of the atlas? Could the space have been better used for additional maps?
   C. Does it provide information not readily available elsewhere? Attention is called to the fact that many statistical tables, charts, and other data rapidly go out of date and are readily obtainable in other compilations.
   D. What is the quality of the supplementary materials?
      1. Is the text clear, accurate, and informative?
      2. Are bibliographies up to date? Annotated?
      3. Are charts, tables, and other features well done?
      4. Are illustrations of good quality? Well placed? Pertinent?

85. BIBLIOGRAPHIC REFERENCE SOURCES

I. *Scope*
   A. How many actual entries or titles are provided? If it is not feasible to give a precise figure, approximately how many are covered?
   B. Is the work comprehensive or selective in its coverage of the literature?
   C. If the work is purported to be comprehensive in coverage, does it include material published in all forms, in all languages, in all countries, regardless of date or publication? Are both popular and scholarly, adult and juvenile publications covered?
   D. If the work is selective in coverage, what are the criteria for selection? Are they followed? The canons of selection should be appropriate in terms of the needs of the audience to whom the work is addressed and in terms of limitations of subject, language, time, place, and type of material included.
   E. To what extent does the work achieve the coverage claimed for it? Base the evaluation on comparison of a portion of the text with other sources. By way of illustration, if the work under review is purported to list all major reference books in a given subject area, entries should be compared with those appearing in such standard lists of reference sources as *Sheehy*, in order to determine whether important authors or titles are omitted. Similarly, if an index under review is supposed to cover the contents of a particular group of journals, the entries in the index might be compared with the actual contents of selected issues of some of the journals. Such comparisons can also prove useful in checking the bibliographical accuracy of the entries in the work under review.

II. *Authority*
   A. What are the qualifications of the compiler? Is the compiler a bibliographer primarily or incidentally? Is he or she a subject specialist? What is his or her academic or other position?
   B. Who are the sponsors of the work, and what is the nature of their contribution to it?

III. *Arrangement*
   A. How is the main body of the work arranged, e.g., by author, organization, classification or other method?
   B. Does the arrangement facilitate retrieval of information?
   C. If subject headings are used, is the terminology based on a common vocabulary or authorized list?
   D. Are headings consistent, with adequate and accurate cross-references from variant forms?

IV. *Nature of Entries*
   A. What is the content of entries?
   B. Are all significant bibliographic elements included? (Author, title, imprint, collation, series)
   C. Are prices given?
   D. Is out-of-print status indicated?
   E. Are library locations given, where this would be appropriate?
   F. Are entries limited to bibliographic data, or are they annotated? Are annotations descriptive, evaluative, or a combination of both? Do they reflect sound knowledge of the works being annotated?

V. *Aids to Facilitate Use*
   A. What approaches are offered in addition to the basic arrangement of entries? If needed indexes or other devices to make information readily accessible have not been provided, the review should point this out. Indexes should be described and evaluated; their accuracy and fullness should not be assumed.
   B. Are geographical and biographical index entries adequate?
   C. Are index entries specific enough that excessive numbers of references do not follow any entries?

VI. *Frequency and Cumulation*
   A. Is the work serial in nature? If so, what is the pattern of publication? Failure to meet publication schedules may be noted where this detracts significantly from the usefulness of the work.
   B. What plans are there for supplements, cumulations, cumulated indexes, and the like?
   C. What is the relationship of date of issue and date of coverage?

VII. *Format*
   A. Are typography and layout well designed?
      1. Is the type adequate in size and properly leaded for optimum legibility?
      2. If the text had been reproduced from typewritten copy, is the result a uniformly clear and legible page?
      3. Are special typographical devices employed to facilitate interpretation of the text?
   B. Is the paper heavy enough to withstand anticipated use?
   C. Is the binding acceptable?
      1. Will it withstand heavy use?
      2. Does the volume lie flat when opened?
      3. Are contents of volumes clearly indicated on the spine?

VIII. *Relationship to Existing Works*
    A. To what extent does the work duplicate the contents of existing works?
    B. What unique features does the work under review contain?

86. ENGLISH-LANGUAGE DICTIONARIES

I. *Authority*
    A. Is the publishing house identified with works of quality, particularly in lexicography or closely related fields?
    B. Does the dictionary identify those having major responsibility for editing and contributing to it? What are their qualifications? Is their authority acceptable?

II. *Scope, Purpose, and Objectives*
    A. How many entries does the work claim to include? Is the claim supported by a sampling count by the reviewer?
    B. What special elements are covered, e.g., slang, dialect, obsolete forms, technical terms?
    C. Does the dictionary include word definitions only, or are there additional listings of a biographical, geographical, or other nature?
    D. Is there a full statement of the purposes, audience and bases of selection? Does the dictionary fulfill its purpose?

III. *Vocabulary*
    A. What is the extent of the vocabulary? Is it, for example, restricted to current usage? Are new words included? If so, is there a designation of "slang" or "colloquialism" when there is some doubt as to the propriety of listing the word?
    B. How is the vocabulary counted? Is it based on main words only or does it include all derived and compound forms?
    C. How is the vocabulary arranged? Is arrangement letter-by-letter or word-by-word in alphabetical sequence?

IV. *Word Treatment*
    A. Spelling
        1. What authority or guidelines are given for spelling?
        2. Are variant spellings given?
        3. Is capitalization indicated?
        4. Is British or American, conservative or simplified, practice followed?
    B. Parts of Speech
        1. Are parts of speech clearly indicated?
        2. Are past tenses of irregular verbs, compounding, and phrase forming shown in full or made clear?
    C. Syllabication and Hyphenation
        1. Is syllabication plainly illustrated?
        2. Is hyphenation clear and easily interpreted?
    D. Pronunciation
        1. What device is used to indicate pronunciation, e.g., diacritical marks, phonetic alphabet?

    2. Is the key to pronunciation easy to use and readily accessible to the user?

    3. Are important variations in pronunciation noted?

E. Standard and Usage

    1. Are obsolete, specialized, and colloquial words and meanings clearly indicated?

    2. Is the dictionary prescriptive or descriptive? Does it establish rules as to how the words are to be used or does it tell how they are being used?

F. Etymology and History

    1. Are the etymology and history of words given in sufficient detail with changes in meanings and usage marked and dated?

G. Definitions

    1. Are definitions accurate, complete, clear, and precise?

    2. Are they geared to the level of the expected user?

    3. In what sequence are definitions given? Are they in historical sequence with the earliest meanings first or are current meanings given first?

H. Illustrative Quotations

    1. Is an adequate number of quotations provided?

    2. Are quotations selected which illustrate precisely the use of the word defined?

    3. Are specific citations to sources and dates of quotations given?

    4. Are the sources authoritative?

I. Illustrations

    1. Are all types of illustrations of good quality?

    2. Do the selection and placement of illustrations complement the definitions effectively?

    3. If colored illustrations are used, are the quality and selection good?

J. Synonyms and Antonyms

    1. Are synonyms and antonyms listed?

    2. Are they listed under the word entries or are they in a separate listing?

    3. Are they well selected?

    4. Are important variations in meaning noted?

V. *Supplementary Material*

A. Types and Quality

    1. What kinds of supplementary material are provided (e.g., lists of signs, symbols, and abbreviations; statistical tables; lists of colleges and universities; maps)?

    2. Does the supplementary material contribute significantly to the achievement of the primary purpose of the dictionary?

    3. Is the supplementary information unique, or is it readily available in other publications?

    4. Is the supplementary information accurate? Is it up to date? Will it go out of date rapidly? Are sources cited?

      5. Is the supplementary information presented clearly and interestingly?

  B. Personal Name Entries

      1. Approximately how many personal name entries are provided?

      2. Is pronunciation given?

      3. Are birth and death dates given?

      4. Is adequate, up-to-date identification provided?

  C. Place-Name Entries

      1. Approximately how many place-name entries are provided?

      2. Is pronunciation given?

      3. Is up-to-date, adequate identification provided?

VI. *Format*

  A. Is the publication a single volume or a multivolume set? Is it physically easy to use?

  B. If the volume is bulky, is the binding substantial? Will it withstand heavy use? Does the volume lie flat when opened? Are margins adequate for rebinding?

  C. Is the type clear, legible, and sufficiently leaded?

  D. Is page make-up conducive to easy reference and pleasing in appearance? Are headings clear, simple and easy to follow?

  E. Is the paper of adequate weight and quality?

87. GENERAL ENGLISH-LANGUAGE ENCYCLOPEDIAS

  I. *History of the Publication*

    A. Is the encyclopedia a new work or is it an abridgment or a revision of a previous publication?

    B. Is there a distinction among imprint, copyright, and revision dates?

    C. If an abridgment, what selection criteria were applied for inclusion of material and what kinds of revision, modifications, and additions to the original material were made?

    D. If a revised work, what is the extent of revision, and updating of maps and illustrations? *See* V-A.

    E. Is it kept up to date through continuous revision, yearbook, or other means?

  II. *Authority.* Reviewers are reminded that authority is but one of the many interrelated guidelines and is in itself and in isolation not meaningful.

    A. Publisher. Standing and Qualifications.

      1. Is the publisher identified with works of quality, particularly encyclopedic or closely related kinds of publications? Reviewers who do not have this background information should so advise the Secretary.

      2. Is the publisher qualified by professional competence and/or experience for these assignments?

    B. Editors and Editorial Staff. Standing and Qualifications.

      1. Does the encyclopedia list the editors and editorial staff and designate their specific editorial competencies?

      2. Are they qualified by professional competence and/or experience?

       a. Have they qualified previously, published, edited, or taught in these fields?

       b. Are they recognized authorities in the fields in which they are editing?

C. Contributors. Standing and Qualifications. Can information in the encyclopedia's list of contributors be verified in recognized biographical sources?

  1. Are articles signed or is any listing of contributors and their contributions to the encyclopedia provided? Reviewers are reminded that unsigned articles are not necessarily less authoritative than signed articles, but the fact that articles are signed and/or contributors listed should be noted.

  2. If contributors are identified, are they qualified by background and experience to write the articles they have contributed? Reviewers should ascertain the competence of contributors in a number and variety of subject fields and should take into consideration the professional reputation of each author and his or her previous contributions to the field in which he or she has written.

  3. Reviewers are advised to read carefully the publisher's statement on authority, signing of articles, and the meaning of signatures. In revised sets, are articles signed by well-known contributors actually written by them? What is the actual extent of the contribution?

III. *Scope and Treatment*

A. What are the major objectives or purposes of the encyclopedia?

  1. Are they stated in the work and to what extent are they accomplished?

    Reviewers should bear in mind that the purpose of the review is not to evaluate promotional literature or sales practice but to evaluate the work itself. However, if there is any marked discrepancy in claims made in the work itself and in the publisher's promotional literature, the difference should be noted.

  2. To what audience or level of readership is the encyclopedia primarily directed? Do range and depth of coverage, literary style, organization of material, and supplementary features successfully gear the encyclopedia to this primary audience? If, for example, intended primarily for children in elementary grades, are topics relevant to subjects taught in school covered adequately? If intended for general home use, are practical subjects covered adequately? If for a more sophisticated audience, are the range and depth of treatment adequate? *See* IV-A.

  3. Do the articles show balance in selection and treatment? Are there longer articles for important subjects, briefer ones for less important?

B. Organization and Arrangement

  1. Are pages numbered consecutively through the entire work, or by volume, or by letter of the alphabet? Are pages added to an earlier edition lettered, e.g., 361a, b, c, d?

2. Is arrangement alphabetical (letter-by-letter or word-by-word), classified, thematic?

3. If alphabetical, is material presented under broad or specific subjects?

4. If classified or thematic, is material presented logically and consistently? Is there a Table of Contents showing the arrangement?

5. Are the arrangement and organization of material adapted to the primary purposes and audience of the encyclopedia?

C. Cross-References

1. Are cross-references facilitating use and location of information consistently provided?

2. Are cross-references accurate?

3. Do they bring out proper relationships among topics and lead to further pertinent information?

D. Index

1. An index is especially crucial in a non-alphabetically arranged set. Is an index provided? If there is no index, do the cross-references or other devices adequately substitute for it?

2. What type of index is provided, e.g., dictionary, classified, or fact index?

3. Does the index provide ready access to pertinent content, e.g., facts, concepts, illustrations, overlays, maps, etc.? Check by an adequate sampling.

4. Is the index accurate? Are there blind references? The accuracy of the index should be checked by an adequate sampling.

IV. *Range and Quality of Contents*

A. Text.

1. Is adequate coverage provided in the subject fields within the intended scope of the encyclopedia?

2. Is the encyclopedia international in scope? Does it provide adequate coverage of foreign events, persons, places?

3. Are articles factually correct? Are authorities or sources cited when they are pertinent?

4. In areas of controversy, are opposing views given adequate treatment and consideration?

5. Is there any indication of national, political, or religious bias that affects the objectivity of the articles? If there is evidence of subjectivity, the reviewer should determine whether such bias sets the general tone of the set or whether it is limited to a few articles or to a particular subject.

6. Is information up to date? Are recent events or contemporary figures given adequate coverage? Is there a tendency to give cursory treatment to recent happenings?

7. Are statistical data accurate and reasonably up to date? Are sources cited? Are they reliable sources?

B. Style and Quality of Writing
1. Is the style of writing uniformly clear, understandable, and interesting?
2. Are the vocabulary and sentence structure suitable for the intended audience? Note the use of technical and abstract terms and the use of personal pronouns such as *we* and *you*. Are technical and abstract terms clearly defined?

C. Bibliographies
1. Are they consistently provided for major topics?
2. What is their purpose? Describe and evaluate bibliographies noting bibliographic information provided; form of material included, e.g., documents, maps, periodicals; countries of origin; type of annotation.
3. Where are they placed? At the ends of articles? Grouped together?

D. Study Guides
1. Where are they placed?
2. What is the basic arrangement of the guides?
3. Will they help the user significantly in understanding the text and in further study?

E. Illustrations
1. What kinds of illustrations are provided?
2. Are they consistently of high quality?
3. Are they well selected to explain or clarify the text?
4. Are they placed in proper relation to the text?

F. Maps. (*See also* Guidelines for Reviewing Atlases)
1. Were the maps produced by a recognized cartographic authority?
2. Do the maps accompany the text, or are they placed in separate sections?
3. Is a sufficient number of maps provided? Are important geographical areas adequately represented? Are various types of maps included—physical, political, historical, etc.?
4. Are the maps adequate in size and scale? Are enough details shown?
5. Are the maps clear, and is color employed effectively?
6. Do they provide reliable, up-to-date information?
7. Are inserts used? Are they adequate in size, number, and quality?

V. *Comparison with Previous Editions and Similar Works*
A. If this is a revised set,
1. Have there been significant changes in scope and purpose and intended audience?
2. Have range and depth of information changed significantly? Has the set been enlarged?
3. Is it significantly rearranged?
4. Are there added features, e.g., a new or improved index?
5. Have there been improvements in its format? If old plates have been revised and used, what are the extent and quality of alterations?

6. Has it been significantly updated? *See also* IV-A-7.
    B. What is the relation of the work to other general encyclopedias of similar purpose, audience, and price range?
VI. *Physical Format*
    A. Is the set durably and attractively bound? Do volumes lie flat when opened? Are lettering or volume numbers on spines?
    B. Is the paper of good quality and does it make for legibility?
    C. Is type attractive, clear, legible, and of proper size for ease of reading? Are type sizes judiciously used?
    D. Is page makeup attractive, and are inner margins sufficient to display double-page maps and illustrations?

Index

Prepared by Wayne F. Moquin

Page numbers in **boldface** indicate the location of complete bibliographical information and annotation, if any, for the title listed.

Abbreviations, 164–65
Abbreviations Dictionary, **165**
Abridged Readers' Guide to Periodical Literature, **68**
Abstract of British Historical Statistics, **259**
Abstracts, 22
  sources of bibliographic information, 62–81
Abstracts and Abstracting Services, **64**
Academia Española, *Diccionario Histórico de la Lengua Española,* **177**
Access, **68**
Access Index to Little Magazines, **73**
Access to the World, 312
Acquisition of Maps and Charts Published by the U.S. Government, **276**
Acronyms, Initialisms and Abbreviations Dictionary, **164–65**
Across the Board, **262**
ACSM Bulletin, 278
Acta Cartographica, **282**
Adams, James Truslow, 300

Adler, Mortimer J., 145
Africa, **272**
Africa, biographical information on, 106–7
Agricultural atlas, 301
Agricultural Situation, **246**
Agricultural Statistics, **246**
Aids to Geographical Research **274**
Akademiia Nauk SSSR, *Slovar' Sovremennogo Russkogo Literaturnogo Iazyka,* **176**
ALA Glossary of Library Terms, 2, **167**
ALA Yearbook, 9
Alexander, Gerald
  Guide to Atlases, **277, 295**
  Mapping, 283
All Asia Guide, **311**
All Possible Worlds, **265**
Allgemeine Deutsche Biographie, **109**
Almanack, **258**
Almanacs, 257–58
America at the Polls, **251**
America: History and Life, **71**

America Votes, **250**
American Antiquarian Society, *Proceedings*, 47
American Architects Directory, 113
American Authors, 1600–1900, **116**
American Automobile Association, *Tour Book*, **310**
American Bibliographical Center's Subject Profile Index, 71
American Bibliography, **39**
American Bibliography: A Chronological Dictionary, **40**
American Book Publishing Record, 32, **35**, 38
American Book Publishing Record Cumulative, **35**
American Cartographer, 284
American Catalogue of Books, 1861–1871, **40**
American Catalogue of Books, 1876–1910, **40**
American Council of Learned Societies, 18
American Dictionary of the English Language, 125
American Documentation, 73
American Geographical Society, 265
  Current Geographical Publications, **274–75**
  Index to Maps in Books and Periodicals, **278–79**
  Research Catalogue, **274**
American Glossary, 141, **142**
American Guide Series, **310**
American Heritage Dictionary of the English Language, 133, 135–36, 137, 145, **146**, 163
American Heritage Pictorial Atlas of United States History, **299**
American Heritage School Dictionary, **151**
American Historical Association, *Guide to Historical Literature*, **56**
American History Atlas, **300**
American Language, 161
American Libraries, 113
American Library Association
  Reference and Adult Services Division, 8, 65
  Reference and Subscription Books Review Committee, 13–14
  Statistics Coordinating Project, *Library Statistics*, **241**
American Medical Directory, 112
American Men and Women of Science, 94, 113, **120–21**
American Newspapers 1821–1936, **46–47**, 52
American Notes and Queries, 157

American Place Names, **307**
American Reference Books Annual, **11**, 194, 197
American Speech, 130, 157
American Society for Information Science
  Bulletin, **67**
  Journal, 67
American Society of Indexers, 63
  Newsletter, 196
American Statistics Index, **244**
American Textbook Publishers Institute, Reference Book Section, 14
American Thesaurus of Slang, **162**
American Women, 106
American Writers, **115**
Americana Annual, **204**
Ammer and Ammer, *Dictionary of Business and Economics*, **168**
Amsden, Diana, 6
Analysis of variance, 233; *see also* Statistics
Analytical Bibliography of Universal Collected Biography, 96, **99**
Andrews, E. A., 175
Andriot, *Guide to U.S. Government Publications*, **42**
Annals of the Association of American Geographers, 284
Annotated World List of Selected Current Geographical Serials, **279**
Annual Abstract of Statistics, **259**
Annual Review of Information Science and Technology, 67
Antique Maps and Their Cartographers, **281**
Applied Science and Technology Index, **76**, 112–13
Appleton's New Cuyás English-Spanish and Spanish-English Dictionary, **177**
Arfwedson, *The United States and Canada in 1832, 1833, and 1834*, **310**
Art Index, **69**, 112
Artists, biographical information on, 113–14
Arts and Humanities Citation Index, **71–72**
Ash, *Subject Collections*, **54**
Ashmore, Harry S., 180
Asimov, Isaac, 203
Association of American Geographers, 265
  Directory, **305**
  Guide to Graduate Departments of Geography, **306**
  Handbook, 112
Atherton, *Librarians and Online Services*, **67**
Atlante Internazionale, **294**
Atlas International Larousse Politique et Economique, **293–94**
Atlas Mira, **291**

Atlas of American History, **300**
Atlas of Early American History, **299**
Atlas of the Bible, **297**
Atlas of the Classical World, **299**
Atlas of the Historical Geography of the United States, **300–1**
Atlas of World History, **298–99**
Atlases, 262, 275–79
  English and American, 288–93
  for the visually handicapped, 303
  foreign language, 293–95
  national, 295–96
  school, 293
  selection of, 284–87
  thematic, 297–303
Australia, biographical information on, 107
Australian Dictionary of Biography, **107**
Author and Titles, **22**
Author Biographies Master Index, **116**
Author-Title Index to Joseph Sabin's "Dictionary of Books Relating to America," **39**
Author's and Writer's Who's Who, **115**
Authors, biographical information on, 114–17
Average Monthly Weather Outlook, **255**
Avery, Catherine B., 177
Ayer Directory of Publications, **47**, 52

Baedeker Handbook for Travelers, 308, **310**
Baker's Biographical Dictionary of Musicians, **118**
Ball, *Foreign Statistical Documents*, **244–45**
Banki, Ivan S.
  Dictionary of Administration and Supervision, **168**
  Dictionary of Supervision and Management, **168**
Banks, Arthur, 300
Bantam New College Spanish and English Dictionary, **178**
Barnhart, Clarence L., 101, 126, 127, 148, 152
Barnhart, Robert K., 148
Barnhart Dictionary of New English since 1963, **149**
Barraclough, Geoffrey, 299
Bartholomew, John, 288
Bartholomew/Scribner Atlas of Europe, **301**
Bartlett, *Familiar Quotations*, **87**
Bartz, Barbara S., 266
Barzun, Jacques, 156, 180
Battaglia, *Grande Dizionario della Lingua Italiana*, **174**
Becker, Joseph, 23
Bede, *Ecclesiastical History*, 16
Bederman, *Africa*, **272**

Bell, Marion V., 12
Bender, James F., 160
Benét, *Reader's Encyclopedia*, 94
Berlitz, Charles, 171
Berry, *American Thesaurus of Slang*, **162**
Bertelsmann Verlag, Cartographical Institute, 286
Besterman, *World Bibliography of Bibliographies*, **89–90**, 91
Betteridge, Harold T., 173
Biblical atlases, 297
Biblio, 37
Bibliographic Guide to Government Publications, **42**
Bibliographic Index, **54**, 90, 91, 270
Bibliographic information, sources of, 15–91
Bibliographical Services throughout the World, **31**
Bibliographical Society of America, *Papers*, 73
Bibliographie de la France, **30**, 37
Bibliographie de la France—Biblio, **37**, 38
Bibliographies
  abstracts, 22–81
  concordances, 22, 81–89
  current selective, 61–62
  definitions, 18–22
  descriptive and systematic, 18–20
  development of, 15–18
  films/microfilms, 49–50
  government publications, 41–43
  indexes, 21, 62–89
  library catalogs, 20, 22–31
  manuscripts, 50
  music, 50–51
  national, 21, 31–40
  newspapers, 46–47
  of bibliographies, 89–91
  of geography, 308–12
  pamphlets, 43
  paperbound books, 47–48
  periodicals, 43–46
  reprints, 48
  selective, 21, 57–60
  subject, 21, 52–57
  translations, 51
  union catalogs/union lists, 20, 25–31
Bibliography, **15**, 52
Bibliography: Tiger or Fat Cat?, **19**
Bibliography, Documentation, Terminology, **17**, 31
Bibliography of Cartography, **279**
Bibliography of Dissertations in Geography, **280**
Bibliography of Geography, **273**
Bibliography of Library Economy, **73**

Bibliography of Philosophical Bibliographies, **57**
Bibliography of Place-name Literature, **280–81**
Bibliography of Publications Issued by UNESCO or under Its Auspices, **17**
Bibliography of Statistical Literature, 239
Bibliography of the Fig, 54
Bibliotheca Americana, **40**
Bibliothèque Nationale, *Catalogue Général des Livres Imprimés*, **29**
Biographical Dictionaries, **122**
Biographical Dictionaries and Related Works, **96**
Biographical Dictionaries Master Index, **97**
Biographical Dictionary of American Educators, **117**
Biographical Dictionary of Republican China, **108**
Biographical Directory of American Labor Leaders, **118**
Biographical Directory of Librarians in the United States and Canada, **118**
Biographical Directory of the American Psychiatric Association, 112
Biographical Encyclopedia & Who's Who of the American Theater, **122**
Biographical information
  current indexes, 96–98
  current sources, 102–4
  evaluation of, 95
  generalizations on, 93–95
  indexes to, 95–99
  international sources, 99–102
  national sources, 104–12
  nature of, 92–93
  retrospective indexes, 98–99
  sources of, 92–123
Biographie Universelle, Ancienne et Moderne, **100**
Biography Index, 96, **97**
Biography News, **102**
Biological Abstracts, **66**
Biological Abstracts from the World's Biological Research Literature, **69**
Biological and Agricultural Index, **69**
BioResearch Index, **66**
BIOSIS PREVIEWS, 66
Birth, Still Birth and Infant Mortality Statistics, **254**
Bishop, Morris, 136
Bishop, William Warner, 2
Black American Writers Past and Present, **115**
Blaeu, *Light of Navigation*, 283
Blanchard, *Literature of Agricultural Research*, **246**

Blanco-González, Manuel, 178
Blue-Backed Speller, 125
Blue Guides, **311–12**
Boehm, Erich H., 71
Bol'shaia Sovetskaia Entsiklopediia, **222–24**
Book of Knowledge, 181, 209
Book of the States, **250–51**
Book Review Digest, **82–83**
Book Review Index, **83**
Book reviews, indexes of, 82–84
Booklist, **12**, 14, **61**, 123, 194, 197–98
Bookman's Glossary, **167**
Books for Children, 60
Books for College Libraries, 58, **60**
Books for Public Libraries, **58**
Books for Secondary School Libraries, **59**
Books in Print, 32, **33–34**, 38, 47, 51
Boorman, Howard L., 108
Bottle, *Use of Biological Literature*, **55**
Bowden, *Dictionary of American Religious Biography*, **120**
Bowers, Fredson, 19
Bowker Annual of Library and Book Trade Information, **251–52**
Bradley, Henry, 141
Bramwell, Martyn, 302
Brett, Lewis, 177
Breul, Karl, 173
Brewer, *Literature of Geography*, **273**
Brewton, *Index to Poetry for Children and Young People*, **86**
Bricker, *Landmarks of Mapmaking*, **281**
Brigham, *History and Bibliography of American Newspapers 1690–1820*, **47**
Britannica Atlas, **290**
Britannica Book of the Year, 157, **204**
Britannica Junior Encyclopedia, 184, 211, **216**, 217
British Authors before 1800, **116**
British Authors of the Nineteenth Century, **116**
British Books in Print, **36**, 38
British Museum
  General Catalogue of Printed Books, **28–29**
  Subject Index of the Modern Works Added to the Library, 29
British National Bibliography, **23**, 32, 36, 38
British Travel Association, *Hotels and Restaurants in Britain*, **312**
British Union-Catalogue of Periodicals, 165
British Writers, **115**
Broadcasting, **262**
Brockhaus, *Konversations-Lexikon*, 180
Brockhaus Enzyklopädie in Zwanzig Bänden, 195, **220**, 221

Brown, L. A., *Story of Maps*, **281**
Brown, Peter, 165
Browning, *Bibliography of Dissertations in Geography*, **280**
Bryan's *Dictionary of Painters and Engravers*, 113
Bryant, *Current American Usage*, **156**
Buckland, *Dictionary of Statistical Terms*, **240**
Buckley, *Historical Statistics of Canada*, **246**
Bulletin of Bibliography, 73
Bulletin of the Institute of Historical Research, 110
Bulletin of the Public Affairs Information Service, **77–78**, 256
Burchfield, R. W., 141, 154
Bureau of the Census Catalog, **244**, 253
Burgess, *Cumulative Paperback Index 1939–1959*, **48**
Burkholder, Clyde, 162
Buros, *Statistical Methodology Review*, **239**
Burrington, *How to Find Out about Statistics*, **242**
Business Information Sources, **56**, **247**, 249
Business men and women, biographical information on, 117
Business of Enlightenment, 180
Business Periodicals Index, **69–70**, **255**
Business Statistics, 263
Business Week, **262**

Cadillac Modern Encyclopedia, 205, **208**
Calvert, *Subject Collections*, **54**
Cambridge Bibliography English Literature, 192
Cambridge History of English Literature, 94, **116**, 192
Cambridge Italian Dictionary, **175**
Cameron, *Guide to Graphs*, **239**
Campbell, *Psychiatric Dictionary*, **168**
Canaday, *Lives of the Painters*, **114**
Canadian Almanac and Directory, **257**
Canadian Library Journal, 11
Canadian Reference Sources, **11**
Canadian Who's Who, **108**
Canadians, biographical information on, 107–8
Cannons, *Bibliography of Library Economy*, **73**
Cappon, Lester J., 299
Card catalogs, 25
Carhart, Paul W., 143
Carrington, *Map Collections in the United States and Canada*, **306**
Cartographic history, 281–87
Casares, Julio, 177

Cass, Lewis, 267
Cassell's New Latin-English, English-Latin Dictionary, **176**
Catalog of Copyright Entries, 51
Catalogue de l'Édition Française, **36–37**
Catalogue Général des Livres Imprimés, **29–30**
Catholic Periodical and Literature Index, **75–76**
Cattell, Jaques, 117, 120
Caught in the Web of Words, 140
CBS News Almanac, 257
Census data, 253–54
Census of Housing, **252**
Census of Population, **235**, 240, **252**
Century Cyclopedia of Names, **101**
Chambers's Biographical Dictionary, **100**
Chambers's Encyclopaedia, 100, **201**
Chambers's Encyclopaedia Yearbook, **204**
Chambers's Twentieth Century Dictionary, **149**
Chapman, Robert L., 159
Checklist of American Imprints for 1820–1829, **39**
Checklist of American Imprints for 1830–1861, **39–40**
Chemical Abstracts, 22, **70**
Chi è?, **111**
Chicago Sun-Times, 80
Chicago Tribune, 80
Chicorel, Marietta, 85
Chicorel Index to Abstracting and Index Services, **79**
Chicorel Index to Biographies, **97**
Chicorel Theater Index to Plays in Anthologies, **85**
Children's Book Review Index, **84**
Children's Books in Print, **34**
Children's Catalog, **59**
Children's Literature Review, **84**
Chinese, biographical information on, 108
Choice, 11, **12**, 46, **62**
Christian, Roger, 65–66, 67
  Electronic Library, 66
  Librarians and Online Services, **67**
Christian Science Monitor, 80
Clark, Thomas D.
  Travels in the New South, **309**
  Travels in the Old South, **309**
Clark, William, 267
Coast and Geodetic Survey, 268
Colby, *European Authors 1000–1900*, **116**
College and Research Libraries, 10
Collier's Encyclopedia, 186, 187, 197, **201–2**
Collier's Encyclopedia Year Book, **204**
Collison, Robert L., 63, 81
  Abstracts and Abstracting Services, **64**

Collison, Robert L. (cont.)
  Dictionaries of English and Foreign Languages, 170
  Encyclopedias, 182, 195, 218
  Indexes and Indexing, 63
Collocott, T. C., 100
Colson, Publishing Library Catalogues, 31
Columbia Lippincott Gazetteer of the World, 304–5
Columbia University
  Dictionary Catalog, 53
  Geographical Research Staff, 304
Coman, Sources of Business Information, 247
Commire, Anne, 115
Committee on Wilson Indexes, 65
Commodity Prices, 248, 262
Commodity Year Book, 246
COMPENDEX, 66
Composers of Tomorrow's Music, 119
Composers since 1900, 119
Comprehensive Dictionary of Psychology and Psychological Terms, 168
Comprehensive Dissertation Index, 66, 84
Comprehensive Etymological Dictionary of the English Language, 154
Comprehensive Index to English-Language Little Magazines, 73
Compton's Encyclopedia, 181, 186, 187, 210, 212–13
Compton's Precyclopedia, 213
Compton's Yearbook, 211
Computer Output Microform Catalog (COMCAT), 24
Computer-readable Bibliographic Data, 67
Concise Cambridge Italian Dictionary, 175
Concise Dictionary, 110
Concise Heritage Dictionary, 151
Concise Oxford Dictionary, 150
Concordances, 22
  sources of bibliographic information, 81–89
Conference Board Record, 262
Congressional Directory, 119
Congressional District Data Book, 261
Consumer Price Index, 263
Contemporary Artists, 114
Contemporary Authors, 115
Contemporary Dramatists, 116
Contemporary Novelists of the English Language, 116
Contemporary Poets, 116
Cooper, G., Checklist of American Imprints for 1830–1861, 39–40
Cooper, M. Francis, 39
Copperud, American Usage, 156

Corporation Records, 249
Corpus of Present-Day Edited American English, 146
Cosmographia, 282
Cote, Directory of Business and Financial Services, 249
Coulson, Jessie, 149
Coulter, Travels in the Confederate States, 309
Council on Library Resources, 18
Country Authors Today, 115
County and City Data Book, 261
Covey, Alma A., 13
Cox, Reference Guide to the Literature of Travel, 309
Coxill, H. Wakelin, 254
CPI Detailed Report, 263
Craigie, W. A.
  Dictionary of American English on Historical Principles, 141–42
  Oxford English Dictionary, 141
Crawford, Fourth Book of Junior Authors and Illustrators, 116
Creative Cartography, 303
Crime and criminals, statistics on, 246
Critical Bibliography of French Literature, 192
Critical Bibliography of German Literature in English Translation, 51–52
Crowell, Thomas Lee, 160
Crowell's Spanish-English and English-Spanish Dictionary, 177
Crowley, Ellen T., 165
Cummings, Dictionary of Contemporary American Artists, 114
Cumulative Book Index, 21, 32, 33, 38, 47, 51, 89
Cumulative Book Review Index, 83–84
Cumulative Index to Periodical Literature, 68
Cumulative Paperback Index 1939–1959, 48
Cumulative Subject Index to Monthly Catalog of U.S. Government Publications, 41–42
Current Biography, 103
Current Book Review Citations, 83
Current events indexes, 80–81
Current Geographical Publications, 274–75
Current Index to Journals in Education, 70
Current Index to Statistics, 242–43
Current Information Services in Mathematics, 56
Current National Bibliographies, 31
Current National Statistical Compendiums, 260-61
Current selective bibliographies, 61–62

Current Slang, **162**
Cuyás, *Appleton's New Cuyás English-Spanish and Spanish-English Dictionary*, **177**

Daily Weather Maps, **255**
Dale, Edgar, 210
Daniells, *Business Information Sources*, **56**, **247**, 249
Darton, *Business Enlightenment*, 180
Data bases, 65–67
Data User News, 253
Database, **67**
Deane, *Abstract of British Historical Statistics*, **259**
De George, *Guide to Philosophical Bibliography and Research*, **57**
De Montreville, Doris
  Fourth Book of Junior Authors and Illustrators, **116**
  Third Book of Junior Authors, **116**
De Sola, *Abbreviations Dictionary*, **165**
Delpar, Helen, 112
Demographic Yearbook, **254**
Denver Post, 80
Descripive bibliography, 18–19
Descriptive statistics, 228
Deskbook of Business Management Terms, **169**
Detroit News, 80
Deutsches Wörterbuch, **172**
Devoto, *Vocabolario Illustrato della Lingua Italiana*, **175**
Dialect dictionaries, 162–64
Diccionario Histórico de la Lengua Española, **177**
Dick, *Current Information Sources in Mathematics*, **56**
Dickie, John, 107
Dictionaries, 124–78
  abridged, 145–53
  American, 146–49
  British, 149–50
  dialect, 162–64
  foreign-language, 169–78
  historical, 140–45
  levels of word usage, 135–36
  making of, 127–38
  of abbreviations, 164–65
  of etymologies, 134–35, 153–54
  of geographical terms, 307–8
  of statistics, 255
  of synonyms and antonyms, 137, 157–60
  order of word senses, 132–33
  pronunciation, 136–37, 160–61

reasons for, 125–27
  school, 150–53
  scope, 130–37
  slang, 161–62
  sources used, 129–30
  specialized subject, 165–69
  staff responsibilities, 128–29
  unabridged, 138–45
  usage guides, 155–57
  vocabulary selection, 130–31
  wording of definitions, 131–32
Dictionaries and That Dictionary, 125
Dictionaries, British and American, 134, 154, 161
Dictionaries, Encyclopedias and Other Word-Related Books, **167**
Dictionaries of English and Foreign Languages, **170**
Dictionary Catalog of the Map Division, **278–79**
Dictionary Catalog of the Schomberg Collection of Negro Literature and History in the New York Public Library, **53**
Dictionary for Accountants, **169**
Dictionary of Administration and Supervision, **168**
Dictionary of American Biography, 94, 99, **104**, 105, 129
Dictionary of American English, 129, 141, 142
Dictionary of American English on Historical Principles, **141–42**
Dictionary of American-English Usage, 155, **157**
Dictionary of American History, 300
Dictionary of American Library Biography, **118**
Dictionary of American Regional English, 163
Dictionary of American Religious Biography, **120**
Dictionary of American Slang, 161, **162**
Dictionary of Americanisms on Historical Principles, 129, 130, 141, **142**
Dictionary of Australian English, 141
Dictionary of Behavioral Science, **169**
Dictionary of Books Relating to America, **39**
Dictionary of Business, Finance and Investment, **169**
Dictionary of Business and Economics, **168**
Dictionary of Canadian Biography, **107**
Dictionary of Canadianisms on Historical Principles, 141, **143**
Dictionary of Contemporary American Artists, **114**

Dictionary of Contemporary Quotations, 87–88
Dictionary of Economic and Statistical Terms, 241–42
Dictionary of Economics, **169**
Dictionary of Education, **168**
Dictionary of Foreign Terms, **171**
Dictionary of Geography, 283
Dictionary of Modern English Usage, 155, **157**
Dictionary of National Biography, 96, **99**, **110**, 120
Dictionary of Occupational Titles, **240**
Dictionary of Quotations, **87**
Dictionary of Scientific Biography, 94, **120**, 184
Dictionary of Slang, 126
Dictionary of Sociology, **169**
Dictionary of South African Biography, 106
Dictionary of Statistical Terms, **240**
Dictionary of Statistics, **257**
Dictionary of Supervision and Management, **168**
Dictionary of the History of Ideas, **190**
Dictionary of the Natural Environment, **307**
Dictionary of the Social Sciences, **168**
Dictionary of Universal Biography, 96, **99**
Dictionnaire Alphabetique et Analogique, **171**
Dictionnaire Biographique Française Contemporain 109
Dictionnaire de Biographie Française, **108–9**
Dictionnaire de la Langue Française, **171**
Digest of Educational Statistics, **250**
Dill, Stephen H., 162
Directory of American Philosophers, **119**
Directory of American Scholars, **117**, 119, 120
Directory of Business and Financial Services, **249**
Directory of Federal Statistics for Local Areas, **242**
Directory of Federal Statistics for States, **244**
Directory of Post Offices, **305**
Directory of Published Proceedings, **86–87**
Dissertation Abstracts International, **85**
Dissertation indexes, 84–85
Dizionario Biografico degli Italiani, **111**
Doig, *Bibliography of Statistical Literature*, **239**
Drama indexes, 85
Drazniowsky, Roman, 286
Dubois, Marguerite-Marie, 172
Duckles, *Music Reference and Research Materials*, **57**
Dunkin, Paul S., 25
  Bibliography: Tiger or Fat Cat?, **19**
Dutch, Robert A., 159

Eastin, *Government Publications and Their Use*, **276**
Eaton, Helen S., 177
Ebbitts, Wilma R., 125
Ecclesiastical History, 16
Economic atlases, 301–2
Economic Censuses, **248**
Economics and Commerce, **247**
Economics and business statistics, 246–49
Editor & Publisher, *Market Guide*, **247**
Education Index, **70–71**
Education statistics, 249–50
Educators, biographical information on, 117
Educators Guide to Free Films, **50**
Election statistics, 250–51
Elementary School Library Collection, **60**
Elementary Teachers Guide to Free Curriculum Materials, **50**
Elements of Cartography, **284**
El-hi Textbooks in Print, **34**
Enciclopedia Italiana de Scienze, Lettere ed Arti, **221–22**
Enciclopedia Universal Illustrada Europeo-Americana, 186, 191, **224–25**
Encyclopaedia Britannica, 180, 181, 184, 186, 187, 195, 196, **197–200**, 218, 219
Encyclopaedia Britannica World Atlas, 290
Encyclopaedia Judaica, **191**
Encyclopaedia Universalis, **219**
Encyclopaedia World Survey, **204**
Encyclopedia Americana, 160, 181, 185, 187, 192, **200–1**
Encyclopedia Buying Guide, **193–94**, 196, 199, 211
Encyclopedia International, 187, 210, **214–15**
Encyclopedia of American Biography, **104–5**
Encyclopedia of Anthropology, **168**
Encyclopedia of Computer Science, **168**
Encyclopedia of Education, 188
Encyclopedia of Information Systems and Services, **18**, 67
Encyclopedia of Latin America, **112**
Encyclopedia of Library and Information Science, 91, **193**
Encyclopedia of Philosophy, 167, **189–90**, 196
Encyclopedia of the Third World, 186
Encyclopedia of World Art, **113**, **193**, 221, 224
Encyclopedia supplements, 203–4
Encyclopedia World Atlas International, 290
Encyclopedia Yearbook, 211
Encyclopedias, 182, **195**, 218
Encyclopedias and Dictionaries for Specialists, **194**

Encyclopedias
  children's/young adults, 210–17
  foreign language, 217–25
  general reference features, 225
  guide to buying, 193–94
  indexes of, 196–97
  making of, 182–93
  multivolume adult, 197–203
  one-three volume, 204–9
  scope of contents, 184–93
  sources of information on, 193–97
  staff of, 182–84
  yearbooks, 203–4
Encyclopédie, 180
Encyclopédie Française, 180
Encyclopédie Larousse des Enfants, 218
English and English, *Comprehensive Dictionary of Psychology and Psychological Terms*, **168**
English-Modern Greek and Modern Greek-English Dictionary, **174**
English-Russian Dictionary, **176**
Enoch Pratt Free Library, *Reference Books*, **12**
EPILEPSYLINE, 66
Erskine, Robert, 267
Espasa, *see* Enciclopedia Universal Illustrada EuropeoAmericana
Essay and General Literature Index, **85–86**
Essay indexes, 85–86
Etymological Dictionary of the English Language, 153, **154**
Etymologies, 134–35
Europa Year Book, **259**
European Authors 1000–1900, **116**
European Historical Statistics, **245**
Evans, Bergen
  Dictionary of Contemporary American Usage, **156**
  Dictionary of Quotations, **87**
Evans, Charles, *American Bibliography*, 40
Evans, Cornelia, *Dictionary of Contemporary American Usage*, **156**
Evans, Luther, 18, 20
Ewen, *Musicians since 1900*, **119**
Extensive Library Guide to English and Foreign Encyclopedias, 218

Fact Finder for the Nation, 227
Facts on File, **80–81**, 187
Familiar Quotations, **87**
Febvre, Lucien, 180
Federal Reserve Bulletin, **247**
Fellmann, *International List of Geographical Serials*, **279–80**
Ferguson, Elizabeth, 251
Ferguson, Jack, 266
Fiction Catalog, **86**

Fiction indexes, 86
Fielding's Travel Guide to Europe, **310–11**
Fieux, *Oceanographic Atlas*, **279**
Films/microfilms, sources of bibliographic information, 49–50
Fink, *Biographical Directory of American Labor Leaders*, **118**
Five Centuries of Map Printing, **282–83**
Flexner, *Dictionary of American Slang*, 161, **162**
Focke, Helen M., 5
Fodor's Travel Guides, **311**
Follett, *Modern American Usage*, 155, 156, **157**
Foreign-language dictionaries, 169–78
Foreign-language encyclopedias, 218–25
Foreign Statistical Documents, **244–45**
Forthcoming Books, **35**, 38
Fortune, **263**
FOSDIC, 227
Foskett, *Subject Approach to Information*, **23**
Fourth Book of Junior Authors and Illustrators, **116**
Fowler, H. W., 149, 156
  Dictionary of Modern English Usage, 155, **157**, 163
France, biographical information on, 108–9
Fremont, John C., 267
French atlases, 293–94
French dictionaries, 171–72
French encyclopedias, 219
Freund, *Dictionary Outline of Basic Statistics*, **239**
Friedrichsen, G. W. S., 154
Frommer, Arthur, 311
Fuller, *More Junior Authors*, **116**
Function of Bibliography, **19**
Funk, I. K., 143
Funk & Wagnalls Modern Guide to Synonyms, **159**
Funk & Wagnalls New Encyclopedia, **202–3**
Funk & Wagnalls New Encyclopedia Yearbook, **204**
Funk & Wagnalls New Standard College Dictionary, 137, **143**
Funk & Wagnalls Standard College Dictionary, 126, 128, 131, 132, 133, 134, 135, 136, 137, 145, **146–47**

G & C Merriam Company, 125
Galen, 16
Galperin, I. A., 176
Gaméz, Tana de, 177
Garraty, John A., 104
Gates, *Guide to the Use of Books and Libraries*, **11**
Gazetteers, 303–5

General Censuses and Vital Statistics of the Americas, 245
General Cartography, **284**
General Catalogue of Printed Books, **28–29**
General Science Index, **76**
General World Atlases in Print, **277**
Geo Abstracts, **279**
Geographers: Biobibliographical Studies, **306**
Geographical and Geological Survey of the Rocky Mountain Region, 268
Geographical Bibliography for American College Libraries, 273, **274**
Geographical Review, 273, **284**
Geographical Survey West of the One Hundredth Meridian, 266
Geography
    atlases, 288–303
    bibliographies, 271–73, 308–12
    cartographic history/map librarianship, 281–87
    dictionaries of terms, 307–8
    dissertations, 280
    encyclopedias/dictionaries/handbooks, 305–7
    gazetteers, 303–5
    general reference works, 271–81
    government publications, 275–76
    library catalogs, 274–75
    literature guides, 273–74
    maps/atlases, 276–79
    overview of sources, 270–71
    place names, 280–81
    selection aids for sources, 274
    serial publications, 279–80
    sources of information, 264–313
    travel guides, 308–13
    U.S. mapmaking, 266–69
Geography and Cartography, **274**
Geography and Earth Sciences Publications, **280**
Geography of China, **272**
Geological and Geographical Survey of the Territories, 267–68
Geological Expedition of the Fortieth Parallel, 267
German dictionaries, 172–74
German encyclopedias, 220
Germany, biographical information on, 109–10
Gilbert, *Recent History Atlas*, 298
Gillhoff, Gerd A., 177
Gillispie, Charles C., 120
Ginsburg, Norton, 265
Girard, Denis, 172
Glavnoe Upravlenie Geodezii i Kartografii, **294–95**

Glossary of Geographical Terms, 307
Goggin, Margaret Knox, 13
Gómez-Ibáñez, Daniel A., 285, 287
Good, *Dictionary of Education*, **168**
Goode's World Atlas, **290**, 293
Gould, Julius, 168
Gove, Philip B., 144
Government activities, statistics on, 250–51
Government Publications and Their Use, **276**
Government Publications Monthly Catalog, 276
Government publications, sources of bibliographical information in, 41–43
Governmental Affairs Institute, *America at the Polls*, **251**
Gowers, Ernest, 155
Grammatical Institute of the English Language, 125
Grand Dictionnaire Universel, 192
Grand Larousse Encyclopédique, 186
Grande Dizionario della Lingua Italiana, **174**
Grande Encyclopédie, **219**, 221
Granger's Index to Poetry, **86**
Grant, *Directory of Business and Financial Services*, **249**
Graphic History of the Americas, **298**
Graphics Simplified, **239**
Gray, Jack C., 139
    Words, Words, and Words about Dictionaries, 145
Gray, Richard, 198
    Guide to Book Review Citations, **84**
    Serial Bibliographies in the Humanities and Social Sciences, **90**, 192
Great Composers 1300–1900, **119**
Great Britain
    biographical information 110–11
    dictionaries, 149–50
———. Central Statistical Office
    Annual Abstract of Statistics, **259**
    Guide to Official Statistics, **245**
    Monthly Digest of Statistics, **259**
Great Men of Popular Song, **119**
Great Soviet Encyclopedia, 186, **221–23**
Greek dictionaries, 174
Greek-English Lexicon, **174**
Green, Samuel, 4
Greenhood, *Mapping*, **283**
Greenwald, Douglas, 168
Greet, W. Cabell, 156
Greg, Walter, 19
Gregory, Winifred, 46
Grimm and Grimm, *Deutsches Wörterbuch*, **172**
Grimsted, Patricia K., 186

Grollenberg, *Atlas of the Bible,* **297**
Grosse Bertelsmann Weltatlas, 286
Grove, *Dictionary of Music and Musicians,* **193**
Groves, Paul A., 303
Grubb, Kenneth, 254
Guerry, *Bibliography of Philosophical Bibliographies,* **57**
Guide to Atlases, **277,** **295**
Guide to Basic Information Sources in the Visual Arts, **55**
Guide to Book Review Citations, **84**
Guide to Catholic Literature, 75
Guide to Foreign Language Courses and Dictionaries, **170**
Guide to Geographical Bibliographies, **272**
Guide to Graphs, **239**
Guide to Historical Literature, **56**
Guide to Microforms in Print, **49**
Guide to National Bibliographical Information Centers, **18**
Guide to Official Statistics, **245**
Guide to Philosophical Bibliography and Research, **57**
Guide to Reference Books, **10,** 98, 122, 139, 256, 258, 262, 271
Guide to Reference Books for School Media Centers, **12**
Guide to Reference Materials, **10,** 38, 122, 256, 258, 262, 271
Guide to Reprints, **48,** 52
Guide to Sources of Educational Information, **56,** 250
Guide to the Use of Books and Libraries, **11**
Guide to U.S. Government Maps, **276**
Guide to U.S. Government Publications, **42**
Guralnik, David B., 148

Hackman, *Practical Bibliographer,* **91**
Hagen, C. B., 265
Hale, *Subject Bibliography of the Social Sciences and the Humanities,* 52
Hall, R. B., *Japanese Geography,* **272**
Hall, Veronica, 85
Halsey, William D., 151, 188, 196, 213
Hammond Almanac, **257**
Hammond Ambassador World Atlas, **292**
Hammond Citation World Atlas, **292**
Hammond International World Atlas, **292**
Hammond Medallion World Atlas, **292**
Harder, Kelsie B., 306
Hare, *Walks in Rome,* **308**
Harmless Drudges, 125, 41
Harper Dictionary of Contemporary Usage, 156, **157**

Harper's Latin Dictionary, 175
Harrap's New Standard French and English Dictionary, **171–72**
Harrap's Standard German and English Dictionary, **173**
Harris, Chauncy D., 265
Annotated World List of Selected Current Geographical Serials, **279**
Bibliography of Geography, **273**
Guide to Geographical Bibliographies, **272**
International List of Geographical Serials, **279–80**
Harris, William H., 205
Harrison, Richard Edes, 284, 304
Harrod, L. M., 23, 196
Librarian's Glossary of Terms, **64,** **167**
Harvey, *Sources of Statistics,* **243**
Havlice, Patrice
Index to Artistic Biography, **114**
Index to Literary Biography, **117**
Hayakawa, S. I., 137, 159
Haycraft, Howard, 116
Hayden, F. V., 268, 310
Hayes, Grace P., 118
Hayes, R. M., 23
Health and welfare statistics, 251
Heise, Jon O., 308
Héraucourt, *New Wildhagen German Dictionary,* **173–74**
Herman, Theodore, 272
Herzberg, *Reader's Encyclopedia of American Literature,* **116**
Hines, Theodore C., 25
Hinojosa, Ida Navarro, 178
Hinsie, *Psychiatric Dictionary,* **168**
Historian's Handbook, **56**
Historical Abstracts, **71**
Historical Atlas, **298**
Historical Atlas of the United States, **300**
Historical atlases, 297–98
Historical Statistics of Canada, **246**
Historical Statistics of the United States, **261–62**
History and Bibliography of American Newspapers, 1690–1820, **47**
History of Bibliographies of Bibliographies, **90**
Hoefer, 100
Home Book of Quotations, **87**
Hotel and Motel Redbook, **312**
Hotels and Restaurants in Britain, **312**
Householder, Fred W., 126
Housing statistics, 252
Houston Post, 80
How to Find Out about Statistics, **242**
How to Identify Old Maps and Globes, **282**

Hulbert, James R.
  Dictionaries, British and American, 134, 154, 161
  Dictionary of American English on Historical Principles, **141–42**
Humanities Index, **72**
Humphrey, Edward, 214
Hunter, David F., 168
Hyamson, *Dictionary of Universal Biography*, 96, **99**

Illustrated Dictionary of Place Names, **306**
Index Bio-bibliographicus Notorum Hominum, **98**
Index-Gazetteer of the World, 304
Index Medicus, **74**
Index to Artistic Biography, **114**
Index to Maps in Books and Periodicals, **278–79**
Index to Poetry for Children and Young People, **86**
Index to Religious Periodical Literature, 76
Index to Women of the World from Ancient to Modern Times, **98**
Index to Young Readers' Collective Biographies, **99**
Index Translationum, **51**, 52
Indexed Periodicals, **46**
Indexer, 73
Indexers and Indexing, 196
Indexes
  book review, 82–84
  drama, 85
  evaluation of, 65
  fiction, 86
  literary form, 82–88
  nonliterary forms, 88–89
  of proceedings, 86–87
  of quotations (collections), 87–88
  poetry, 86
  single author, 82
  single book, 81–82
  short story, 88
  to biography, 95–99
  to dissertations, 84–85
  to essays, 85–86
  to sources of bibliographical information, 62–89
  to speeches, 88
Indexes and Indexing, **63**
Indexing, **63**
Industrial Arts Index, 76
Inferential statistics, 228, 231–32
Information Market Place, **67**
Information Please Almanac, 203, **257–58**
Instructional Materials, **275**
Insurance statistics, 251
Interior Department surveys, 267–68

International Authors and Writers Who's Who, **115**
International Bibliography of Reprints, **49**
International Bibliography of Translations, **51**
International Dictionary of Management, **168**
International Directory of Philosophy and Philosophers, **119**
International Encyclopedia of Statistics, **239–40**
International Encyclopedia of the Social Sciences, 187
International Federation of Library Associations and Institutions, 265
International Geographic Encyclopedia and Atlas, **304**
International Geographical Union, 265
  Commission on National Atlases, 295
International List of Geographical Serials, 273, **279–80**
International Maps and Atlases in Print, **276–77**
International Microforms in Print, 49
International Periodicals Directory, 78, 79
International Phonetic Alphabet, 136, 160
International Statistical Yearbook of Large Towns, **259**
International Who's Who, 93, **103**
International Yearbook and Statesmen's Who's Who, **103**
Introduction to Reference Books, **26**
Introduction to Reference Work, **11**, 122, 187, 194, 271
Introduction to United States Public Documents, **276**
Ireland, *Index to Women of the World from Ancient to Modern Times*, **98**
Irregular Serials and Annuals, 45
Italian atlases, 294
Italian dictionaries, 174–75
Italian encyclopedias, 221
Italy, biographical information on, 111
Ives, Sumner, 126, 131, 132, 135, 136

Jackson, Kenneth T., 300
Jackson, William V., 54
James, *All Possible Worlds*, **265**
Japanese Geography, **272**
Johannsen, *International Dictionary of Management*, **168**
John Bartholomew & Son, Edinburgh, 286
Johnson, Samuel, 130, 137
  Dictionary of the English Language, 125
Johnson Reprint Corporation, 125
Joint Population and Housing Reports, **252**
Jones, H. G., *Second Abstract of British Historical Statistics*, **259**

Jones, Trevor, 173
Journal of Documentation, 73
Journal of Geography, 266, 275, 284
Journal of Library Automation, 67
Journals, 12–13
Junior Book of Authors, **116**
Junior High School Library Catalog, **59**

Katz, William A., 9
  Introduction to Reference Work, **11**, 122, 187, 194, 271
  Magazines for Libraries, **46**
Keesing's Contemporary Archives, **80–81**, 188
Kelly, *American Catalogue of Books*, **40**
Kemmerling, *Commodity Prices*, **248**
Kendall, Maurice
  Bibliography of Statistical Literature, **239**
  Dictionary of Statistical Terms, **240**
Kenner, Hugh, 206
Kenyon, *Pronouncing Dictionary of American English*, **160**
King, Clarence 267, 310
King, Geraldine B., 4
King Survey, 267
Kingsbury, Robert
  Creative Cartography, **303**
  Sources of Information and Materials, **275**
Kirk, *Library Research Guide to Biology*, **56**
Kister, Kenneth
  Dictionary Buying Guide, 138, **151**
  Encyclopedia Buying Guide, **193–94**, 196, 199, 211
Klein, *Comprehensive Etymological Dictionary of the English Language*, **154**
Knapp, Sara D., 4
Knight, *Indexing*, **63**
Knott, Thomas A., 143
  Pronouncing Dictionary of American English, **160**
Kohler, *Dictionary for Accountants*, **169**
Kolb, William L., 168
Konversations-Lexikon, 180
Kruskal, William H., 239
Kruzas, Anthony T., 18
——— et al., *Encyclopedia of Information Systems and Services*, **67**
Kujoth, *Subject Guide to Periodical Indexes and Review Indexes*, **78**
Kunitz, *European Authors 1000–1900*, **116**
Kurian, *Encyclopedia of the Third World*, 186
KWIC index, 65
Kykkōtēs, *English-Modern Greek and Modern Greek-English Dictionary*, **174**

Labor leaders, biographical information on, 117–18
Lampert, Felicia, 139, 145
Landau, Sidney, 139
Landis, Martha, 4
Landmarks of Mapmaking, **281**
Lands and Peoples, **306**
Lang, John Hamilton, 299
Langescheidt's New Muret-Sanders Encyclopedic Dictionary of the English and German Languages, **173**
Langlois, Charles Victor, 15
Language of the Foreign Book Trade, **167**
Large-Type Hammond-Jennison World Atlas, **303**
La Roche, Nancy, 159
Larousse, Pierre, 218
Larousse, *Modern French-English Dictionary*, **172**
Larsgaard, *Map Librarianship*, **283**
Latin America, biographical information on, 111–12
Latin dictionaries, 175–76
Leaders in Education, **117**
Lebed, Andrew I., 112
Lee, Sidney, 110
Le Gear, *United States Atlas*, **296**
Leidy, *Popular Guide to Government Publications*, **42**
Let's Go, **311**
Levey, Judith S., 205
Lewis, Charlton T., 175
Lewis, Meriwether, 267
Lewis, Peter R., *Literature of the Social Sciences*, **256**
Lewthwaite, *Geographical Bibliography for American College Libraries*, **274**
Lewytkyj, *Who's Who in the Socialist Countries*, **108**, **112**
Librarian and Reference Service, **9**
Librarians and Online Service, **67**
Librarians, biographical information on, 118
Librarian's Glossary of Terms, 64, **167**
Librairie Française des Livres de l'Année, 37
Library and Information Science Abstracts, **22**, 72
Library catalogs, 20, 22–31
  American theories of, 24–25
Library Journal, 9, 11, **12**, **62**
Library Literature, 24, **72–73**, 196
Library of Congress, *see* U.S. Library of Congress
Library of Congress, 1978, **28**
Library of Congress Catalog—Music and Phonorecords, **50–51**
Library of Congress Subject Catalog, **26–27**

Library of World Biography, **100–1**
Library Research Guide to Biology, **56**
Library Science Abstracts, 72
Library statistics, 251–52
Library Statistics, **241**
Library Trends, 20, 73
Liddell, *Greek-English Lexicon*, **174**
Light of Navigation, 282
Lincoln Library of Essential Information,
    187, 204, **209**; see also *New Lincoln
    Library Encyclopedia*
Linder, *Rise of Current Complete National
    Bibliographies*, **31**
Linderman, W. B., 5
*List of Frequently Used Federal Govern-
    ment World, United States and Histor-
    ical Maps*, **278**
Lister, Raymond
    Antique Maps and Their Cartographers,
        281
    How to Identify Old Maps and Globes,
        282
Literary History of the United States, 192
Literature of Agriculture, **246**
Literature of Geography, **273**
Literature of the Social Sciences, **256**
Little, William, 149
Littre, *Dictionnaire de la Langue Française*,
    171
Lives of the Painters, **114**
Livres de l'Année—Biblio, 37
Livres Disponibles, **37**
Livres du Mois, 37
Livres du Trimestre—Biblio, 37
Lobies, *Index to Bio-bibliographicus Noto-
    rum Hominum*, **98**
Lock, C. B. M.
    Geography and Cartography, **273–74**
    Modern Maps and Atlases, **277**, 295
Long Beach (Calif.), City College Travel
    Geography Program, 266
Longman's Dictionary of Geography, **308**
Lord and Lord, *Historical Atlas of the
    United States*, **300**
Los Angeles Times, 80
Lottman, Herbert R., 218
Lovell, Sir Bernard, 302
Low, *Acquisition of Maps and Charts Pub-
    lished by the U.S. Government*, **276**
Lynam, *Mapmaker's Art*, **282**
Lynch, Michael, 311

Macdonald, A. M., 149
McGowan, Frank M., 31
*McGraw-Hill Dictionary of Modern Eco-
    nomics*, **168**

*McGraw-Hill Encyclopedia of Science and
    Technology*, **121**, 184
*McGraw-Hill Encyclopedia of World
    Biography*, **101**
McGraw-Hill International World Atlas, **286**
*McGraw-Hill Modern Scientists and En-
    gineers*, **121**
MacGregor, *Graphics Simplified*, **239**
McHenry, Robert, 105
Machine-Assisted Reference Service Sec-
    tion, Reference and Adult Services Di-
    vision, ALA, 8–9
McKerrow, Ronald, 19
Macmillan Dictionary, **151–52**
Macmillan Dictionary for Children, 152
*Macmillan Dictionary of Canadian Biogra-
    phy*, **108**
Macmillan School Dictionary, 152
Magazines for Libraries, **46**
Malclès, Louise-Nöelle, 16
    Bibliography, **15**, 52
    Sources du Travail Bibliographique, **10**
Mallett's Index of Artists, **114**
Maltby, *Economics and Commerce*, **247**
Mansion, J. E., 171
Manuscripts, sources of bibliographical in-
    formation on, 50
"Map Collections," **283**
*Map Collections in the United States and
    Canada*, **306**
Map librarianship, 281–87
"Map Librarianship," **283–84**
Map Librarianship, **283**
Mapmaker's Art, **282**
Mapmaking, U.S., 266–69
Mapping, **283**
Maps, **282**
Maps
    national, 295–96
    thematic, 297–303
    volumes of, 276–79
Maps and Diagrams, **283–84**
Maps and Man, **282**
Maps for America, **269**
Marconi, *Indexed Periodicals*, **46**
Mark, Linda, 11
Market Guide, **247**
Marquis Who's Who Publications, **97–98**
Martell, Paul, 118
Martin, Gilbert, *American History Atlas*,
    300
Martin, Lowell, 196
Martin, Marvin, 216
Mathematical Reviews, **73–74**
Mathews, Mitford M., 138, 145
    *Dictionary of Americanisms on Historical
        Principles*, **142**

Mawson, *Dictionary of Foreign Terms*, **171**
Maxwell Scientific International, 218
Media Review Digest, **50**
MEDLARS, 74
MEDLINE, 66
Mencken, *American Language*, 161
Merit Students Encyclopedia, 184, 210, **213–14**
Merit Students Year Book, **204**, 211
Messages from MARSS, 9
Michaud, Joseph François, 100
Michaud, **100**
Michelin Travel Guides, **311**
Microfilm Abstracts, 85
Microform Marketplace, **49**
Miller, *Graphic History of the Americas*, **298**
Military leaders, biographical information on, 118
Mitchell, B. R.
   Abstract of British Historical Statistics, **259**
   European Historical Statistics, **245**
   Second Abstract of British Historical Statistics, **259**
Mitchell, G. D., *Dictionary of Sociology*, **169**
Miuller, Vladimir K., 176
Mobil Travel Guides, **311**
Modern American Usage, 155, 156, **157**
Modern English Usage, 163
Modern Maps and Atlases, **277**, 295
Molnar, *Author-Title Index to Joseph Sabin's "Dictionary of Books Relating to America,"* **39**
Monkhouse, F. J.
   Dictionary of Geography, 283
   Dictionary of the Natural Environment, **307**
   Maps and Diagrams, **283–84**
Monthly Bulletin of Statistics, **260**
Monthly Catalog of United States Government Publications, **41–42**, 52
Monthly Checklist of State Publications, **42–43**, 276
Monthly Digest of Statistics, 259
Monthly Labor Review, **262–63**
Monthly Vital Statistics, 263
Moody's Investor's Service, *Moody's Manual of Investments*, **249**
Mooney, *National Index of American Imprints Through 1800*, **40**
Moore, N. D., *Dictionary of Business, Finance and Investment*, **169**
Moore, Patrick, *Rand McNally New Concise Atlas of the Universe*, **302**
More Junior Authors, **116**

Morehead, *Introduction to United States Public Documents*, **276**
Morgan, *Critical Bibliography of German Literature in English Translation*, **51–52**
Morris, Mary, *Harper Dictionary of Contemporary Usage*, 156, **157**
Morris, William, 146
   Harper Dictionary of Contemporary Usage, 156, **157**
Mortality Statistics, 254
Motion Pictures and Filmstrips, 49
Mott-Smith, George, 137
Mudge, Isadore, 10
Muesham, *Guide to Basic Information Sources in the Visual Arts*, **55**
Muirhead's Blue Guides, **311–12**
Mulhall, *Dictionary of Statistics*, **257**
Multi-Media Reviews Index, **50**
Municipal Year Book, **251**
Murra, Kathrine, 17
Murfin, *Reference Service*, **9**
Murray, James A. H., 141
   New English Dictionary on Historical Principles, **140**; *see also* Oxford English Dictionary
   Shorter Oxford Dictionary, **149–50**
Murray, K. M., *Caught in the Web of Words*, 140
Murray, Wallace S., 183, 215
Music, sources of bibliographic information on, 50–51
Music Index, 74
Music Reference and Research Materials, **57**
Musicians, biographical information on, 118–19
Musicians since 1900, **119**
Myers, *Black American Writers Past and Present*, **115**

Nagel's Travel Guides, **312**
Nakata, *From Press to People*, 42
Name into Word, 153, **154**
National Academy of Sciences, 268–69
National Atlas of the United States of America, 295–96
National bibliography
   American, 33–35
   British, 36
   current, 31–38
   French, 36–37
   retrospective, 38–40
National book bibliographies, 27, 31–40
National Cartographic Information Center, 296
National Censuses and Vital Statistics in Europe, **245**

National Conference on Library Statistics, 241
National Council for Geographic Education, 266
  Pacesetter series, **275**
National Cyclopedia of American Biography, **105**
National Endowment on the Arts and the Humanities, 18
National Geographic Magazine, 266, 270, **280**
National Geographic Society
  National Geographic Atlas of the World, **291–92**
  Picture Atlas of Our Fifty States, **300**
National Index of American Imprints through 1800, 40
National library catalogs, 25–31
National Newspaper Index, 80
National Ocean Survey, 268, 296
National Union Catalog, **20, 26–28,** 38, 51, 196, 223
National Union Catalog of Manuscript Collections, **50,** 52
National Zip Code and Post Office Directory, **305**
Nature of Maps, **283**
Nault, William H., 196
Nault-Caswell-Brain Curriculum Analysis, 210
Naylor, *Contemporary Artists,* **114**
NBC Handbook of Pronunciation, **160**
Neilson, William Allan, 143
Neue Deutsche Biographie, **109**
New Book of Knowledge, 184, 211, **215–16,** 217
New Cassell's French Dictionary, **172**
New Cassell's German Dictionary, **173**
New Catholic Encyclopedia, **191,** 193
New Century Cyclopedia of Names, **101**
New Columbia Encyclopedia, 182, 185, 187, **205,** 206, 207, 304
New Dictionary of Statistics, **257**
New Encyclopaedia Britannica, see Encyclopaedia Britannica
New English Dictionary on Historical Principles, **140–41;** see also *Oxford English Dictionary*
New English-Russian Dictionary, **176**
New Geographical Literature and Maps, **280**
New Guide to Popular Government Publications for Libraries and Home Reference, **42**
New Information Systems and Services, **18, 67**
New Lincoln Library Encyclopedia, **209**
New Orleans Times-Picayune, 80

New Periodicals Index, **68**
New Pronouncing Dictionary of the Spanish and English Languages, **178**
New Sabin, **39**
New Serial Titles, **44–45,** 52
New Velásquez Spanish and English Dictionary, **178**
New Wildhagen German Dictionary, **173–74**
New York Public Library, *Dictionary Catalog of the Map Division,* **278–79**
New York Times, 80, 94, 249
New York Times Atlas of the World, **288**
New York Times Biographical Service, **103**
New York Times Book Review Index, **84**
New York Times Encyclopedic Almanac, **257**
New York Times Index, **79**
New York Times Information Bank, **66**
New York Times Obituaries Index, 94, **98**
Newsome, *New Guide to Popular Government Publications for Libraries and Home Reference,* **42**
Newspaper Index, **80**
Newspaper indexes, 79–80
Newspapers in Microfilm 1948–72, **47**
Newspapers, sources of bibliographic information on, 46–47
Nicholson, *Dictionary of American-English Usage,* 155, **157**
Nineteenth Century Reader's Guide to Periodical Literature, **68**
Noh, *Japanese Geography,* **272**
Notable Names in American History, 105
Notable Names in the American Theatre, **121–22**
Notes and Queries, 157
Nouvelle Biographie Générale, **100**

Obituaries from the Times, **98**
Occupational Outlook Handbook, **252**
Occupations, statistics on, 252
Oceanographic Atlases, **279**
Official Airline Guide, **312**
Official Associated Press Almanac, **257**
Official Map Publications, **269**
Ohles, John F., 117
Oli, *Vocabolario Illustrato della Lingua Italiana,* **175**
Onions, C. T., 141, 149
Online, 67
Orne, Jerrold, 54
  Language of the Foreign Book Trade, **167**
Orridge, *Contemporary Artists,* 114
Ortelius, *Theatrum Orbis Terrarum,* **283**
Ostvold, *Literature of Agricultural Research,* **246**
Owen, David Dale, 267

Oxford Atlas of the World, 286
Oxford Companions, **116**
Oxford Dictionary of English Etymology,
150, 153, **154**
Oxford Economic Atlas of the World, 262,
302
Oxford English Dictionary, 125, 126, 129,
134, **140–41,** 153, 162
Oxford Regional Atlases, 302
Oxford Russian-English Dictionary, **176–77**
Oxford University Press, Cartographic De-
partment, 286

Pacesetter series, **275**
Pacific Tourist, **310**
Page, *International Dictionary of Manage-
ment,* **168**
Palmer, R. R., 298
Pamphlets, sources of bibliographic in-
formation on, 43
Papazian, Pierre, 5–6
Paperbacks in Print, **48**
Paperbound Books in Print, **48,** 52
Paperbound books, sources of bibliographic
information on, 48
Parametric statistics, 233
Paris, Matthew, 282
Partridge, Eric
    Dictionary of Slang, 126
    *Dictionary of Slang and Unconventional
    English,* **162**
    Name into Word, 153, **154**
    *Origins: A Short Etymological Dictionary
    of Modern English,* 153, **154**
    Slang, Today and Yesterday, 161, 164
    Usage and Abusage, 156, **157**
Pater, Alan F., 88
Pater, Jason R., 88
Paullin, *Atlas of the Historical Geography
of the United States,* **300–1**
Pei, Mario, 125
    Dictionary of Foreign Terms, **171**
Periodical indexes
    art, 69
    biological sciences, 69
    business, 69–70, 255
    chemistry, 70
    education, 70–71
    general, 67–68
    history, 71
    humanities, 71–72
    library and information sciences, 72–73
    literature, 73
    mathematics, 73–74
    medicine, 74
    music, 74
    philosophy, 74
    psychology, 75

    religion, 75–76
    science and technology, 76–79
    social sciences, 77–78
    statistics, 254
Periodical indexing and abstracting ser-
    vices, 64–65
Periodicals for School Media Programs, **46**
Periodicals, sources of bibliographical in-
    formation on, 43–46
Permanent Committee on Geographic
    Names, 285
Perrin, Porter, 145
Petchenik, Barbara Bartz, 299
    Nature of Maps, **284**
Peters, Jean, 167
Peterson, *Reference Books for Elementary
    and Junior High School Libraries,* **12**
Petit Robert, **171**
Philosophers, biographical information on,
    119
Philosopher's Index, **74**
*Philosopher's Index: A Retrospective Index
    to U.S. Publications from 1940,* **74**
Physics Literature, **57**
Picture Atlas of Our Fifty States, **300–1**
Pike, Zebulon, 267
Pirie, *Books for Junior College Libraries,*
    60
Place names, 280–81
*Planning for a Nationwide System of Lib-
    rary Statistics,* **241**
Platt, *Aids to Geographical Research,* **274**
Play Index, 85
Plumb, J. H., 100
Poetry indexes, 86
Political leaders, biographical information
    on, 119–20
Poole's Index to Periodical Literature, **68**
Popular Guide to Government Publications,
    42
Popular Periodical Index, **68**
Population Characteristics, **254**
Population/housing statistics, 252
Population Index, **252**
Population Index Bibliography, 252
Post, J. B., 284
Poulton, *Historian's Handbook,* **56**
Powell, John Wesley, 268
Practical Bibliographer, **91**
Practical Charting Techniques, **239**
PRECIS, 23
Preece, Warren E., 179, 180, 181, 197
Price, E. T., *Geographical Bibliography for
    American College Libraries,* **274**
Price, Frank Williams, 254
Probability sampling, 232
Problems in Lexicography, 126
Proceedings indexes, 86–87

Producer Prices and Price Indexes, 263
Professional Geographer, 284
Professions, biographical information on, 113–23
Profile of the U.S. Economy, 249
Progress in Library Science, 63
Projections of Educational Statistics, 250
Prokhorov, A. M., 222
Przebienda, Words and Phrases Index, 157
Psychiatric Dictionary, 168
Psychological Abstracts, 66, 75
Ptolemy, Cosmographia, 283
Public Affairs Information Service, 65, 238, 262
    Bulletin, 77–78, 256
Public Library Catalog, 58
Published Library Catalogues, 31
Publishers' Trade List Annual, 32, 33, 38
Publishers Weekly, 35
Pulp and Paper, 263

Quarterly Journal, 278
Queneau, Raymond, 179
Quotations, collections of, 87–88

Rainbow Dictionary, 152
Raisz, General Cartography, 284
Rake, Alan, 107
Ralston, Anthony, 168
Ramondino, Dictionary of Foreign Terms, 171
Rand McNally and Company Atlas of World History, 298–99
Rand McNally Atlas of World Wildlife, 302
Rand McNally Commercial Atlas and Marketing Guide, 261–62, 270, 302
Rand McNally New Concise Atlas of the Universe, 302
Random House College Dictionary, 147
Random House Dictionary of the English Language, 126, 132, 133, 144–45, 163
Random House Encyclopedia, 184, 185, 186, 188, 204, 206–7
Ranganathan, S. R., 7
Rather, Statistics of Libraries, 252
Ray, Jean M., 266
Read, Allen Walker, 135
Reader's Adviser, 58
Reader's Digest Almanac and Yearbook, 258
Reader's Digest Family Word Finder, 159
Reader's Encyclopedia, 94
Reader's Encyclopedia of American Literature, 116
Readers' Guide to Periodical Literature, 67–68

Reader's Guide to the Social Sciences, 265
Recent History Atlas, 298
Rees, Alan M., 5
Reference and Information Services: A Reader, 9
Reference and Subscription Books Review Committee, ALA, 13–14
Reference and Subscription Books Reviews 1976–1977, 13, 61, 123
Reference Book Review, 12
Reference books, evaluation of, 13–14
Reference Books for Elementary and Junior High School Libraries, 12
Reference Books for Small and Medium-sized Libraries, 12, 122
Reference Books in Paperback, 12
Reference environment, 3
Reference evaluation, 3
Reference Guide to the Literature of Travel, 309
Reference interview, 4
Reference librarian, 5
Reference Manual on Population and Housing Statistics, 253
Reference materials, guides to, 9–12
Reference personnel, 3
Reference resources, 3
Reference services
    current reviewing journals, 12–13
    definition, 2–6
    indirect, 2
    search, 6–9
Reference Services, 2, 9
Reference Services Review, 11, 12
Reference Sources, 11
Reference Work, 2
Reginald, Cumulative Paperback Index 1939–1959, 48
Regression analysis, 233
Reinhart, Vocational-Technical Learning Materials, 60
Religion Index One, 76
Religion Index Two, 76
Religion statistics, 254
Religious Bodies: 1936, 254
Religious leaders, biographical information on, 120
Repertoire des Livres de Langue Française Disponibles, 37
Repertoire International des Traductions, 51
Reprints, bibliographical information on, 48
Research Catalogue, 274
Research Librarianship, 53
Rettig, James, 6
Reynolds, Cambridge Italian Dictionary, 175

Concise Cambridge Italian Dictionary, **175**

Richards, B. G., *Magazines for Libraries,* **46**

Richards, I. A., 145

Richardson, *Periodicals for School Media Programs,* **46**

Riches, *Analytical Bibliography of Universal Collected Biography,* 96, **99**

Rigdon, Walter, 122

Rise of Current Complete National Bibliographies, 31

Ristow, Walter W., 285, 307

Robert, *Dictionnaire Alphabetique et Analogique,* **171**

Roberts, A. D., *Introduction to Reference Books,* **26**

Roberts, Charles G. D., 107

Roberts' Dictionary of Industrial Relations, **169**

Robinson, A. H.
    Elements of Cartography, **284**
    Nature of Maps, **284**

Robinson, A. M. L., *Systematic Bibliography,* **53**

Rodale, *Synonym Finder,* **159**

Roget's International Thesaurus, 157, **159**

Roorbach, *Bibliotheca Americana,* **40**

Rothman, John, 63

Rothstein, Samuel, 8

Rowland, Arthur Ray
    Librarian and Reference Service, **9**
    Reference Services, **2**

Royal Geographic Society, *New Geographical Literature and Maps,* **280**

RQ, **13,** 17

Rush, *Black American Writers, Past and Present,* **115**

Russian atlases, 294–95

Russian dictionaries, 176–77

Russian encyclopedias, 222–24

Russkii biograficheskii slovar', **112**

Ryder, *Canadian Reference Sources,* **11**

Sabin, *Dictionary of Books Relating to America,* **39**

Sales and Marketing Management, *Survey of Buying Power,* **247**

San Francisco Chronicle, 80

Saporta, Sol, 126

Sarton, George, 179

Schmeckebier, *Government Publications and Their Use,* **276**

School atlases, 293

School dictionaries, 150–53
    selection aids, 150–51

Schoolcraft, Henry Rowe, 267

Schorr, Alan E., 269

Schulz, Heinrich E., 112

Science Citation Index, **66, 77**

Scientists/social scientists, biographical information on, 120–21

Scott, *Greek-English Lexicon,* **174**

Scott, *Foresman Beginning Dictionary,* **152**

Screen, *Guide to Foreign Language Courses and Dictionaries,* **170**

Scribner-Bantam English Dictionary, 145, **147**

Scullard, H. H., 299

SDIC, 65

Seaberg, Lillian M., 13

Sealock, *Bibliography of Place-name Literature,* **280–81**

Search, 6–9
    variables, 7–8

Sears' List of Subject Headings, **24,** 83

Second Abstract of British Historical Statistics, **259**

Seely, *Bibliography of Place-name Literature,* 280–81

Selected U.S. Government Publications, **42**

Selection aids, bibliographic, 57–60

Selective bibliographies, 21

Seltzer, Leon, 304

Senior High School Library Catalog, **58–59**

Serial Bibliographies in the Humanities and Social Sciences, **90–91,** 192

Shapp, Martha G., 215

Shaw, *American Bibliography,* **39**

Shearer, F. E., 310

Sheehy, *Guide to Reference Books,* **10,** 55, 78, 122, 139, 196, 218, 256, 258, 262, 271, 302

Shenker, *Harmless Drudges,* 125, 141

Shepherd, *Historical Atlas,* **298**

Shipton, *National Index of American Imprints through 1800,* **40**

Shoemaker, Richard H.
    American Bibliography, **39**
    Checklist of American Imprints for 1820–1829, **39**

Shores, Louis, 196
    Instructional Materials, **275**

Short, Charles, 175

Short stories, indexes for, 88

Short Story Index, **88**

Shorter Etymological Dictionary of Modern English, 153, **154**

Shorter Oxford English Dictionary, **149–50**

Showers, *World Facts and Figures,* **306–7**

Sidney, Sir Philip, 130

Silverman, *Index to Young Readers' Collected Biographies,* **99**

Simon and Schuster's International Dictionary, **177–78**
Simpson, D. P., 176
6000 Words, **144**
Skeat, *Etymological Dictionary, 153,* **154**
Skelton, *Maps,* **282**
Slang dictionaries, 161–62
Slang, Today and Yesterday, 161, 164
Sledd, James H., 125
Sloan, *Dictionary of Economics,* **169**
Slocum, *Biographical Dictionaries and Related Works,* **96, 122**
Slonimsky, Nicholas, 118
Slovar' sovremennogo russkogo literaturnogo iazyka, **176**
Small, *Dictionary of the Natural Environment,* **307**
Small Area Data Notes, 253–54
Smith, Logan P., 164
Smithsonian Institution, 268
Social conditions, statistics on, 255
Social Indicators, **255**
Social Science Citation Index, 77, **78**
Social Sciences and Humanities Index, 72, **78**
Social Sciences Index, **78**
Social Security Bulletin, **251**
Society of Indexers, 63
Something about the Author, **115**
Sources du Travail Bibliographique, **10**
Sources of Business Information, **247**
Sources of Information and Materials, **275**
Sources of Information in the Social Sciences, 53, **57,** 265, 271, 293
Sources of Insurance Statistics, **251**
Sources of Serials, **45**
Sources of Statistics, **243**
South Asia, **272**
Southern Illinois University, Map Room, 266
Soviet World Atlas, 286, **290–91,** 294–95
Space atlas, 302
Spanish dictionaries, 177–78
Spanish encyclopedias, 224–25
Special Libraries Association, Geography and Map Division, 265
Speech Index, **88**
Speer, *Practical Charting Techniques,* 239
Sprach-Brockhaus, **172–73**
Springer, Otto, 173
Stamp, L. Dudley, 307, 308
Standard and Poor's Corp., *Corporation Records,* **249**
Standard Catalog series, 57, 151
Standard Dictionary of Canadian biography, 107–8
Standard Education Almanac, **249–50**

Standard Industrial Classification Manual, **240–41**
Statesman's Yearbook, 256, **259**
Statistical Abstract, 256
Statistical Abstract of Latin America, **260**
Statistical Abstract of the United States, 236, **261**
Statistical Abstract Service, 246
Statistical bibliographies, 242–55
Statistical Bulletins, **245**
Statistical Methodology Reviews, **239**
Statistical reference service, 228–39
Statistical Reporter, **244**
Statistical Services of the United States Government, **244**
Statistical sources
  evaluation of, 228–39
  frequently consulted titles, 237–38
  general types, 238–39
  notes in, 236–37
  types of, 256–63
Statistical Sources, 261
Statistical Theory and Method Abstracts, **243**
Statistical Yearbook, **260**
Statistical yearbooks, 259–62
Statistical Yearbooks, **245**
Statistics
  almanacs, 257–59
  analysis of variance, 233
  atlases, 261
  chi-square test, 234
  confidentiality of records, 235
  correlation, 233
  descriptive, 228
  dictionaries of, 257
  encyclopedias and dictionaries, 239–42
  F test, 233
  frequency polygon, 229
  general sources, 242–43
  government sources (foreign), 244–46
  government sources (U.S.), 244
  hypothesis, 232
  index number, 236
  inferential, 228
  mean/median/mode, 229
  measures of central tendency, 229
  nonparametric tests, 234
  normal distribution, 230
  null hypothesis, 232
  parameters, 231
  Pearson product-moment correlation, 233
  periodical sources, 262–63
  periodicals indexes, 255–56
  population/universe, 228, 231 ·
  probability sample, 231
  regression analysis, 233

sources of, 226–63
subject sources, 246–55
terminology of, 228–42
variability, 229
Statistics of Libraries, 252
Statistics Sources, **243,** 262
Stecchini, Livio C., 221, 224
Stein, Jess, 126, 147
Stephen, Leslie, 110
Stephenson, *Map Collections in the United States and Canada,* **306**
Stevenson, *Home Book of Quotations,* 87
Steward, Harry, 291
Stewart, *American Place Names,* **307**
Stokes, *Function of Bibliography,* **19**
Stommel, *Oceanographic Atlases,* **279**
Stone, Adolf, 266
Story of Maps, **281**
Stratton, George B., 165
Stroynowski, *Who's Who in the Socialist Countries,* **108, 112**
Subject Approach to Information, **23**
Subject bibliographies, 21, 52–57,
retrospective-comprehensive, 53–54
retrospective-selective, 55–57
Subject Bibliography of the Social Sciences and the Humanities, 52
Subject Collections, **54**
Subject Guide to Books in Print, 32, **34,** 38
Subject Guide to Children's Books in Print, **34**
Subject Guide to Forthcoming Books, **35,** 38
Subject Guide to Microforms in Print, **49**
Subject Guide to Periodical Indexes and Review Indexes, 78
Subject Headings Used in the Dictionary Catalogs of the Library of Congress, 23
Subject Index of the Modern Works Added to the Library, **29**
Subscription Books Bulletin Reviews, 61
Sukhwal, *South Asia,* **272**
Supplement to the Oxford English Dictionary, **141**
Survey of Buying Power, **247**
Survey of Current Business, 236, **263**
Surveying and Mapping, 278
Sutton, *Speech Index,* **88**
Swiden, Eleanor, A., 12
Synonym Finder, **159**
Systematic bibliography, 19, 20
Systematic Bibliography, **53**

Tait, *Author & Titles,* **22**
Tanur, Judith N., 239
Tarr, Andrea, 9

Taylor, Archer, 90
Textbooks in Print, 34
Theater, biographical information on the, 121–22
Theatrum Orbis Terrarum, 282
Theatrum Orbis Terrarum, Ltd., Amsterdam, 282
Thesaurus, 158
Thiele, *Official Map Publications,* **269**
Third Book of Junior Authors, **116**
Thomas, Calvin, 143
Thomas, Joseph, *Universal Pronouncing Dictionary of Biography and Mythology,* **101**
Thompson, A., *Vocabularium Bibliothecarii,* **168**
Thompson, M. M., *Maps for America,* **269**
Thorndike-Barnhart Advanced Dictionary, **152–53**
Thorndike-Barnhart Beginning Dictionary, **152**
Thorndike-Barnhart Intermediate Dictionary, **152**
Thorne, J. O., 100
Thornton, John L., 63
Thornton, R. H., *American Glossary,* 141, **142**
Thrower, *Maps and Man,* **282**
Times Atlas of the World, 286–87, **288**
Times Atlas of World History, **299**
Times Index-Gazetteer of the World, **304**
Times (of London), *Official Index,* **79–80**
Titus, Edna Brown, 44
Toomey, *World Bibliography of Bibliographies,* **90**
Topographic Maps, 296
Tour Book, **310**
Touring Club Italiano, *Atlante Internazionale,* **294**
Training in Indexing, **63**
Translations, sources of bibliographic information on, 51
Travel Guidebooks in Review, **308–9**
Travel guides, 308–12
Travels in the Confederate States, **309**
Travels in the New South, **309**
Travels in the Old South, **309**
Tunnell, Arthur L., 107
Twentieth Century Authors, **116**
Tyner, *World of Maps and Mapping,* **284**
Types of Maps Published by Government Agencies, **296**

Ulrich's International Periodicals Directory, **45,** 52, 262
Ulrich's Quarterly, **46**
Unbegaun, B. O., 176

UNESCO, 17–18
  Bibliographical Services throughout the
    World, 31
  Bibliography, Documentation, Terminol-
    ogy, 17, 31
  Conference on the Improvement of Bib-
    liographical Services, 17
  Guide to National Bibliographical In-
    formation Centers, 18
Unger, Leonard, 115
Uniform Crime Reports, 246
Union catalogs/union lists, 20, 25–31
Union List of Serials, 28, 44, 52
United Nations
  Demographic Yearbook, 254
  Documents Index, 43
  Monthly Bulletin of Statistics, 260
  Statistical Yearbook, 260
  UNDEX, 43
  World Statistics in Brief, 260
United States
  biographical information, 104–6
  dictionaries, 146–49
United States Atlases, 296
United States Catalog, 40
Universal Pronouncing Dictionary of
    Biography and Mythology, 101
University Desk Encyclopedia, 188, 204,
    207–8
University of California at Los Angeles,
    Map Library, 266
Urban, Paul K., 112
Urdang, Laurence, 159, 216
Urquhart, Historical Statistics of Canada,
    246
U.S. Board on Geographic Names, 269,
    285, Gazetteer, 305
———. Bureau of Land Management, 296
———. Bureau of the Census, 227
  Bureau of the Census Catalog, 244, 253
  Census of Housing, 252
  Census of Population, 252
  Congressional District Data Book, 261
  County and City Data Book, 261
  Current Industrial Reports, 247–48
  Directory of Federal Statistics for Local
    Areas, 242
  Economic Censuses, 248
  Fact Finder for the Nation, 227
  Guide to Foreign Trade Statistics, 248
  Historical Statistics of the United States,
    261
  Joint Population and Housing Reports,
    253
  Population Characteristics, 254
  Reference Manual on Population and
    Housing Statistics, 253

Religious Bodies: 1936, 254
Statistical Abstract of the United States,
    260
———. Bureau of Labor Statistics, Occu-
    pational Outlook Handbook, 252, 253
———. Congress, Biographical Directory
    of the American Congress 1774–1971,
    119
———. Copyright Office, Catalog of Copy-
    right Entries, 51
———. Department of Agriculture, 296
  Agricultural Situation, 246
  Agricultural Statistics, 246
  Yearbook of Agriculture, 246
———. Employment Service, Dictionary of
    Occupational Titles, 240
———. Environmental Data and Informa-
    tion Service, Daily Weather Maps, 255
———. Federal Bureau of Investigation,
    Uniform Crime Reports, 246
———. Geological Survey, 269, 296
———. Lake Survey, 296
———. Library of Congress, 17, 265
  Bibliography of Cartography, 279
  Films and Other Materials for Projection,
    49
  General Censuses and Vital Statistics of
    the Americas, 245
  Library of Congress Catalog—Music and
    Phonorecords, 50–51
  Monthly Checklist of State Publications,
    42–43
  National Censuses and Vital Statistics in
    Europe, 245
  Newspapers in Microfilm 1948–1972, 47
  Quarterly Journal, 278
  Statistical Bulletins, 245
  Statistical Yearbooks, 245
  Subject Catalog, 26–27
  Union List of Serials, 45
———. National Center for Education Sta-
    tistics, Digest of Educational Statistics,
    250
———. National Center for Health Statis-
    tics, Vital Statistics of the United States,
    254
———. National Meteorological Center,
    Average Monthly Weather Outlook,
    255
———. National Ocean Survey, List of
    Frequently Used Federal Government
    World, United States and Historical
    Maps, 278
———. Office of Federal Statistical Policy
    and Standards, Social Indicators, 255
———. Office of Management and Budget
  Social Indicators, 255

Standard Industrial Classification Manual, **240**

Statistical Services of the U.S. Government, **244**

————. Postal Service, *National Zip Code and Post Office Directory,* **305**

————. Social and Economic Statistics Administration, *Dictionary of Economic and Statistical Terms,* **241–42**

————. Social Security Administration, *Social Security Bulletin,* **251**

————. Superintendent of Documents, *Cumulative Subject Index to Monthly Catalog of United States Government Publications,* **41–42**

Monthly Catalog of United States Government Publications, **41–42**

Selected U.S. Government Publications, **42**

U.S. Fact Book, **261**

U.S. Geological Survey, 269

U.S. Government Publications, **269**

Usage, books on, 155–57

Usage and Abusage, 156, **157**

Use of Biological Literature, **55**

Use of Earth Science Literature, **56**

USSR (Soviet Union)
biographical information, 112
Chief Directorate of Geodesy and Cartography, 286

Van Balen, *Geography and Earth Sciences Publications,* **280**

Van den Bark, *American Thesaurus of Slang,* **162**

Van Der Heyden, A. A. M., 299

Van Doren, Charles, 105, 180

Variables, 7–8

Velázquez de la Cadena, Mariano
New Pronouncing Dictionary of the Spanish and English Languages, **178**
New Revised Velázquez Spanish and English Dictionary, **178**

Venezky, R. L., 163

Vertical File Index, **43**, 52

Vinson, James, 116

Vital and Health Statistics, 254

Vital Statistics of the U.S., **254**

Vizetelly, F. H., 143

Vocabolario Illustrato della Lingua Italiana, **175**

Vocabularium Bibliothecarii, **168**

Vocational-Technical Learning Materials, **60**

Volume Library, **209**

Wakeman, John, 116

Walford, A. J.
Guide to Reference Materials, **10**, 38, 55, 122, 196, 256, 258, 262, 271, 302
Guide to Foreign Language Courses and Dictionaries, **170**

Walks in Rome, **308**

Wall, *Words and Phrases Index,* **157**

Wall Street Journal, 80, **249**
Index, **80**

Wallace, W. S., 108

Walsh, James P., *General World Atlases in Print,* **277**

Walsh, P., *Anglo-American General Encyclopedias,* **195**

War Department Surveys, 267–68

Washington, George, 267

Washington Post, 80

Wasserman, *Commodity Prices,* **248**

Watson, Paula, 4

Weather statistics, 255

Weaver, Warren, 145

Webb, *New Dictionary of Statistics,* **257**

Webster, Noah, 125
American Dictionary of the English Language, **125**
Blue-Backed Speller, 125
Grammatical Institute of the English Language, 125

Webster's American Biographies, **105**

Webster's Biographical Dictionary, 93, 94, **101–2**, 189

Webster's Collegiate Thesaurus, 158, 159, **160**

Webster's Elementary Dictionary, 131

Webster's Intermediate Dictionary, 153

Webster's New Collegiate Dictionary, 137, 145, **147–48**, 163

Webster's New Dictionary of Synonyms, 158, **160**

Webster's New Elementary Dictionary, 153

Webster's New Geographical Dictionary, 304, **305**

Webster's New International Dictionary of the English Language, **143–44**

Webster's New Students Dictionary, **153**

Webster's New Twentieth Century Dictionary of the English Language, **132**

Webster's New World Dictionary, 138, **148**, 152

Webster's Third New International Dictionary, 125, 129, 130, 131, 132, 133, 134, 135, 136, 137, **144**, 166

Weekly Business Statistics, 263

Weekly Record, 32, **35**, 38

Weiss, *Access to the World,* **312**

Wentworth, *Dictionary of American Slang,* 161, **162**

Wer 1st Wer, **110**

Western Association of Map Libraries, 265
What They Said, **88**
Wheeler, George M., 268
Wheeler, M., *Oxford Russian-English Dictionary*, **176–77**
Whitaker, *Almanack*, **258**
White et al., *Sources of Information in the Social Sciences*, **57**, 265, 271, 293
Whitelock, Otto, 182
White's Conspectus of American Biography, 105
Whitford, *Physics Literature*, **57**
Whitmore, Harry E., 13
Whittaker, Kenneth, 6, 127
Whitten, Phillip, 168
Who Did What, **102**
Who Was Who, **110–11**
Who Was Who in America, **105**
Who Was Who in the Theatre, 1912–1976, **122**
Who Was Who in the USSR, **112**
Wholesale Prices and Price Indexes, 263
Who's Who among Black Americans, **106**
Who's Who in Africa, **107**
Who's Who in America, **106**
Who's Who in American Art, **114**
Who's Who in American Politics, **119**
Who's Who in Art, **113–14**
Who's Who in Australia, **107**
Who's Who in Canada, **108**
Who's Who in Commerce and Industry, 117
Who's Who in Finance and Industry, **117**
Who's Who in France, **109**
Who's Who in Germany, **110**
Who's Who in Government, **119–20**
Who's Who in Labor, **117–18**
Who's Who in Latin America, **111–12**
Who's Who in Library Service, **118**
Who's Who in Religion, **120**
Who's Who in the Socialist Countries, **108, 112**
Who's Who in in the Theatre, **122**
Who's Who in the World, **103–4**
Who's Who of American Women, **106**
Wiedell, Joseph W., 303
Wiener, Philip P., 190
Wiezell, Richard John, 178
Wildhagen, *New Wildhagen German Dictionary*, **173–74**
Wildlife atlas, **302–3**
Wilkinson, H. R., *Maps and Diagrams*, **283–84**
Williams, Edwin B., 147
    Bantam New College Spanish and English Dictionary, **178**
Williams, F. J., *Dictionary Outline of Basic Statistics*, 239
Wilson, H. W., Co., 64

Wilson Author series, 98, **116**
Wilson Library Bulletin, **13**
Winch, Kenneth, 277
Winchell, Constance, 10
Winters, *Geographical Bibliography for American College Libraries*, **274**
Wolman, *Dictionary of Behavioral Sciences*, **169**
Wood, *Use of Earth Science Literature*, **56**
Woodbury, Marda, *Guide to Sources of Educational Information*, **56, 250**
Woodward, David, 282
Word List of Scientific Periodicals Published in the Years 1900–1960, **165**
Words, sources on, 124–78
Words and Phrases Index, **157**
Words, Words, and Words about Dictionaries, 139, 145
World Almanac and Book of Facts, 203, **258**
World Atlas of Agriculture, **301**
World Authors, **116**
World Bibliography of Bibliographies, **89–90**, 91
World Book Atlas, **293**
World Book Dictionary, **148–49**
World Book Encyclopedia, 184, 185, 210, **211–12**
World Book Year Book, 211
World Christian Handbook, 254
World Directory of Map Collections, **307**
World Facts and Figures, **306–7**
World Health Organization, *World Health Statistics Annual*, **251**
World Military Leaders, **118**
World of Maps and Mapping, **284**
World Statistics in Brief, **260**
World Who's Who in Commerce and Industry, 117
World Who's Who in Finance and Industry, 117
World Who's Who in Science, **121**
World Language Catalog, **170**
Wortman, *Deskbook of Business Management Terms*, **169**
Woytinsky, *Profile of the U.S. Economy*, **249**
Wright, John K., 285, 300
    Aids to Geographical Research, **274**
Wright, Joseph, *English Dialect Dictionary*, **163**
Wright, Wendell W., 152
Wyer, *Reference Work*, **2**
Wynar, B. S., *Reference Books in Paperback*, **12**
Wynar, C. L., *Guide to Reference Books for School Media Centers*, **12**
Wynar, L. R., *Reference Service*, **9**

Yearbook of Agriculture, **246**
*Yearbook of American and Canadian
    Churches,* **254**
Yearbooks, statistical, 257–60
Young Students Encyclopedia, 211, **217–18**

Young Students Encyclopedia Yearbook,
    211

Zurcher, *Dictionary of Economics,* **169**

Designed by Vladimir Reichl
Composed by Modern Typographers, Inc.,
  in Linotype Times Roman
Printed on Warren's 50# 1854,
  a pH neutral stock,
and bound by Braun-Brumfield, Inc.